801 Questions Kids Ask About God

FAMILY DESK REFERENCE

801

Questions
Kids Ask
About God

with answers
from the Bible

TYNDALE HOUSE PUBLISHERS | CAROL STREAM, ILLINOIS

Visit Tyndale online at www.tyndale.com.

TYNDALE and Tyndale's quill logo are registered trademarks of Tyndale House Publishers, Inc.

801 Questions Kids Ask about God

Cover illustration by Lil Crump. "Jason and Max" copyright © 1989 Impartation Idea, Inc. All rights reserved.

Designer: Jacqueline L. Nuñez
Compilation Editor: Anisa Baker

This book was compiled from the following books published by Tyndale House Publishers, Inc., in cooperation with the Livingstone Corporation and Lightwave Publishing, Inc.:
101 Questions Children Ask about God, 1992
102 Questions Children Ask about the Bible, 1994
103 Questions Children Ask about Right from Wrong, 1995
104 Questions Children Ask about Heaven and Angels, 1996
105 Questions Children Ask about Money Matters, 1997
106 Questions Children Ask about Our World, 1998
107 Questions Children Ask about Prayer, 1998
108 Questions Children Ask about Friends and School, 1999

Library of Congress Cataloging-in-Publication Data

801 questions kids ask about God: with answers from the Bible/[compiled] by David R. Veerman; editor, Anisa Baker.
    p. cm.
    Includes index.
    ISBN 978-0-8423-3788-5
    1. Christian education—Home training.   2. Christian education of children.   3. God—Biblical teaching—Miscellanea.   4. Children's questions and answers.
I. Title: Eight hundred one questions kids ask about God.   II. Title: Eight hundred and one questions kids ask about God.   III. Veerman, David.   IV. Baker, Anisa.
BV1590.A16 2000
248.8'45—dc21   00-044705

Printed in the United States of America

15
16   15   14

CONTENTS

Questions
Kids Ask

From Beginning
to End

1

Creation

Q 1: Why did God create the world?

A: God created the world and everything in it because he enjoys making things, and he wanted to be with us. God created people because he wanted to have friends, men and women, and boys and girls with whom he could share his love. He created the world for them to live in and enjoy.

KEY VERSES: *In the beginning God created the heavens and the earth. . . . Then God looked over all he had made, and he saw that it was excellent in every way. (Genesis 1:1, 31)*

NOTE TO PARENTS: This question is a good opportunity to tell your children that God's plan involves them. God created the world and everything in it—including your children—so that he could have people to love.

Q 2: How did God make people?

A: The Bible tells us that God made Adam from the "dust of the ground." In other words, God took something he had already made, dust, and formed a man's body out of it and then gave that body life. God made Adam, the first man, just the way he wanted him. Then God made Eve from part of Adam, just the way he wanted her. We're all made by God. And he has made us just right.

SCULPTURE
(not the way God did it)

KEY VERSE: *The LORD God formed a man's body from the dust of the ground and breathed into it the breath of life. And the man became a living person. (Genesis 2:7)*

Q 3: Why did God make people?

A: People are special creations, not just different animals. God created people to be his friends and to take care of the world. Unlike animals, human beings can talk to each other and to God. People are the only part of God's marvelous creation that can be friends with God. And he created them perfect—that's why Adam and Eve were not ashamed of their nakedness. But people are also the only ones who can sin.

KEY VERSES: *Then God said, "Let us make people in our image, to be like ourselves. They will be masters over all life—the fish in the sea, the birds in the sky, and all the livestock, wild animals, and small animals." So God created people in his own image; God patterned them after himself; male and female he created them. (Genesis 1:26-27)*

Q 4:

How did God make Adam and Eve?

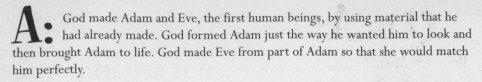

A: God made Adam and Eve, the first human beings, by using material that he had already made. God formed Adam just the way he wanted him to look and then brought Adam to life. God made Eve from part of Adam so that she would match him perfectly.

KEY VERSES: *The LORD God formed a man's body from the dust of the ground and breathed into it the breath of life. And the man became a living person. . . . So the LORD God caused Adam to fall into a deep sleep. He took one of Adam's ribs and closed up the place from which he had taken it. Then the LORD God made a woman from the rib and brought her to Adam. (Genesis 2:7, 21-22)*

NOTE TO PARENTS: A young child's concrete understanding can be a barrier to understanding this because the creation of Adam and Eve was a miracle. Explaining it as such may be the best approach, especially if your child is asking about the exact process that God used.

Q 5:

How did God make everyone else after Adam and Eve?

A: When God created animals and plants, he gave them the ability to reproduce themselves. The same is true with Adam and Eve—God created them with the ability to make babies. Adam and Eve had babies; then, when those children grew up, they got married and also had children. Those children also grew up and had babies. As time went on, there were more and more people on the earth. And although God didn't make each person the same way he created Adam and Eve, he was still involved with the creation of each one. He watched over and put him or her (and you) together just right. Just think—God carefully formed you in your mother's womb. You are very special to him!

KEY VERSES: *Now Adam slept with his wife, Eve, and she became pregnant. When the time came, she gave birth to Cain, and she said, "With the LORD's help, I have brought forth a man!" Later she gave birth to a second son and named him Abel. When they grew up, Abel became a shepherd, while Cain was a farmer. (Genesis 4:1-2)*

NOTE TO PARENTS: Many parents avoid this issue because they are uncomfortable talking about sex. Don't communicate nonverbally that this is a dirty or embarrassing topic. But at the same time, don't give children more information than they want or need.

Q 6:

How did Adam know what to name the animals?

A: God gave Adam the job of naming the animals, much like when your parents might ask you to name your pet. Adam named the animals whatever he wanted. But Adam didn't speak English, so the names he used are not the ones we use today. Adam lived a very long time ago, and today each language has its own words for the animals in our world.

KEY VERSES: *The LORD God formed from the soil every kind of animal and bird. He brought them to Adam to see what he would call them, and Adam chose a name for each one. He gave names to all the livestock, birds, and wild animals. (Genesis 2:19-20)*

Q 7:

What made the Garden of Eden prettier than other gardens today?

A: The Garden of Eden was more beautiful than any garden today because God made it that way. Eden was perfect, and God was there. The whole world was perfect because it hadn't yet been spoiled by sin. When Adam and Eve sinned, God made them leave the Garden, and the whole world changed because of their sin. Thistles and thorns began to grow, animals began to eat each other, and human beings had to work hard at living in the world.

KEY VERSE: *The LORD God banished Adam and his wife from the Garden of Eden, and he sent Adam out to cultivate the ground from which he had been made. (Genesis 3:23)*

Q 8:

What did Adam and Eve "dress" the land with?

A: The word *dress* that is used in some Bible versions means "take care of" or "tend." So when God told Adam and Eve to "dress" the land, he was telling them to take care of the rest of his creation.

KEY VERSE: *The LORD God placed the man in the Garden of Eden to tend and care for it. (Genesis 2:15)*

NOTE TO PARENTS: This kind of question is a good example of why it is important to choose an age-appropriate translation of the Bible for your child. There are many excellent translations from which to choose. The best one for your child is the one that uses words that he or she already knows.

Q 9:

How did God create the earth?

A: Whenever we make something, like a craft, a drawing, or a sand castle, we have to start with special materials, like clay, string, glue, paper, crayons, and sand. We can't even imagine creating something out of nothing—by just saying the words and making it appear. But God is so powerful that he can do what is impossible for us. That includes making anything he wants, even creating things from nothing. That's what it means to be God—he can do anything.

KEY VERSES: *In the beginning the Word already existed. He was with God, and he was God. He was in the beginning with God. He created everything there is. Nothing exists that he didn't make. (John 1:1-3)*

Q 10:

Why did God make mosquitoes?

A: When we're being attacked by mosquitoes, it's easy to wonder why God made pests and other animals that can harm us. When God created the world, it was perfect. Only after sin entered the picture did animals and human beings become enemies, causing humans to protect and defend themselves. So now mosquitoes try to feed off of us. They, in turn, become food for birds and bats. In the future, in the new heaven and new earth, animals won't hurt people or each other.

KEY VERSES: *In that day the wolf and the lamb will live together; the leopard and the goat will be at peace. Calves and yearlings will be safe among lions, and a little child will lead them all. The cattle will graze among bears. Cubs and calves will lie down together. And lions will eat grass as the livestock do. Babies will crawl safely among poisonous snakes. Yes, a little child will put its hand in a nest of deadly snakes and pull it out unharmed. Nothing will hurt or destroy in all my holy mountain. And as the waters fill the sea, so the earth will be filled with people who know the LORD. (Isaiah 11:6-9)*

Q 11:

Why do sharks eat people?

A: Sharks attack people because they are meat-eaters. When they are hungry, they will attack anything that looks good to eat. Sharks don't go looking for people to attack—they just react to what comes near them. The best thing to do is to be smart and stay away from sharks. When we go where we shouldn't go, we get into trouble—like walking in poison ivy or playing in a thunderstorm. There are dangers in the world, and we should be careful to avoid them.

KEY VERSES: *Wisdom will enter your heart, and knowledge will fill you with joy. Wise planning will watch over you. Understanding will keep you safe. (Proverbs 2:10-11)*

NOTE TO PARENTS: The question of why God made animals that can harm us is answered in Question 10. The answer according to Scripture is that we live in a sinful world (Genesis 3:14-19).

Q 12:

If God made spiders, why do people squish them?

A: God created spiders just as he made all the other animals. But there's a great difference between animals and human beings. People are created in God's image and are supposed to take care of all creation—including all animals and plants. God put people in charge of creation, but this does not mean we can harm and kill for fun or destroy the world as we please. We can kill animals and plants for food and to control their population; we can remove or kill spiders, insects, and so forth that threaten us or make it difficult for us to live. But we should be kind to animals when possible and take good care of the world.

KEY VERSE: *God blessed them and told them, "Multiply and fill the earth and subdue it. Be masters over the fish and birds and all the animals." (Genesis 1:28)*

NOTE TO PARENTS: Some children want to hurt animals, while others want to be compassionate. God's desire is for us to be compassionate and wise rulers of all animal life (Proverbs 12:10). This should not be taken to such an extreme that we think eating meat is wrong. God has provided animals as a source of food and has given us permission to eat meat (see Acts 10).

Q 13:
Why did God make people red and yellow, black and white?

A: Can you imagine a world in which everyone looked the same—the same height, weight, color of hair, length of nose, color of eyes, size of ears, and color of skin? That would be boring—and how would we tell people apart? Instead, God created all kinds and colors of people. Some are tall; some are short; some are brown; some are pink; some have straight black hair; some have curly red hair. They are all special to God. He created them, and he wove each person together in their mother's womb. Don't you just love the differences and what makes you special? God does!

KEY VERSE: *In this new life, it doesn't matter if you are a Jew or a Gentile, circumcised or uncircumcised, barbaric, uncivilized, slave, or free. Christ is all that matters, and he lives in all of us. (Colossians 3:11)*

Q 14:
Did God make people in outer space?

A: Although people may talk about creatures in outer space, no one really knows whether there is life on other planets. Most of the talk about other life forms comes from make-believe movies and what people imagine *might* be true. But if there is life in other parts of the universe, God is in charge of it because God is in charge of the whole universe. God created *everything,* and he is the God of all life everywhere, no matter where it may be.

KEY VERSE: *Christ is the one through whom God created everything in heaven and earth. He made the things we can see and the things we can't see—kings, kingdoms, rulers, and authorities. Everything has been created through him and for him. (Colossians 1:16)*

Q 15:
How does God make the sun and moon go up and down?

A: God made powerful laws to govern the universe. These laws control the movements of the sun, moon, earth, and other planets and stars. For example, one law called "gravity" draws objects toward each other. Other natural laws control the weather. Many forces determine whether the day will be sunny or cloudy, or warm or cold, such as the heat from the sun, the currents in the ocean, the wind, and many others. God set up the rules that make all these forces work together. And because God controls the entire universe, he can interrupt the laws if he wants to—bringing rain to dry land or bright sunshine to flooded areas. How powerful God must be to control all that!

KEY VERSE: *The heavens tell of the glory of God. The skies display his marvelous craftsmanship. (Psalm 19:1)*

NOTE TO PARENTS: Part of this is a science issue. If your children are wondering how the forces of nature work, don't be afraid of encouraging them to learn more about the natural sciences. The power and wonder of nature can be used to inspire awe and worship of God. The heavens declare his glory! (See Psalm 19.)

Q 16:

Why do some people believe that humans came from monkeys?

A:

Many people today believe that human beings descended from apelike creatures millions of years ago. In other words, they believe that way, way back in time certain animals changed so that they eventually became human. This is known as the theory of evolution.

There are three main reasons that people believe this: (1) They prefer *not* to believe that God created Adam and Eve and that all people descended from those two people, so they need another explanation. (2) Many scientists tell us that the theory of evolution explains the fossil record. Therefore, it seems reasonable to people. (3) So many *other* people believe the theory of evolution that they assume it must be true.

The Bible teaches, however, that God created human beings at a certain time and that he created them "in his own image" (Genesis 1:27). This means that humans are not just smart animals. Every human being is a special creation of God, from a tiny unborn baby to the oldest person on Earth. The Bible also says that only God was witness to creation.

KEY VERSE: *God created people in his own image; God patterned them after himself; male and female he created them. (Genesis 1:27)*

NOTE TO PARENTS: Evolution is merely a theory—one way of explaining the past. Many textbooks and teachers today present it as fact, but it is not. Explain this to your children so they will be prepared for discussions in school.

Q 17:

Can you figure out how old the earth is by yourself?

A:

No. Scientists have come up with ways to figure out how old the world is, but no one can know for sure whether these ways are true, and it is impossible to test them because no one can go back in time. There is no book that tells about everything that happened since the creation of the earth. Not even the Bible has an unbroken record of history. Many people think that the earth is billions of years old; others think it is much younger. But no one really knows how old the earth is, and there is no foolproof way to find out.

What we do know is this: God created Adam and Eve and all life on earth many thousands of years ago. It was not an accident or a product of time—it was God's doing.

KEY VERSES: *[God said,] "Where were you when I laid the foundations of the earth? Tell me, if you know so much. Do you know how its dimensions were determined and who did the surveying? What supports its foundations, and who laid its cornerstone as the morning stars sang together and all the angels shouted for joy?" (Job 38:4-7)*

Q 18:

Why is the world getting overpopulated?

A: Some people say the world is getting overpopulated, but it is not true. There is plenty of room for everyone. It is true that many *cities* have too many people. In fact, in some places thousands of poor people live in an area that is much too small for them. And in some areas people do not get enough food. But the world itself has enough room for everyone, and it has enough farmland to grow food for everyone too.

Selfishness is a bigger problem than the threat of overpopulation. If people would help each other and always be kind to each other, hunger and overcrowding would not be so much of a problem. God loves each person and has a special place for all of us—from the tiniest unborn baby to the oldest person alive.

KEY VERSES: *Children are a gift from the LORD; they are a reward from him. Children born to a young man are like sharp arrows in a warrior's hands. How happy is the man whose quiver is full of them! He will not be put to shame when he confronts his accusers at the city gates. (Psalm 127:3-5)*

Q 19:

How come God makes storms with lightning and thunder?

A: God made laws that control how the weather works. Thunder storms are part of our weather. Without rain, the grass, flowers, and crops wouldn't grow. The lightning and thunder in those storms come from the electricity in the air and on the earth. Of course, God can interrupt his laws of nature. But he made those laws so the earth would work. God doesn't send storms to scare us or hurt us. But storms can be dangerous, so we should stay out of their way and find cover when they come.

KEY VERSES: *The clouds poured down their rain; the thunder rolled and crackled in the sky. Your arrows of lightning flashed. Your thunder roared from the whirlwind; the lightning lit up the world! The earth trembled and shook. (Psalm 77:17-18)*

NOTE TO PARENTS: Many natural disasters are the result of sin in the world. Of course we don't know all the reasons for hurricanes, earthquakes, tornadoes, and other terrible calamities. But some natural disasters are clearly the result of misusing the environment (for example, strip mining) or poor planning (for example, building on a flood plain).

God

Q 20:
How was God created?

A: God was not created; he has always existed. This is impossible for us to understand because everything else we know about has a beginning and an end. But God had no beginning, and he has no end. He always was, and he always will be.

Imagine going on a deep-sea dive and being able to talk to the fish at the bottom of the sea. Imagine trying to explain to the fish what life is like for humans above the surface of the water and on land. The fish would not be able to understand, no matter how hard you tried to explain it. Everything he knows is in the water. *You* can breathe air and walk on the land, but the fish knows nothing about that. So the fish thinks it's silly or impossible.

That is the way it is with God. God created everything we know, including time. Beginnings and endings are limitations of our world, but not of God. That is one of the great things about him—he is so much greater than we are!

KEY VERSES: *In the beginning the Word already existed. He was with God, and he was God. He was in the beginning with God. He created everything there is. Nothing exists that he didn't make. (John 1:1-3)*

Q 21:
What does God look like?

A: No one knows what God "looks like" because God is invisible and doesn't have a physical body as we do. But we can learn about God and see what God acts like by learning about his Son, Jesus. In the Bible we can read about how Jesus lived, how he treated people, and what he taught. That's what God is like.

KEY VERSE: *Jesus replied, "Philip, don't you even yet know who I am, even after all the time I have been with you? Anyone who has seen me has seen the Father! So why are you asking to see him?" (John 14:9)*

Q 22:
Does God have friends or is he alone?

A: God doesn't have other "gods" to be friends with. He is the only God there is. God doesn't need friends the way we do; he is perfectly happy being alone. But God also wants to have friendship with us. In fact, God wants to be our closest friend. So he has done a lot to make friends with us and to have our friendship. That's why he created us, sent Jesus to save us, gave us the Bible, and gave us the church.

KEY VERSES: *[Jesus said,] "You are my friends if you obey me. I no longer call you servants, because a master doesn't confide in his servants. Now you are my friends, since I have told you everything the Father told me." (John 15:14-15)*

Q 23:
Where does God live?

A: Sometimes we think of God as though he were another person like us. And just as we can only be one place at a time and we need a place to live, we think that God is the same way. But God isn't limited to a physical body or to one place at a time. In fact, God lives everywhere, especially inside people who love him. We call church "God's house" because that's where people who love God gather together to worship him. But no matter where we are, God is with us. We can never be lost to his love. God also lives in heaven. Eventually, we will live there, too.

KEY VERSES: *[Solomon said,] "Will God really live on earth? Why, even the highest heavens cannot contain you. How much less this Temple I have built! Listen to my prayer and my request, O LORD my God. Hear the cry and the prayer that your servant is making to you today. May you watch over this Temple both day and night, this place where you have said you would put your name. May you always hear the prayers I make toward this place. May you hear the humble and earnest requests from me and your people Israel when we pray toward this place. Yes, hear us from heaven where you live, and when you hear, forgive."(1 Kings 8:27-30)*

Q 24:
Why can't we see God?

A: We can't see God because he's invisible. But we *can* see what he does. Balloons are filled with air that we can't see, but we see the balloon get big as the air is put in. Radio waves are invisible, but they exist. Just because we can't see God doesn't mean he isn't real. Believing that God is there even though we can't see him is *faith*. Someday, in heaven, we will see God face-to-face.

KEY VERSE: *Now we see things imperfectly as in a poor mirror, but then we will see everything with perfect clarity. All that I know now is partial and incomplete, but then I will know everything completely, just as God knows me now. (1 Corinthians 13:12)*

NOTE TO PARENTS: Young children struggle with this because of their concrete way of thinking. Using illustrations like the ones here are helpful, but still imperfect; we can't see air because its molecules don't form a solid enough image for us to see, not because it has no physical form. In contrast, God is invisible to us because he is a spirit.

Q 25:

Can Christians hear God talking to them?

A: In the Bible we read about people hearing God's voice. Today, the main way that God speaks to us is through the Bible. That's why it's called "God's Word"—the Bible is God's message to us. God may also speak to us through people and circumstances and in other ways. But God will never tell us to do something that goes against what he says in the Bible. And don't forget, God is with us all the time.

KEY VERSES: *Long ago God spoke many times and in many ways to our ancestors through the prophets. But now in these final days, he has spoken to us through his Son. God promised everything to the Son as an inheritance, and through the Son he made the universe and everything in it. (Hebrews 1:1-2)*

Q 26:

Dad, why do I need two fathers, you and God?

A: We call God "our Father" because he created us, watches over us, and provides everything we need. He's like a human father, only perfect. God has given us human fathers and mothers to take care of us on earth. That's why God tells children to obey their parents and their heavenly Father—it's for their own good.

KEY VERSE: *[Jesus said,] "If you sinful people know how to give good gifts to your children, how much more will your heavenly Father give good gifts to those who ask him." (Matthew 7:11)*

Q 27:

Does God see everything that we do?

A: Yes, God sees everything we do, both good and bad. We can't hide from him. God is happy when we do what is right and sad when we do wrong. God can reward us for doing what's right, even when no one else knows about it.

KEY VERSES: *God carefully watches the way people live; he sees everything they do. No darkness is thick enough to hide the wicked from his eyes. (Job 34:21-22)*

NOTE TO PARENTS: This question may arise from a guilty conscience. Your child may want to talk about something that he or she did.

Q 28:

Does God have things to do at nighttime?

A: God does not have a body like ours, so he does not need to sleep. And because God is everywhere and lives in eternity, there's no night or day for him (and when it's night here, it's day somewhere else). So God is always working when we are sleeping. When you go to sleep, you can be sure that God is awake, watching over you and taking care of you.

KEY VERSES: *He will not let you stumble and fall; the one who watches over you will not sleep. Indeed, he who watches over Israel never tires and never sleeps. (Psalm 121:3-4)*

Q 29:

Does God have a sense of humor?

A: Yes. One clue that God has a sense of humor is that men, women, boys, and girls love to laugh. Genesis 1:26-27 says that God created human beings in his image. That means that in many ways we are like God—and he is like us. So if we have a sense of humor, God probably does, too. What's more, in his Word, God talks quite a bit about joy, happiness, fun, and laughter: "Sarah declared, 'God has brought me laughter!'" (Genesis 21:6); "We were filled with laughter, and we sang for joy!" (Psalm 126:2); "Always be full of joy in the Lord. I'll say it again—rejoice!" (Philippians 4:4). It is clear that God wants his people to enjoy life.

But the fact that God has a sense of humor doesn't mean that he enjoys all the things that we think are funny or that he likes all our jokes. Some people are cruel with their humor; they laugh when people are hurt, or they make fun of others. That's wrong. We should laugh *with* people, not at them. Tell good jokes, laugh, enjoy life; God wants you to be filled with joy.

KEY VERSE: *A cheerful heart is good medicine, but a crushed spirit dries up the bones. (Proverbs 17:22)*

Q 30:

How do I become even closer to God than I am now?

A: Think of God as someone who wants to be your very close friend. For that to happen, you will need to spend time together. You can spend time with God by reading his Word, the Bible. You can ask your parents to help you know where and how to read. Also, you can talk with God about your life (called praying). When you pray, tell God about your fears and hopes. Thank him for loving you. Tell him that you are sorry for disobeying him, and ask him to help you to get closer to him and do what he wants. You can also tell him about other people and their problems, asking him to help those people, too.

You also get closer to God through worship. That's why churches have worship services. There, with other Christians, you can sing praises to God, talk to him, think about him, remember how much he loves you and what Jesus did for you, and learn from his Word.

Remember that God will draw closer to you if you draw closer to him. Tell him you want to get to know him better. Ask him to draw you closer to himself. You can't get closer to God just by doing a few "Christian" things. But you can get closer to him by having a relationship with him and asking him to help you get to know him better!

KEY VERSE: *Draw close to God, and God will draw close to you. Wash your hands, you sinners; purify your hearts, you hypocrites. (James 4:8)*

Q 31:

How is God always there?

A: God can always be with us because he does not have a physical body. God does not have to stay in one place the way we do. We don't know exactly how this works, but that's OK. God is much, much greater and more amazing than we can imagine. Isn't it great to know that God is there . . . and here?

KEY VERSE: *[Jesus said,] "Teach these new disciples to obey all the commands I have given you. And be sure of this: I am with you always, even to the end of the age." (Matthew 28:20)*

Jesus

Q 32:
Is Jesus God?

A: Jesus is fully God. When he came to earth and was born of the Virgin Mary, Jesus also became a human being, a person like you. So Jesus is both God and man. As God, Jesus has always existed—he was not created when he was born. Instead, he willingly chose to take on a human body.

KEY VERSES: *In the beginning the Word already existed. He was with God, and he was God. He was in the beginning with God. (John 1:1-2)*

Q 33:
How can God be three persons and one person at the same time?

A: We don't know *how* God can be three persons at the same time, but we know he is because the Bible tells us so. The idea of three in one (the Trinity) is very hard to understand. Some people use the example of water. Water can be a liquid, a gas, or a solid. We usually see water in liquid form, as when we use it for drinking or for taking a bath. But water can also be a gas, as when it turns to steam. And it can be a solid, in the form of ice. But whether liquid, gas, or solid, it's still water. In some ways God is like a family with father, mother, and child—three persons and one family. Just remember that the Trinity does not mean that we have three gods. There is one God with three persons. The Trinity also does not mean that God wears three hats, or takes on three roles, at different times. All three persons—Father, Son, and Holy Spirit— have always existed.

KEY VERSE: *[Jesus said,] "Go and make disciples of all the nations, baptizing them in the name of the Father and the Son and the Holy Spirit." (Matthew 28:19)*

Q 34:
Do God and Jesus cry?

A: As a man, Jesus cried real tears when he was sad. God does not shed tears today, but he feels sad when people are hurting, when they disobey him, and when they don't believe in him. We can bring God joy by living as we should, showing love to others, and telling people about Christ.

KEY VERSE: *Then Jesus wept. (John 11:35)*

Q 35:

Did Jesus really live just like me, or was he pretend?

A: Jesus is real. He came to earth and was born as a baby (we celebrate Jesus' birth at Christmas). And he lived like other ordinary people. Some stories we read and hear are made up and weren't meant to be taken as true. But the stories in the Bible really happened, and that's where we can read about Jesus.

KEY VERSE: *The one who existed from the beginning is the one we have heard and seen. We saw him with our own eyes and touched him with our own hands. He is Jesus Christ, the Word of life.* (1 John 1:1)

Q 36:

Why was Jesus born in a stinky stable?

A: God sent his own Son, Jesus, when the time was right. Jesus' birth tells us the kind of Savior he is. At the time Jesus was born, the Roman ruler of Palestine (where the Jews lived—Israel's Promised Land) was Herod, an evil man. Herod had great forts and palaces built so he could feel safe and powerful. One of the huge forts was right outside Bethlehem. But Jesus—the *true* king and ruler of the universe—came to earth and was born in a stinky stable. Herod's kingdom and power were very temporary; he's dead and his buildings are in ruins. But Jesus' kingdom and power last forever. So one reason Jesus was born in such a place was to show us that he and his ways are the opposite of the world's. Jesus' kingdom doesn't come by force but by God working in each person. Jesus' birth in a stable also lets us know that he came for *all* people, not just the rich and famous.

KEY VERSES: *While they were there, the time came for her baby to be born. She gave birth to her first child, a son. She wrapped him snugly in strips of cloth and laid him in a manger, because there was no room for them in the village inn.* (Luke 2:6-7)

NOTE TO PARENTS: Children may ask the related question, "How could Mary have a baby if she wasn't married to God?" The best answer is, "I don't know." Exactly how Mary conceived is a mystery. Jesus was unique—the only Son of God. Jesus' birth was a miracle.

Q 37:

Did Jesus ever do anything bad when he was little?

A: Jesus was born as a baby and grew up as a little boy and into a young man. When he was a child, Jesus had to learn many things, like how to hold a cup, how to talk, and how to count. He learned things from his parents and went to school to learn, too. But though Jesus was a real human being, he never did anything wrong—he never sinned—like stealing, lying, disobeying his parents, or saying bad words. Sometimes Jesus did things that *others* said were bad—like helping certain people and speaking out against wrong. But Jesus always did what was right—he always obeyed God.

KEY VERSES: *This suffering is all part of what God has called you to. Christ, who suffered for you, is your example. Follow in his steps. He never sinned, and he never deceived anyone. He did not retaliate when he was insulted. When he suffered, he did not threaten to get even. He left his case in the hands of God, who always judges fairly. (1 Peter 2:21-23)*

Q 38:

Why did Jesus dress so funny?

A: The clothes worn by Jesus and his followers may look different to us today, but they were in style back then. Jesus wore what people wore at that time. His clothes fit the climate and culture of the day. No one who lived in Jesus' time told him that he dressed funny, and they should know.

KEY VERSES: *When the soldiers had crucified Jesus, they divided his clothes among the four of them. They also took his robe, but it was seamless, woven in one piece from the top. So they said, "Let's not tear it but throw dice to see who gets it." This fulfilled the Scripture that says, "They divided my clothes among themselves and threw dice for my robe." (John 19:23-24)*

NOTE TO PARENTS: Children get their idea of how Jesus dressed from Bible and Sunday school art. This is what we think Jesus might have looked like, but we have no pictures or descriptions of his physical appearance, so we don't know exactly what he looked like.

Q 39:

Why did the Holy Spirit come down on Jesus like a dove?

A: When Jesus was thirty years old, John the Baptist baptized him. When Jesus came up out of the water, the Holy Spirit came down on him in the form of a dove. The Holy Spirit is a spirit and doesn't have a body, so the Spirit took a form that people could see. A dove was a great form to take because when people saw doves, they thought of peace and purity, and that's exactly what the Holy Spirit brings to people. After Jesus left the earth, he sent the Holy Spirit to live here in his place. But now, instead of taking a special form, the Holy Spirit lives inside us. When a person trusts in Christ as Savior, the Holy Spirit comes to live inside him or her.

KEY VERSE: *The Holy Spirit descended on him in the form of a dove. And a voice from heaven said, "You are my beloved Son, and I am fully pleased with you." (Luke 3:22)*

Q 40:

Why did Jesus get tempted by the devil?

A: When someone tempts you, that person is trying to get you to do something. Because Satan is against Jesus, he tried to get Jesus to do something wrong, to sin. But Jesus didn't give in—he didn't sin. Being tempted isn't sin; giving in to temptation is.

KEY VERSES: *This High Priest of ours understands our weaknesses, for he faced all of the same temptations we do, yet he did not sin. So let us come boldly to the throne of our gracious God. There we will receive his mercy, and we will find grace to help us when we need it. (Hebrews 4:15-16)*

Q 41:

Why does Jesus want us to follow him?

A: Jesus told the people to follow him because he is the way to God, heaven, and eternal life. When Jesus was on earth, the disciples and others followed him by walking close to him and listening to his words. Today, we follow Jesus by copying his example and by doing what he says.

KEY VERSES: *Jesus said to the disciples, "If any of you wants to be my follower, you must put aside your selfish ambition, shoulder your cross, and follow me. If you try to keep your life for yourself, you will lose it. But if you give up your life for me, you will find true life. And how do you benefit if you gain the whole world but lose your own soul in the process? Is anything worth more than your soul?" (Matthew 16:24-26)*

Q 42:

How did Jesus do miracles?

A: Jesus was able to do miracles because he was God's Son. The miracles weren't magic or tricks; they really happened. Jesus performed miracles because he had compassion on people and because he wanted to show the people that he was the Messiah, the promised one from God. Only God can do real miracles. Sometimes God worked his miracles through special people, like the prophets or apostles. We read in the Bible about a lot of miracles, but miracles didn't happen every day. More miracles happened when Jesus was on earth than at any other time, but only during the three years that he was preaching and teaching in public. Jesus didn't do miracles to show off, and he didn't heal everybody. He had a purpose for everything he did.

KEY VERSES: *Jesus' disciples saw him do many other miraculous signs besides the ones recorded in this book. But these are written so that you may believe that Jesus is the Messiah, the Son of God, and that by believing in him you will have life. (John 20:30-31)*

Q 43:

If Jesus doesn't want us to get hurt, why did he tell us to chop our hands off and poke our eyes out?

A: When Jesus spoke about cutting off a hand or poking out an eye, he was purposely exaggerating to make his point. This is called *hyperbole*. It's like saying, "I'd give *anything* to have an ice cream cone right now." Even though you wouldn't actually do *anything,* you want everyone to know how badly you want it. Jesus wanted to make people realize how bad sin is; it's so bad that you should get rid of *anything* that makes you sin. Jesus didn't want us actually to cut off our hands or poke out our eyes. Cutting off your hand won't get you to heaven and won't get rid of sin in your life. But saying it that way shows us how important it is to sacrifice habits, friendships, or attitudes that cause us to sin.

KEY VERSE: *[Jesus said,] "If your hand or foot causes you to sin, cut it off and throw it away. It is better to enter heaven crippled or lame than to be thrown into the unquenchable fire with both of your hands and feet."(Matthew 18:8)*

NOTE TO PARENTS: Jesus was also addressing the issue of legalism; the religious leaders were very concerned about keeping every letter of the law, and they had added hundreds of rules and regulations of their own. In effect, Jesus was saying that if they were serious about keeping the law, they should take drastic action. The point? Putting out an eye doesn't stop a child from envying his friend's bike; envy comes from the heart and involves the mind and imagination, not just what a person sees.

Q 44:

How did Jesus walk on water?

A: Jesus did a lot of miracles. We don't know how he did them. Jesus is God, so he can do anything. Walking on the water was not Jesus' ordinary way of getting around. He did this miracle, like other miracles, to teach his disciples and to show them his power. Jesus is Lord of the laws of the universe—he's in charge of the water, too, so he can walk on it whenever he wants to.

KEY VERSES: *That evening his disciples went down to the shore to wait for him. But as darkness fell and Jesus still hadn't come back, they got into the boat and headed out across the lake toward Capernaum. Soon a gale swept down upon them as they rowed, and the sea grew very rough. They were three or four miles out when suddenly they saw Jesus walking on the water toward the boat. They were terrified, but he called out to them, "I am here! Don't be afraid." Then they were eager to let him in, and immediately the boat arrived at their destination! (John 6:16-21)*

NOTE TO PARENTS: Lots of well-meaning people have tried to explain miracles (such as Jesus' walking on the water) to make them believable to children. But this is a tragic mistake. The fact that miracles are incredible is exactly the point—they show us that God is awesome and powerful.

Q 45:

Why did the disciples tell the people Jesus was too busy to see the kids?

A: Many parents brought their children to see Jesus, and Jesus always welcomed them. The disciples tried to stop them because they didn't understand how much Jesus loved children and wanted all people to come to him. Sometimes adults act like kids aren't important or that children get in the way. But Jesus thinks kids are very important. He thinks *you* are important. Don't be afraid to bring your requests to him.

KEY VERSE: *Jesus said, "Let the children come to me. Don't stop them! For the Kingdom of Heaven belongs to such as these." (Matthew 19:14)*

NOTE TO PARENTS: Remember that Jesus told us to be like children in our belief in him. Watch your kids for clues about how this is done.

Q 46:

Why did Judas betray Jesus?

A: Judas turned against Jesus and betrayed him because Judas did not care about what Jesus had come to earth to do. Judas had hoped that Jesus would be a military leader and free the Jews from the Romans. Also, Judas loved money, and the religious leaders who wanted to kill Jesus offered Judas money to help them capture Jesus. If Judas had been one of Jesus' true disciples, he would not have betrayed him. Afterward, when he saw that Jesus was going to be killed, Judas was so upset at what he had done that he killed himself.

KEY VERSES: *Judas Iscariot, one of the twelve disciples, went to the leading priests and asked, "How much will you pay me to betray Jesus to you?" And they gave him thirty pieces of silver. From that time on, Judas began looking for the right time and place to betray Jesus. (Matthew 26:14-16)*

Q 47:

Why were the Roman soldiers so mean?

A: The Roman soldiers were mean for the same reason that people are mean today—they didn't love God or care about his ways. Roman soldiers were trained to keep people in line and kill if they had to. The Roman soldiers were mean to Jesus because they treated all criminals that way and they thought Jesus was a criminal just like all the others. (Some religious leaders wanted Jesus crucified because they didn't like what he was saying and because he claimed to be the Son of God.) And the soldiers felt pressure from each other; one started and the others joined in. Though the Roman authorities found Jesus innocent, they went along with the crowd and killed him on the cross, just as the prophets had predicted (see Psalms 22:16-18; 34:20; Zechariah 12:10).

KEY VERSE: *They beat him on the head with a stick, spit on him, and dropped to their knees in mock worship. (Mark 15:19)*

Q 48:

Why did the people say, "Come down off the cross if you are the Son of God"?

A: The people who said this didn't believe in Jesus and thought he was lying when he claimed to be God. Actually, Jesus had the power to come down off the cross, but he didn't come down because he loved us and wanted to pay for our sins. When Adam and Eve sinned, everybody was separated from God. Jesus died so everyone could have the chance to be forgiven and be with God again. If Jesus had saved himself and had come off the cross, we couldn't be saved from our sins. Jesus showed his power in a much greater way—by rising from the dead three days later. Aren't you glad Jesus stayed on the cross?

KEY VERSES: *The people passing by shouted abuse, shaking their heads in mockery. "Ha! Look at you now!" they yelled at him. "You can destroy the Temple and rebuild it in three days, can you? Well then, save yourself and come down from the cross!" (Mark 15:29-30)*

NOTE TO PARENTS: A child's questions about Jesus' death on the cross may be a good opportunity to explain that he died for *them,* in *their* place, to pay for *their* sins. Explain that your children, individually, can trust in Jesus for salvation. You can lead them in a prayer confessing their sin, expressing trust in Jesus to save them, and thanking him for eternal life.

Q 49:

Why did God let them hurt Jesus?

A: When Jesus was being hurt, he could have called on angels to save him. After all, he was God's Son. But Jesus chose to suffer and die *for us.* Jesus loved us so much that he did what it took to pay for our sins. Jesus and the Father agreed that it was necessary for him to die on the cross.

KEY VERSES: *He is so rich in kindness that he purchased our freedom through the blood of his Son, and our sins are forgiven. He has showered his kindness on us, along with all wisdom and understanding. God's secret plan has now been revealed to us; it is a plan centered on Christ, designed long ago according to his good pleasure. And this is his plan: At the right time he will bring everything together under the authority of Christ—everything in heaven and on earth. (Ephesians 1:7-10)*

Q 50:

Why do they call it "Good Friday" if that's the day Jesus died?

A: The day Jesus died is called "Good Friday" because it was a good day for us—Jesus died for us, in our place. That day was both a happy day and a sad day. It was sad because Jesus suffered and died. But it was happy because Jesus paid the penalty for our sins. At the time, the day was not seen as Good Friday. But by Easter morning, after Jesus had been raised from the dead, everybody knew it was good.

KEY VERSES: *Carrying the cross by himself, Jesus went to the place called Skull Hill (in Hebrew, Golgotha). There they crucified him. There were two others crucified with him, one on either side, with Jesus between them. (John 19:17-18)*

Q 51:

If Jesus died on the cross, how can he be alive today?

A: Jesus lived as a real human being. Jesus' death was a real death, too (he really died on the cross)—the people who killed him made sure of that. When Jesus was killed, all of his followers were very sad. Jesus' body was put in a grave. But three days later, God brought Jesus back to life. Jesus showed his wounds to his disciples. Jesus lives in his special "glorified" body in heaven today. Isn't that great?

KEY VERSES: *I passed on to you what was most important and what had also been passed on to me—that Christ died for our sins, just as the Scriptures said. He was buried, and he was raised from the dead on the third day, as the Scriptures said. (1 Corinthians 15:3-4)*

NOTE TO PARENTS: We call Jesus' post-resurrection body a "glorified" body. Jesus was recognized by the disciples, and he ate a meal with them. But he also was able to appear suddenly in their midst—he wasn't limited by space and time. We really don't know anything more about what his body was like or what our body will be like. (See Luke 24:36-43 and John 20:19-31.)

Q 52:

Did Jesus know that he would come to life again?

A: He sure did! He not only knew he would come to life again, he also told his disciples about it at least three times. But the disciples didn't seem to hear Jesus or understand what he was talking about because they were totally shocked by his death. They didn't expect Jesus to come back to life, so when they saw him, they didn't recognize him at first. But when Jesus came up close, talked with them, and ate with them, they knew it was him. After the Resurrection, Jesus appeared first to Mary Magdalene in the garden. Later, he appeared to two men walking on a road and then to the disciples gathered together in a room. He appeared to hundreds of others, too.

KEY VERSE: *[Jesus said about himself,] "They will mock him, spit on him, beat him with their whips, and kill him, but after three days he will rise again."(Mark 10:34)*

Q 53:

Why can't I see Jesus now?

A: Jesus went back to heaven to be with his Father, but he has *not* forgotten about his people. In fact, he is preparing a place for all who believe in him, getting it ready for when they die and go to be with him. Also, Jesus is acting as our High Priest (like in the Old Testament)—whenever his people sin, he presents his own death as a payment so God can forgive them.

You may remember that the Bible calls Satan the Accuser. That's because he tells God the believers' faults to get God to reject his people. (There's an example in Job 1:6-11.) Whenever the devil accuses a believer, Jesus defends that person. We can't see Jesus now because it's not a part of God's plan.

Meanwhile, Jesus has not left his people alone. He has sent the Holy Spirit to be with them wherever they go. That's why Jesus said, "It is best for you that I go away" (John 16:7). When Jesus comes back, he will take all believers to live with him forever. Then you *will* be able to see Jesus in person.

KEY VERSE: *[Jesus said,] "It is actually best for you that I go away, because if I don't, the Counselor won't come. If I do go away, he will come because I will send him to you."(John 16:7)*

Q 54:

Why did Jesus go up to heaven instead of staying here on earth?

A: Jesus is the Son of God, and his home is in heaven. He left his Father (and his home) to become a human being and live on the earth. So it's quite natural that Jesus would leave the earth and go back home. Jesus also went to heaven to prepare a place for us. And although Jesus left us, he also sent the Holy Spirit to take his place and be with us. Though Jesus couldn't be in two places at once, the Holy Spirit can; he can be everywhere because he lives inside all people who have trusted in Christ as Savior. Because Jesus went back to heaven, the Holy Spirit can be with you and in you, everywhere you go.

KEY VERSES: *[Jesus said,] "There are many rooms in my Father's home, and I am going to prepare a place for you. If this were not so, I would tell you plainly. When everything is ready, I will come and get you, so that you will always be with me where I am."(John 14:2-3)*

Q 55:

Why hasn't God told us when Jesus is coming back?

A: Jesus promised his disciples (and us) that he would return to earth some day. But when they asked *when,* he told them, "The Father sets those dates, and they are not for you to know" (Acts 1:7). Rather than be concerned with when Jesus will return, we should always live as though Jesus can return at any moment. In other words, we should always do what is right and tell others about God's salvation. Although God doesn't say exactly when Christ will return, he did say that certain things need to take place first. One of these is that Christ will not come back until the Gospel has been preached to the whole world. God has promised that Jesus will return soon, and every day that is passed is a day closer to his return.

KEY VERSE: *[Jesus said,] "No one knows the day or the hour when these things will happen, not even the angels in heaven or the Son himself. Only the Father knows."(Matthew 24:36)*

Salvation

Q 56:

Why do God and Jesus love people?

A: God loves us because that's what he decided to do. God doesn't love us because we're good or nice people. In fact, no one could ever be good enough to be worthy of God's love. Isn't it amazing that God loves us even though we sometimes ignore him and disobey him?

KEY VERSE: *God showed his great love for us by sending Christ to die for us while we were still sinners. (Romans 5:8)*

NOTE TO PARENTS: The best way to help children understand God's love is to demonstrate it to them. Hug them, train them, cheer them, guide them, discipline them, talk to them, spend time with them, accept them, forgive them, help them, stand by them, and provide for them—then they'll understand.

Q 57:

How can Jesus fit in my heart?

A: When we say "heart," we mean deep down inside us—where we really feel and believe. So when someone says, "Jesus lives in my heart," the person means that he has asked Jesus to be his Savior— to forgive and take care of him—and that Jesus is in charge of his life. When someone asks Jesus to take over, God really does come inside—the Holy Spirit comes and lives inside that person. And the Holy Spirit can be in all of the people who love God at the same time. Jesus wants to be very close to you, too, like a good friend. Through his Holy Spirit, he wants to "live in your heart."

KEY VERSES: *This message was kept secret for centuries and generations past, but now it has been revealed to his own holy people. For it has pleased God to tell his people that the riches and glory of Christ are for you Gentiles, too. For this is the secret: Christ lives in you, and this is your assurance that you will share in his glory. (Colossians 1:26-27)*

NOTE TO PARENTS: Children are often told that Jesus comes to live inside their hearts when they believe in him. Young children take this literally and think that a miniaturized Jesus actually lives in their chest. "Jesus lives in my heart" is a shorthand way of calling Jesus Savior and Lord. "Jesus goes with you everywhere" may be a better way of phrasing it for young children.

Q 58:
How do you get Jesus in your heart?

A: You become a Christian by asking Jesus to take over your life. You know that you have done wrong things, that you have sinned, and you recognize that you need Jesus to forgive your sins. So you tell Jesus about your sins and that you are sorry, and you ask for his forgiveness. Then you do what Jesus says.

KEY VERSES: *Now God has shown us a different way of being right in his sight—not by obeying the law but by the way promised in the Scriptures long ago. We are made right in God's sight when we trust in Jesus Christ to take away our sins. And we all can be saved in this same way, no matter who we are or what we have done. For all have sinned; all fall short of God's glorious standard. Yet now God in his gracious kindness declares us not guilty. He has done this through Christ Jesus, who has freed us by taking away our sins. (Romans 3:21-24)*

Q 59:
Why doesn't God take us to heaven as soon as we get saved?

A: God doesn't take his people to heaven right away because he wants them to grow in their faith. He also wants them to tell others about Christ, to help others, and to make the world better. God has work for his people to do.

KEY VERSE: *We are God's masterpiece. He has created us anew in Christ Jesus, so that we can do the good things he planned for us long ago. (Ephesians 2:10)*

Q 60:
Would God send nice people to hell if they are not Christians?

A: Compared to each other, some people are nice and some are mean. But compared to God, all people are not very good. All people need to be forgiven for their sins, not just "mean people." To be fair, God has to punish sin. God doesn't *want* to send anyone to hell. That's why he sent Jesus—to pay the penalty for our sins by dying on the cross. But, unfortunately, not all people are willing to admit that they sin and ask for forgiveness. They don't accept the payment of Jesus' death for them. So God lets them experience the results of their choice.

KEY VERSES: *As the Scriptures say, "No one is good— not even one. No one has real understanding; no one is seeking God. All have turned away from God; all have gone wrong. No one does good, not even one."(Romans 3:10-12)*

Q 61:

What is hell like?

A: According to the Bible, hell is very dark and very painful. It is a place of eternal suffering and separation from God. It is a place of grim loneliness. The worst thing about hell is that it is separate from God and from all that is good. There is no love, joy, fun, laughter, or celebration in hell. Some people make jokes about hell and say that they want to go there to be with their friends. But no one will have any friends in hell. No one should want to go there.

KEY VERSE: *His soul went to the place of the dead. There, in torment, he saw Lazarus in the far distance with Abraham. (Luke 16:23)*

NOTE TO PARENTS: Be very serious when you explain hell to your children. At the same time, however, tell them about heaven, a place of eternal love, joy, fun, laughter, and celebration. And assure them that they can go to heaven if they trust in Jesus.

Q 62:

Why is hell dark if they have fires?

A: The Bible uses a lot of pictures to give us an idea of what heaven and hell are like. Fire means burning and pain. Do you remember having a fever? You felt like you were burning up, but there was no flame. Darkness means loneliness. Can you imagine anything more lonely than sitting by yourself in total darkness? What God is telling us is that hell is a terrible place. We certainly don't want to go there.

KEY VERSE: *[Jesus said,] "Many Israelites—those for whom the Kingdom was prepared—will be cast into outer darkness, where there will be weeping and gnashing of teeth." (Matthew 8:12)*

NOTE TO PARENTS: Children hear conflicting descriptions of hell. They hear that hell is a dark place (Matthew 8:12) and yet a lake of fire (Revelation 19:20). (They may also have heard that it is cold.) Instead of grasping the meanings of these metaphors, the child is taking the images concretely.

Q 63:

Who ends up in hell?

A: Hell is the place where God will punish Satan and his followers—and all those who refuse to follow God. We don't know exactly who will go there because we don't make that judgment; God does. But God has made it possible for everyone to escape punishment in hell. He gives everyone the opportunity to go to heaven. That's why he sent Jesus to die on the cross. When Jesus suffered and died, he took our place—he paid the penalty for our sins. So if we trust in Jesus, we can escape hell and go to heaven. It sure would be great if all our friends, family, and neighbors would end up in heaven. Let's tell them how to get there.

KEY VERSE: *Anyone whose name was not found recorded in the Book of Life was thrown into the lake of fire. (Revelation 20:15)*

Q 64:

If I swear, will I go to hell when I die?

A: Although it is very important to watch what we say, God doesn't decide who goes to hell because of our speech. Instead, our forgiveness and eternal life are based on the death and resurrection of Jesus Christ. If we trust Jesus to save us, we are forgiven. Of course that doesn't make it all right to swear. We should always try to speak and do what is right.

KEY VERSES: *God saved you by his special favor when you believed. And you can't take credit for this; it is a gift from God. Salvation is not a reward for the good things we have done, so none of us can boast about it. (Ephesians 2:8-9)*

NOTE TO PARENTS: Many children think they are too bad or evil to be forgiven by God. If you sense that your child feels this way, he or she needs to know that God can forgive *any* sin. Tell your children that they are not uniquely bad—all people sin.

Q 65:
Will all of my friends go to heaven?

A: God loves your friends just as he loves you. Only God knows who will go to heaven and hell; we don't. But there is only one way to heaven—through Jesus. So we can go to heaven only if we have given our life to Christ. If your friends don't follow Jesus, you can help them understand by telling them the Good News about Jesus and how he died for them. Heaven is worth going to even if your friends don't. There will be no good times in hell.

KEY VERSE: *Jesus told him, "I am the way, the truth, and the life. No one can come to the Father except through me." (John 14:6)*

NOTE TO PARENTS: This may be a good opportunity to encourage your child to invite a friend to church or Sunday school.

Q 66:
Why isn't everyone a Christian?

A: Not everyone wants to be a Christian, and God doesn't force people to follow Jesus. Some people don't just reject Christ—they also act mean to Christians. That's because they don't understand the love that God has for them. We should try to tell these people about God's love for them.

KEY VERSES: *[Jesus said,] "Now I am coming to you. I have told them many things while I was with them so they would be filled with my joy. I have given them your word. And the world hates them because they do not belong to the world, just as I do not. I'm not asking you to take them out of the world, but to keep them safe from the evil one. They are not part of this world any more than I am." (John 17:13-16)*

NOTE TO PARENTS: You can pray with your child for others to become Christians.

Q 67:

Why didn't God just forgive everybody?

A: It would not be right or fair for God to just forgive everyone. There is a penalty that must be paid for doing wrong. The penalty for sinning against God is death, eternal death. But God loved us so much that he sent Jesus, his only Son, to pay our penalty. Jesus did this by dying on the cross in our place. Now everyone can be forgiven by trusting in Christ.

KEY VERSES: *All have sinned; all fall short of God's glorious standard. Yet now God in his gracious kindness declares us not guilty. He has done this through Christ Jesus, who has freed us by taking away our sins. For God sent Jesus to take the punishment for our sins and to satisfy God's anger against us. We are made right with God when we believe that Jesus shed his blood, sacrificing his life for us. God was being entirely fair and just when he did not punish those who sinned in former times. (Romans 3:23-25)*

Q 68:

Why doesn't God just zap the bad people?

A: God loves people so much, even the worst people in the world, that he is giving them time to turn away from being bad and to turn to him. God is very patient. Someday, however, the time will be up, and all those who refuse to live God's way and give their lives to Christ will be punished. That will be a very sad day, but it will come.

KEY VERSE: *The Lord isn't really being slow about his promise to return, as some people think. No, he is being patient for your sake. He does not want anyone to perish, so he is giving more time for everyone to repent. (2 Peter 3:9)*

Q 69:
How long is eternity?

A: We can't even imagine how long eternity is. Eternity goes on forever. Sometimes we have good times that we wish would never end—such as a party or a vacation or a visit by a friend from out of town. But they do come to an end. Eternity, however, never ends. God is eternal, and he has given us eternal life. If we know Jesus, we will live forever with him, someday in heaven, after our life on earth comes to an end.

KEY VERSE: *You must not forget, dear friends, that a day is like a thousand years to the Lord, and a thousand years is like a day. (2 Peter 3:8)*

Q 70:
What does God want us to do?

A: In the Bible, God's Word, God tells us what he wants us to do, how he wants us to live. Although there are a lot of messages and information in the Bible, God's four main instructions for our lives are: (1) believe in Jesus and trust him every day; (2) obey Jesus and do what he says; (3) love God and others; (4) be fair and honest and live for God without being proud about it.

KEY VERSES: *They replied, "What does God want us to do?" Jesus told them, "This is what God wants you to do: Believe in the one he has sent." (John 6:28-29)*

Suffering

Q 71:

Why do I feel afraid if Jesus is with me?

A: Jesus is always with us even though we don't see him and often we don't feel any different. Jesus wants us to learn to trust him, to believe and know that he is there. It's natural to feel afraid. In fact, being afraid can be good. We should be afraid of danger. For example, fear can keep us a safe distance from a mean dog or something else that might hurt us. God wants our fears to remind us to trust him. Being afraid should be a signal to trust God and do what he wants us to do. But it doesn't mean that Jesus isn't with us.

KEY VERSE: *May the Lord of peace himself always give you his peace no matter what happens. The Lord be with you all. (2 Thessalonians 3:16)*

Q 72:

Why do some people die before they are old?

A: Death entered the world when sin came in. Ever since Adam and Eve, pain and death have been part of life. Eventually, everything that is alive in our world has to die. Plants die. Animals die. People die. Death can come from a lot of different causes: automobile accidents, sickness, old age, and so forth. And life is short, no matter how long a person lives. Just ask someone who is sixty or seventy or eighty. Remember that because life is short, we should make the most of every day we are alive. Each breath is a gift from God. But also remember that this life is not all there is. After we die we can live forever with God.

KEY VERSES: *For to me, living is for Christ, and dying is even better. Yet if I live, that means fruitful service for Christ. I really don't know which is better. I'm torn between two desires: Sometimes I want to live, and sometimes I long to go and be with Christ. That would be far better for me. (Philippians 1:21-23)*

Q 73:

Why are some people different from others?

A: Bad things happen in this world, and people suffer. Some people are hurt in accidents. Some are injured in sports. Some are born with physical problems. You can probably think of many ways that people can be harmed. Today there are many doctors, nurses, and other people who can help us when we are hurt or need special help. They can give us medicine and bandages, and they can operate if necessary. And scientists are always working on special tools to help. Glasses, wheelchairs, hearing aids, and artificial legs are just a few of their wonderful inventions. These doctors and scientists are gifts from God.

KEY VERSES: *"Teacher," his disciples asked him, "why was this man born blind? Was it a result of his own sins or those of his parents?" "It was not because of his sins or his parents' sins," Jesus answered. "He was born blind so the power of God could be seen in him." (John 9:2-3)*

NOTE TO PARENTS: God planned for people to be healthy. Disease, death, and disasters are a result of sin in the world. Everyone living in this sinful world suffers the effects of sin, even Christians. God may allow us to go through difficult times to teach us to rely on him or other lessons. Whatever our struggles, God can be glorified in them. In fact, God delights in demonstrating his strength in weak people.

Q 74:

Why does God let wars happen?

A: Wars are a result of sin in the world. Because people aren't perfect, sometimes they get angry and fight. When leaders of countries do this, wars start. Wars are like fights between people, only much, much bigger. If people followed God's instructions for living, there would not be wars. God wants people to get along, not to fight and kill each other. But if we ignore God and break his rules, we suffer. God could stop all wars and fights in the world. But God wants human beings to trust him, to listen to him, to obey him, and to live in peace with each other.

KEY VERSES: *What is causing the quarrels and fights among you? Isn't it the whole army of evil desires at war within you? You want what you don't have, so you scheme and kill to get it. You are jealous for what others have, and you can't possess it, so you fight and quarrel to take it away from them. And yet the reason you don't have what you want is that you don't ask God for it. (James 4:1-2)*

Q 75:
Why does God let us get sick?

A: Sometimes sickness is the body's way of telling us that we should stop living a certain way. Perhaps we ate too much (or we ate something bad), or we didn't get enough sleep. Sickness and disease are problems that came into the world with sin. All kinds of people get sick: good and bad, rich and poor, old and young. God wants us to take care of ourself and be healthy so we can live for him. And when we are sick, we can pray to God and ask him to help us.

KEY VERSES: *Are any among you sick? They should call for the elders of the church and have them pray over them, anointing them with oil in the name of the Lord. And their prayer offered in faith will heal the sick, and the Lord will make them well. And anyone who has committed sins will be forgiven. (James 5:14-15)*

Q 76:
Does God know about people who are hungry?

A: God knows everything. He even knows how many hairs you have on your head. God knows about all the hungry people in the world, and it makes him sad. Remember, he put *us* in charge of the world. God wants us to care about people and help those who need it. This includes helping to feed those who are hungry. Think about what you can do to feed the hungry people in your community.

KEY VERSES: *He is the one who made heaven and earth, the sea, and everything in them. He is the one who keeps every promise forever, who gives justice to the oppressed and food to the hungry. The LORD frees the prisoners. (Psalm 146:6-7)*

Q 77:

Who feeds people who don't have enough to eat?

FOOD BANK

A: Although there is plenty of food in the world, thousands of people go hungry every day. Maybe they live far from food or they just don't have money to buy food.

Many people who care about this work hard to feed those who don't have enough to eat. This is the main purpose of many relief organizations. Some government agencies, churches, and other organizations also help. If you know of a hungry family, you could take them a bag of groceries or a special meal. You could also support the work of a Christian organization that is working with the poor. Some people sponsor children through agencies; some donate money; others take food to food pantries; and some donate time at homeless shelters, soup kitchens, and other places that help poor people.

KEY VERSES: *Suppose you see a brother or sister who needs food or clothing, and you say, "Well, good-bye and God bless you; stay warm and eat well"—but then you don't give that person any food or clothing. What good does that do? (James 2:15-16)*

NOTE TO PARENTS: It is good to get involved as a family to help meet the needs of the poor. It helps people in a tangible way and also shows God's love to them. Consider options available to you through your church or another organization that you trust.

Q 78:

Why do you get mad at me if you have Jesus in your heart?

A: Not all anger is wrong. We should be angry with the bad things in the world, and we should try to make them right. When children disobey their parents and do other things that are wrong, sometimes their parents get angry. Good parents want their children to do what is right, and so they try to teach children right from wrong. Sometimes, of course, parents get angry at children for the wrong reasons. Maybe the parents are grouchy because they've had a bad day. Or maybe they misunderstood what their child did. Parents are human too; they can make mistakes. Even Christian parents who have God living in them and guiding them can do what is wrong at times. That happens when they don't do what God wants them to do. No matter how your parents act, you should love them and pray for them.

KEY VERSE: *"Don't sin by letting anger gain control over you." Don't let the sun go down while you are still angry. (Ephesians 4:26)*

Q 79:

Why does God kill nature with forest fires?

A: Forest fires don't kill nature. They are part of the life cycle that God built into our world. Raging forest fires can destroy many thousands of trees and wild-life. But forest fires also help life continue. For example, they burn away dead growth and open seed pods, such as those of jack pines, which can't be opened any other way. Forest fires are a little like lightning— they may be dangerous, but they do important work.

Some forest fires start naturally, and some are started by people. We should not try to start forest fires just to destroy property. And we should try to keep them from damaging property or endangering people's lives. But some fires start naturally, and we know now that they are necessary. This is just part of God's plan for us and our world.

KEY VERSES: *God said, "Let the land burst forth with every sort of grass and seed-bearing plant. And let there be trees that grow seed-bearing fruit. The seeds will then produce the kinds of plants and trees from which they came." And so it was. The land was filled with seed-bearing plants and trees, and their seeds produced plants and trees of like kind. And God saw that it was good. (Genesis 1:11-12)*

NOTE TO PARENTS: Whenever your children ask about fire, be careful not to overplay fear to keep them from it. Fire can be used for good purposes, even though it is dangerous. Simply teach them to respect these dangers, to use fire responsibly, and to handle it wisely.

Q 80:

Why do floods and hurricanes kill innocent people?

A: Most floods, and all hurricanes, are natural disasters that can't be prevented. They are simply events that happen when water strikes with great force (for example, from storms at sea, heavy rains, or melting snow). The forces of nature go to work, and those forces are very powerful.

Sometimes people die in these natural disasters because they have not listened to a warning. Some live too near the water and in areas that flood easily. Some ignore storm warnings and stay in the path of danger when they should leave. Some even try to get *close* to a powerful storm, risking their lives because they think it will be exciting. Too many people die in floods and hurricanes because they are foolish.

But others die through no fault of their own; they are in the wrong place at the wrong time. It is not because God overlooked them; it is because we live in a broken world. We have suffering and death because of sin.

Deaths from floods and hurricanes are tragedies. That is why we need to be wise and do what we can to avoid unnecessary risks. As long as we have sin in this world we will have these dangers, and we need to avoid them.

KEY VERSE: *[Jesus said,] "Anyone who listens to my teaching and obeys me is wise, like a person who builds a house on solid rock." (Matthew 7:24)*

Q 81:

Why does God send earthquakes?

A: Like hurricanes, earthquakes are a natural part of the way the earth works. Huge pieces of the earth's surface, called tectonic plates, are shifting and rubbing against each other all the time. Sometimes their movements release great amounts of energy stored up in the friction between them. The release of this energy produces an earthquake. It is not that God sends earthquakes so much as that they happen as part of the world God has made.

Earthquakes can do a lot of damage to buildings and other structures not made to handle the mighty rumblings and shocks. If possible, people who live in earthquake areas should have homes built with earthquakes in mind. They should also plan how they will get to safety the next time an earthquake happens. This is simply an example of planning wisely and being careful.

KEY VERSE: *When the earth quakes and its people live in turmoil, I am the one who keeps its foundations firm. (Psalm 75:3)*

NOTE TO PARENTS: If you live in an area prone to earthquakes, teach your children what to do in the event of a tremor. Be familiar with basic safety steps— including where to go and what not to do—and explain them to your children. You can even make a game of practicing them!

Q 82:

Why do people die in hot weather?

A: Temperatures over 100 degrees Fahrenheit (35 degrees Celsius) put a lot of stress on the human body. In hot weather, bodies need more water than normal because they lose water more quickly. Older people and those who are sick suffer the most because their bodies are not as strong as younger, healthier people. Most of the people who die in hot weather become overheated because they can't get cooled off. If they would go to a cooler place or to a building with air-conditioning, they could cool off.

This is one way people can look out for each other. If you have older relatives, make sure they have a way to get cool on a really hot day.

KEY VERSE: *O God, you are my God; I earnestly search for you. My soul thirsts for you; my whole body longs for you in this parched and weary land where there is no water. (Psalm 63:1)*

NOTE TO PARENTS: Children tend to think of themselves as invulnerable and often don't know the dangers that high heat can pose. Make sure your kids know how to handle themselves in hot weather. They should drink plenty of fluids, try to stay cool, stay out of the sun, and limit their exercise.

Q 83:

Why do people commit crimes?

A:

The main reason people commit crimes is that they are selfish. They want what others have and take it by force. Another big reason is anger. People get so angry that they lose their temper and do things that they would not normally do. Both selfishness and uncontrolled anger are sin.

Crime happens when people get cut off from God and his love. Some people do not know God at all and do not know that they can trust him to take care of them. Some people know him but lose touch with him, then fail to trust and obey him. God's way is for us to know him, to ask and trust him for the things we need, and then to love and help others. If everyone did things God's way all the time, crime would never happen. That is why we need to trust God to provide for us instead of selfishly trying to get what we want regardless of how it affects others.

KEY VERSE: *When they refused to acknowledge God, he abandoned them to their evil minds and let them do things that should never be done. (Romans 1:28)*

NOTE TO PARENTS: It is important to teach children to *talk* their way through conflicts with others instead of forcing their way by hitting, screaming, or threatening. On the playground, at school, and among siblings, they will get into conflicts of will every day. Most things are not worth fighting for. It is OK to try to persuade; it is not OK to use force on those who disagree. Remind them that they *can* control their temper (Proverbs 12:16).

Q 84:

Why is the world so violent and evil?

A:

Sin is the root cause of all evil. Because people sin, the world is filled with sin and evil. It has been this way since Adam and Eve's first sin. In fact, God flooded the world in Noah's day because of violence and evil. These things are not new.

In some ways it may seem that violence is worse today than in the past. Weapons are more destructive than ever before. There are more guns and knives and more ways of hurting people than ever before. As these weapons get more powerful, so does the power to hurt others.

But in reality, violence and evil come out of evil hearts that are separated from God, and the world has always had that. As long as people rebel against God, we will have violence and evil in the world.

KEY VERSE: *Don't let evil get the best of you, but conquer evil by doing good. (Romans 12:21)*

NOTE TO PARENTS: When your children ask a question like this, make sure they get a balanced view. Talk about all the good that is happening in the world. Many believers are telling others about Christ, helping to relieve suffering through health care, serving as missionaries, praying for leaders, and working behind the scenes to achieve good. God has not abandoned our world.

Q 85:

Why are there so many accidents and people getting killed?

A: Because of sin in the world. When God created the world, everything was perfect. But when the first people disobeyed God, sin threw things out of order. This is what it means to say we live in a *fallen world*. It is full of dangers. If it weren't for sin, we would not have suffering or death at all.

Some of our own creations have also brought new dangers. The fact that we can go faster in cars and planes means that accidents can have bigger and worse results. People also have lots of accidents when they are in a hurry. As they rush from place to place, they run into others.

It is important to be careful. This means looking both ways before crossing streets, watching where you are going, wearing seat belts, and using common sense. As long as accidents happen in this world, we must be careful.

KEY VERSE: *A prudent person foresees the danger ahead and takes precautions. The simpleton goes blindly on and suffers the consequences. (Proverbs 27:12)*

NOTE TO PARENTS: Whenever you pray with your children about God protecting them, ask God for the wisdom and common sense they need to live safely. This helps them remember that they have a role to play in staying safe.

The Church

Q 86:

Why do we go to church if God is everywhere?

A: In the Bible, God tells us to join other Christians and worship him. We should spend time alone, praying and reading his Word. But it is also very important to get together with others who follow Christ. We can encourage and strengthen each other. We can pray for each other. We can learn from each other. We can sing and praise God together. We can serve and help each other. All of this can happen in church. Church is also a place where Christians of all ages and types can come together—babies, grandparents, children, poor, wealthy, brown, black, white, American, Asian, African, weak, strong, and so on. Something very special happens when God's family gets together.

KEY VERSE: *Let us not neglect our meeting together, as some people do, but encourage and warn each other, especially now that the day of his coming back again is drawing near. (Hebrews 10:25)*

NOTE TO PARENTS: Many children find church boring. That's because the service is usually geared for adults. But it also may be because children have not been taught *how* to worship. Take time to explain the purpose behind the church programs (like Sunday school, church dinners, the worship service, and so forth) and each part of the worship service (for example, songs, Communion, offering, and so forth). Help your child understand what he or she should be doing and why.

Q 87:

Why do we worship God?

A: Worship means praising and thanking God for who he is and for what he has done. People worship in many different ways. Worship can involve group singing, group reading, special music, giving money, prayer, Communion, Bible reading, teaching, preaching, and other activities. God has given us everything good that we have. He loves us and wants the very best for us. Shouldn't we spend time with him and tell him how grateful we are? We play with our friends because we enjoy them. We worship God because we enjoy him.

KEY VERSES: *Jesus replied, "Believe me, the time is coming when it will no longer matter whether you worship the Father here or in Jerusalem. You Samaritans know so little about the one you worship, while we Jews know all about him, for salvation comes through the Jews. But the time is coming and is already here when true worshipers will worship the Father in spirit and in truth. The Father is looking for anyone who will worship him that way. For God is Spirit, so those who worship him must worship in spirit and in truth." (John 4:21-24)*

Q 88:

How come my friends go to a different church?

A: In most homes, parents decide where children will go to church if they go. Some people go to a certain church because they grew up in that church. Even after moving across town, they drive there every Sunday to be with friends and family. Some people choose a church because they enjoy a certain style of worship. There are many reasons for choosing a church. But some churches really aren't true churches according to the Bible's teachings. Real churches honor Jesus, study God's Word, tell people to give their lives to Christ, and emphasize obeying God. Churches are groups of God's people, meeting together to worship, fellowship, serve, and learn.

KEY VERSES: *If someone says, "I love God," but hates a Christian brother or sister, that person is a liar; for if we don't love people we can see, how can we love God, whom we have not seen? And God himself has commanded that we must love not only him but our Christian brothers and sisters, too. (1 John 4:20-21)*

Q 89:

What part of the body of Christ am I?

A: The Bible uses word pictures to explain how Christians relate to each other. We are a "family," with brothers and sisters in Christ. We are a "building," with Christ as the cornerstone. We are a "body," with each person serving as a special part. God talks about us being a body to show how Christians should treat each other and work together. God has given each Christian special gifts. That means each of us has talents and abilities that can be used to help other believers. Not everybody has the same gifts. And, like the parts of a body, we need each other. All of our gifts are important.

KEY VERSES: *Just as our bodies have many parts and each part has a special function, so it is with Christ's body. We are all parts of his one body, and each of us has different work to do. And since we are all one body in Christ, we belong to each other, and each of us needs all the others. (Romans 12:4-5)*

NOTE TO PARENTS: This is a question usually asked only by older children (junior high or older) who have heard teaching on the body of Christ. Encourage them to get involved with a gift or talent they have.

Q 90:

Why do people get baptized?

A: People get baptized because Jesus was baptized, and they want to follow his example. They also get baptized because Jesus told his followers to go into all the world, telling people about him and baptizing them. Some Christians believe that babies from Christian families should be baptized to show that they belong to Christ. Some Christians think that only believers in Christ should be baptized, to show that Jesus is their Savior. Either way, baptism is a very important event in a Christian's life.

KEY VERSE: *Peter replied, "Each of you must turn from your sins and turn to God, and be baptized in the name of Jesus Christ for the forgiveness of your sins. Then you will receive the gift of the Holy Spirit." (Acts 2:38)*

Q 91:

What happens to people who don't go to church?

A: Going to church doesn't get a person into heaven. And not going to church doesn't send a person to hell. A person becomes a Christian by faith—believing in Christ—not by doing good things. Most Christians go to church because of what happens there. At church you can meet other Christians. You can find help for your problems and encouragement. You can learn from God's Word and help others. And you can experience wonderful worship, singing, and praying that glorifies God. People who don't go to church miss all that. They miss a very special meeting with God.

KEY VERSES: *Can we boast, then, that we have done anything to be accepted by God? No, because our acquittal is not based on our good deeds. It is based on our faith. So we are made right with God through faith and not by obeying the law. (Romans 3:27-28)*

The End of the World

Q 92:

When will the world end?

A: The world will not end until God is ready to take all believers home to heaven. It will happen when God decides that it is the right time. And no one knows when that time will come. Only God the Father knows. People who trust in God should not be afraid about the world coming to an end because it will be God's time of rescuing them from trouble and pain.

KEY VERSES: *[Jesus said,] "Heaven and earth will disappear, but my words will remain forever. However, no one knows the day or hour when these things will happen, not even the angels in heaven or the Son himself. Only the Father knows." (Mark 13:31-32)*

JASON'S PRAYER
Lord, please come quickly To end all sin and hurt. But if you're coming today PLEASE, after dessert.

Q 93:

If Jesus has already won, why is everyone still fighting?

A: Jesus won over sin and death when he rose from the dead. But some people still sin and fight because they don't love or follow Jesus. Jesus is waiting for them to change their minds and follow him. As Jesus waits, they do what their sinful desires tell them to—they sin and fight. Satan has not surrendered, and he still tries to trick people. Jesus hasn't come back yet because he loves us all and wants many more people to trust in him as Savior so they can be saved from hell and go to heaven.

Jesus has won over sin and death, but he won't *make* us live at peace with each other. The more we love him, the more we learn to live at peace and not fight.

KEY VERSE: *When you bow down before the Lord and admit your dependence on him, he will lift you up and give you honor. (James 4:10)*

Q 94:

How will the world end?

A: We don't know exactly *how* the world will end, but we know that it *will* end—the world will not go on forever. This is not bad news; it is part of God's plan. The world will not be destroyed by people or by things getting out of control. It will be God's doing and in God's timing. It will end in a blaze of fire! God will replace this world with a new one.

But it will not happen until Jesus comes back. He will return, just as he promised, to judge all people who have ever lived and to set up his kingdom. He will replace our damaged world with a new, perfect one, where his people will live with him forever. For those who love him, the end of the world will really be a beginning—a wonderful, awesome beginning!

KEY VERSE: *[Jesus said,] "Everyone will see the Son of Man arrive on the clouds with great power and glory." (Mark 13:26)*

Q 95:

What happens to the bad people when Jesus comes back?

A: When Jesus comes back to earth, people who know Jesus will be glad. But people who don't know Jesus will be very sad and afraid because they will be judged for their sin. Those who have not believed in Jesus as their Savior will be punished and sent to hell, far away from God. That is one of the reasons God urges us to tell our friends about Jesus—so they can join us and God in heaven.

KEY VERSE: *They will be punished with everlasting destruction, forever separated from the Lord and from his glorious power. (2 Thessalonians 1:9)*

NOTE TO PARENTS: Be careful not to divide the world between "good people" and "bad people." Many so-called good people don't trust in Christ, and they will be judged for their sin. Meanwhile, some Christians do bad things, yet they will receive eternal life because of their faith in Christ.

Q 96:

How can God move a whole city down to earth?

A: The apostle John had a vision of God bringing the new Jerusalem, the Holy City, down from heaven. We don't know exactly how this will work, but it will happen—God can do anything. He created all the stars and planets, as well as all the plants, animals, and human beings. He can certainly create a new city and bring it to earth.

KEY VERSE: *I saw the holy city, the new Jerusalem, coming down from God out of heaven like a beautiful bride prepared for her husband. (Revelation 21:2)*

Q 97:

When Jesus comes to get us, what will happen to earth and everyone else?

A: When Jesus comes back to rescue all who believe in him, several things will happen: (1) Jesus will bring life on earth to an end. (2) Jesus will judge everyone. (3) Jesus will create a new heaven and new earth. (4) We will begin eternal life with God. (5) The devil, his demons, and all unbelievers will begin their eternal death in hell.

KEY VERSE: *I saw a new heaven and a new earth, for the old heaven and the old earth had disappeared. And the sea was also gone. (Revelation 21:1)*

Q 98:

When will Jesus come back?

A: No one knows when Jesus will come back, not even the angels. God has chosen not to tell us. God has also warned us not to listen to people who say they know when Jesus will return. The day of Christ's return will come "like a thief in the night," when no one is expecting it. People who say they know the date of Christ's return are just trying to trick you. You don't have to worry about missing Jesus when he returns. When Jesus comes back, it will be obvious to everyone. All people all over the world will know.

KEY VERSE: *[Jesus said,] "I will come as unexpectedly as a thief! Blessed are all who are watching for me." (Revelation 16:15)*

Q 99:

Why does eternity last for a long, long, long, long time?

A: It doesn't. It lasts forever, and that's longer than a long time. That's what the word *eternity* means—"infinite or endless time."

It is impossible for people to understand eternity. It's beyond what our brain can imagine because everything we imagine has limits. But God knows because he has no limits, and he is eternal.

KEY VERSE: *God has made everything beautiful for its own time. He has planted eternity in the human heart, but even so, people cannot see the whole scope of God's work from beginning to end. (Ecclesiastes 3:11)*

Q 100:

If the Bible says we'll live for eternity, why is there an end on earth?

A: The earth was not made to last forever. Things only last forever if God wants them to. God has determined that the world the way it is now will be destroyed and then made new again. God will give us a new heaven and a new earth to replace the old one. The new earth will be perfect in every way, as God intended it to be.

But people *will* last forever. When Jesus returns to make the world new, he will judge every person who has ever lived. Those who have received his forgiveness will be welcomed into his home to live with him forever. And those who have refused his forgiveness will be cast into the lake of fire. That is why Jesus came—"so that everyone who believes in him will not perish but have eternal life" (see John 3:16).

KEY VERSES: *All creation is waiting eagerly for that future day when God will reveal who his children really are. Against its will, everything on earth was subjected to God's curse. All creation anticipates the day when it will join God's children in glorious freedom from death and decay. For we know that all creation has been groaning as in the pains of childbirth right up to the present time. (Romans 8:19-22)*

Questions Kids Ask

God's Word

2

The Bible

Q 101:
What is a Bible?

A: The Bible is God's message to us. Actually, the Bible is not just one book but a collection of many books that have been put together. It came to be called *the* Book because it is so important, because it is *God's* book. (The word *Bible* means "book".) The Bible serves as an instruction manual for living God's way; it tells us what's right and what's wrong. It has many stories and lessons that he wants us to know. The Bible tells us about God and Jesus and how we are supposed to live. You can look in the Bible to find out what God wants you to do.

KEY VERSE: *Your word is a lamp for my feet and a light for my path. (Psalm 119:105)*

Q 102:
Why do we have the Bible?

A: God gave us the Bible because he wanted to talk to us in a way that we would understand. Because God gave us his Word in a book, we can read it over and over. We can share it with a friend. The Bible is like a map—it shows us the direction to go in life. The Bible is like a love letter—it tells us about God's love for us. The Bible is like food—it gives us strength to live. To find out what God is like and how he wants us to live, read the Bible.

KEY VERSE: *The word of God is full of living power. It is sharper than the sharpest knife, cutting deep into our innermost thoughts and desires. It exposes us for what we really are. (Hebrews 4:12)*

Q 103:

Did the Bible stories really happen, or are they like fairy tales?

A: The stories in the Bible really happened. Some of the events seem amazing to us because they're miracles, but they still happened. We know that the stories are true because the Bible is God's Word, and God wouldn't lie to us or fool us. The Bible also says that every word in it is true. Some people don't believe the Bible because they haven't read it. Some don't believe it because they don't think miracles can happen. Others don't believe because they don't want to; they don't want to learn about God and do what he tells them to do. But we know that God can do anything, and he's the best one to tell us how to live. We should pray for those who don't believe the Bible or who think it's full of fairy tales.

KEY VERSE: *All these events happened to them as examples for us. They were written down to warn us, who live at the time when this age is drawing to a close. (1 Corinthians 10:11)*

NOTE TO PARENTS: This question presents a good opportunity to take out a Bible and look at it together.

Q 104:

When was the Bible made?

A: God wrote the Bible over many, many years, a long time ago—long before computers, cars, and even before books. The people who wrote down God's words used scrolls of paper made from papyrus leaves and animal skin. They wrote it over a period of 1,500 years, from the time of Moses to the apostle John. Even though the Bible was written hundreds of years before we were born, it is still up-to-date. When we read the stories and understand what God is saying, we learn how we should live today.

KEY VERSES: *Long ago God spoke many times and in many ways to our ancestors through the prophets. But now in these final days, he has spoken to us through his Son. God promised everything to the Son as an inheritance, and through the Son he made the universe and everything in it. (Hebrews 1:1-2)*

Q 105:

How did they write the Old Testament without paper or pencils?

A: When the oldest books in the Bible were written, they didn't have typewriters, computers, or printing presses. And there weren't any ballpoint pens, felt-tipped pens, or number-two pencils. But the people who lived back then did have other tools for writing. The paper they used was different, too. The paper they first wrote the Old Testament on was probably either *papyrus* or *parchment*.

KEY VERSES: *After the king had burned Jeremiah's scroll, the LORD gave Jeremiah another message. He said, "Get another scroll, and write everything again just as you did on the scroll King Jehoiakim burned." (Jeremiah 36:27-28)*

Q 106:

Where did they get the scrolls from?

A: Today, we use pencils and pens to write, and we write on paper. But the Bible was written a long time ago, long before these things were invented. Instead of using paper, people would write on long strips of *papyrus* or *parchment*. Papyrus was made from a plant that grows in Bible lands. Parchment was made from animal skins. Both papyrus and parchment could be sewn together and rolled up into long scrolls. Museums have some of these ancient scrolls. People read from these scrolls like books. But there weren't a lot of them because each one had to be copied by hand. Today, everyone can have his or her own Bible to read. But in those days, most synagogues and churches would only have one copy each. So the scrolls were very valuable, and the priests took good care of them. We should take care of our Bibles, too.

KEY VERSE: *When you come, be sure to bring the coat I left with Carpus at Troas. Also bring my books, and especially my papers. (2 Timothy 4:13)*

Q 107:

Who wrote the Bible?

A: The words in the Bible came from God. That's why it is called "God's Word." God used people to write down the ideas, thoughts, teachings, and words that he wanted to put in the Bible. The writers were very special people, chosen by God for this very important task. And God used many people, writing over many, many years. These people wrote in their own style and in their own language, but they wrote God's Word. God guided their thoughts as they wrote. And God made sure that what they wrote was exactly what he wanted. He kept them from making any mistakes. Today we can read the Bible, God's Word, which he wrote through those special people so many years ago.

KEY VERSES: *Above all, you must understand that no prophecy in Scripture ever came from the prophets themselves or because they wanted to prophesy. It was the Holy Spirit who moved the prophets to speak from God. (2 Peter 1:20-21)*

Q 108:
What does inspired mean?

A: *Inspired* describes the way God used the Bible writers to write down what he wanted them to write. It doesn't mean "dictated"; that is, God didn't say the words out loud while the writers copied them down. Inspired means that God guided the writers, helping them to write everything he wanted them to write, so that all the words in the Bible would tell us what we need to know. He gave the writers the ideas and the desire to write; then he guided them so that every word they wrote was what he wanted.

KEY VERSE: *All Scripture is inspired by God and is useful to teach us what is true and to make us realize what is wrong in our lives. It straightens us out and teaches us to do what is right. (2 Timothy 3:16)*

Q 109:
If lots of different people in different places wrote the Bible, how did it get together in one big book?

A: The first books of the Bible, the Old Testament, were written to the Jewish people. The Jews took care of and protected these books and spent countless hours carefully copying them again and again. Jesus often quoted from the Old Testament and said it was all true and that it was the Word of God. The books that we find in the New Testament were written by people who had seen Jesus or who were close to those who had contact with Jesus. Their stories about Jesus (the Gospels) and their letters (the Epistles) were read in the local churches. Church leaders collected the writings and guarded them carefully. For nearly 2,000 years now, all these Bible books have been together.

KEY VERSE: *Yes, being a Jew has many advantages. First of all, the Jews were entrusted with the whole revelation of God. (Romans 3:2)*

Q 110:

Why can't we put new books in the Bible?

A: We can't put new books in the Bible because the Bible is *God's* message, not ours. It contains his words, which he inspired his people to write in a special way. Some people have tried to put new books in the Bible, but others who recognized that the Bible is a special book kept them from changing it. The story about how God has saved us is complete. God has already told us all we need to know and do.

KEY VERSE: *I solemnly declare to everyone who hears the prophetic words of this book: If anyone adds anything to what is written here, God will add to that person the plagues described in this book. (Revelation 22:18)*

NOTE TO PARENTS: While Protestants and Catholics differ on the question of including the intertestamental books in the Bible, no Christian denomination is arguing for new books to be added to the Bible. Many heretical teachers and leaders have tried to add their words to those of Scripture. Many others have tried to give additional writings the same status as the books of the Bible. But God's people recognize that the Bible contains God's words, not our own, so it's not up to us what goes in it.

Q 111:

Will people write about us in a special Bible, too?

A: There is only one Bible (or "revelation from God"), and it has already been written. But remember, the Bible is far more than a collection of stories about people who lived a long time ago—it's God's message about Jesus; it tells how we should live today. The Bible also tells us about the future, not just the past. So in one sense, we *are* in the Bible. We are important in God's plan. Also, the Bible tells us that those who believe in Jesus have their names written in the "Lamb's Book of Life"—that's another book that God has. It tells who will live with God in heaven.

KEY VERSE: *Nothing evil will be allowed to enter—no one who practices shameful idolatry and dishonesty—but only those whose names are written in the Lamb's Book of Life. (Revelation 21:27)*

Q 112:
Why did God put scary stories in the Bible?

A: The Bible tells true stories about real people who actually lived and died. Sometimes those stories can seem scary to us. God included those stories because he wanted to teach us something from them. That is, they weren't put there to scare us but to serve as a warning of what to avoid, to show us what we should do, and to help us learn how to live. Some teachings in the Bible seem scary to people, especially people who disobey God, because the stories reveal the bad that can happen when we choose to do evil. Hopefully, these teachings will show us how important it is to listen to God.

KEY VERSE: *All these events happened to them as examples for us. They were written down to warn us, who live at the time when this age is drawing to a close. (1 Corinthians 10:11)*

Q 113:
What is the Bible's biggest story?

A: The Bible's biggest story is the story of Jesus. In fact, the whole Bible tells his story—about God creating people and saving them from sin. Jesus came to the world to die in our place, to pay the penalty for our sins. If we trust in Christ as Savior, God gives us eternal life. The Old Testament Bible writers told us that Jesus would be born, live, die, and rise again. Even the sacrifices described in the book of Leviticus show us what the death of Christ would be, the perfect "Lamb of God who takes away the sin of the world." No matter where you look in the Bible, you can learn about Jesus. Have you put your faith in him?

KEY VERSE: *[Jesus said,] "God so loved the world that he gave his only Son, so that everyone who believes in him will not perish but have eternal life." (John 3:16)*

NOTE TO PARENTS: The Bible's biggest story is also a parent's biggest responsibility. In order to be ready for the day when a child asks a question like this one, plan what you will say and which Scriptures you will use to introduce him or her to Jesus.

Q 114:

Were there any crimes in the Bible?

A: Ever since Adam and Eve sinned against God, sin, and therefore crime, has been in the world. In fact, every person ever born has been born a sinner. That means that it is natural for boys, girls, men, and women to do wrong—to lie, cheat, steal, and hurt others. So crimes have been committed by people since the beginning. That's why we need Jesus. Only Jesus can take away our sin, teach us to do right, and help us love and respect one another. It all starts when we admit our sin, ask Jesus to forgive us, and invite him to rule our lives. If everyone did that and tried to obey God, there would be a lot less crime in the world!

KEY VERSE: *Now the earth had become corrupt in God's sight, and it was filled with violence. (Genesis 6:11)*

Q 115:

Why do some Bibles have pictures and some don't?

A: The people who wrote the Bible didn't put pictures in them. But in recent years, the people who print Bibles wanted to help us better understand the Bible stories. So they put pictures at various places in the Bible to help us see what Bible people and places may have looked like. The pictures are drawings or paintings, not photographs. These pictures were made recently—they're not very old. The artists knew what to draw by learning about that part of the world and by reading what the Bible says about how people lived in Bible times.

KEY VERSE: *If I bring you some revelation or some special knowledge or some prophecy or some teaching—that is what will help you. (1 Corinthians 14:6)*

Q 116:

Does Satan know about the Bible?

A: Satan knows all about the Bible. He even knows what it says. But Satan certainly doesn't follow what the Bible teaches. In fact, he does everything he can to stop people from obeying God's Word. Just because someone knows the truth doesn't mean that he or she will do it. Satan is a liar, the father of lies. He has lied and twisted the truth so much that he has fooled himself into thinking that what the Bible predicts won't happen. Satan thinks that he can beat God and escape his punishment. But the Bible tells the truth. Eventually God will totally wipe out Satan and his demons.

KEY VERSES: *Do you still think it's enough just to believe that there is one God? Well, even the demons believe this, and they tremble in terror! Fool! When will you ever learn that faith that does not result in good deeds is useless? (James 2:19-20)*

Studying the Bible

Q 117:

Why do we study the Bible?

A: It's important to study the Bible because the Bible is God's message to us and studying it helps us know and understand it better. If you want to learn more about butterflies, you study butterflies. Studying the Bible helps us find out how to live and to find out what God wants. When we only read the Bible (without studying it), we may not see the meaning right away. *Studying* helps us learn lessons for life—we learn God's will so we can obey him. Studying the Bible is like reading a story many, many times—each time you see something different and learn more.

KEY VERSE: *So Paul stayed for a year and a half, teaching them the Word of God. (Acts 18:11)*

Q 118:

How can kids study the Bible?

A: Studying the Bible is not as difficult as it may sound. In fact, it can be fun! First, start out by just reading the Bible. Read short portions—a paragraph or story—and read it in a translation you understand. Second, ask a parent to explain big words to you that you don't understand. Third, memorize verses that tell you what you should do. As you read and study, you will have questions about what the Bible means. Save your questions and find someone to answer them, like a parent, teacher, or pastor. It's good to read the Bible every day. Make it a habit. And if you get really ambitious, you can use a Bible dictionary and atlas; a dictionary tells what Bible words mean, and an atlas shows where Bible places are.

KEY VERSE: *Study this Book of the Law continually. Meditate on it day and night so you may be sure to obey all that is written in it. Only then will you succeed. (Joshua 1:8)*

NOTE TO PARENTS: A child asking this question may provide a good opportunity to introduce him or her to study. Get out a Bible and start a study together. Some Bible books that many kids will find interesting include Genesis, Mark, Romans, and James. If you are unfamiliar with the Bible, you can use this book to help you get an overview.

Q 119:

Why do so many people keep translating the Bible?

A: The Old Testament first was written in the Hebrew language, and the New Testament was written in Greek. If no one had ever translated the Bible, only people who could read ancient Hebrew and Greek would be able to understand the Bible today. Fortunately, over the years men and women have taken the time to put the Bible into other languages, including English, so that speakers of almost *all* languages can read it.

But some people still don't have the Bible in their own language—some don't even have a written language. For them to read God's Word, somebody has to put their language into written words. Then someone has to translate the Bible into their language so they can read it. Imagine if there were no Bibles in your language— how would you read it? God wants us to take the message about Jesus to everyone all over the world, and that means translating the Bible into every language there is. That's why people keep translating the Bible.

KEY VERSES: *[Jesus said,] "Go and make disciples of all the nations, baptizing them in the name of the Father and the Son and the Holy Spirit. Teach these new disciples to obey all the commands I have given you. And be sure of this: I am with you always, even to the end of the age."* (Matthew 28:19-20)

Q 120:

Why isn't there just one kind of Bible?

A: There are many kinds of Bibles because there are many kinds of people. But they all contain the same message. Different Bibles meet different needs. Some Bibles are very small so you can carry them with you. Others are big so you can see the words better. Some Bibles use everyday words to make the Bible easy to read and the lessons easy to learn. Some Bibles have notes, maps, and charts to help people understand the parts that are different from today. The purpose of all these different Bibles is to help people understand what God is saying so they can obey him.

KEY VERSE: *Until I get there, focus on reading the Scriptures to the church, encouraging the believers, and teaching them.* (1 Timothy 4:13)

NOTE TO PARENTS: It is very important for children to have a translation of the Bible that they can read and understand themselves. If they ask this question because they can't understand their own Bible, consider getting them a translation that they can understand.

Q 121:

What is a Living Bible?

A: *The Living Bible* is an English version of the Bible. The words and sentences in *The Living Bible* reflect the way people speak today so that most people can understand them. The Bible talks about the Scriptures as being "living and active," so that's where the name came from. There are many other English translations of the Bible. Some of the most well-known are: the New International Version, the *New American Standard Bible,* the King James Version, the New King James Version, and the New Revised Standard Version.

KEY VERSE: *The word of God is full of living power. It is sharper than the sharpest knife, cutting deep into our innermost thoughts and desires. It exposes us for what we really are. (Hebrews 4:12)*

Q 122:

Is archaeology the study of Noah's ark?

A: Archaeology is the study of ancient cultures. It tells us about Bible times and people who lived long ago and what life was like back then. Archaeologists are the people who study and teach about archaeology. They find out about Bible times by digging up old cities to find buildings and things people used long ago. They are even trying to find Noah's ark. Archaeologists study other places, too, and have shown us many interesting things about people and places all over the world.

KEY VERSES: *So the flood gradually began to recede. After 150 days, exactly five months from the time the flood began, the boat came to rest on the mountains of Ararat. (Genesis 8:3-4)*

Q 123:

Why is the Bible in two parts instead of in one part?

A: The Bible has two main parts: the Old Testament and the New Testament. The Old Testament tells the story of the beginning of the world and the beginning of the nation of Israel. It also tells about how the people of Israel obeyed and disobeyed God over many, many years. All of the stories and messages from God in the Old Testament lead up to Jesus Christ. The New Testament tells the story of Christ, the early Christians, and the future. You can think of the Old Testament and New Testament as "before Christ" and "after Christ," or as volume 1 and volume 2. Old doesn't mean out-of-date—it means that it happened before Jesus. But remember, even though the Bible has two main parts, it is all one book—God's book.

KEY VERSE: *[Jesus said,] "You search the Scriptures because you believe they give you eternal life. But the Scriptures point to me!" (John 5:39)*

NOTE TO PARENTS: If your kids aren't already familiar with the two parts, pick up a Bible and show them the Old Testament and New Testament.

Q 124:

Why are there four books about Jesus in the Bible?

A: The Gospels are the books in the Bible that tell us about Jesus' birth, life, death, and resurrection. God used *four* books because each book tells the story of Jesus from a unique point of view. Each one shows us something different about Jesus. When we read all the Gospels, we see the whole picture. It's like seeing a house from all four sides.

The four stories about Jesus are all named after their writers: Matthew, Mark, Luke, and John. Matthew and John knew Jesus, went places with him, and were his close friends; they were two of Jesus' original twelve disciples. Matthew was a tax collector; Mark was a friend of the twelve disciples; Luke was a doctor; John was a fisherman.

KEY VERSE: *I suppose that if all the other things Jesus did were written down, the whole world could not contain the books. (John 21:25)*

NOTE TO PARENTS: If this question arises, open your Bible and show your kids where the four Gospels are.

Q 125:

How do we know that what the Bible says is true?

A: The Bible is true because it is God's Word, and God always speaks the truth. When you read the Bible, you will see that it says it is the Word of God. The Bible also says that every word in it is true. But if that doesn't convince you, read the Bible and see for yourself that everything makes sense. When you read it, you will think, *This sounds right! This is true.* The Bible has also proven to be true over the many hundreds of years since it was written. For example, many events predicted in the Bible have happened, just as it said they would.

KEY VERSE: *All Scripture is inspired by God and is useful to teach us what is true and to make us realize what is wrong in our lives. It straightens us out and teaches us to do what is right. (2 Timothy 3:16)*

NOTE TO PARENTS: Children usually will not raise this question as a matter of curiosity until they are older. Most will only ask a question like this if they are (1) mocked for believing the Bible, or (2) don't want to do something God wants them to do. If your children ask it, you might want to probe further before or after answering.

Q 126:

Why do we memorize verses?

A: We memorize Bible verses because we want to remember what God has told us. When we have the Bible in our head, God's Word will be with us when we're out playing, at the pool, or doing anything—it's with us wherever we go. Then, when we face a problem or a tough situation, we will be able to remember what God has told us to do. It's also fun to memorize verses—then during the day, we can think about the verses and what they mean.

KEY VERSE: *I have hidden your word in my heart, that I might not sin against you. (Psalm 119:11)*

NOTE TO PARENTS: Don't make Bible memorization feel like a chore, and never use it as a punishment for bad behavior. Instead, make it into a game. The goal is for children to *enjoy* reading the Bible and memorizing verses, not merely that they have a lot of Bible knowledge. Some good ones to start with include John 3:16, Genesis 1:1, and Romans 12:9.

Q 127:

What's a concordance?

A: A concordance is an index of words in the Bible. It lists the words that appear in the Bible and all the verses where those words appear. Many study Bibles include a concordance in the back. If you know part of a verse but don't know where to find it in the Bible, you can look up one of the verse's words in the concordance, and it'll tell you where the word is used. For example, if you want to find the verse, "God so loved the world that he gave his only Son, so that everyone who believes in him will not perish but have eternal life," you could look up the word *believes* in the concordance. It would tell you all the places where *believes* is used, and you could see if any of them is the one you're looking for. For practice, see if you can find it now!

KEY VERSE: *Work hard so God can approve you. Be a good worker, one who does not need to be ashamed and who correctly explains the word of truth. (2 Timothy 2:15)*

From Adam to Moses

Q 128:

Why did Adam and Eve eat the forbidden fruit if God said not to?

A: Adam and Eve were sinless and perfect when God created them. But they still could choose to do what was wrong (just like you can choose to do what you aren't supposed to). When the devil tempted them to eat the forbidden fruit, they chose to do it. Although people talk about Adam and Eve eating an "apple" in the Garden of Eden, we don't know what the fruit looked like or how it tasted. All we know is that it was the one fruit in that big, beautiful garden that they weren't supposed to eat. Adam and Eve ate the fruit because the devil started them thinking about what it would be like. Then he lied about God's rule to make them think that God was keeping something good from them. Pretty soon they wanted to eat the fruit more than they wanted to obey God's rule.

KEY VERSES: *Now the serpent was the shrewdest of all the creatures the LORD God had made. "Really?" he asked the woman. "Did God really say you must not eat any of the fruit in the garden?" "Of course we may eat it," the woman told him. "It's only the fruit from the tree at the center of the garden that we are not allowed to eat. God says we must not eat it or even touch it, or we will die." "You won't die!" the serpent hissed. "God knows that your eyes will be opened when you eat it. You will become just like God, knowing everything, both good and evil." The woman was convinced. The fruit looked so fresh and delicious, and it would make her so wise! So she ate some of the fruit. She also gave some to her husband, who was with her. Then he ate it, too. (Genesis 3:1-6)*

Q 129:

Why did Eve disobey God when she knew she would die?

A: Eve disobeyed God because Satan *deceived* her. That is, the devil used lies and tricks to get her to disobey God. God had said that Adam and Eve would die if they ate of the "Tree of Conscience," but Satan said they wouldn't. Because Eve believed Satan, she wasn't sure what would happen. Another trick Satan used was to promise that it would do great things for her; he said that if she ate the forbidden fruit, she would be as God. That sounded good to Eve, and so she did what Satan suggested. Temptation tells you that feeling good right now is better than anything that might happen in the future. Satan still deceives people by twisting God's words and making people believe lies.

Satan wants us to think that once we sin, God can't forgive us. But even though Eve sinned, and even though we sin, God had a plan for taking away our sin. That plan was to send Jesus.

KEY VERSE: *[Jesus said,] "You are the children of your father the Devil, and you love to do the evil things he does. He was a murderer from the beginning and has always hated the truth. There is no truth in him. When he lies, it is consistent with his character; for he is a liar and the father of lies." (John 8:44)*

Q 130:

Why didn't Adam die when God said he would?

A: When Adam and Eve disobeyed God and ate the fruit, sin entered the world. That was the first sin ever! And when sin came into the world, death came with it. There are two kinds of death, and both came to Adam and Eve and to the world. First, there is physical death. Although Adam and Eve didn't die immediately when they took a bite of the fruit, eventually they *would* die. From that moment on, all plants, animals, and humans would die eventually. Second, there is spiritual death. That means being separated from God, being his enemies instead of his friends. This death came to Adam and Eve, and to all of us, the moment they disobeyed God. The only way to avoid this death forever is to trust in Christ. That's why Jesus came to earth—to die in our place, for our sin, so that we might have eternal life!

KEY VERSES: *When Adam sinned, sin entered the entire human race. Adam's sin brought death, so death spread to everyone, for everyone sinned. . . . And what a difference between our sin and God's generous gift of forgiveness. For this one man, Adam, brought death to many through his sin. But this other man, Jesus Christ, brought forgiveness to many through God's bountiful gift. And the result of God's gracious gift is very different from the result of that one man's sin. For Adam's sin led to condemnation, but we have the free gift of being accepted by God, even though we are guilty of many sins. (Romans 5:12, 15-16)*

Q 131:

Did God know Adam and Eve were going to sin?

A: God knows everything, even before it happens, so he knew that Adam and Eve were going to sin. Still, God was very disappointed with what Adam and Eve did. But because God loved them (and because he loves us), he made a way for the sin to be forgiven. God's plan was to send Jesus to die on the cross for Adam's, Eve's, and our sins. By trusting in Christ, we can have eternal life.

KEY VERSES: *Long ago, even before he made the world, God loved us and chose us in Christ to be holy and without fault in his eyes. His unchanging plan has always been to adopt us into his own family by bringing us to himself through Jesus Christ. And this gave him great pleasure. (Ephesians 1:4-5)*

NOTE TO PARENTS: The knowledge that God knows everything can give your children a sense of security. Children can't do anything that will surprise God. He may be happy or disappointed, but he won't be surprised. Also, be aware that your children may not understand what the word *penalty* means. So be prepared to offer a simple explanation.

Q 132:

If Adam and Eve hadn't sinned, would people sin today?

A: We really don't know what would have happened if Adam and Eve hadn't sinned in the Garden of Eden, but their temptation was a very important test. Unfortunately, they failed the test, and sin entered the world; the perfect world became damaged, broken, and dirty. Because of Adam and Eve's sin, every person who has ever lived has been born a sinner. Sin is passed on from parents to their children. We do wrong things because we're sinners.

KEY VERSE: *Because one person disobeyed God, many people became sinners. But because one other person obeyed God, many people will be made right in God's sight. (Romans 5:19)*

NOTE TO PARENTS: Though Adam and Eve sinned, God made a way for all people to come back to him—to be forgiven—by sending Jesus.

Q 133:

Why did Cain kill his brother?

A: The story of Cain and Abel shows the effects of sin in the world. The first sin was when Adam and Eve disobeyed God and ate from the Tree of Conscience. After that, every person has been born a sinner, someone who will often do what's wrong instead of what's right. Cain's sins of jealousy and hatred led to murder. Both Cain and Abel had presented gifts to God, but Abel's gifts had pleased God, while Cain's had not. Cain became jealous of God's favor; this made Cain very angry (Genesis 4:5). Cain's jealousy and anger led him to kill his brother. We can see from this story that jealousy and anger can cause people to do terrible harm, even to people they love. Watch out for those feelings, and take care of them before they hurt you, too!

KEY VERSE: *We must not be like Cain, who belonged to the evil one and killed his brother. And why did he kill him? Because Cain had been doing what was evil, and his brother had been doing what was right. (1 John 3:12)*

Q 134:
How did Noah build a boat that was so big?

A: We don't know exactly *how* Noah built the huge boat (which we call the "ark"). But God told him what size to make it and what materials to use, and Noah obeyed God's instructions to the letter. The boat had to be very large because it would have to hold Noah, his children, their families, and hundreds of animals. It had to be a boat because God was going to flood the whole earth. It took a long time for Noah to build the boat. He probably used his whole family in the building project.

Why did Noah build the ark? Because everyone in the whole world had become so evil and violent, God was going to kill everyone with a flood. Noah was the only good man in the world, so he and his family would survive in the boat. And all the animals Noah brought on the ark would survive, too. Noah did everything God told him—he obeyed God.

KEY VERSE: *Noah did everything exactly as God had commanded him. (Genesis 6:22)*

Q 135:
Why did God flood the whole earth?

A: God made the rain fall and the water rise in order to flood the whole earth so that all the evil people in the world would drown. Because of sin, the world had gotten worse and worse. It was so bad that God became very sad; God was even sorry that he had created human beings. People were evil, mean, cruel, and violent. God gave them 120 years to improve; they had many chances to obey God, but they only got worse. Only Noah and his family were trying to live God's way (only one family in the whole world!). Noah tried to tell people about God, but no one would listen. So God decided to destroy all the human beings except Noah and his family.

KEY VERSE: *Now the earth had become corrupt in God's sight, and it was filled with violence. (Genesis 6:11)*

Q 136:

Why did God put a rainbow in the sky?

A: After the rains stopped, the flood waters went down, and Noah, his family, and the animals left the ark, God promised that he would never again send a flood to destroy the earth. Then God put a rainbow in the clouds as a sign of this promise. Whenever we see a rainbow, it reminds us of the Flood, the reason for it, and God's promise never to flood the earth again.

KEY VERSES: *"I solemnly promise never to send another flood to kill all living creatures and destroy the earth." And God said, "I am giving you a sign as evidence of my eternal covenant with you and all living creatures. I have placed my rainbow in the clouds. It is the sign of my permanent promise to you and to all the earth." (Genesis 9:11-13)*

NOTE TO PARENTS: God gives us symbols and images to remind us of his love and promises. The cross, for example, reminds us of Christ's death for us. The empty tomb reminds us of his power over sin and death. His throne in heaven reminds us of his authority.

Q 137:

Why did God choose Abraham to go to the Promised Land instead of someone else?

A: God chose Abraham (called Abram at first) to go to the Promised Land (which would later be called Israel) and to become the father of a great nation. Abraham was chosen, not because he was especially good, but simply because God wanted him—the Bible doesn't give us God's reasons. God doesn't always tell us why he does what he does. God knows everything and can do anything he wants. God knew that Abraham would obey.

KEY VERSES: *Then the LORD told Abram, "Leave your country, your relatives, and your father's house, and go to the land that I will show you. I will cause you to become the father of a great nation. I will bless you and make you famous, and I will make you a blessing to others." (Genesis 12:1-2)*

Q 138:

Why was Abraham willing to kill his own son?

A: One day God told Abraham to take his son, Isaac, up into the mountains and offer him as a sacrifice. Abraham took the trip and was willing to kill his own son because he knew that he had to obey God. Isaac was a miracle child, a special gift from God, and Abraham loved him very much. It was *very difficult* for Abraham to take Isaac and prepare him to be killed. But Abraham loved and obeyed God; he had faith and expected a miracle. Abraham believed that God could and would raise Isaac from the dead. This request from God was a test of Abraham's faith. Abraham believed that God's plan wouldn't be stopped. The good news, of course, is that Abraham didn't have to kill Isaac—God provided an animal to be sacrificed instead. Many years later, God sacrificed his own Son, Jesus, for us.

KEY VERSE: *Abraham assumed that if Isaac died, God was able to bring him back to life again. And in a sense, Abraham did receive his son back from the dead. (Hebrews 11:19)*

Q 139:

Why did Jacob trick his dad?

A: Isaac had two sons, Jacob and Esau. Jacob tricked his father because he wanted the inheritance that should have gone to his brother. Jacob was selfish and greedy. Also, he was his mom's favorite child, and when his mother told him how to trick his father, he went along and did what she said. Although Jacob received the inheritance, his actions broke up the family and caused everyone a lot of grief.

KEY VERSES: *[Rebekah said,] "Now, my son, do exactly as I tell you. Go out to the flocks and bring me two fine young goats. I'll prepare your father's favorite dish from them. Take the food to your father; then he can eat it and bless you instead of Esau before he dies." (Genesis 27:8-10)*

Q 140:

Why did Joseph's brothers sell him?

A: Joseph had ten older brothers (and one younger brother, Benjamin). Joseph's older brothers didn't like him because Joseph was their father's favorite son. (Joseph was Jacob's favorite because Joseph was born when Jacob was an old man.) They were jealous of him. Joseph's father even gave him a special gift—a beautiful coat. Joseph also made his brothers angry because he would tell his father about some of the bad things they would do, and he would tell his older brothers about his dreams in which the brothers bowed down before him. Eventually the brothers became so upset with Joseph that they decided to kill him. But one brother, Reuben, talked the others into putting Joseph into a well instead of killing him. He planned to set Joseph free later. But while Reuben was gone, the other brothers sold him to some foreign traders as a slave.

KEY VERSES: *"Here comes that dreamer!" they exclaimed. "Come on, let's kill him and throw him into a deep pit. We can tell our father that a wild animal has eaten him. Then we'll see what becomes of all his dreams!" (Genesis 37:19-20)*

Q 141:

Why didn't Joseph go back home?

A: Joseph may have wanted to go back home (certainly he missed his father, mother, and little brother), but he couldn't—first because he was a slave, then because he was in prison, and finally because he was in government service. He also was a long way from home, and transportation was different from today; Joseph couldn't just hop on a bus or train and go home. Also, Joseph may have been afraid of facing his brothers again; remember, they had wanted to kill him and then had sold him into slavery. It's good that Joseph stayed in Egypt because God used him in his powerful position in the government to save his family (and thousands of others) from starvation. And eventually God brought the whole family back together again in Egypt with Joseph—all part of God's plan to bring Jesus to earth.

KEY VERSE: *[Joseph said,] "Yes, it was God who sent me here, not you! And he has made me a counselor to Pharaoh—manager of his entire household and ruler over all Egypt." (Genesis 45:8)*

Q 142:

Why didn't the bush burn up?

A: One day while watching sheep, a man named Moses saw a bush on fire that would not burn up. The bush didn't turn into ashes because God was present, doing a miracle to get Moses' attention. When Moses saw the bush and heard God's voice, he was ready to listen. God used the burning bush to help Moses see that God had the power to do what he said he would do—rescue the people of Israel from slavery in Egypt.

KEY VERSES: *Suddenly, the angel of the LORD appeared to him as a blazing fire in a bush. Moses was amazed because the bush was engulfed in flames, but it didn't burn up. "Amazing!" Moses said to himself. "Why isn't that bush burning up? I must go over to see this." When the LORD saw that he had caught Moses' attention, God called to him from the bush, "Moses! Moses!" "Here I am!" Moses replied. (Exodus 3:2-4)*

Q 143:

Why wasn't Moses afraid to go to Pharaoh?

A: Moses probably was afraid to go to Pharaoh, but he went anyway out of obedience to God. When God said he was going to send Moses to Pharaoh to demand that he let the Israelites go, Moses was very frightened at the idea. In fact, he tried to get out of the job by using all sorts of excuses: He said he wasn't the right person, the people would wonder why he should be the one to lead them, the people wouldn't believe that God had sent him, and he wasn't a good speaker. Finally, when Moses had run out of excuses, he simply pleaded: "Lord, please! Send someone else" (Exodus 4:13). But God wanted Moses to go, and Moses did go—God gave him strength and stayed with him. Moses was able to lead God's people out of slavery and to the Promised Land. The Bible doesn't say Moses wasn't afraid; it says he obeyed God.

KEY VERSE: *[God said,] "Now go, for I am sending you to Pharaoh. You will lead my people, the Israelites, out of Egypt." (Exodus 3:10)*

Q 144:

Why wouldn't Pharaoh let the people go?

A: Pharaoh is a title, like "king." The pharaoh in charge of Egypt when Moses lived was different from the pharaoh whom Joseph served—that pharaoh was kind and generous to the Israelites. But this pharaoh was mean; he forced the Israelites to serve the Egyptians as slaves. When Moses went to see Pharaoh and asked him to let the Israelites leave Egypt to worship in the wilderness, Pharaoh was furious. He was too proud to give in to a slave, and he thought he would lose his slave labor, so he refused. Moses went back to him with the request and did special signs to prove that he had been sent by God, but Pharaoh still said no. Finally God sent a series of plagues to convince Pharaoh to let the people go. After each plague, Pharaoh would agree to let the people go, but then he would change his mind and refuse. The Lord hardened Pharaoh's heart in order to punish him and demonstrate God's power.

KEY VERSE: *"This is the finger of God!" the magicians exclaimed to Pharaoh. But Pharaoh's heart remained hard and stubborn. He wouldn't listen to them, just as the LORD had predicted. (Exodus 8:19)*

Q 145:

Why did God send plagues on Egypt?

A: God sent the plagues to Egypt to punish Pharaoh and to show God's power. The plagues were miracles—fantastic demonstrations of God's power. Pharaoh saw himself as a god, and God was showing him who the true God was. Also, God was answering the prayers of the Israelites to deliver them from slavery. The Egyptians were holding the Israelites captive and did not want to let them go. Each time Pharaoh would refuse to let the people go, God would send a plague on the Egyptians (but not the Israelites) to help convince Pharaoh to change his mind. After each plague, Pharaoh would agree to release the Israelites, but then he would harden his heart and say no. Eventually, after the death of the firstborn male children, the Israelites were allowed to leave Egypt. But even then, Pharaoh changed his mind and chased after them. Pharaoh was an evil man.

KEY VERSES: *"Go back to Pharaoh," the LORD commanded Moses. "Tell him, 'This is what the LORD, the God of the Hebrews, says: Let my people go, so they can worship me. If you continue to oppress them and refuse to let them go, the LORD will send a deadly plague to destroy your horses, donkeys, camels, cattle, and sheep. But the LORD will again make a distinction between the property of the Israelites and that of the Egyptians. Not a single one of Israel's livestock will die!'" (Exodus 9:1-4)*

Q 146:

Why did the Israelites smear blood on their doors?

A: The blood on the doors helped the Israelites prepare for God's final plague on Egypt. That plague would kill all the firstborn males in Egypt except those who lived in the homes marked by the blood on the doors. The blood came from a perfect lamb that they killed and ate that night. The blood showed their faith that God would do as he said and rescue them from slavery. Though the people at that time didn't know it, the blood also represented Christ's death on the cross. By trusting in Jesus, men and women and boys and girls can be rescued from slavery to sin . . . and receive *eternal* life.

KEY VERSE: *The LORD will pass through the land and strike down the Egyptians. But when he sees the blood on the top and sides of the doorframe, the LORD will pass over your home. He will not permit the Destroyer to enter and strike down your firstborn. (Exodus 12:23)*

NOTE TO PARENTS: It is sometimes difficult for children to understand why God asked his people to sacrifice animals. Explain that God does everything for our good—God is love, and he does whatever benefits us all. He's just and kind, and his plans for us are good.

Q 147:

How did Moses part the Red Sea?

RED SEA FUN POOL

A: After Moses and the Israelites left Egypt, Pharaoh changed his mind and sent soldiers to bring them back. When the fleeing Israelites came to the Red Sea, it looked as if they would be caught by the soldiers because there seemed to be no way across the water. But Moses held his rod over the edge of the sea, and God made the waters part so the people could march across to the other side on dry ground. Moses himself didn't part the Red Sea—it was a miracle that God did through him. God used Moses to lead the people to safety. Once the Israelites were safe on the other side, God allowed the water to return to normal, and the Egyptian army was drowned.

KEY VERSES: *Then Moses raised his hand over the sea, and the LORD opened up a path through the water with a strong east wind. The wind blew all that night, turning the seabed into dry land. So the people of Israel walked through the sea on dry ground, with walls of water on each side! (Exodus 14:21-22)*

Q 148:

Why did God give Moses so many laws for the Israelites to obey?

A: Moses led the Israelites to Mount Sinai, where God met with Moses and gave him laws that are recorded in the book of Leviticus. When we read Leviticus, it seems as if God gave the Israelites a lot of laws to obey. Actually, today most cities and towns have far more laws than are listed in Leviticus. (The basic laws are the Ten Commandments—many of the other laws grew out of these.) Some of the laws God gave helped organize the Israelites into a nation; some helped keep the people healthy; others told them (and us) how to live. God knew what was best for the people, and he wanted what was best for them, so he gave them many instructions.

KEY VERSE: *Moses called all the people of Israel together and said, "Listen carefully to all the laws and regulations I am giving you today. Learn them and be sure to obey them!" (Deuteronomy 5:1)*

NOTE TO PARENTS: The law guided the Israelites, but it also shows us that we are sinners. That is, it shows us that we can't obey perfectly. You can use this to explain how we all break God's law, making us guilty before God and in need of salvation through faith in Christ.

Q 149:

Why did the Israelites who left Egypt have to wander in the wilderness until they died?

A: Through Moses, God led the Israelites right to the Promised Land, the land he had promised to Abraham. (This is also the land that Jacob and his sons left when they went to live with Joseph in Egypt.) Moses had sent twelve spies into Canaan to see what the land and the Canaanites were like. Ten spies reported that the Canaanites were giants that the Israelites shouldn't try to fight. But Joshua and Caleb, who knew God would help them, said, "Let's go at once to take the land. . . . We can certainly conquer it!" (Numbers 13:30). Unfortunately, the people listened to the report of the ten and refused to obey God and march into the land. Those Israelites never saw the Promised Land because they didn't have faith to do what God wanted them to do; they wandered in the wilderness for forty years.

KEY VERSES: *[God said to the Israelites,] "Because the men who explored the land were there for forty days, you must wander in the wilderness for forty years—a year for each day, suffering the consequences of your sins. You will discover what it is like to have me for an enemy." I, the LORD, have spoken! I will do these things to every member of the community who has conspired against me. They will all die here in this wilderness! (Numbers 14:34-35)*

The Nation of Israel

Q 150:
Did the Israelites have lawyers and courts for their judges?

A: Joshua was the Israelites' leader when they first got to the Promised Land. After Joshua died, God used judges to lead his people. The judges that we read about in the book of Judges were not like the judges we have today, so they didn't have courts or listen to lawyers. The Israelite judges were their nation's spiritual leaders and sometimes military leaders. Their main job was to organize the people, rescue them from enemies, and lead the people to God. This was how God led the Israelites, much the way parents lead their children.

KEY VERSE: *The LORD raised up judges to rescue the Israelites from their enemies. (Judges 2:16)*

Q 151:
Was Samson a good guy or a bad guy?

A: One of Israel's judges was a man named Samson. Samson served God and wanted to please him, but he wasn't perfect. God had chosen him to do a special service for the nation of Israel—to rescue his people from cruel enemies. Samson fulfilled that job well. But Samson also did some cruel and foolish things, just as most people do. God didn't force him to do everything right. Like us, Samson had the freedom to choose to use his God-given abilities (in his case, strength) for good or bad. Sometimes Samson chose to go his own way instead of God's.

KEY VERSE: *[The angel of the LORD said,] "You will become pregnant and give birth to a son, and his hair must never be cut. For he will be dedicated to God as a Nazirite from birth. He will rescue Israel from the Philistines."(Judges 13:5)*

Q 152:

Why did Samson tell Delilah his secret?

A: Samson was in love with a woman named Delilah even though Delilah did not really love him and was a friend of his enemies. When some of those enemies offered her money to help them capture Samson, Delilah agreed and asked him for the secret of his strength. At first he gave her the wrong answers, but she nagged him and prodded him until finally Samson told her the truth—his strength came from God as part of a vow that included not cutting his hair. He told her that if his hair were cut, the Lord and his strength would leave him. Samson let himself be tricked because he was blinded by his feelings for Delilah. We need to be careful about our friends; even people we care about and like may sometimes want us to do bad things. Whenever that happens, we should obey God.

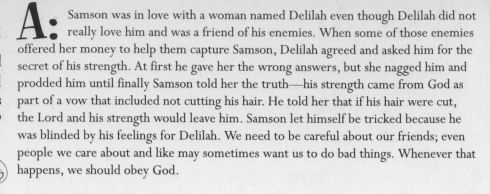

KEY VERSES: *Day after day she nagged him until he couldn't stand it any longer. Finally, Samson told her his secret. "My hair has never been cut," he confessed, "for I was dedicated to God as a Nazirite from birth. If my head were shaved, my strength would leave me, and I would become as weak as anyone else." (Judges 16:16-17)*

Q 153:

Why did Hannah leave her son at the church?

A: For a long time, Hannah was unable to have children, and that bothered her very much. One day, while crying and praying to God, she vowed that if God would answer her prayer and give her a son, she would give the boy back to God, dedicating his life to serving God. When Samuel was born, Hannah remembered her promise to God; a few years later, when Samuel was old enough to eat solid food, she brought Samuel to the tabernacle (the place where God's people worshiped). Leaving Samuel there was like leaving him at a boarding school, with people who would love and care for him and teach him God's ways. Hannah wasn't abandoning Samuel; she was leaving him with teachers who would train him to become a priest and servant of God. Hannah's son was in good hands. Samuel grew up to be a leader of Israel and a spokesman for God.

KEY VERSES: *[Hannah said,] "I asked the LORD to give me this child, and he has given me my request. Now I am giving him to the LORD, and he will belong to the LORD his whole life." And they worshiped the LORD there. (1 Samuel 1:27-28)*

NOTE TO PARENTS: Questions like this one may have others hidden underneath: Will I be left alone with strangers? Does God think it's good for children to be left with strangers? Do my parents care about me? Be sensitive to this concern and reassure your children of God's care and your commitment to love and nurture them.

Q 154:

Why did the people want to have a king?

A: The people of Israel were unhappy with God as their king and wanted to be like all the other nations—to have a human king who would lead them in battle. Times were tough, and Samuel's sons were turning out to be bad judges. They were accepting bribes and making wrong decisions. Samuel knew that God wanted the people to trust in God and not in a king, but God told Samuel to give them one anyway, along with a warning that a king would bring them many hardships. The man chosen to be Israel's first king was Saul; he was tall and handsome, but very shy. Saul started out to be a good king, but then became bad because he disobeyed God.

KEY VERSE: *"Do as they say," the LORD replied, "for it is me they are rejecting, not you. They don't want me to be their king any longer." (1 Samuel 8:7)*

Q 155:

What did Goliath eat that made him so big?

A: Goliath was a very big man—over nine feet tall. If he were alive today, he would be able to dunk a basketball without jumping, and his head would touch the net. We don't know how Goliath got to be so big, but he was a giant of a man. Goliath was as nasty as he was big; he hated the Israelites and would make fun of them and God. King Saul and his soldiers were afraid of fighting him. But a young man named David wasn't afraid. He knew that he had to fight against this man who stood against God, no matter how big he was. And he knew he would win because God would fight for him.

KEY VERSE: *Then Goliath, a Philistine champion from Gath, came out of the Philistine ranks to face the forces of Israel. He was a giant of a man, measuring over nine feet tall! (1 Samuel 17:4)*

Q 156:

How did David fight Goliath if he was so small?

A: Although David wasn't a big man or a soldier, he wasn't afraid to fight the giant Goliath because he trusted in God, not in his own strength or in a soldier's weapons and armor. In fact, he wouldn't wear the king's armor when it was offered to him. David remembered that he had defeated lions and bears while protecting his father's sheep. David also knew that he would not fight Goliath in hand-to-hand combat; instead, he would use a sling and a stone. Also, David was about sixteen, not a little boy. David trusted in God and knew that he had to fight Goliath because Goliath was mocking the armies of Israel and God.

KEY VERSE: *David shouted in reply, "You come to me with sword, spear, and javelin, but I come to you in the name of the LORD Almighty—the God of the armies of Israel, whom you have defied." (1 Samuel 17:45)*

Q 157:

Why was Saul jealous of David?

A: After Saul made David an army commander, people were singing, "Saul has killed his thousands, and David his ten thousands!" (1 Samuel 18:7). It angered Saul that David had become so popular with the people; in fact, it seemed as though everyone liked David more than Saul. This made Saul jealous. Saul knew that David was a better man—a better warrior and a better person. This jealousy made Saul a very cruel and deceitful person, and he tried for years to kill David. Eventually God told Saul he couldn't be king anymore, and after Saul died, David became king. We must be careful to be content with whom God has made us and not become jealous of others.

KEY VERSES: *This made Saul very angry. "What's this?" he said. "They credit David with ten thousands and me with only thousands. Next they'll be making him their king!" So from that time on Saul kept a jealous eye on David. (1 Samuel 18:8-9)*

Q 158:

Why did Saul go to a fortune-teller?

A: King Saul went to see a medium, or fortune-teller, because he was desperate. He did not trust in God to lead him. Saul wanted to find out things that he didn't have a right to know. In the law, God had told his people that they should never get involved with witchcraft, mediums, and fortune-tellers. Saul disobeyed God and did it anyway.

KEY VERSE: *Saul then said to his advisers, "Find a woman who is a medium, so I can go and ask her what to do." His advisers replied, "There is a medium at Endor." (1 Samuel 28:7)*

NOTE TO PARENTS: Dabbling in the occult is *not* a harmless pastime. Satan and demons are real beings that can influence the physical world, and occult practices only invite them to do so. Don't have Ouija boards, tarot cards, or other forms of occult fortune-telling in your home, and don't let your kids use them either. Remind your child that God loves us, has good plans for us, and has given us the Holy Spirit. He will give us wisdom if we ask him (James 1:5).

Q 159:

Why did Solomon want to cut the baby in half?

A: After David died, his son Solomon became king. God told Solomon that he could have anything he asked for. Solomon asked for wisdom. One day two women came to King Solomon arguing over who was the real mother of a baby, and Solomon suggested that he cut the baby in half and give one half to each mother. Solomon didn't want to kill the baby. He just suggested that they cut the baby in half in order to find out who was the baby's real mother. Solomon knew that the real mother would never let such a thing happen to her baby. Solomon's trick worked, and the baby was given to his real mother. This story is in the Bible to show how wise Solomon was, in answer to his prayer. God made him the wisest man who ever lived.

KEY VERSES: *So God replied, "Because you have asked for wisdom in governing my people and have not asked for a long life or riches for yourself or the death of your enemies—I will give you what you asked for! I will give you a wise and understanding mind such as no one else has ever had or ever will have!" (1 Kings 3:11-12)*

Q 160:

Were prophets the people in Bible days who made lots of money?

A: It's easy to confuse words that sound alike but have different meanings. *Profit* refers to making money; *prophet* means a person who represented God to the people in Bible times. A prophet spoke God's messages and told the people to obey God. People never became prophets in order to become rich or famous. Most of the time—especially when they had to give bad news—prophets were very unpopular; some were even put in prison. But God's prophets were willing to risk everything for God. Some of the most famous prophets include Moses, Elijah, Elisha, Isaiah, Jeremiah, Ezekiel, and Daniel. Some less well-known prophets also wrote books of the Bible: Hosea, Joel, Amos, Obadiah, Jonah, and Malachi. Even though these prophets spoke hundreds of years ago, their messages apply to us, too, and we should listen to what they had to say.

KEY VERSE: *Long ago God spoke many times and in many ways to our ancestors through the prophets. (Hebrews 1:1)*

NOTE TO PARENTS: Many children think prophets mainly foretold the future. But their main job was to "forth-tell" God's word to the people, to challenge the people to turn back to God. Often the prophets' messages contained predictions about the future, but most of the messages were calls or challenges to obey God and live right.

Q 161:

Why did Elijah go up to heaven so early?

A: Elijah was a famous prophet who spent most of his life telling others about God. He is one of only two people mentioned in the Bible who didn't die before going to heaven (Enoch is the other one—see Genesis 5:21-24). Instead, God took them. God used a chariot of fire and a whirlwind to take Elijah to heaven. The whirlwind and fire didn't kill Elijah or burn him; rather, the chariot and horses separated Elijah from his good friend and student, Elisha. Then the whirlwind carried Elijah to heaven. This showed that God approved of Elijah and that Elijah was a good man who loved God. And God took Elijah to heaven at just the right time, not early. We don't know how old Elijah was when God took him; he may have been an old man.

KEY VERSE: *As they were walking along and talking, suddenly a chariot of fire appeared, drawn by horses of fire. It drove between them, separating them, and Elijah was carried by a whirlwind into heaven. (2 Kings 2:11)*

NOTE TO PARENTS: Children often imagine that the chariot of fire would have killed Elijah and burned Elisha because it was on fire. We don't know what the "fire" was like. The point of the image is that God used a dramatic and miraculous event to separate Elijah and Elisha and to take Elijah to heaven.

Q 162:

Why did God send the Jews to Babylon?

A: The people of Judah (the Jews) didn't listen to the prophets. They turned away from God, worshiped idols, and mistreated the poor. So God allowed a wicked nation, Babylon, and a wicked king, Nebuchadnezzar, to capture their cities and take many of the people to Babylon. The Babylonians often did this to the people they conquered; they removed the best young people from their own country and trained them in Babylonian ways. Prophets like Jeremiah predicted that this would happen, and they were very sad about it. The Jews spent seventy years in Babylon, just as God said they would. God's warnings are for our good. When we ignore them again and again, we end up being hurt, just like the people of Judah did.

KEY VERSE: *King Nebuchadnezzar took ten thousand captives from Jerusalem, including all the princes and the best of the soldiers, craftsmen, and smiths. So only the poorest people were left in the land. (2 Kings 24:14)*

NOTE TO PARENTS: The Babylonian captivity came as a result of Israel's failure to heed the prophets. It shows God's willingness to discipline his people for their own good. In Judah's case, the time in Babylon taught them not to worship idols anymore.

Q 163:

Whose hand made the writing on the wall?

A: It was a miracle of God, performed to announce judgment on the king of Babylon for his pride. Belshazzar was holding a great feast and serving a lot of wine. During the eating and drinking, he sent for the gold and silver cups that had been taken from the temple in Jerusalem many years before by a king who ruled before him, King Nebuchadnezzar. As he was using these cups to drink a toast to idols of wood and stone, fingers of a man's hand appeared and began writing on the wall. The king was shocked and frightened, and he called for Daniel (one of God's prophets) to interpret the writing. It contained a message for the king: He had been evil and proud, and soon his enemies would defeat him (which they did). God used the hand and the writing to get the king's attention, and it certainly worked!

KEY VERSES: *At that very moment they saw the fingers of a human hand writing on the plaster wall of the king's palace, near the lampstand. The king himself saw the hand as it wrote, and his face turned pale with fear. Such terror gripped him that his knees knocked together and his legs gave way beneath him. (Daniel 5:5-6)*

Q 164:

How did Daniel sleep with the lions without being afraid?

A: Daniel was a young man when he was captured and taken to Babylon. He lived the rest of his life there, serving four kings, but he always remained true to God. One day, when he was an old man, the last of these kings, Darius, signed a law stating that no one could ask a favor of (or pray to) anyone except him, the king. (This was a trick by some powerful men to get rid of Daniel.) Because Daniel ignored the new law and continued to pray to God, the king had to punish him by putting him into a den of lions. Daniel spent all night with the lions but wasn't hurt.

The Bible doesn't say that Daniel wasn't afraid. Rather, Daniel was willing to face the lions because he trusted in God. Daniel had seen what God could do (see Daniel 3:1-30 and 5:1-31) and believed that obeying God was right, even if it meant being in danger. Even if Daniel was afraid, he faced the lions *bravely* because of his confidence in God.

KEY VERSE: *[Daniel said,] "My God sent his angel to shut the lions' mouths so that they would not hurt me, for I have been found innocent in his sight. And I have not wronged you, Your Majesty." (Daniel 6:22)*

Q 165:

Why didn't the Jews ever change their clothes while they were rebuilding the walls?

A: After seventy years in Babylon, God had the king begin to let his people go back home again. Although Nehemiah lived in Babylon and served the king there, he still loved his own country, Israel, especially the capital city, Jerusalem. When he heard that the walls were still torn down, he became very upset. (In those days, a city's walls helped protect it from invading armies, and good, solid walls showed that the city was doing well.) So Nehemiah asked for and received permission from the king to return to Jerusalem to organize the wall-building project. Not everyone in Jerusalem and the surrounding areas wanted the wall to be rebuilt; some were trying hard to stop the project. So all the workers had to be on guard constantly and to be organized so that the work could continue twenty-four hours a day. Nehemiah and the workers were so determined to rebuild the walls that they didn't change their clothes (except to wash) and always kept their weapons with them. Soon the wall was rebuilt.

KEY VERSE: *During this time, none of us—not I, nor my relatives, nor my servants, nor the guards who were with me—ever took off our clothes. We carried our weapons with us at all times, even when we went for water. (Nehemiah 4:23)*

Q 166:

What's a Maccabee?

A: The Maccabees were a courageous and heroic family of Jews who lived between the time of the Old and New Testaments. The events in the Old Testament ended about four hundred years before the events in the New Testament began. But during that time, Israel was still ruled by other nations, and most of the rulers were cruel to them. One ruler from Greece even made fun of the Jewish religion by sacrificing a pig in the temple. This greatly upset the Jews, and so they rebelled. The revolt was led by Judas Maccabee (who, by the way, was no relation to the Judas who betrayed Jesus). Under his leadership, the Jews were able to win many battles and eventually restore the temple to the way it was. They celebrated with a great festival, which came to be called Hanukkah, or the "Feast of Lights" (referred to as the "Feast of Dedication" in the New Testament). It became an annual event, beginning in December and lasting eight days.

KEY VERSE: *It was now winter, and Jesus was in Jerusalem at the time of Hanukkah. (John 10:22)*

New Testament Events and People

Q 167:

Did people in the Bible have Christmas?

A: Christmas is a celebration of the birth of Christ. Many years after Jesus was born, Christians decided to celebrate his birth. They chose December 25 as the day to observe it. December 25 is probably not the exact day Jesus was born, but that's not important. What is important is that we remember and celebrate the birth of Jesus, our Savior, not that we get presents, get time off from school, or get to eat a lot of sweets.

KEY VERSES: *Jesus was born in the town of Bethlehem in Judea, during the reign of King Herod. About that time some wise men from eastern lands arrived in Jerusalem, asking, "Where is this newborn king of the Jews?" (Matthew 2:1-2)*

NOTE TO PARENTS: If your children ask about Santa Claus, explain that he was a person whom people have used to help celebrate Christmas. Many years ago, the real St. Nicholas was a man who helped poor children at Christmastime by giving them gifts. Since that time, the story has grown so that today we talk about Santa Claus, with his flying reindeer, who delivers presents to children all over the world. Santa isn't real, but Jesus is.

Q 168:

How come Zacharias couldn't talk until his son was born?

A: Zacharias was a priest who served in the temple. One day he entered a part of the sanctuary where only the priest could go. There the angel Gabriel appeared to him and announced that Zacharias's wife, Elizabeth, would have a son. Zacharias doubted the angel's promise, and so he was silenced until the birth of the baby. This would be a sign to the people that Zacharias had met with God. When Zacharias's son was born, he asked for a writing tablet to write down the boy's name. As soon as he wrote, "His name is John!" as Gabriel had told him to do, Zacharias was able to talk again.

KEY VERSE: *When he finally did come out, he couldn't speak to them. Then they realized from his gestures that he must have seen a vision in the Temple sanctuary. (Luke 1:22)*

Q 169:

Why did John the Baptist live in the desert?

A: John the Baptist was a prophet. God had given him the important job of preparing the way for Jesus. So John wanted to preach away from where people were living so they would have to go out to see him and hear his message. Living in the desert also kept him from having a lot of arguments with the religious leaders in Jerusalem who didn't like what he was saying. And by living in the desert, John was showing that he was serious about his message and that a person's relationship with God was much more important than having a nice, comfortable life on earth.

KEY VERSES: *In those days John the Baptist began preaching in the Judean wilderness. His message was, "Turn from your sins and turn to God, because the Kingdom of Heaven is near." (Matthew 3:1-2)*

Q 170:

Are "Beatitudes" short for bad attitudes?

A: Jesus taught a short sermon called "the Beatitudes" to describe good attitudes, the attitudes that God wants us to have. The word *beatitude* means "blessed." Jesus said that whoever followed him should be poor in spirit, merciful, honest, and should expect rejection from others for being his follower. Jesus' disciples may have been thinking that they would become rich, famous, and powerful by following him, but Jesus was telling them that they should expect their rewards in heaven.

KEY VERSE: *One day as the crowds were gathering, Jesus went up the mountainside with his disciples and sat down to teach them. (Matthew 5:1)*

Q 171:

What's a parable?

Good Samaritan
PAIR APPLE

A: A parable is a short story with a surprise ending that makes a point. Jesus told many parables for two reasons: (1) to hide the truth from people who weren't really interested, and (2) to teach the truth to listeners who were interested and wanted to learn. Whenever Jesus told parables, those who weren't interested or who didn't want to listen didn't understand. But those who wanted to learn asked Jesus to explain the story, and then they got the point. We can learn from the Bible if we want to do what God says. But if we don't want to listen to God, the Bible won't make much sense.

KEY VERSE: *He used many such stories and illustrations to teach the people as much as they were able to understand. (Mark 4:33)*

NOTE TO PARENTS: Many younger children (preadolescents) may not fully understand parables. That's OK. Part of what makes parables powerful is that they can teach us more and more as we gain experience in life. Whenever you read a parable with your children, help them see how it teaches us to live. For example, the parable of the Good Samaritan is about a hurt man who receives help from an unlikely stranger after being bypassed by two religious leaders. Simply explain that Jesus wants us to be like the helper—compassionate toward others.

Q 172:

What does Passover mean?

A: Just before Jesus died, he had a Passover meal with his disciples. *Passover* is the special celebration Jews hold every year to remember when the Israelites left Egypt and started their trip to the Promised Land. Moses had told Pharaoh that because he wouldn't let the Jews go, all the firstborn boys would die. But God told the Jews to put the blood of a lamb over the door and on the sides of the door so the angel of death would see the blood and pass over them and spare the Jewish children. Today, Jews still celebrate Passover. Christians celebrate the Lord's Supper (Holy Communion) rather than Passover.

KEY VERSE: *[God said to the Israelites,] "Celebrate this Festival of Unleavened Bread, for it will remind you that I brought your forces out of the land of Egypt on this very day. This festival will be a permanent regulation for you, to be kept from generation to generation." (Exodus 12:17)*

NOTE TO PARENTS: The Christian celebration of Communion comes from Jesus' celebration of Passover. Just before Jesus died, he had a Passover meal with his disciples. As they ate bread and wine, he told them that the bread was his body that would be broken for them and the wine was his blood that would be shed for them. Jesus is our Lamb that was killed; because of his blood, we can have eternal life.

Q 173:

Didn't the tongues of fire on the apostles' heads burn them?

A: The tongues of fire that appeared on the heads of the disciples (after Jesus had gone back to heaven) symbolized the Holy Spirit who had come into their lives. The "tongues" weren't mouth tongues, but tongues of fire. This "fire" wasn't real fire that burns things; it looked like fire, so that's how people described it. Everyone watching knew that something very special was happening. And when they listened, they heard their own language being spoken by people who hadn't learned the language. It was obvious that God was speaking through these people.

KEY VERSES: *What looked like flames or tongues of fire appeared and settled on each of them. And everyone present was filled with the Holy Spirit and began speaking in other languages, as the Holy Spirit gave them this ability. (Acts 2:3-4)*

Q 174:

How could the angel unlock Peter out of jail without keys?

A: The angel freed Peter through God's power. Herod wanted to kill Peter to make some of the other leaders happy. He had Peter arrested and sentenced to death. The night before he was going to be killed, God sent an angel to rescue Peter. He woke Peter up, and the chains fell off Peter's wrists. Then Peter and the angel walked away from the soldiers without waking any of them up. God made the iron gate open up when they walked up to it. The angel left him when they got outside. Peter could hardly believe what had happened—and neither could his friends who were praying for him! (Acts 12:12-16)

KEY VERSES: *The night before Peter was to be placed on trial, he was asleep, chained between two soldiers, with others standing guard at the prison gate. Suddenly, there was a bright light in the cell, and an angel of the Lord stood before Peter. The angel tapped him on the side to awaken him and said, "Quick! Get up!" And the chains fell off his wrists. (Acts 12:6-7)*

Q 175:

How big were the worms that ate King Herod?

A: King Herod had become very popular with many of the people because he had been hurting the Christians. Later, some people who were trying to get on his good side told him that he looked and sounded like a god. Already a very proud man, Herod enjoyed hearing what the people said, and he accepted their worship as though he really were a god. Because Herod did this instead of honoring God, God caused him to be filled with tiny worms, or maggots, that ate him from the inside out. In the Bible, worms are a sign of pain and punishment.

KEY VERSE: *Instantly, an angel of the Lord struck Herod with a sickness, because he accepted the people's worship instead of giving the glory to God. So he was consumed with worms and died. (Acts 12:23)*

Q 176:

How could Peter kill and eat animals that were in a vision?

A: Peter never actually ate the animals he saw in his vision; he received *permission* to eat them. You see, the animals Peter saw were the types that the Jews were not supposed to eat (called "unclean" animals). In his vision, a voice told Peter to kill and eat any of the animals he wished. Peter didn't actually eat the animals that he saw because they weren't real, but soon after seeing the vision, Peter learned its meaning. Three men who weren't Jews came to the door and asked Peter to come and talk to their leader, an officer in the Roman army. Normally Peter, a Jew, would not have anything to do with non-Jews (Gentiles) because they, like the animals, were considered unclean. But the vision made him realize that he should go with the men. Because Peter obeyed God and went with the men, the Roman soldier (Cornelius), his family, and his servants all became followers of Christ.

KEY VERSES: *In the sheet were all sorts of animals, reptiles, and birds. Then a voice said to him, "Get up, Peter; kill and eat them." (Acts 10:12-13)*

Q 177:

Why was it against the law to make friends with a Gentile?

A: A Gentile was anyone who was not a Jew. It *wasn't* against the law to make friends with a Gentile. Instead, God wanted the Jewish people not to copy and be like Gentiles because they didn't follow the Jewish laws and didn't worship the true God. Some Jews wouldn't even walk through Gentile towns. Jews did accept some Gentiles into their religion. They were called "God-fearers." By breaking down this barrier, the message about Jesus could be taken to everybody, not just Jews. God wants us to accept all people and not think we're superior just because we know God.

KEY VERSE: *Peter told them, "You know it is against the Jewish laws for me to come into a Gentile home like this. But God has shown me that I should never think of anyone as impure." (Acts 10:28)*

Q 178:

Why was Saul blinded by a bright light?

A: At first, Saul (also known as Paul) was totally against Jesus and anyone who followed him. In fact, he watched and approved when a Christian named Stephen was killed for believing in Christ. Saul hated Christians so much that he got permission to capture them and put them in jail. But God had other plans for Saul's life. One day, while Saul was traveling to another city to look for Christians, he was blinded by a bright light. God used the light to get Saul's attention. Then Jesus appeared to him. Through this experience, Saul believed in Jesus. He became a strong follower of Christ and a great missionary. Instead of trying to get rid of Christians, he went all over the world helping people become Christians. He wrote many letters to those Christians; some of those letters are in our Bibles today.

KEY VERSES: *As he was nearing Damascus on this mission, a brilliant light from heaven suddenly beamed down upon him! He fell to the ground and heard a voice saying to him, "Saul! Saul! Why are you persecuting me?" (Acts 9:3-4)*

NOTE TO PARENTS: Paul wrote Romans, 1 and 2 Corinthians, Galatians, Ephesians, Philippians, Colossians, 1 and 2 Thessalonians, 1 and 2 Timothy, Titus, and Philemon.

Q 179:

Why did Paul want to tell the Romans about Jesus?

A: Many people in Rome had become followers of Christ after visiting Jerusalem and hearing the message from the apostles there. Some had become Christians in other cities and had then moved to Rome. Paul wanted to meet these believers and encourage them in their faith. Rome was the most important city in the world at that time—the capital city of the Roman Empire. Paul knew that Christ's message had to go all over the world, and Rome would be a key place for helping to make that happen. Also, Paul was a Roman citizen, and he spoke Greek just as many people in Rome did, so he knew people would listen to him. Paul went on several trips all over the Roman Empire, including one to Rome, to tell people about Jesus.

KEY VERSE: *That night the Lord appeared to Paul and said, "Be encouraged, Paul. Just as you have told the people about me here in Jerusalem, you must preach the Good News in Rome." (Acts 23:11)*

Q 180:

How did Paul send letters to churches if they didn't have mailboxes?

A: In Paul's time, they didn't have a postal service like the one we have today. Instead, people sent letters by messengers or friends. Many of Paul's friends delivered his letters to churches. These friends included Timothy, Tychicus, and others. Paul wrote some letters, such as Philemon and Titus, to individuals. He wrote others, such as Romans and Philippians, to specific churches. And he wrote still others, such as Galatians and Colossians, to specific churches with the idea that the letters would be passed along to other churches. Paul's letters teach us about other parts of the Bible, about Jesus, about how Christians should live, and about how churches should be organized. Paul's letters have a lot to teach us!

KEY VERSE: *Remember, the Lord is waiting so that people have time to be saved. This is just as our beloved brother Paul wrote to you with the wisdom God gave him. (2 Peter 3:15)*

Bible Times

Q 181:

When did Bible times happen?

GRANDPA, WERE YOU ALIVE WHEN JESUS WAS HERE?

A: Everything in the Bible happened a long time ago—hundreds and hundreds of years before your grandparents were born. In fact, when you say what year it is right now, that tells about how many years have passed since Jesus lived on earth, and that's about when the New Testament was written. But many, many years also separate the Old Testament from the New. The events described in the Old Testament took place over thousands of years, and there are four hundred years between the last event in the Old Testament and the first event in the New. Although people who lived long ago didn't have TV, cars, computers, and other modern inventions, they weren't stupid. In fact, they were a lot like us. Those things just hadn't been invented yet.

KEY VERSE: *When we were utterly helpless, Christ came at just the right time and died for us sinners. (Romans 5:6)*

Q 182:

How did Bible people travel?

A: People in Bible times didn't have cars, trains, buses, or airplanes, but they still had to travel from town to town. Usually they walked. If you've ever taken a hike, you know that you walk until you're tired, and then you rest. You may even have to pitch a tent and camp out for the night before getting to your destination. Then you start hiking again the next day. That's what people did back then whenever they walked a long way. If they could afford it, people also rode on donkeys, camels, or horses. Sometimes people (usually kings, soldiers, or rich people) would ride in chariots that were pulled by horses. And, of course, when they had to travel over water, they went in boats or ships.

KEY VERSE: *[God said to the Israelites,] "Wear your traveling clothes as you eat this meal, as though prepared for a long journey. Wear your sandals, and carry your walking sticks in your hands. Eat the food quickly, for this is the LORD's Passover."(Exodus 12:11)*

Q 183:

Why did Bible people give their kids such funny names?

A: In ancient times, especially among the Jewish people, a person's name was very special. Usually it said something about the person or about the parents' dreams for their child. For example, Jedidiah means "lover of God." Sometimes God told prophets to give their children names with special messages. Hosea named his children Lo-ruhamah and Lo-ammi. Lo-ruhamah means "not loved," and Lo-Ammi means "not my people." By giving his children these unusual names, Hosea was giving God's message to the people. But usually names from other countries and cultures sound strange to us because we're not used to them. Names may sound funny to us, but not to the people in that country. Your name would probably sound funny to the people of Israel.

KEY VERSES: *Soon Gomer became pregnant again and gave birth to a daughter. And the LORD said to Hosea, "Name your daughter Lo-ruhamah—'Not loved'—for I will no longer show love to the people of Israel or forgive them. But I, the LORD their God, will show love to the people of Judah. I will personally free them from their enemies without any help from weapons or armies." After Gomer had weaned Lo-ruhamah, she again became pregnant and gave birth to a second son. And the LORD said, "Name him Lo-ammi—'Not my people'—for Israel is not my people, and I am not their God." (Hosea 1:6-9)*

Q 184:

Did children in Bible times color?

A: Children in Bible times didn't color with crayons like the ones we have today, but they did draw pictures. They also played games. Archaeologists (people who study ancient cities and cultures) have found some of the games. Children back then dressed differently from the way we do, their houses and schools were made differently, and they had different kinds of games. But they were just like kids today in many ways. They liked to have fun. They had family chores to do. When they were bad, their parents disciplined them. They studied. They had times of happiness and sadness. They were real kids.

KEY VERSE: *The streets of the city will be filled with boys and girls at play. (Zechariah 8:5)*

Q 185:

Do people live in the land of Israel today?

A: Today, millions of people live in the lands where the Bible events took place, including Israel. Egypt, Iraq, Jordan, and Israel are some of the nations that now make up where Abraham, Isaac, Jacob, Joseph, Moses, Joshua, Gideon, Samuel, David, Solomon, Isaiah, Jonah, and Jesus lived. The cities that Paul visited are in parts of what we know today as Turkey, Greece, and Italy. Thousands of people go to these lands every year to visit places mentioned in the Bible. Some of the people there still dress much as they did in Bible times, but the big cities are very modern, with skyscrapers, telephones, fax machines, and computers.

KEY VERSE: *[God said,] "I will never abandon the descendants of Jacob or David, my servant, or change the plan that David's descendants will rule the descendants of Abraham, Isaac, and Jacob. Instead, I will restore them to their land and have mercy on them." (Jeremiah 33:26)*

NOTE TO PARENTS: If you can find a Bible map or atlas, show your kids where this all happened. Compare it to where you live. Tell them that Israel, Jordan, and other areas are called the "Holy Land" because that's where Bible events took place, but God isn't there more than anywhere else. Jesus told the disciples to take his message to the whole world, and we can serve God anywhere.

Q 186:

Why did people in Bible times bow down to welcome each other?

A: In Bible times, people usually greeted each other with a hug or a kiss on the cheek. That's like a handshake today. They almost never bowed down unless they wanted to show humility, service, or great respect toward someone. People always bowed before a king or another important official. But when they were just meeting on the street or visiting one another's homes, they usually just hugged or kissed.

KEY VERSE: *Greet all the brothers and sisters in Christian love. (1 Thessalonians 5:26)*

Q 187:

Why did people used to go to wells instead of using the water at home?

A: In Bible times, people went to rivers, streams, wells, and cisterns for their water because they didn't have indoor plumbing. (They also used candles and lanterns at night because they didn't have electricity.) A well was a hole dug deep into the ground to an underground spring. A cistern was a huge hole in the ground that collected rain water. Many people today use wells. Water from wells and cisterns is very clean. Although the people didn't have pipes and faucets, or chlorine and fluoride in their water like we have, they had plenty of good, clean water. And God gave them rules to follow that protected their health.

KEY VERSE: *"But sir, you don't have a rope or a bucket," she said, "and this is a very deep well. Where would you get this living water?" (John 4:11)*

NOTE TO PARENTS: Don't give the impression that this was crushing poverty. Due to the Old Testament laws, things were clean and sanitary.

Q 188:

Did people have shoes in Bible days?

A: Because it is very sunny, hot, and dry in the Middle East (Bible lands), people usually wore sandals rather than shoes. Their sandals, made of leather, would be fastened to the feet with strips of leather attached to the bottom and wrapped up around the shins. Sandals protected their feet without making them hot. This also meant that their feet got dirty quite easily. Whenever people entered a home, they had to clean off the dust and dirt that had stuck to their sweaty feet. That's why Jesus spoke of washing others' feet as an act of service—it was a dirty job!

KEY VERSES: *He got up from the table, took off his robe, wrapped a towel around his waist, and poured water into a basin. Then he began to wash the disciples' feet and to wipe them with the towel he had around him. (John 13:4-5)*

Q 189:

How come there are no Bible stories that take place in winter?

A: Because the Bible doesn't mention snow very often, we might assume that none of the Bible stories took place in the winter. But, in fact, they took place at all times throughout the year. Bible lands are a bit too warm in the winter for snow, so that's why it's rarely mentioned. But it does rain in the winter. Though the winters aren't as cold as they are in the northern United States and Canada, there is snow on some of the mountains of Israel, especially in the northern area (where Lebanon is today).

KEY VERSE: *Does the snow ever melt high up in the mountains of Lebanon? Do the cold, flowing streams from the crags of Mount Hermon ever run dry? (Jeremiah 18:14)*

Q 190:

Did people have ice cream in Bible times?

A: No. Ice cream was invented only about 200 years ago. But the Israelites had lots of good food to eat. Before God brought the Israelites out of slavery in Egypt, he promised Moses that he would give them "a land flowing with milk and honey" (Exodus 3:8), and that's exactly what they got. Their land was very fertile, with rich soil for growing crops and grazing animals. The Hebrews had all kinds of delicious foods— figs, dates, honey, grapes, raisins, venison, bread, rice, lamb, milk, cheese, all kinds of vegetables, and other foods. They made cakes out of barley, raisins, and figs. Often they would flavor their food with salt and spices too, just as we do today. The Hebrews didn't have supermarkets, microwaves, or refrigerators, but they had plenty of healthy, delicious food.

KEY VERSE: *This was their report to Moses: "We arrived in the land you sent us to see, and it is indeed a magnificent country—a land flowing with milk and honey. Here is some of its fruit as proof." (Numbers 13:27)*

Q 191:

How come the husbands could have so many wives?

A: Actually, very few husbands had more than one wife. Most had only one wife and lived with their families just as people do today. But some men, usually kings or rich men, would marry several women at once. A king might marry a princess from a neighboring country, for example, to ensure peace with that country. Other men married more than one wife because their first wives couldn't have children. No matter what the reason, God never wanted men to live this way. His plan is for a man to have one wife and for a woman to have one husband. Today people don't usually have more than one wife or husband.

KEY VERSE: *This explains why a man leaves his father and mother and is joined to his wife, and the two are united into one. (Genesis 2:24)*

Q 192:

Why did people kill animals for church?

A: Before Jesus came, God's people had to sacrifice animals in worship to make payment for their sins. All of us sin against God, and that sin must be paid for. The animal took the person's place. (Not all sacrifices involved killing animals; some people would offer grain as a praise offering to God.) But when Jesus came, he died for every person's sin for all time. That's why John the Baptist called him "the Lamb of God who takes away the sin of the world!" (John 1:29). The sacrifice of animals in Old Testament times represented Jesus' future death for us; the animals could not actually take away sins, as Jesus could (see Hebrews 10:4-7). Because Jesus died and rose again, we never have to sacrifice animals again. Instead, we worship and praise Jesus for all he's done for us.

KEY VERSE: *Our High Priest offered himself to God as one sacrifice for sins, good for all time. Then he sat down at the place of highest honor at God's right hand. (Hebrews 10:12)*

NOTE TO PARENTS: Kids are going to be repulsed at the idea of killing, but they would also be appalled if they found out where they get their hamburger, the details of which we hide from them. Actually, most of the meat sacrificed to God was given to the priests and Levites for food.

Q 193:

Did people in Bible times have music?

A: People had music in Bible times and loved it! Although they didn't have compact discs, tapes, pianos, or electric guitars, they did have many kinds of instruments. They also loved to sing. Singing praise to God was a very important part of their worship. They also sang songs to express their feelings. (All of the Psalms are songs—150 of them.) Often dirges (sad songs) would be sung when people were very sad. Perhaps the most well-known musician in the Bible is King David. He played the harp and wrote many songs, some of which are in the book of Psalms.

KEY VERSES: *Sing your praise to the LORD with the harp, with the harp and melodious song, with trumpets and the sound of the ram's horn. Make a joyful symphony before the LORD, the King! (Psalm 98:5-6)*

Q 194:
What language did they speak in Bible days?

A: At one time, everyone in the world spoke the same language. But they became proud and thought they were as good as God. When they tried to build a tower to heaven (the Tower of Babel), God gave them all different languages. That caused them to become confused, so they quit the project and scattered all over the earth. Ever since then, in Bible times just as today, each different group of people has spoken a different language. The most common languages the people of the Bible spoke were Hebrew, Aramaic, and Greek. In heaven, there will be people "from every tribe and language and people and nation" (Revelation 5:9).

KEY VERSES: *They were beside themselves with wonder. "How can this be?" they exclaimed. "These people are all from Galilee, and yet we hear them speaking the languages of the lands where we were born!" (Acts 2:7-8)*

Q 195:
When did "Bible times" stop?

A: The last book in the Bible was written about seventy years after the time Jesus lived on earth. That's a very long time ago, almost two thousand years. In one way that's when Bible times stopped. But in other ways we are still in Bible times. God still speaks to us through his Word, he still cares about us, and he still does miracles. We may not see God divide a sea like he did for Moses, and we may not see anyone walk on water like Jesus did, but God still answers prayer and changes lives.

KEY VERSE: *You are always the same; your years never end. (Psalm 102:27)*

**Questions
Kids Ask**

Prayer

3

What Prayer Is

Q 196:
What is prayer?

A: Prayer is talking with God. When we have a good friend, we talk to that person about all sorts of things. That's part of being a friend. In the same way, we should talk to God about what is happening in our life. God wants us to share our life with him, to tell him about what makes us happy, sad, and afraid. He wants to know what we want and what we would like him to do, for ourself and for others. Also, when we pray, we open ourself up to God so that he can make good changes in us.

KEY VERSES: *Don't worry about anything; instead, pray about everything. Tell God what you need, and thank him for all he has done. If you do this, you will experience God's peace, which is far more wonderful than the human mind can understand. His peace will guard your hearts and minds as you live in Christ Jesus. (Philippians 4:6-7)*

NOTE TO PARENTS: *Practical Christianity* (LaVonne Neff and others, Tyndale House Publishers) and *What Is Prayer?* (Carolyn Nystrom, Moody Press) are two good resources for more on the topic of prayer.

Q 197:
What is prayer for?

A: The purpose of prayer is for us to get closer to God. When we tell God that we are sorry for our sins, thank him for all he has done, and ask for his help, God begins to change us. He changes our thoughts and desires, and he shows us what he wants us to do. We come to love him more and to see things from his point of view. Also, prayer gives us an opportunity to say, "Your will be done." It is a way for us to work with God to change the world. Think about it this way: God is our Father. He loves us and wants to meet our needs, to teach us how to live, to take care of us, and to use us. He wants to be our friend. Prayer asks him to do that in our lives. We pray because it invites our loving Father to work in our lives and in our world.

KEY VERSE: *[Jesus said,] "You haven't done this before. Ask, using my name, and you will receive, and you will have abundant joy." (John 16:24)*

NOTE TO PARENTS: Prayer is a lot like a conversation between a parent and a child. This analogy will help you explain prayer.

Q 198:

Why do we have to pray instead of just asking God?

A: Prayer does not have to be very formal and serious. Prayer can be natural, like having a talk with a friend. Whenever we have a need, we can just talk to God. We can tell him what we are excited about, tell him what worries us, or ask him for help. So when we pray, we *are* just asking God. We are talking to our best Friend.

We can pray about anything, anytime, anywhere, because God loves us.

KEY VERSE: *I prayed to the Lord, and he answered me, freeing me from all my fears. (Psalm 34:4)*

NOTE TO PARENTS: Prayer should be a very normal part of a child's life. The more conversational and real-life we make it, the easier it will be for children to understand. Prayer should not be so overly formalized that it becomes detached from the rest of their lives.

Q 199:

Why do we have to pray to God?

A: We have to pray to God because he is the only one who can answer. He is the only one who can give us what we need. And only God can satisfy our *deepest* needs—the needs we don't even know we have. God is everywhere and knows everything and can do anything, so he can hear everyone's prayers and answer them. Praying to ancestors, idols, angels, or people does not make sense because only God can answer prayer.

Praying to God is an awesome privilege. God made it so that we could get to know him, our heavenly Father, and have him care for us, teach us, and meet our needs. It's not a bad thing that we "have to pray." It's a good thing!

KEY VERSES: *Bend down, O LORD, and hear my prayer; answer me, for I need your help. Protect me, for I am devoted to you. Save me, for I serve you and trust you. You are my God. (Psalm 86:1-2)*

NOTE TO PARENTS: Although prayer is to be an important part of our disciplined daily routine, we should always present it as an awesome privilege and encourage our children to see it that way. Making them pray or being stern about it won't give them a long-term desire to pray.

Q 200:

Why is it good to pray?

A:
Praying is good because it brings us closer to God, our heavenly Father. Being a Christian means having a relationship with God. Prayer is a part of that relationship. Friends talk with each other, and God is our friend. Prayer makes our relationship with God better. We wouldn't have a very good relationship with him if we never talked to him.

It is also good to pray because God tells us to do it. All that God is and wants is good. Those who love God know this. They try to obey God and do what pleases him. So even though we may not always feel like praying, we should pray anyway because God says it is good to do. And if he says we should do it, then that is what is best for us and our lives.

KEY VERSES: *But you, dear friends, must continue to build your lives on the foundation of your holy faith. And continue to pray as you are directed by the Holy Spirit. Live in such a way that God's love can bless you as you wait for the eternal life that our Lord Jesus Christ in his mercy is going to give you. (Jude 1:20-21)*

NOTE TO PARENTS: Our relationship with God is to be the foundation of our whole life, and prayer is the communication element of that relationship. Therefore, prayer is the key to life the way God meant it to be. Our children need to realize how important prayer is. We wouldn't forget to eat, sleep, or dress every day, and prayer is more important to our lives than those things.

Q 201:

Why do people pray to idols?

A:
Some people pray to idols because they believe that idols have power to change things. That is, they believe in a false god. They believe that their god hears and answers their prayers.

Other people pray to idols out of habit or superstition. They do not really know or believe in their idol. They just hope something will happen if they pray.

Praying to idols is wrong because idols are not really gods. They are just things. They are not alive and do not hear. They cannot answer prayers or bring good fortune. God wants us to place our trust in him and not in idols or superstitious beliefs.

KEY VERSES: *Yes, they knew God, but they wouldn't worship him as God or even give him thanks. And they began to think up foolish ideas of what God was like. The result was that their minds became dark and confused. Claiming to be wise, they became utter fools instead. And instead of worshiping the glorious, ever-living God, they worshiped idols made to look like mere people, or birds and animals and snakes. (Romans 1:21-23)*

NOTE TO PARENTS: Making a wish when blowing out birthday candles, wishing on a star, or throwing coins into a well can be used as an example of why some people believe prayers to idols will bring them good luck. If your children wish at these times, let them know it's just for fun. If they really want something, encourage them to talk to God about it.

Q 202:

Who do we pray to—God or Jesus?

A: When a person prays, it is all right to talk with God the Father, with Jesus, or with the Holy Spirit. You can find prayers to all three in the Bible. Some prayers are addressed to God the Father, some to God the Son, and some to God the Holy Spirit. That is because God is one. We have one Lord, not three. So when we pray to God the Father, we are praying to God. And when we pray to God the Son, we are praying to God. And when we pray to God the Holy Spirit, we are praying to God. We cannot mess it up by saying the wrong name.

The important thing is that the person prays to the Lord of heaven and earth, the living God. It is what is in a person's heart that counts. Beyond our words, God sees our hearts and knows our thoughts and desires.

KEY VERSE: *Dear friends, I urge you in the name of our Lord Jesus Christ to join me in my struggle by praying to God for me. Do this because of your love for me, given to you by the Holy Spirit. (Romans 15:30)*

NOTE TO PARENTS: Jesus taught his disciples to talk to the Father in Jesus' name. This is a good way to guide our children because most of them can understand a father-child relationship. God wants to love them, care for them, and teach them as their heavenly Father.

Q 203:

Why did Jesus pray?

A: Jesus is the God-man. That is, he is fully God and fully man, a whole human being. Because Jesus lived on earth as a man, he had human needs. It made sense for him to pray just as it makes sense for us to pray. He depended on his Father for all his needs. He also loved his Father and enjoyed being with him, so he wanted to spend time talking with him.

Jesus was also perfect. He did everything that God wanted. God told his people to pray, so Jesus obeyed his Father and prayed.

In other words, Jesus prayed for the same reasons we do—he needed God, he loved God, and he wanted to please God.

KEY VERSE: *While Jesus was here on earth, he offered prayers and pleadings, with a loud cry and tears, to the one who could deliver him out of death. And God heard his prayers because of his reverence for God. (Hebrews 5:7)*

NOTE TO PARENTS: God doesn't stand on the sidelines and judge our every move. He is our loving Father. He is alongside us, helping us, teaching us, caring for us. When we fall, he is right there to help us up, strengthen us, teach us, and encourage us forward.

Q 204:

When we're bad, can we still pray?

A:
A person can pray at any time and in any need. When people do bad things or make mistakes, they need God more than at any other time. When we do something wrong, we need to talk with God about it. We need to admit that what we did was wrong, say that we're sorry, and ask him to forgive us. That is the first thing we should pray when we do something bad. Then God can help us learn so that we can do better next time. God knows we are not perfect, and he wants to help us by giving us wisdom and helping us change.

If we wait until we are good enough to pray, we will never pray.

KEY VERSES: *[Jesus said,] "The tax collector stood at a distance and dared not even lift his eyes to heaven as he prayed. Instead, he beat his chest in sorrow, saying, 'O God, be merciful to me, for I am a sinner.' I tell you, this sinner, not the Pharisee, returned home justified before God. For the proud will be humbled, but the humble will be honored." (Luke 18:13-14)*

Q 205:

Who is not allowed to pray?

A:
No one is so bad that he or she is not allowed to pray. God is always willing to accept the person who comes and asks for forgiveness. God does not ban people from praying.

Some people have turned away from God so much that they never pray. They do not pray because they don't feel any need to pray and don't want to.

Are there any prayers that God does not welcome? Yes. God does not welcome the prayers of people who disobey him all the time and are happy about it. (They may even brag about their sins.) When these people pray, they do not really mean to have a relationship with God. Instead, they just go through the motions. Prayers from people like that are just empty words. The first *real* prayer that God wants to hear from them is *I have sinned. I was wrong. I am sorry. Please forgive me.*

KEY VERSE: *The LORD is far from the wicked, but he hears the prayers of the righteous. (Proverbs 15:29)*

Q 206:

Why do we have to pray when God already knows what we are going to pray?

A: When we pray, we talk to God about the things that we and God are doing together. God designed the universe to work a certain way, and prayer is part of his plan for how it works.

One of the most important reasons for praying is that it changes the person who is praying. When we pray, we become more like God wants us to be. *We* learn something from *God!*

Also, God wants to have a friendship with us. No one would say, "Why do we have to talk to our friends?" Talking with God just grows out of loving him and being cared for by him.

KEY VERSE: *[Jesus said,] "Your Father knows exactly what you need even before you ask him!" (Matthew 6:8)*

NOTE TO PARENTS: Help and encourage your children to say prayers that do not always involve asking for something. They can talk to God about what is going on in their lives and tell him what they are excited about. Also, encourage them to ask for needs that are intangible, such as wisdom, guidance, and help.

Q 207:

If God is invisible, how can we know he is around us?

A: It is a little bit like believing in a country you have never been to. Other people have told you about it, you have read about it, and perhaps you have even met people from that land. All of this together tells you that the country is real. You yourself have never been there, but that does not stop you from believing it exists. You have plenty of good reasons to believe that it does.

Although we cannot see God, we know by faith that he is around us. That is, we accept that God is there because the Bible says so, because we have met God's people, and because it makes sense to us. So by faith we believe and trust that he is there even though he is invisible.

KEY VERSE: *From the time the world was created, people have seen the earth and sky and all that God made. They can clearly see his invisible qualities—his eternal power and divine nature. So they have no excuse whatsoever for not knowing God. (Romans 1:20)*

NOTE TO PARENTS: When your children ask why they can't see God, make sure you explain that God is invisible because he does not have a body like ours, not because he is trying to hide from us. As we get to know him better, we begin to see how he works on our behalf and how he shows his love.

Q 208:

How does God feel when we pray?

A: God is very happy when we pray. The Bible makes it clear that God is glad to hear from us and rejoices over us. He loves us and wants us to love him. So God is delighted when we come before him, just as a loving father is happy when his children come to him. The father welcomes his children with open arms and listens carefully to everything they say because he loves them so much.

KEY VERSE: *The Lord hates the sacrifice of the wicked, but he delights in the prayers of the upright. (Proverbs 15:8)*

NOTE TO PARENTS: This is a good opportunity to reinforce God's extravagant love for us. Take every opportunity to tell your children how much God loves and cares for them.

How to Pray

Q 209:

Why did Jesus say we should pray the Lord's Prayer?

A: When the disciples asked Jesus to teach them how to pray, Jesus gave them the Lord's Prayer. It is a sample prayer that shows how we should pray. In other words, it is a guide and an example, not the exact words we must say every time. It shows us a good way to pray and some good topics to pray about.

For example, it tells us that we should ask God to meet our needs. It shows us that we should pray for God's will to be done in everything that happens. And it tells us to pray that we will be strong and resist temptation. It is always good to pray that way. And it is OK for us to use our own words when we do.

KEY VERSES: *Once when Jesus had been out praying, one of his disciples came to him as he finished and said, "Lord, teach us to pray, just as John taught his disciples." He said, "This is how you should pray: Father, may your name be honored. May your Kingdom come soon. Give us our food day by day. And forgive us our sins— just as we forgive those who have sinned against us. And don't let us yield to temptation." (Luke 11:1-4)*

Q 210:

How does God know what we're saying if we're praying in our head?

A: God knows everything, even what we keep to ourselves. He knows every thought of every person on earth. He knows what is in everyone's head. Nothing that anyone thinks or feels is hidden from God.

Praying silently means focusing our thoughts on God and talking to him in our head. He hears every silent prayer.

Of course, sometimes it is better to pray aloud, such as when we are praying with another person. And praying aloud can help us concentrate when we are praying on our own. But God hears us either way, whether we say the words or just think them.

KEY VERSES: *O LORD, you have examined my heart and know everything about me. You know when I sit down or stand up. You know my every thought when far away. (Psalm 139:1-2)*

NOTE TO PARENTS: From time to time your children may ask if they can pray a certain prayer silently or to themselves. Encourage them to do so. It is a good sign that they are trusting God with things close to their heart that they may feel embarrassed to say even to you.

Q 211:

Is it OK if we pray really fast or slow?

THANK YOU GOD, AMEN.

A: The speed of a prayer is not important. What matters is that we pray in a thoughtful manner.

Sometimes we pray fast because we are excited. That is fine. But people who pray *very* fast may just be repeating a memorized prayer or saying certain words out of habit and trying to finish quickly. Whenever we pray, God is listening right then, and he does not want us to just speed through some words that we always say.

Sometimes we pray slowly because we are being thoughtful about what we want to say to God. But sometimes we pray slowly because we are letting our thoughts wander. It is always best to keep our attention on God.

Fast, medium, or slow, prayer should be a real talk with our heavenly Father.

KEY VERSES: *As you enter the house of God, keep your ears open and your mouth shut! Don't be a fool who doesn't realize that mindless offerings to God are evil. And don't make rash promises to God, for he is in heaven, and you are only here on earth. So let your words be few. (Ecclesiastes 5:1-2)*

NOTE TO PARENTS: Before praying with your children, help them think of a few things they are concerned or excited about, and encourage them to talk to God about these things. This will help make each day's prayers sincere and relevant and not just something to get done.

Q 212:

Does how we pray matter?

A: Yes. We should pray *sincerely, secretly,* and *respectfully.* To pray sincerely means to pray in plain words that say just what we mean to say. It means we do not try to use fake language or fancy words. We tell God whatever is on our mind in the words that we would normally use, because he loves us and knows us and wants to care for us.

To pray secretly means to make a habit of praying alone. (Some people call it quiet time.) It means we take time out of every day to talk to God all by ourselves. We do not limit our prayers to church, meals, or bedtime with Mom or Dad.

To pray respectfully means to treat God as God. It means we do not make light of prayer or act silly. We are talking to God, the Maker of all creation, the Lord of the universe, and the King of kings, so we show him honor and respect.

KEY VERSE: *The sacrifice you want is a broken spirit. A broken and repentant heart, O God, you will not despise. (Psalm 51:17)*

NOTE TO PARENTS: If we get wrapped up in exactly how our kids must behave, position themselves, or talk when praying, they may get the idea that God expects a performance instead of a sincere expression. Give your children room to grow in the exact way they pray.

Q 213:

Can God help us pray?

A: Yes. Many times we want to talk with God but just don't know what to say or how to put our feelings into words. The Holy Spirit can help us think of the right words and say them. But even if we still don't know what to say, God knows what we are feeling and thinking. He knows that we sincerely want to talk with him, and he understands what we *would* say if we could.

The best way to pray is just to pray. That is, we should not wait until we think we have all the right words. We should just speak to God from the heart as best we can. He will understand what we mean even if we get the words messed up.

KEY VERSES: *The Holy Spirit helps us in our distress. For we don't even know what we should pray for, nor how we should pray. But the Holy Spirit prays for us with groanings that cannot be expressed in words. And the Father who knows all hearts knows what the Spirit is saying, for the Spirit pleads for us believers in harmony with God's own will. (Romans 8:26-27)*

NOTE TO PARENTS: Encourage your children to pray even if they do not feel that they are good at it. Remind them that God is gentle and kind and always ready to hear their prayers and that God will never make fun of them for how they pray.

Q 214:

Why do pastors pray long prayers?

A: Pastors pray long prayers because they have a lot to pray about. They are responsible for caring for a lot of people and want to pray for the concerns those people have.

Also, a lot of people ask pastors to pray for them. Many churches have a "pastor's prayer" as part of the worship service. At that time the pastor prays aloud for the needs of the people. At the same time, the people in the congregation should also pray, silently, for each need that the pastor mentions.

Keep in mind that God listens to kids just as much as to pastors. If you pray, God hears and answers your prayers the same as he does for the pastor.

KEY VERSES: *So we have continued praying for you ever since we first heard about you. We ask God to give you a complete understanding of what he wants to do in your lives, and we ask him to make you wise with spiritual wisdom. Then the way you live will always honor and please the Lord, and you will continually do good, kind things for others. All the while, you will learn to know God better and better. (Colossians 1:9-10)*

NOTE TO PARENTS: God hears and answers your child's prayers as much as he does a pastor's. Be careful not to give your children the idea that their prayers are not as effective as those of "important" people.

Q 215:

Why do people pray on their knees?

A: The Bible tells of people praying in all sorts of positions. Some stood and raised their hands. Some lay down on the ground. Some put their head between their knees. Some sat down. Some kneeled. Some stood but bowed their head and beat on their chest. We can pray in almost any position.

Some people kneel in prayer to show respect for God. It is their way of saying that they want to do things God's way. Kneeling makes them feel humble and submissive to God, which is the right attitude to have in prayer.

KEY VERSES: *[Jesus] walked away, about a stone's throw, and knelt down and prayed, "Father, if you are willing, please take this cup of suffering away from me. Yet I want your will, not mine."* *(Luke 22:41-42)*

Q 216:

Do we have to fold our hands to pray?

A: No. Our hands can be in any position when we pray. It is not the position of our hands that God loves but the attitude of our heart.

But most people fold their hands for a good reason. Some fold their hands to show respect and that they are bringing a request. Sometimes people fold their hands to keep them from doing anything else that might distract them from focusing on their prayer. So folding hands during prayer can be a good idea, but God does not require it. In the Bible, God's people often raised their hands to pray, as some people do today.

KEY VERSE: *So wherever you assemble, I want men to pray with holy hands lifted up to God, free from anger and controversy. (1 Timothy 2:8)*

NOTE TO PARENTS: It is not that a particular position for your hands or body must be followed, but once a position is chosen, a reminder to stay in that position until the "amen" can really help concentration.

Q 217:

Should we make the sign of the cross when we pray?

A: Some people make the sign of the cross when they pray to show that their prayer is in "Jesus' name" (because Jesus died on the cross). It is a bit like folding hands or kneeling—God does not require it of us, but some people do it to help them pray. It reminds them that God hears their prayers because Jesus died for them.

Always remember that God cares more about our being honest and sincere than about the exact way we sit, stand, kneel, or move when we pray.

KEY VERSE: *We do this by keeping our eyes on Jesus, on whom our faith depends from start to finish. He was willing to die a shameful death on the cross because of the joy he knew would be his afterward. Now he is seated in the place of highest honor beside God's throne in heaven. (Hebrews 12:2)*

NOTE TO PARENTS: If you teach your children certain traditions in prayer, take the time to explain what they mean and why you feel they are important. Helping your children understand a tradition will help them get more out of it.

Q 218:

Why do we shut our eyes when we pray?

A: We shut our eyes mainly to help us concentrate on our prayers. Whenever our eyes are open, we can see everything going on around us, and then we think about those things. We don't think so much about God or about talking to him. So people close their eyes when they pray because it helps them concentrate on what they are saying.

We can pray with our eyes open. Eyes open or shut doesn't matter to God. It's just that we need help concentrating, and closing our eyes helps us do that.

KEY VERSE: *The tax collector stood at a distance and dared not even lift his eyes to heaven as he prayed. Instead, he beat his chest in sorrow, saying, "O God, be merciful to me, for I am a sinner." (Luke 18:13)*

NOTE TO PARENTS: Some young children have trouble keeping their eyes closed. Don't fret about it. Try having them put their hands over their eyes, or just have them keep their head and hands still.

Q 219:

What is a prayer closet?

A: A prayer closet is a private place where a person can pray without anyone else around. It is a place where a person can get away from the busyness and noise of life. The peace and quiet helps a person spend quiet time with God, praying honestly in private without being distracted or watched by others.

A prayer closet can be a real closet where a person can shut the door, but it can also be other kinds of places. It can be a quiet spot in the house, outdoors, or somewhere else. It can be any special spot where you and God can talk. Where do you get away from everything to talk with God?

KEY VERSE: *[Jesus said,] "When you pray, go away by yourself, shut the door behind you, and pray to your Father secretly. Then your Father, who knows all secrets, will reward you."* (Matthew 6:6)

NOTE TO PARENTS: One of the best ways to encourage children to pray is to let them see you do it. Tell them where you like to spend time with God alone. Talk to them about your prayer times.

Q 220:

Can't we pray anywhere?

A: Yes, we can pray anywhere. Prayers do not have to be spoken aloud, so we can pray while we are sitting at a desk with our eyes wide open, or anywhere else. We can pray silently because God knows our thoughts. We can pray in school, on the playground, at basketball practice, in a choir concert, in church, at home, on vacation—anywhere! God is glad when we ask him for help right when and where we need it.

KEY VERSE: *Pray at all times and on every occasion in the power of the Holy Spirit. Stay alert and be persistent in your prayers for all Christians everywhere.* (Ephesians 6:18)

NOTE TO PARENTS: Our children can learn spontaneous prayer from us. Next time you are with the kids and you think of something you should pray about, ask them to join in and just do it briefly and naturally.

Q 221:

Do we have to pray certain prayers?

A: No. We do not have to pray certain prayers, but it is OK to have certain prayers that we pray often. Written prayers can be helpful. The Lord's Prayer and the Psalms, for example, are good things to pray, and they help us think of ways to pray and things we can talk to God about. Some people memorize prayers and recite them at mealtimes or at bedtime. We just need to be careful that we really mean the words as we say them. If we say them over and over again, we may not pay attention to what we are saying.

KEY VERSE: *Give thanks to the LORD and proclaim his greatness. Let the whole world know what he has done. (1 Chronicles 16:8)*

NOTE TO PARENTS: Children will often say things a certain way or pray certain prayers because they imagine the words themselves to have power, like magic spells. Encourage your children to pray with their own words, from the heart, and not to get stuck in a pattern of praying only certain prayers. Remind them that they are talking to their heavenly Father—someone who loves them!

Q 222:

Is it bad to memorize a prayer and say it every time we pray?

A: It is never bad to pray a sincere and humble prayer, and memorized prayers can surely be part of that. The problem with memorized prayers is that we might get to know the prayers so well that we only say the words without thinking about them.

What matters is our attitude. Jesus wants us to say what we mean and mean what we say, not "babble on" in prayer. Our prayers should be sincere and express our true thoughts.

KEY VERSE: *[Jesus said,] "When you pray, don't babble on and on as people of other religions do. They think their prayers are answered only by repeating their words again and again." (Matthew 6:7)*

NOTE TO PARENTS: Memorized prayers can be very inspirational and educational. Take the time to help your children understand their meaning and what they are asking. Then encourage them to add their own words on the same topic to help make the memorized prayers relevant.

Q 223:

Does God listen to any prayer, big or small?

A: Yes, God listens to all prayers, no matter how big or small they are. In the Bible, Nehemiah prayed that he would say the right words when he talked to the king one day. Solomon prayed for wisdom. Hannah prayed for a child. Each one of these people prayed for something that mattered to him or her. It did not matter whether the prayer was big or small. They just brought their cares to God.

That is what God wants us to do. The important question is, what is on our mind? What do we care about? God will listen to any prayer if it is sincere.

KEY VERSE: *Give all your worries and cares to God, for he cares about what happens to you. (1 Peter 5:7)*

NOTE TO PARENTS: Always encourage your children to take their concerns to God, even if those concerns seem small or simple.

Q 224:

Why do people say "thee" and "thou" when they pray?

A: Some people say "thee" and "thou" because they are used to it. Many years ago, the King James Version was the only English Bible. When it was written, everyone used *thee* and *thou* when they talked, so that version of the Bible has many "thees," "thous," and other words that people do not say anymore. People learned to talk to God that way because that is the way they read it in the King James Version.

Some people also feel that praying in this older style helps them show respect to God; they feel it is a more appropriate way to speak to him than to use normal language because God is a holy and awesome God. Still, God does not care about the exact words or style of English we use as long as we say what we mean. He understands.

KEY VERSE: *Since we are receiving a Kingdom that cannot be destroyed, let us be thankful and please God by worshiping him with holy fear and awe. (Hebrews 12:28)*

NOTE TO PARENTS: If we talk to God in plain, sincere language, our children will feel more comfortable praying than if they hear us use formal language. Using special words or tones for prayer will give them the impression that these details matter more than the content.

Q 225:

Why do we say "amen" when we're done praying?

A: *Amen* means "So be it" or "It is true." It is simply a way of closing a prayer. We close letters with a similar word, *sincerely. Amen* means that we have said what we mean and believe that God has heard our prayer.

To say *amen*—"So be it"—is a way of saying that we trust God to answer. It reminds us that God has everything under control.

KEY VERSE: *Blessed be the LORD, the God of Israel, from everlasting to everlasting! Let all the people say, "Amen!" Praise the LORD! (Psalm 106:48)*

NOTE TO PARENTS: Be sure to explain to your children what *amen* means and that it is a declaration of their trust in God's love for them.

When to Pray

Q 226:

Why do we call it "saying grace"?

A: The word *grace* means "thanks to God." It can also be used to mean "I ask for God's favor." This is how the apostle Paul used it to close some of his letters, such as Galatians, 1 Timothy, Philemon, and others. When we pray before meals, we are thanking God for the food and asking for his blessing on that time of eating. So this prayer is called grace.

Praying before meals is a way of showing that we depend on God. It reminds us that all we have comes from God. This is an important part of prayer—thanking God for life and everything else he gives us.

KEY VERSE: *Let us come boldly to the throne of our gracious God. There we will receive his mercy, and we will find grace to help us when we need it. (Hebrews 4:16)*

NOTE TO PARENTS: *Thank-you* prayers are important, and it is important to teach children to include them in their prayers every day. It helps them learn that God loves and cares for them and that he is the source and owner of all they have.

Q 227:

What is the difference between food that we pray for and food that we have not prayed for?

A: There is no difference between the two kinds of food. Praying at meals does not change the food. It changes us. We pray over the food to thank God for it and to ask his blessing on those who eat it, just the way Jesus did. We are saying, "God, we know that you have provided this food. We are thankful for it, and we ask you to use it to make us strong and healthy." We are asking God to bless the people at the meal.

Praying at meals reminds us that every bit of food we get comes from God's hand and that God provides everything we need.

KEY VERSE: *As they sat down to eat, [Jesus] took a small loaf of bread, asked God's blessing on it, broke it, then gave it to them. (Luke 24:30)*

Q 228:

Why do we have to thank God at every meal when he already knows we're thankful?

DITTO FROM THE PRAYER I PRAYED AT BREAKFAST.

A: Thanking God for food is a good habit to form because it reminds us to be thankful for all that God gives us. Sometimes we think we are thankful when we really aren't. Pausing to say thank you helps us renew our thankfulness. If we just sit down and eat without thanking God every time, we can easily and quickly forget to be thankful. We can forget that our food comes from God.

It is also a nice thing to do. We say thank you to God because he is our friend and he has done something kind for us. Don't you like it when your friends say thank you to you?

KEY VERSE: *Whatever you do or say, let it be as a representative of the Lord Jesus, all the while giving thanks through him to God the Father. (Colossians 3:17)*

NOTE TO PARENTS: Mealtime prayer with the family is a good time for your children to start learning to pray with others. Wait until they're ready, and help them out the first few times. Take turns, and encourage adding a new prayer about something current to the regular mealtime prayer.

Q 229:

Do we still have to thank God if we don't like the food?

A: We should thank God for our food because we need food to live and God kindly gives it to us. He meets our needs even when we are not too thrilled with the way he does it.

When we pray at meals, we do not have to say that we like the food when we really do not. But it is good to say thank you to God anyway. We need to eat. Some people have very little to eat. It only makes sense to thank God that we have a meal.

KEY VERSE: *No matter what happens, always be thankful, for this is God's will for you who belong to Christ Jesus. (1 Thessalonians 5:18)*

Q 230:

Why do we pray before we go to bed?

A: Because nighttime is a good time to pray. We can think about the day we had. We can thank God for all that he did and tell him about our problems and struggles. Also, we can pray for protection. We can ask God for a good night's sleep and for good dreams and to keep us from nightmares. Praying before going to bed is a good habit to form and keep. But not all people pray before going to bed. We can pray anytime.

KEY VERSE: *I will lie down in peace and sleep, for you alone, O LORD, will keep me safe. (Psalm 4:8)*

NOTE TO PARENTS: Nighttime is a good time to teach your children to pray. It gives you an opportunity to set aside a regular, special, quiettime of prayer without a lot of distractions. It lets you model how to pray and what kinds of concerns to bring to God. And it lets you review how God has blessed you as a family that day.

Q 231:

Why do we have to pray when we don't want to?

A: Eating foods that are good for us, brushing our teeth, getting up when the alarm goes off, working hard in school, practicing the piano, and cleaning up our messes are all good. We are glad we did them after they are done, but often we do them only because they need to be done, not because they are fun.

God tells us to pray because it draws us closer to God. It changes us. It helps us understand God's will better. It helps us give our worries to God. So we should pray even when we do not feel like it.

If we wait until we feel like praying, we may never do it. This is true of all good activities, not just prayer. We have to work at things that are good and important. But the rewards are always worth it.

KEY VERSE: *No discipline is enjoyable while it is happening— it is painful! But afterward there will be a quiet harvest of right living for those who are trained in this way. (Hebrews 12:11)*

NOTE TO PARENTS: It is important to make learning fun. But children need to understand that we pray not because it is fun but because it is vital to life. Our relationship with God is life's foundation, and prayer is the key to that relationship.

Q 232:

Why do we have to give thanks for things we don't like?

DON'T FORGET TO THANK GOD FOR THAT ADORABLE OUTFIT AUNTIE GERTRUDE GOT FOR YOU.

A: God tells us to thank him *in* all things, not *for* all things. That means that when something bad happens, we should thank God for being there with us through those bad times. This helps us remember that God is in control and that he still loves us and has a plan for us, no matter what happens.

We do not have to thank God for bad events. If something bad happens, it is bad. God does not ask us to be glad for that. Maybe a pet or a relative died. That is a bad thing, and it is OK to cry about it.

But God also tells us to be grateful for him and his plan. Some of the things we do not like are actually good for us. Maybe it is good even if we do not like it. Or maybe God has a plan that we cannot see. We need to trust in God's goodness; that is why we thank him in all things.

KEY VERSE: *Whatever you do or say, let it be as a representative of the Lord Jesus, all the while giving thanks through him to God the Father. (Colossians 3:17)*

Q 233:

Why should we go to God for help?

A: We should ask God for help because we need him. Asking why we should go to God for help is like asking "Why should I go to the gas station for gas?" God is the one who gives us life, the one who makes us able to walk, talk, and move; he is the one who gives us knowledge and the one who gives us all we need. In a sense, he is the *only* one who can help us. That is why we should go to God for help.

KEY VERSE: *In my distress I prayed to the LORD, and the LORD answered me and rescued me. (Psalm 118:5)*

NOTE TO PARENTS: The world does not teach children to recognize God as their source of help. They will need to learn it from you. Point your children to God in prayer as the first stop on the way to getting help and finding answers.

Q 234:
Why do people wait until the last minute to pray?

A: Some people wait till the last minute to pray because they forget or because they do not think they need God's help. They rely on themselves so much that they think they can do almost anything on their own. Or they may have forgotten about God. Then, when things get worse, they cry out to God for help as a last resort.

Instead of doing those things, we should remember that we need God's help all the time. We should talk with him *first* in every situation we face.

Of course, we should not wait until we have a huge problem to pray. We should talk with God about everything. We should praise the Lord every day because it reminds us that he is there, he loves us, and he is in charge of everything that happens. That helps us avoid a lot of problems in the first place.

KEY VERSE: *Praise the LORD, I tell myself, and never forget the good things he does for me. (Psalm 103:2)*

NOTE TO PARENTS: People begin to grow in prayer when they turn to God during times of calm. Pray together with your children even when you have everything you need. This will help them mature in their prayer habits.

Q 235:
What happens if we don't pray at all?

A: People who do not pray at all grow distant from God, like friends who grow apart because they never talk to each other. Friends keep their friendship close by talking with each other. People who never talk to each other become almost like strangers. People who do not pray miss out on getting to know God better.

Also, people who do not pray miss out on God's help. It is the people who call out to God who get to see God work most. They see him change things and people in awesome ways. They learn things that they could not have learned on their own. People who do not pray cut themselves off from this special part of God's plan.

We need to stay close to God, and we need his power. Prayer meets those needs.

KEY VERSE: *[Jesus said,] "I tell you, keep on asking, and you will be given what you ask for. Keep on looking, and you will find. Keep on knocking, and the door will be opened." (Luke 11:9)*

NOTE TO PARENTS: We need to be very clear with our children on this issue. God will not force himself into our lives. It is not true that a person can walk with God without prayer. Prayer is God's plan and program for having a relationship with him.

Q 236:

What happens if we're interrupted when we're praying?

A: It is just like a conversation with somebody else—we stop until we can pick up where we left off. Of course, if we keep getting interrupted in our prayers, we should try to find a place and time where we can pray without any distractions. But it is OK to start praying again if we get interrupted in the middle of a prayer.

KEY VERSE: *Jesus often withdrew to the wilderness for prayer. (Luke 5:16)*

Q 237:

What does "praying continually" mean?

A: When the Bible talks about praying continually, it means always being ready to pray. It means checking in with God throughout the day. It means that our *first* response when something happens is to pray. When something bad happens, we ask for help. When something good happens, we thank God. When we do not know what to do, we ask God to give us wisdom. It means talking to him as a friend and as a loving Father who is always around.

When you think about it, it makes perfect sense. God *is* our Friend and loving Father who is always around!

KEY VERSE: *Keep on praying. (1 Thessalonians 5:17)*

NOTE TO PARENTS: Our children need to know that we pray because of our relationship with God. We pray to get to know him better and to develop our relationship with him. That is prayer's purpose. Do not leave your children with the impression that prayer is always a dry time of merely covering the day's issues.

Q 238:

Does praying a lot make a person better?

A: Yes. Praying a lot makes a person better because it draws that person closer to God. Prayer makes a person more sensitive to God's will, to others, and to what is important. Praying gets the focus off one's self and onto God. When we spend time with God, we become more like him, just the way we become more like the friends we hang around with.

We just need to be careful not to compare ourselves with others. We need to concentrate on praying more, not on praying more than someone else we know.

KEY VERSE: *Devote yourselves to prayer with an alert mind and a thankful heart. (Colossians 4:2)*

NOTE TO PARENTS: Longer prayers come from sincere conversation with God, not from a concern with longer prayers. Let your children grow in prayer as a result of their growing relationship with God. Do not focus on how many minutes they spend praying each day.

Q 239:

Can we pray anytime we want?

A: Yes, we can pray to God anytime we want. God does not mind if we pray between meals, after bedtime prayer (when we can't sleep), or in school. Because of Christ, the door to God is always open. We can always go to him.

Of course, we need to respect others. We should not start praying out loud in the middle of a conversation with our friends. But if we are in a group, we can still take a moment to pray silently if we need to.

KEY VERSE: *Pray at all times and on every occasion in the power of the Holy Spirit. Stay alert and be persistent in your prayers for all Christians everywhere. (Ephesians 6:18)*

NOTE TO PARENTS: Keep affirming how pleased God is with your children when they pray and how much he loves to talk to them. We want to spend time with the people we love, and so does God. He is pleased when his children come to him in prayer.

What to Pray For

Q 240:

What do we need to pray for?

DEAR GOD, I DON'T FEEL LIKE PRAYING FOR ALL THE USUAL STUFF TODAY. CAN WE JUST TALK?

A: We need to pray for three things: (1) our needs, (2) the needs of others, and (3) God's will to be done. Many of the requests we bring to God will be one of these kinds of prayers.

For example, we need food, clothing, and shelter. So do other people. We also need forgiveness and help in resisting temptation, doing good, and becoming what God wants us to be.

We also need to pray for God's will to be done on earth. Jesus taught us to pray, "May your will be done here on earth, just as it is in heaven" (Matthew 6:10). This is also one reason the Bible tells us to pray for leaders. We can affect events in the world by praying this way.

We do not have to limit our prayers to needs. We can praise God and tell him how wonderful he is. God is our friend. He wants to hear from us.

KEY VERSES: *[Jesus] said, "This is how you should pray: Father, may your name be honored. May your Kingdom come soon. Give us our food day by day. And forgive us our sins—just as we forgive those who have sinned against us. And don't let us yield to temptation." (Luke 11:2-4)*

NOTE TO PARENTS: You can introduce your children to different prayer needs one at a time. When they get a handle on one, you can move them on to the next. That way they have time to learn each one well.

Q 241:

Are there some things that we shouldn't pray about?

A: If something is important to us, we should feel free to pray about it. God does not laugh at people when they pray. He does not have a list of topics that people should not pray about.

Prayer is one of the main ways God changes people for the better. If there is something wrong with the way we are praying, God will reveal it to us in a kind way. In fact, our prayer will draw us closer to God, and he will use our relationship with him to help us change. Of course, prayer should be sincere, not silly or selfish. But God will not make fun of us for talking to him about this or that topic. He will always listen to what we have to say.

It would not make sense to ask God to do something that is wrong or bad because God never sins. But we can talk to God about anything that concerns us.

KEY VERSE: *Let us come boldly to the throne of our gracious God. There we will receive his mercy, and we will find grace to help us when we need it. (Hebrews 4:16)*

NOTE TO PARENTS: Concentrate on teaching your children to turn to God in prayer as a way of life, not on restricting their prayers to a certain type. It is much more important that they develop the habit of prayer than that they "get it perfect" at a young age.

Q 242:

Can we tell God everything we want to?

A: Yes, we can talk to God about any joy, sorrow, need, feeling, worry, doubt, or fear that is on our mind. It is important to be honest with God and say what we are thinking.

But whenever we are angry or upset, we should also try to remember that God is on our side. Job did this when he was hurt and confused. He told God how he felt, but he did not accuse God of doing something wrong just because he was so upset. He knew God was good and loved him, so Job did not take out his anger on God. David's psalms are this way too; Psalm 22 is a good example. If we are hurt or angry, we should tell God, but we should also say that we know he is good. We can also ask him to help us understand and trust him. We should not accuse God of evil or of doing bad things.

KEY VERSES: *Don't worry about anything; instead, pray about everything. Tell God what you need, and thank him for all he has done. If you do this, you will experience God's peace, which is far more wonderful than the human mind can understand. His peace will guard your hearts and minds as you live in Christ Jesus. (Philippians 4:6-7)*

NOTE TO PARENTS: Help your children talk openly with God, just like they do with people they trust when they feel deeply about something. But also encourage them to be ready to learn and change.

Q 243:

How come some people are asking for sunshine while other people are asking for rain?

A: People ask God for different things because they have different needs and different concerns. A softball player might ask God for sunshine so she can play her game. At the same time, a farmer nearby might ask God for rain to help his crops to grow. Fortunately, God sees everything and knows what is best. He can work out all things everywhere for everyone's best because he is infinite and all-powerful. We can be thankful that God is wiser than we are and that he sees the whole picture, not just one part of it!

KEY VERSE: *Our God is in the heavens, and he does as he wishes. (Psalm 115:3)*

NOTE TO PARENTS: Do not discourage your children from praying for things like weather just because the answers may not come as asked. Explain that God hears and cares but must consider what is best. Have them pray something like "God, if it is possible, I'd really like sunshine for our camping trip. But I trust you can work things out in another way too. Please work it out in the way that is best."

Q 244:

Can we pray for snow so we can't go to school?

A: We can talk with God about anything that is on our mind. But we should not make silly, selfish, or foolish requests. For example, we *could* pray that money would fall from the sky, but that would be both silly and selfish. Praying for school to be called off would be foolish. We should do what is good and wise, and that includes going to school. We should try to match our desires with God's. Instead of treating him like a genie, we should treat him like our loving Father and wise, almighty God.

KEY VERSE: *Take delight in the LORD, and he will give you your heart's desires. (Psalm 37:4)*

Q 245:

Can we pray for animals?

A: We can pray about anything that is important to us, and that includes animals. God wants us to talk with him about the things that matter to us. He is our friend, and he cares about us. Also, God created the animals, and he loves them. So if an animal or a pet is important to us, we should feel free to pray for it. Certainly farmers should pray for their animals.

KEY VERSE: *The godly are concerned for the welfare of their animals. (Proverbs 12:10)*

Q 246:

Can we ask God to give us things like toys?

A: It is all right to ask God for fun things such as toys. We can talk with God about anything. But praying for something does not mean that we will get it. God knows if something is good or bad for us. He may not give us something because it is not good for us.

The Bible warns us that we should not ask God for things if we want them only for selfish reasons. Solomon knew this. God promised to give Solomon whatever he asked for. Solomon decided to ask for wisdom. God was very pleased with this. He said Solomon made the right choice because he did not ask for great wealth or power. Then God rewarded him by making him rich and powerful.

Ask for things that help others. God wants us to trust him to meet our needs.

KEY VERSES: *God said to Solomon, "Because your greatest desire is to help your people, and you did not ask for personal wealth and honor or the death of your enemies or even a long life, but rather you asked for wisdom and knowledge to properly govern my people, I will certainly give you the wisdom and knowledge you requested. And I will also give you riches, wealth, and honor such as no other king has ever had before you or will ever have again!" (2 Chronicles 1:11-12)*

NOTE TO PARENTS: Help your children look to God, not things, as the source of happiness. Whenever they want to pray for toys or other fun things, guide them to ask God to do what he thinks best. This is part of teaching them to trust God to rule in their lives.

Q 247:

Is it OK to pray to get something that our friends have?

DEAR GOD, PLEASE GIVE ME FREDA'S SENSE OF HUMOR, GOOD VALUES LIKE SUSIE'S, AND A BASEBALL CARD COLLECTION LIKE TOMMY'S.

A: It is good to tell God what is on our mind, but it is not good to think that we need to have certain things to be happy. Having things does not make us happy. God knows this. So we should not think that if we suddenly had a new toy or piece of clothing we would be happy forever. Knowing God and obeying him is what makes us happy.

Craving what others have is called envy. God tells us not to envy because people who envy are never satisfied; they never think they have enough, even after they get all that they want. Instead of envying, God tells us to be content with what we have.

But we should still tell God how we feel. When a friend has something that we would like, we should talk with God about it, especially if it is something that we need. Then we should trust that God will give us what is best for us.

KEY VERSE: *Do not covet your neighbor's house. Do not covet your neighbor's wife, male or female servant, ox or donkey, or anything else your neighbor owns. (Exodus 20:17)*

NOTE TO PARENTS: Make sure your children know about advertising and how it works. If they can learn to recognize the hard sell, they will be more prepared to handle it correctly.

Q 248:

Is it bad to ask God for something we don't really need?

A: It is not the *best* way to pray, but it is not bad. God invites us to come to him with our needs and concerns. He invites us to tell him how we feel. He promises to meet our needs, to care about our cares, and to work out his good plan in our lives.

That means we should ask him to meet our true needs and talk to him about our problems. It does not mean we should treat God like Santa Claus and always be asking for a long list of things that we want only for ourselves.

Sometimes we ask God for things that we *think* we need, but really we do not need them at all. It is OK to tell God we wish we had this or that thing. Whenever we pray, we should be honest and tell God our real feelings. But we should accept his answers and be content with what he gives us.

KEY VERSES: *I know how to live on almost nothing or with everything. I have learned the secret of living in every situation, whether it is with a full stomach or empty, with plenty or little. For I can do everything with the help of Christ who gives me the strength I need. (Philippians 4:12-13)*

NOTE TO PARENTS: Listen to your children's heart when they ask a question like this. Some children need encouragement to ask God for anything, and others come to prayer time with a long list. Encourage a balance, and, most important, teach kids to trust in God.

Q 249:

If we prayed to find something we lost, would we really find it?

A: If it was part of God's plan for us, yes. No job is too small for God. It is good to pray for what matters to us, even something small that is lost. God may help us find it right away, or he may help us remember where we put it. He also might have us retrace our steps to find it so we will be more careful next time.

But prayer does not substitute for being careful. We should not be careless and think, "Oh, well, if I lose it, I can just ask God to find it for me." That would be using prayer the wrong way.

KEY VERSES: *As one of them was chopping, his ax head fell into the river. "Ah, my lord!" he cried. "It was a borrowed ax!" "Where did it fall?" the man of God asked. When he showed him the place, Elisha cut a stick and threw it into the water. Then the ax head rose to the surface and floated. (2 Kings 6:5-6)*

NOTE TO PARENTS: Let your children hear you pray aloud, in both small matters and big ones. Also talk with them about God's answers. This will help them see how God works in your life and, therefore, in theirs.

Q 250:

Can we ask God to help us pass a test?

A: We can ask God for help on a test because we can talk with God about anything. But God expects us to do our best at whatever we do. We go to school and work as part of his plan to grow us into adults. It is true that we rely on God for strength, wisdom, and life. But that is not the same as asking God to live our lives for us.

We should do our duty as students. We should study for tests and do what the teacher says. Then we should pray and ask God to give us a clear mind to take the test as well as we can, to help us relax, and to remember what we have studied.

God is merciful, and he does help us. But it helps to study for the test more than to pray for God to rescue us from a lack of studying. We can ask God to help us study.

KEY VERSES: *Work hard and cheerfully at whatever you do, as though you were working for the Lord rather than for people. Remember that the Lord will give you an inheritance as your reward, and the Master you are serving is Christ. (Colossians 3:23-24)*

Q 251:

Is it OK to complain to God?

DEAR GOD, PLEASE HELP MY MOM, SHE'S GOING CLEAN CRAZY. IT'S "CLEAN YOUR ROOM, CLEAN YOUR HANDS"...I CAN UNDERSTAND THAT, BUT "CLEAN OUT YOUR GARBAGE CAN"? THAT'S WHAT A GARBAGE CAN IS FOR!

A: Yes, it is all right to complain to God. We should be honest about our feelings, and we certainly cannot hide them from God. Anyone who reads the Psalms and the book of Job can see that the people who prayed told God how they really felt. But they also did not accuse God of doing something wrong. They did not accuse him of losing control or of doing something bad. They told God that they believed in his goodness. That is how we should pray too.

We can and should tell God how we feel. Also, we should tell him that we know he is God and has our best interests in mind. We should thank him for loving us.

God is on our side. He will come alongside and help us if we trust him.

KEY VERSES: *How long, O LORD, must I call for help? But you do not listen! "Violence!" I cry, but you do not come to save. Must I forever see this sin and misery all around me? Wherever I look, I see destruction and violence. I am surrounded by people who love to argue and fight. (Habakkuk 1:2-3)*

NOTE TO PARENTS: There is a difference between complaining to God and lashing out at him in anger. Lead your children to see God as their ally, loving Father, and best friend. Lead them from their complaint to an expression of faith in God and trust in his goodness.

Q 252:

When we're sad, can we pray that someone will come play with us?

A: Yes. God cares for us, he wants us to have good friends, and he wants to comfort us when we are sad. Those are the three main reasons that it is OK to ask God to send someone to play with us when we are sad. We can talk with God about anything. It is especially important to be honest and tell him how we are feeling.

We can also pray that we can be a friend and a comfort to someone else. Maybe someone nearby is feeling lonely and needs a friend. Sometimes the best way to get a friend is to be a friend.

KEY VERSE: *Please keep a guest room ready for me, for I am hoping that God will answer your prayers and let me return to you soon. (Philemon 1:22)*

Q 253:

Why do we pray to God to help us not be bad?

A: Because we all sin. It is natural for us to do bad things. So we need God's help to do good things instead of bad. God can help us, and he wants to. In fact, God is the only one who has the power to help us overcome temptation.

When the disciples asked Jesus how to pray, he gave them what we call the Lord's Prayer. In that prayer he taught them to pray, "Don't let us yield to temptation, but deliver us from the evil one." When we pray a prayer like that, we ask God to help us not be bad.

KEY VERSE: *[Jesus prayed,] "Don't let us yield to temptation, but deliver us from the evil one." (Matthew 6:13)*

Q 254:

Why do we ask Jesus into our heart?

A: When we say "heart," we mean the part of us that decides everything. So when someone says that we ought to ask Jesus into our heart, the person means that we should ask Jesus to be the true master of our lives. It also means that we ask him to be our Savior, to forgive our sins, and to take care of us. That is how a person becomes a Christian. When we do this, the Holy Spirit really does come and live inside us. Then we have him with us all the time.

KEY VERSE: *I pray that Christ will be more and more at home in your hearts as you trust in him. May your roots go down deep into the soil of God's marvelous love. (Ephesians 3:17)*

NOTE TO PARENTS: Whenever a question like this comes up, be prepared to talk about your children's own decision to accept Jesus. Be ready and willing to invite them to pray to receive Christ if they have never done so before.

Q 255:

Do we have to pray to be forgiven?

A: Whenever we ask God to forgive us, he forgives us. That is what the word *confession* means. It means that we tell God what we have done, agree with him that it is wrong, and ask him to forgive us. Because only God can forgive sins, we need to confess them to him in order to be truly forgiven. And we have his promise that he will always forgive if we come to him truly sorry for what we have done.

KEY VERSE: *If we confess our sins to him, he is faithful and just to forgive us and to cleanse us from every wrong. (1 John 1:9)*

NOTE TO PARENTS: There is no better way to teach children about confession than to show them how it is done. Always be willing to seek out forgiveness if appropriate, and let your children hear you confess sins to God.

Answers to Prayers

Q 256:

How can God hear our prayers from heaven?

A: God can do anything. He is all-powerful and unlimited. He is everywhere all the time. He also knows everything. He knows what we think as well as what we say. So God can hear everyone's prayers from all over the world all the time.

Sometimes people think that God is "out there in heaven," far away. But God is not far away; he is always right here with us, living among his people.

KEY VERSE: *I am the LORD, the God of all the peoples of the world. Is anything too hard for me? (Jeremiah 32:27)*

Q 257:

If we talk to God, does he always hear us?

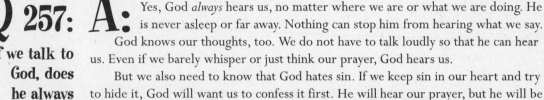

A: Yes, God *always* hears us, no matter where we are or what we are doing. He is never asleep or far away. Nothing can stop him from hearing what we say.

God knows our thoughts, too. We do not have to talk loudly so that he can hear us. Even if we barely whisper or just think our prayer, God hears us.

But we also need to know that God hates sin. If we keep sin in our heart and try to hide it, God will want us to confess it first. He will hear our prayer, but he will be waiting to hear us confess our sin first. Then he will listen to our requests.

God loves us more than we could possibly imagine. He *wants* to hear from us. He is always available and always listening. We can talk to him anytime throughout the day.

KEY VERSES: *If I had not confessed the sin in my heart, my LORD would not have listened. But God did listen! He paid attention to my prayer. Praise God, who did not ignore my prayer and did not withdraw his unfailing love from me. (Psalm 66:18-20)*

NOTE TO PARENTS: Always present the positive side of what God knows, not just the negative. While it is true that the wicked cannot hide from God, it is just as true that God's people never have to fear his inattention. God is always ready and willing to hear our prayers. Comfort your children with this fact.

Q 258:
How can God hear everyone's prayers at once?

A: God can hear everyone's prayers at once because God is everywhere. We can only be in one place at a time, and usually we can't understand more than one person at a time. But God is not like us— he is not limited. Not only can God hear and understand everyone who is praying to him in many different languages, but he also can give each person his full attention. Isn't that great?

KEY VERSES: *"Am I a God who is only in one place?" asks the LORD. "Do they think I cannot see what they are doing? Can anyone hide from me? Am I not everywhere in all the heavens and earth?" asks the LORD. (Jeremiah 23:23-24)*

NOTE TO PARENTS: Many children harbor the misconception that God is limited as we are. This is partly unavoidable because children think concretely. But it is also an opportunity for you to introduce them to the idea that God is infinitely greater than we are. He can even hear thousands of prayers at once! Here's an illustration that might help: When five people touch you, you can feel all five.

Q 259:
Does God usually give us what we pray for?

A: Sometimes we pray for things that will hurt us or others, or we pray with a selfish attitude. It would not be good if God gave us what we asked for in those situations. At other times, what we want is good but not part of God's plan for us. Sometimes God wants us to wait—he may give us what we ask for, but not now. He knows that later is better.

But at other times, God does give us what we ask for because it is a good thing, and God loves to give us good things.

God has already told us how he will answer certain kinds of prayers. He promises to give us what we ask for whenever we ask for food, clothing, help living the Christian life, and wisdom. On the other hand, we know God will answer no whenever we ask for things that go against his will. We can be sure that God will always do what is best.

KEY VERSES: *[Jesus] walked away, about a stone's throw, and knelt down and prayed, "Father, if you are willing, please take this cup of suffering away from me. Yet I want your will, not mine." (Luke 22:41-42)*

NOTE TO PARENTS: Encourage your children to ask God for specific things they are concerned about and to ask God for his will. Then encourage them to trust that God will take care of it. He is faithful and trustworthy.

Q 260:

Does God only give us things that we need?

A: No, he gives us much more. The Bible says that every good thing we have comes from God (James 1:17). That includes all of the things that we need plus all of the extras that he so kindly gives to us.

God loves us and he delights in blessing us. Sometimes he lets us have more than what we need—good things that are just for us to enjoy.

Jesus put it this way: "You fathers—if your children ask for a fish, do you give them a snake instead? Or if they ask for an egg, do you give them a scorpion? Of course not! If you sinful people know how to give good gifts to your children, how much more will your heavenly Father give the Holy Spirit to those who ask him." (Luke 11:11-13)

KEY VERSES: *Praise the LORD, I tell myself, and never forget the good things he does for me. He fills my life with good things. My youth is renewed like the eagle's! (Psalm 103:2, 5)*

NOTE TO PARENTS: Encourage your children to talk to God about fun stuff that is important to them, not merely "serious needs." God is interested in your children as they are. They will have plenty of serious topics to talk about soon enough.

Q 261:

Why doesn't God give us some things we pray for?

A: Because God is much wiser than we are. He knows what will happen if we get some of the things that we pray for. He can see all that is happening all over the world in every person's life all the time. He wants the very best for us. He has a plan for our lives and for the lives of every other person. So sometimes God does not give us what we pray for because it might hurt us or turn us the wrong way. At other times God doesn't give us something *right away*. He wants us to wait patiently for his timing. And sometimes God has plans that we cannot understand, so he waits or works something out that we cannot see.

Remember that God will never ignore our prayers. He loves us, hears our prayers, and works things out the best way possible. We can always trust in God's great care for us.

KEY VERSES: *Trust in the LORD with all your heart; do not depend on your own understanding. Seek his will in all you do, and he will direct your paths. (Proverbs 3:5-6)*

Q 262:

How do we know God is answering our prayer?

A: We know that God is answering our prayers because God said in the Bible that he would. Of course, not all of his answers are yes. Sometimes God answers no. And sometimes he wants us to wait. The answer we receive is not always the one we had in mind, but it is always best.

God is most interested in changing us into his kind of people. That is his main goal for us. Prayer keeps us close to God and helps us understand what he wants us to become. We should pray knowing that God wants to hear from us and that his answer will be best.

KEY VERSE: *I took my troubles to the Lord; I cried out to him, and he answered my prayer. (Psalm 120:1)*

NOTE TO PARENTS: Children tend to take life as it comes, without connecting events. They may not notice the many answers that God gives to their prayers. Watch for God's answers to your children's prayers. And when you see them, hold a little celebration and thank God together.

Q 263:

Why doesn't God answer prayers right away?

A: God knows more than we know. He has more wisdom than we have. So he gives the answer at the time that is best. Sometimes we do not have to wait at all—God answers our prayers even before we put them into words. At other times we must wait.

God has good reasons for his timing. Sometimes it takes awhile for the answer to come because God is using people and circumstances to answer, bringing them all together like a big team. Or God may know that we are not ready for the thing we want, so he spends a lot of time helping us grow and get ready.

And sometimes God waits to answer in order to test our faith and trust in him. He wants to see if we will keep trusting him even when it looks as if he is not answering. When we decide to keep trusting, our faith becomes stronger, and when the answer finally comes, that helps us trust God even more.

KEY VERSE: *There is a time for everything, a season for every activity under heaven. (Ecclesiastes 3:1)*

NOTE TO PARENTS: Every child asks this question eventually. Encourage your children through this time to keep on trusting God. Together, ask God to help them keep trusting.

Q 264:

If we're discouraged and it seems like God doesn't answer our prayers, what should we do?

A: We should keep on praying. If we are discouraged, we should tell him that we are discouraged. Then we should tell him that we know he is good and has not given up on us.

We should not blame God for our problems or for not answering our prayers. Sometimes bad things happen to test our faith or to make our faith stronger. We should remember that God is teaching us. God will give us strength to keep praying and to keep trusting that he is working things out for good.

Sometimes we are expecting things to work out a certain way. Often God answers in a way we are not expecting. We need to keep looking for his answers.

KEY VERSES: *One day Jesus told his disciples a story to illustrate their need for constant prayer and to show them that they must never give up. Then the Lord said, "Learn a lesson from this evil judge. Even he rendered a just decision in the end, so don't you think God will surely give justice to his chosen people who plead with him day and night? Will he keep putting them off?"* (Luke 18:1, 6-7)

NOTE TO PARENTS: When your children are waiting for God to answer their prayers, encourage them by reminding them of times when God has answered past prayers (both theirs and yours).

Q 265:

When we pray for someone not to die and then they die, does that mean that God didn't love them?

A: No, not at all. Every person has to die. That is part of life. When a person dies, it does not mean that God does not love the person or that God does not love the people who wanted that person to live. It also does not mean that someone lacked faith.

The Bible says that God loves *all* people. That is why he sent Jesus to die on the cross. He loved people so much that he sent Jesus to take away the sin of the world.

God hates death, but death is not the end. God's people can look forward to eternal life in heaven with God.

It is OK to cry when our loved ones die. We miss them very much. But if they are Christians, they are going to heaven, and that is much better for them.

KEY VERSE: *The LORD's loved ones are precious to him; it grieves him when they die.* (Psalm 116:15)

NOTE TO PARENTS: Whenever your family prays for someone who is very ill and may die, commit that person to God's care. Ask together that God will do what is best for that person. Ask him also to help friends and family members help and comfort one another.

Q 266:

If God has it all planned, can we really change it by praying for things?

A: The Bible says that God knows everything, even the future. Nothing takes him by surprise. And he is in control of the world. He rules it all.

Yet we also know that we work with God to accomplish his work. He could do it all without our prayers, but he has chosen not to. Our prayers are part of the way God's work will get done. Prayer is his idea. God wants his people to be coworkers with him in this world, and that means we must pray.

No one can see how their prayers affect God. It is better to pray in faith that God will do what is good than not to pray because we think that it might not make any difference. The main reason for praying is for us to get to know God better and to let him teach and care for us, not just to change things.

KEY VERSE: *The earnest prayer of a righteous person has great power and wonderful results.* *(James 5:16)*

NOTE TO PARENTS: Whenever a question like this comes up, remind your children why we pray. We pray to get to know God better and to invite God to change us. That is, we should conform more to God's will, not expect God to conform more to ours.

Q 267:

Why does God not answer our prayers the way we want?

A: God can see into the future and knows the needs of every person everywhere at all times, so sometimes his answers seem strange to us. He sees what we cannot. Sometimes he answers our prayers exactly as we expect; sometimes the answer is so different that we hardly recognize it.

Sometimes God gives us what we were *really* asking for rather than the specific thing we thought we wanted. Maybe we asked for a toy but really we needed to be happy. God may make us happy *without* the toy, or he may send us a friend to play with instead.

If we trust in God's perfect love, we will always be content with his answers to our prayers.

KEY VERSES: *Dear friends, if our conscience is clear, we can come to God with bold confidence. And we will receive whatever we request because we obey him and do the things that please him. (1 John 3:21-22)*

NOTE TO PARENTS: Sometimes we are amazed at how God answers our prayers, but other times the answer comes so subtly that we wonder if God really did it or it just happened. Encourage your children with the fact that God is everywhere, knows everything, and is in control. If you prayed about it, God arranged it, subtly or miraculously.

Q 268:

If we pray for something one night, do we have to pray for it the next night?

A: We do not have to keep praying the same prayers over and over, but it is good to pray every day for the things that really matter to us. It is all right to keep praying for the same thing when we don't see an answer and when it is important. Also, continuing to pray for the same thing has a way of changing us. While we are praying, God may show us a different direction to take or a new attitude to have. God uses prayer to change us. So it is good to keep praying for what matters to us.

KEY VERSE: *Be glad for all God is planning for you. Be patient in trouble, and always be prayerful. (Romans 12:12)*

NOTE TO PARENTS: The Bible tells us what we should pray for regularly (see questions 221–223 and the section "What to Pray For"). Help your children learn and add new kinds of prayers one at a time. Suggest topics (a little different each time) that will help them add to their prayer life slowly and progressively.

Q 269:

How come God answers some people's prayers and not others'?

A: God answers the prayers of the people who love him. The Bible says, "The earnest prayer of a righteous person has great power and wonderful results" (James 5:16). This verse teaches that a person who knows God and obeys him prays the kinds of prayers that God answers.

But not everyone in the world is part of God's family. Only people who have put their faith in Jesus are God's children. People who do not know God may pray, but they do not have the assurance that God will act on their request.

In the end, no one knows why God does what he does. God has plans for every person's life, and he works out those plans in his wisdom. We trust that his plans for us are good, and we trust that his plans for others are good too. We should not judge people or pretend to know why God does something for this person but not for that one.

KEY VERSE: *The LORD hates the sacrifice of the wicked, but he delights in the prayers of the upright. (Proverbs 15:8)*

NOTE TO PARENTS: Children tend to think that God rewards good people with answered prayer and punishes bad people with unanswered prayer. Remind your children that God answers prayers out of his love and grace. He does not use our works to determine who gets this or that blessing.

Q 270:

Why do some people write down when God answers their prayer?

A: Usually people write down God's answers to prayer because they want to remember how God has blessed them. Many passages in the Bible tell about people who did this. These people wrote down what God did for them in the past so that they would not forget and so their children would know about it too.

When we remember what God has done for us, we can thank and praise him. We can also be encouraged to keep praying and to live for him. It helps to go back and read about all the times just like this one when God answered prayers for which we patiently waited, especially if it looks as if God is not answering our prayers now.

KEY VERSE: *Think of the wonderful works he has done, the miracles and the judgments he handed down. (Psalm 105:5)*

NOTE TO PARENTS: You can help your children make a "faith story" book for themselves and record in it the details of God's answering prayer. You might want to do one for the whole family.

Q 271:

How does God answer our prayers?

A: God answers our prayers in many ways. God is all-powerful, so he can use anything he wants to work out his plans. One of the ways he answers prayer is by using other people. For example, God often uses doctors and medicines to bring healing. He uses generous Christians to give money to people in need, in answer to their prayers.

God also uses other means. Sometimes he uses angels to do miracles or to intervene in some invisible way. He also uses events and the forces in nature.

Sometimes God simply changes *us*. For example, we may ask for more money, and God may answer by showing us how to use what we have more carefully. In other words, God gives us wisdom and teaches us; he works inside us to make us more like Christ in the way we think, talk, and act.

KEY VERSE: *You faithfully answer our prayers with awesome deeds, O God our savior. You are the hope of everyone on earth, even those who sail on distant seas. (Psalm 65:5)*

NOTE TO PARENTS: Our children need to know that nothing can stop God from answering their prayers and nothing is too big or too small for him to do. He is always able, and he is always willing to work things out for our good.

Q 272:

When God says we can pray about anything, does he really mean <u>anything</u>?

A: God always means what he says, so indeed we can talk with him about anything at all— feelings, requests, questions, anything we can think of. God invites us to come to him with whatever is on our mind. This does not mean that we will *get* everything we ask for, but we can pray about anything.

Prayer is not magic. It is a talk with God, who is a person. What matters most is that we trust in God and do what he says.

KEY VERSES: *[Jesus said,] "You can ask for anything in my name, and I will do it, because the work of the Son brings glory to the Father. Yes, ask anything in my name, and I will do it!" (John 14:13-14)*

Q 273:

Does it matter how much faith we have?

A: Jesus said that even if we have a very tiny amount of faith, we can accomplish great things in prayer. Having faith just means that we believe that God is faithful. In other words, we decide to trust that he loves us and will do what he said he would do. Great faith in God comes from having a little faith and deciding that God is faithful and that we are going to trust him no matter what.

We should put all our trust in God and depend on him, not on our own words, strength, or clever plans. If we trust even a little in our mighty God, it will make a huge difference.

KEY VERSE: *"You didn't have enough faith," Jesus told them. "I assure you, even if you had faith as small as a mustard seed you could say to this mountain, 'Move from here to there,' and it would move. Nothing would be impossible." (Matthew 17:20)*

NOTE TO PARENTS: A man wanted Jesus to heal his son. Jesus said, "Anything is possible if a person believes." The man replied, "I do believe, but help me not to doubt!" (Mark 9:23-24). Jesus healed his son. Sometimes we, like that man, doubt God. Whenever this happens with your children, let them know that God loves them and is willing to act on their behalf. Then lead them in asking God to overcome their doubt.

Q 274:

Doesn't God ever get tired of answering prayers?

A: Nope. God never gets even a little bit tired of answering prayers. He loves to hear from us because he loves us. Jesus died for our sins so that we could have friendship with him. That does not change no matter how often we ask things of him.

God wants to work in our lives to change our behavior, thoughts, and habits. We should never fear that we are wearing him out with our prayers, even when we pray the same thing over and over. That is because he wants to keep being a part of our lives.

KEY VERSES: *O Israel, how can you say the LORD does not see your troubles? How can you say God refuses to hear your case? Have you never heard or understood? Don't you know that the LORD is the everlasting God, the Creator of all the earth? He never grows faint or weary. No one can measure the depths of his understanding. (Isaiah 40:27-28)*

Praying for Others

Q 275:
How do we know who to pray for?

A: We should pray for whomever we care about, and we should also pray for people in need, for pastors and missionaries, for government leaders, and for ourselves. For example, we can pray for family and friends. We can pray for people that we know are having trouble. We can pray for the pastor of our church, for the missionaries that our church supports, and for our Bible teachers. We can pray for our elected leaders, judges, lawmakers, school board superintendents, teachers, and other leaders. We can even make a list and pray for them regularly.

It is always good to pray for ourselves. We can ask God to teach us, to give us wisdom each day, and to make us grow in our faith.

KEY VERSE: *I urge you, first of all, to pray for all people. As you make your requests, plead for God's mercy upon them, and give thanks. (1 Timothy 2:1)*

Q 276:
Does God want us to pray for our friends?

... AND GOD, PLEASE HELP TOMMY FEEL BETTER IN TIME FOR THE BIG SPELLING TEST TOMORROW.

A: God definitely wants us to pray for our friends. John 17 tells about Jesus praying for his disciples. He prayed that they would be filled with joy, made holy, unified, and protected from the evil one. Jesus thought that it was important to pray for his friends in this way.

We can also pray for our friends' problems, their attitude, that they will come to know Jesus, and that they learn to be better friends. In fact, this is one way we keep them as friends. Whatever our friends need, we can pray for them, and God welcomes such prayers.

KEY VERSES: *[Jesus said,] "I am praying not only for these disciples but also for all who will ever believe in me because of their testimony. My prayer for all of them is that they will be one."* *(John 17:20-21)*

NOTE TO PARENTS: Guide your children in praying for a friend each night.

Q 277:

Do we have to pray for people we haven't met before?

A: We do not have to meet people in order to pray for them. For example, the Bible tells us to pray for government leaders. Surely we have not met all the leaders of the country, but we should pray for them anyway. We should also pray for missionaries we hear or know about, even if we have never met them. So, yes, we should pray for some of the people we have never met before.

Remember that prayer can be an adventure. We can affect decisions of the president or mayor by praying for that person. Try not to look at it as a duty or a job but as a privilege. It is kind of like helping run the country.

KEY VERSES: *Pray this way for kings and all others who are in authority, so that we can live in peace and quietness, in godliness and dignity. This is good and pleases God our Savior, for he wants everyone to be saved and to understand the truth. (1 Timothy 2:2-4)*

NOTE TO PARENTS: From time to time, lead your children in praying for people they know; then, guide them to include someone they don't know. God will help them learn to pray beyond their own experience. After all, prayer is a dialogue with God, and he will teach them as they practice and get to know him better.

Q 278:

What if kids are mean to us and it's hard for us to pray for them?

A: It is not always easy to pray. But praying for kids who are mean to us is one of the best things we can do to help them. We can pray that God will help those who are mean to stop being mean. We can also pray that God will help us to be kind and loving to them so they will learn about God's love through our example. Maybe if they see God's love in us, they will come to know Jesus.

We should let God judge others. In other words, we should not pray for God to punish someone, even our enemies. Instead, we should pray that people will trust in Jesus and that they will develop a love for God. If they love God, they will stop being mean.

KEY VERSES: *[Jesus said,] "I say, love your enemies. Do good to those who hate you. Pray for the happiness of those who curse you. Pray for those who hurt you."(Luke 6:27-28)*

Q 279:

Why do we pray for our enemies?

A: The main reason to pray for our enemies is because God tells us to. In fact, he tells us to *love* our enemies. Praying for our enemies and loving them is God's way.

Another reason is that all people, especially bad people, need prayer. There is no better way to change them. If we want bad people to stop being bad, we need to ask God to do it. We need to pray for them so that they will change.

Jesus prayed for his enemies. He prayed for the religious leaders who wanted him to die, and he prayed for us. He did that because he loved us, even while we were God's enemies.

OH LORD, HELP HIM BE A GREAT GUY, KIND AND CONSIDERATE SO EVERYONE WILL LIKE HIM AND HE'LL BE HAPPY.

KEY VERSES: *[Jesus said,] "Love your enemies! Pray for those who persecute you! In that way, you will be acting as true children of your Father in heaven. For he gives his sunlight to both the evil and the good, and he sends rain on the just and on the unjust, too."* (Matthew 5:44-45)

Q 280:

How does praying help sick people feel better?

A: Sometimes God answers our prayers for a sick person by causing the person to get better. Perhaps we pray that the doctors will have wisdom, and God makes them think of a treatment that cures the disease.

Other times God helps the sick person learn to live with the illness. Perhaps the person cannot walk, but God teaches the person how to be joyful with God's love and care instead of walking again. Or the person becomes kind and caring toward others who are suffering because of what he or she has gone through.

One kind of healing makes the person's *body* better, and the other kind makes the *person* better. So praying for sick people is very important.

KEY VERSES: *Are any among you sick? They should call for the elders of the church and have them pray over them, anointing them with oil in the name of the Lord. And their prayer offered in faith will heal the sick, and the Lord will make them well. And anyone who has committed sins will be forgiven.* (James 5:14-15)

NOTE TO PARENTS: Prayer is a natural response to sickness. Encourage your children to pray for people who are sick, but be sure to explain that the outcome is in God's hands.

Q 281:

How come missionaries need so much prayer?

A: Because their work is very important, and they often run into problems that make their work difficult. They are telling people about Jesus. Only God can change people's minds and hearts. So we pray that God will open the hearts of people to the gospel message that the missionaries are telling. It is very important that people hear and understand the message of Jesus.

At the same time, missionary work is very difficult. Satan does not want missionaries to succeed in what they do. He will give the missionaries trouble and problems that make their work frustrating. For example, some people may speak against the missionaries. Or the missionaries may get sick. So we pray that God will keep Satan away from the missionaries and make them strong and able to do their work.

Missionaries depend on our prayers. If we do not pray, they will have a very hard time telling others about Christ.

KEY VERSES: *Don't forget to pray for us, too, that God will give us many opportunities to preach about his secret plan—that Christ is also for you Gentiles. That is why I am here in chains. Pray that I will proclaim this message as clearly as I should. (Colossians 4:3-4)*

NOTE TO PARENTS: Try to introduce your children to at least one missionary. The best candidates are missionaries who are relationally close to you or are from your church. Go hear them speak at your church the next time you have opportunity to do so. You can also open your home to missionaries who are on furlough. Kids find it easier to pray for people they know than for strangers.

Q 282:

What do prayer warriors do?

A: Some people use the term "prayer warriors" to describe people who seem to pray all the time. They pray for others and for God's work on a regular basis. They know that prayer is important. Because they care about God's work in the world, they make sure that they pray about it often.

God wants all of us to pray for others, for Christian leaders, and for the growth of his kingdom. But some people feel that God has given them an extra special task of spending a lot of time doing this.

KEY VERSE: *Pray at all times and on every occasion in the power of the Holy Spirit. (Ephesians 6:18)*

Praying Together

Q 283:

What should a person do who feels embarrassed to pray in public?

A: It is OK to pray in public as long as we are not showing off. We should not feel ashamed of it or embarrassed. But some people are shy. When they are asked to pray aloud, they feel very awkward. They are afraid that they will say something wrong and that people will laugh at them.

We must remember that we do not pray to impress others. Whatever we pray is all right if it comes from the heart. So when we are asked to pray in public, we can just talk to God in our own words and in our own way.

KEY VERSE: *Then I will declare the wonder of your name to my brothers and sisters. I will praise you among all your people. (Psalm 22:22)*

NOTE TO PARENTS: At a certain age, some children will become self-conscious about praying in public. You can teach them to pray in front of others (and help them get used to it) by having them take turns saying the mealtime prayer. Start simple, and expand it to include a current family issue or two.

Q 284:

If we don't like what someone prayed for, what should we do?

A: Nothing. We should let people lead us in prayer and not judge them or what they say. Some people become used to certain patterns of praying that may seem strange to us. We should be careful not to scorn them just because we do not like their choice of words or style of praying. They may just have a different way of asking God for something. But remember that God cares most about the heart of the people praying, not the specific words they use.

Sometimes we can learn from others' prayers. If we do not like what someone prayed for, we should thank God that the person prayed and then think about what we can learn from the person's prayer. We should always be open to learning new things from others. We should especially be glad that they are praying.

KEY VERSE: *[Jesus said,] "Stop judging others, and you will not be judged. Stop criticizing others, or it will all come back on you. If you forgive others, you will be forgiven." (Luke 6:37)*

Q 285:
Why does God want us to pray together?

A: God enjoys it when his people pray together because it is one of the ways we can help and support one another. The Bible calls Christians a "body." This means that they work best when they work together, like the different parts of a body. When believers pray together, they strengthen and encourage each other. They complement each other. And they can share prayer requests and pray for each other. It is powerful.

KEY VERSES: *[Jesus said,] "If two of you agree down here on earth concerning anything you ask, my Father in heaven will do it for you. For where two or three gather together because they are mine, I am there among them." (Matthew 18:19-20)*

NOTE TO PARENTS: Always be ready to pray with your children. When they have a need or you both see a need, pray about it together. Ask your children to pray for you, too, and give them specifics. Also let your children know that you are praying for them.

Q 286:
Do children have to pray with an adult?

A: Not at all. Jesus said, "Let the children come to me. Don't stop them!" (Luke 18:16). Any believer, no matter how old or young, can talk with God alone. God loves to hear from his children. He welcomes all sincere prayers.

Go ahead and practice praying to God all by yourself. You can start by telling him what is on your mind and asking him to help you solve your problems. You can also ask him to teach you to pray better. You do not have to do it a certain way; it is like talking to your friends— you just tell them what you want to say in your own words. Then thank God for understanding what you want to say, even if you don't know how to say it.

I'M GOING TO PRAY FOR SOME REALLY BIG THINGS! I THINK IT WOULD HELP IF YOU FILLED OUT THIS CONSENT FORM.

KEY VERSE: *You have taught children and nursing infants to give you praise. (Psalm 8:2)*

NOTE TO PARENTS: When your children start praying on their own, you have successfully primed the pump. But do not leave them there. Continue getting together with them for prayer so that you can continue to help them while also encouraging them to pray on their own. If there is something they want to pray about privately, without your hearing it, don't pry it out of them; encourage it. It shows that they are starting to trust God with private and important concerns. That is very good.

Q 287:

Is group prayer more powerful?

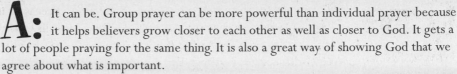

A: It can be. Group prayer can be more powerful than individual prayer because it helps believers grow closer to each other as well as closer to God. It gets a lot of people praying for the same thing. It is also a great way of showing God that we agree about what is important.

Group prayer is one way God helps us. We may not feel like praying, or we may not feel very confident in our prayers. So others pray with us to help us receive God's strength and help. In that way it is more powerful because we can get our prayers answered even when we are feeling weak.

KEY VERSE: *Let us not neglect our meeting together, as some people do, but encourage and warn each other, especially now that the day of his coming back again is drawing near. (Hebrews 10:25)*

NOTE TO PARENTS: A good time to teach your children the importance of group prayer is when your family is going through a tough time. You can call the family together, explain the situation and what you want to tell God, and then pray together.

Q 288:

Why do some people hold hands while they're praying?

A: Holding hands with others when we pray can help us feel together and more like we care for each other. Also, holding hands can be a sign that we all agree in what we are talking to God about. People in a family or small group do not have to hold hands when they pray together, but sometimes they like to.

KEY VERSES: *May God, who gives this patience and encouragement, help you live in complete harmony with each other—each with the attitude of Christ Jesus toward the other. Then all of you can join together with one voice, giving praise and glory to God, the Father of our Lord Jesus Christ. (Romans 15:5-6)*

NOTE TO PARENTS: Holding hands when you are praying with your children can help them concentrate and not fidget so much. But also let your children know that holding hands is not essential.

Bedtime Prayers

Q 289:

Do we have to pray every night?

A: No. God has not set exact times when we *must* pray. Prayer is simply something that we should do every day. A lot of people like to pray every night and try to keep that habit because they know that prayer is important, and the end of the day seems to be a good time for them. Others prefer to pray in the morning before they start the day. Some people set aside special time to pray in the middle of the day. Praying at night is a good habit, but it is not a rule that we have to follow. Each of us should pick the time of day that works best for us.

KEY VERSE: *Timothy, I thank God for you. He is the God I serve with a clear conscience, just as my ancestors did. Night and day I constantly remember you in my prayers.* (2 Timothy 1:3)

NOTE TO PARENTS: As your children get older, they may want to change the time of their devotional prayer. Encourage them to pray during a part of the day when they can concentrate and be consistent.

Q 290:

What if God has already answered all of our prayers?

A: First of all, we can thank him for answering them! We can be glad, tell God thank you, and praise him for being so good to us. Then we can tell someone else about it so they know about the great things God has done for us. And then we should think about new requests we can bring to him. If we cannot think of anything *we* need, we can think of other people who need prayer. We can pray for the people in our family, for our friends, for our leaders, and even for our enemies. Then we can pray for wisdom and that God will teach us new things. There's always something to talk to God about.

KEY VERSES: *Give thanks to the LORD, for he is good! His faithful love endures forever. Has the LORD redeemed you? Then speak out! Tell others he has saved you from your enemies.* (Psalm 107:1-2)

NOTE TO PARENTS: Encourage your children to tell God what is on their mind even if they don't have a request to make. As they get older and develop their relationship with God, they will get more comfortable with different kinds of prayer. And when you pray with them, let them hear you talk to God about what is on your mind so that they can see that not all prayer has to involve a list of needs.

Q 291:

If we've prayed all through the day, do we still need to pray at night?

OPEN 9:30 - 5:00
6:00
7:30
9:00
OR CALL DIRECT

JASON'S PRAYER BOOTH

A: We should try not to think of prayer as a requirement that we have to meet. Instead, we should make a habit of praying. We should pray about things that matter to us. And we should pray honestly and privately.

Remember that prayer is an opportunity to talk to God, who knows us and loves us. If we know him and love him, we will pray often because we know he is on our side. We will pray simply because we love God. But we will not worry whether we have prayed enough.

Bedtime is a good time to pray because we can think through the day and pray about the next day. But we do not need to think of bedtime prayer as a chore to do. If we have already spoken with God about our concerns, we can just thank him for taking care of us as we drift off to sleep.

KEY VERSE: *Keep on praying. (1 Thessalonians 5:17)*

NOTE TO PARENTS: Do not force children to pray. Always present prayer as an opportunity to do something good and pleasing to you and to God. This will help your children see prayer as a positive activity that they can do.

Q 292:

Are your daytime prayers as effective as your night ones?

A: God does not hear prayers better during the day than during the night. And God does not care what time of day we choose to pray. What God cares about is our attitude. He wants our prayers to be honest and heartfelt—he wants us to say what is on our mind.

Some people find it easier to pray at night than during the day. Perhaps they become more easily distracted during the day, thinking about all the things they have to do and the places they have to go. They may have trouble concentrating on their prayer during the day. For them, praying at night may be better.

Others find it easier to pray during the day because they become drowsy at night. They cannot concentrate on praying at night because they too quickly fall asleep.

It is always good to pray, whether it is nighttime or daytime. God always loves to hear from us.

KEY VERSE: *Night and day we pray earnestly for you, asking God to let us see you again to fill up anything that may still be missing in your faith. (1 Thessalonians 3:10)*

Q 293:

After our parents pray with us, do we still need to pray on our own later?

A: We certainly can. We do not have to pray only with our parents. If we have our own private requests that we want to bring to God, we should go ahead and do so. It is OK to tell God whatever we like. He loves us and cares for us and loves to hear anything and everything we want to say to him, as long as it is respectful.

But we do not have to pray on our own in order for God to love us or to answer our requests. If we happen to pray mostly with our parents, God does not mind. The important thing is that we pray.

KEY VERSES: *Jesus said, "Let the children come to me. Don't stop them! For the Kingdom of Heaven belongs to such as these." And he put his hands on their heads and blessed them before he left." (Matthew 19:14-15)*

NOTE TO PARENTS: It is great for you to pray with your children; it lets you lead them to God and teach them how to pray. But be sure your children also know that God welcomes their private prayers. If they are afraid of "not saying it right," tell them that God is very happy with the way they pray all by themselves and that he will help them grow. Remind them that Jesus welcomes children.

Q 294:

Why did I have a bad dream when I prayed before I went to sleep?

A: It's good to pray before falling asleep at night. Praying helps us think through the day and thank God for how much he loves us. We should also pray for the next day. Christians aren't promised that they will be free from all problems and difficulties. God does promise to be with us during hard times. A lot of things can cause bad dreams—something on our mind, something we ate, a noise. Ask God to help you sleep, but remember that whatever happens, he is there with you.

KEY VERSE: *I lay down and slept. I woke up in safety, for the LORD was watching over me. (Psalm 3:5)*

Q 295:

Why are we sometimes forced to pray? Shouldn't we pray when we want to?

A: Prayer is a good thing to do, just like brushing our teeth, taking a bath, and eating good food. We may not always enjoy praying, but we should do it whether we feel like it or not.

Sometimes parents make children pray even if they don't feel like it or want to. There is nothing wrong with that. If we always waited till we *felt* like eating good food, we would probably eat nothing but cookies and ice cream. Then we would get sick, fat, and weak. We simply need to do what we ought to do. This is true of prayer, too. And prayer is much more important than eating good food, taking a bath, or anything else.

The good news is that God rewards those who discipline themselves to pray. They soon find that they miss it when they cannot do it. God changes us as we pray, and that is just one more reason we should work at it.

KEY VERSE: *Devote yourselves to prayer with an alert mind and a thankful heart. (Colossians 4:2)*

NOTE TO PARENTS: Be careful never to use prayer as a punishment. Do not make children pray as penance or as a way of making them think about God. Make prayer something to look forward to. And if they do not want to pray, tell them that's OK, and pray for them aloud as they listen. Lead them; do not push them.

Q 296:

How can we think of something good to pray about if we've had a bad day?

A: Even when we have had a terrible day, we have good things to pray about. For example, God is good—we can thank him for being good, for being in control, and for caring about us. We can tell God about our bad day and what makes us upset about it. Then we can ask him to help us with our bad situation. Also, we can express confidence in God's goodness and in his willingness to help us. We can say that we are glad he is with us.

Praying and praising God is a good way to take our mind off our troubles.

KEY VERSE: *No matter what happens, always be thankful, for this is God's will for you who belong to Christ Jesus. (1 Thessalonians 5:18)*

NOTE TO PARENTS: It is very reassuring to a child for Mom or Dad to pray for him or her. Whenever your children have a bad day, pray for them. Express sadness at the things that have made your children sad, ask God to help, and express confidence that he will help. This will do more to calm and comfort them than making them pray.

Q 297:

Do we have to pray even if we're tired?

A: Just before Jesus was arrested, he asked his disciples to stay awake and pray, but they fell asleep. It is difficult to pray when we are tired, but we should not let tiredness keep us from talking with God. We should try hard to make a habit of praying, even if it is sometimes inconvenient.

KEY VERSE: *"Why are you sleeping?" [Jesus] asked. "Get up and pray. Otherwise temptation will overpower you." (Luke 22:46)*

NOTE TO PARENTS: If your children are too tired to pray, pray for them and let them go to sleep. Tired children do not learn well. And if your children are often too tired to pray, consider changing your family's bedtime routine so they are more awake at prayer time.

Q 298:

Is it bad to fall asleep when we are praying to God?

A: No, it is not bad to fall asleep while praying. In fact, there is no better way to fall asleep. If we are in bed and want to talk to God until we fall asleep, that is a wonderful thing to do. It is always good to pray.

But if we are falling asleep because we pray *only* when we are tired, then we need to find another time to pray so we can also pray when we are awake. It is always good to set aside times for prayer when we can think clearly and not get distracted.

KEY VERSE: *Through each day the LORD pours his unfailing love upon me, and through each night I sing his songs, praying to God who gives me life. (Psalm 42:8)*

Questions Kids Ask

Heaven and Angels

4

Angels

Q 299:

Where did angels come from?

A: God created everything, and that includes angels. The Bible doesn't say, "God created angels," nor does it mention when God created angels. But we know he did because the Bible explains that God created everything that exists. The Bible never says that God created dogs, for example, but we know that he did because he created all things. We also don't know if God created all the angels at once or if he creates them as he needs them. Angels take orders from God and serve him. They aren't equal with God and don't have the same powers as God. Remember, God didn't discover angels—he created them.

KEY VERSES: *Praise him, all his angels! Praise him, all the armies of heaven! . . . Let every created thing give praise to the LORD, for he issued his command, and they came into being. (Psalm 148:2, 5)*

NOTE TO PARENTS: Try to avoid using the word *angel* when it is inaccurate, such as calling your child a "little angel" or saying that a person who died has become an angel. These innocent explanations can easily confuse children.

Q 300:

Do angels have names?

A: The Bible mentions two angels by name— Gabriel and Michael. We don't know if all angels have names, but they probably do since angels are personal beings, like people. Even though they don't have bodies, they have identities, just like people. But they're not human beings. They are God's servants. He created them to do his work. Remember, the only place that we can learn for sure about angels is in the Bible, God's Word.

KEY VERSE: *"Why do you ask my name?" the angel of the LORD replied. "You wouldn't understand if I told you." (Judges 13:18)*

Q 301:

What do angels really look like?

A: The word *angel* means "messenger." Angels are God's messengers. They can also be God's warriors. In the Bible we read about people who saw angels. Sometimes the people knew they were angels, and sometimes they didn't. Some angels described in the Bible have wings. Those angels are called cherubim. But most of the angels in the Bible stories looked like regular people. We don't know what angels look like in heaven.

KEY VERSES: *I, John, am the one who saw and heard all these things. And when I saw and heard these things, I fell down to worship the angel who showed them to me. But again he said, "No, don't worship me. I am a servant of God, just like you and your brothers the prophets, as well as all who obey what is written in this scroll. Worship God!" (Revelation 22:8-9)*

NOTE TO PARENTS: You may want to ask if your child has seen a picture of an angel, perhaps in a children's Bible, in a painting, in the cartoons, etc. Those pictures often leave mental impressions about an angel's appearance.

Q 302:

Do angels have hearts?

A: If you're asking whether angels have feelings, the answer is yes. Angels have feelings just as people do and just as God does. Many Bible passages tell of angels rejoicing whenever someone first believes in Jesus. Others tell of angels singing songs of gladness and praise to God.

Angels can also think. The Bible says they can tell the difference between good and evil. Satan and his demons used to be good angels, but they chose to do evil. (More on that in question 329.) The Bible also says that angels care about us and that they helped Jesus.

But angels don't have real hearts because they don't have physical bodies.

KEY VERSE: *[Jesus said,] "There is joy in the presence of God's angels when even one sinner repents." (Luke 15:10)*

Q 303:
Do angels grow up?

A: You may have seen paintings or cartoons of "baby angels," but those are not true pictures of angels. Angels are never born, they never grow up, and they never die. They don't need to eat or drink, and they don't outgrow their clothes. But they can learn—they can get more knowledge than they started with. The Bible says that angels learn from watching people (they "grow in knowledge"). Angels are learning more and more of God's wisdom all the time.

KEY VERSE: *God's purpose was to show his wisdom in all its rich variety to all the rulers and authorities in the heavenly realms. They will see this when Jews and Gentiles are joined together in his church. (Ephesians 3:10)*

NOTE TO PARENTS: We associate growth with change. That is, we talk about people "growing" spiritually, mentally, and in other areas to describe the changes we see happening in them. When children ask, "Do angels grow up?" however, they are usually referring to physical growth—aging and getting bigger, stronger, faster, etc.

Q 304:
Are angels boys or girls?

A: *People* are either male or female (boys or girls) because of their bodies—the way they are physically. But angels don't have physical bodies, so they are neither boys nor girls. (Jesus explained that angels don't get married.) The angels Michael and Gabriel have male names, but that doesn't mean that they are men. When angels visited people in human form (when Gabriel visited Mary, for example), usually it was as a man.

KEY VERSE: *When the dead rise, they won't be married. They will be like the angels in heaven. (Matthew 22:30)*

Q 305:
Do angels get tired?

A: Angels never get tired, not even a little bit, and they never sleep. They don't need sleep like you do. Good angels are incredibly powerful and always ready to do what God tells them to do. Angels can open locked doors, roll away huge stones, and even wipe out whole armies. That's because they are God's servants, and God gives them the power they need to carry out his work. Angels are not all-powerful, though. The book of Daniel tells of a time when Satan stopped an angel for a little while until the archangel Michael came to help him. But angels never get tired, weak, or sick. And someday they will fight in the final battle against Satan and his demons—and *win*.

KEY VERSE: *Suddenly there was a great earthquake, because an angel of the Lord came down from heaven and rolled aside the stone and sat on it. (Matthew 28:2)*

Q 306:

Do angels have halos?

A: Many drawings of angels or of people in the Bible show them with little rings of light over their heads that look a lot like round fluorescent lightbulbs. Those are called halos. But there is no evidence in the Bible that anyone, human or angel, ever had a halo. Real angels don't look anything like those pictures. Some passages in the Bible describe angels as very bright beings. Their clothes or their faces shine with bright light, glow like hot metal, or gleam like the sun. This is because angels reflect the glory of God. (When Moses met with God on Mount Sinai, his face took on a glow because he had been with God.) Angels don't *have* to come shining brightly, but many of them do. Halos have become a popular way of showing that angels give off God's glory or brightness, but they don't give a very good picture of the glory and power that angels actually have.

KEY VERSES: *I looked up and saw a man dressed in linen clothing, with a belt of pure gold around his waist. His body looked like a dazzling gem. From his face came flashes like lightning, and his eyes were like flaming torches. His arms and feet shone like polished bronze, and his voice was like the roaring of a vast multitude of people. (Daniel 10:5-6)*

Q 307:

Why can't I see angels?

A: The Bible tells of angels appearing to people. Why don't they appear to us today? It may seem unfair or strange that you can't see angels, but angels are spirits. They don't have bodies as we do. Angels appear with physical bodies only when God sends them to speak to people. The times when angels have appeared to people (at least the ones we know about for sure) have been quite rare—only during the Exodus, the time of the judges, the time of Elijah, the time of Jesus' birth, and the time of the forming of the early church. In other words, God doesn't show off his angels. He saves angelic appearances for times when people really need to see them. Angels can do their work without being seen.

KEY VERSE: *As for Philip, an angel of the Lord said to him, "Go south down the desert road that runs from Jerusalem to Gaza."(Acts 8:26)*

NOTE TO PARENTS: The real question here may be, If angels are real, why can't I see them? Explain to your child that there are a lot of things that are real that they can't see, such as electricity, oxygen, etc.

Q 308:
Are there people inside of angels?

A: People and angels are two different kinds of beings altogether. There aren't any people inside angels, nor do people become angels when they die. In cartoons you may see people die and become angels, but that's not what really happens. People have souls. Our souls live forever as spiritual beings. In fact, here's a cool secret: When we get to heaven, we will get to rule the angels!

KEY VERSE: *Don't you realize that we Christians will judge angels? So you should surely be able to resolve ordinary disagreements here on earth. (1 Corinthians 6:3)*

Q 309:
How many angels are in heaven?

A: There's a huge number. We don't know how many angels are in heaven because the Bible doesn't give an exact number. But there are thousands and thousands—as many as God needs. Some people who have seen these large crowds of angels are Elisha and his servant (2 Kings 15-19), the shepherds at Christ's birth (Luke 2:8-14), and the apostle John (Revelation 5:11).

KEY VERSE: *Then I looked again, and I heard the singing of thousands and millions of angels around the throne and the living beings and the elders. (Revelation 5:11)*

Q 310:
How did angels get their wings?

A: Artists often paint angels as having wings, and people have written stories that describe angels as having wings or earning their wings. But the Bible doesn't say that all angels have wings. It does say that angels can fly and that, at times, they appear with wings. But angels don't need wings to fly, like birds or butterflies do. God made sure that they can get where they need to be when they need to be there.

KEY VERSE: *As I was praying, Gabriel, whom I had seen in the earlier vision, came swiftly to me at the time of the evening sacrifice. (Daniel 9:21)*

Q 311:

Can angels die?

A: If angels had bodies like people do, they would die, just like people do. But angels don't have bodies. They're spiritual beings, which means that they have no flesh or blood. Angels are spirits, invisible to us but still very real. Angels aren't born, either—they're created. Because angels don't have bodies, they can't grow old and die. But at the final judgment after the world ends, God will destroy Satan and the bad angels (see Revelation 20:10-14).

KEY VERSES: *[Jesus said,] "Those worthy of being raised from the dead . . . will never die again. In these respects they are like angels. They are children of God raised up to new life."* (Luke 20:36)

Q 312:

Are angels our imaginary friends?

A: Angels are real, not imaginary. Some people think they can talk to angels or that they have special angels who guide them. But the Bible teaches that angels are God's messengers—they serve him and do what he says. Often God tells them to help us. But they're not our friends the way people are or even the way God can be. Angels are God's servants, not people's, but they are as real as God is.

KEY VERSE: *The angel of the LORD guards all who fear him, and he rescues them.* (Psalm 34:7)

NOTE TO PARENTS: A lot of children go through stages when they have imaginary friends, and many children may believe these friends are angels. This can be an ideal time to introduce them to a Friend who will always be with them—Jesus.

What Angels Do

Q 313:
Do angels go to work?

A: The word *angel* means "messenger." Angels don't have jobs where they work for pay the way people do. Instead, they serve God. Angels do nothing but what God wants them to do all the time, without ever getting tired or grumpy. They're happy to do it. They do a lot of work, but they don't "go to work" like your mom or dad does.

KEY VERSE: *Angels are only servants. They are spirits sent from God to care for those who will receive salvation. (Hebrews 1:14)*

Q 314:
Do angels watch television?

A: Angels spend all their time doing what God wants them to do and praising him. They don't take time to relax or do things "just for fun." Keep in mind that angels don't need to relax because they don't get tired. And they enjoy their service to God so much that stopping to do something else wouldn't be "fun" for them anyway. Why would angels want to watch the stuff on TV when they can see the stars up close, fly through the universe doing errands for God, and watch God doing miracles in people's lives? Angels have much better things to do than watch TV—they help us!

KEY VERSE: *Each of these living beings had six wings, and their wings were covered with eyes, inside and out. Day after day and night after night they keep on saying, "Holy, holy, holy is the Lord God Almighty— the one who always was, who is, and who is still to come." (Revelation 4:8)*

Q 315:
Does each angel belong to a person?

A: The Bible says that angels help people, but it doesn't say each angel watches over a certain person like a bodyguard. You may have heard people say that God assigns an angel to watch over each person, but we don't know whether that's true. We only know that God gives angels the job of helping and protecting us. We don't know how they divide that job.

KEY VERSE: *[Jesus said,] "Beware that you don't despise a single one of these little ones. For I tell you that in heaven their angels are always in the presence of my heavenly Father." (Matthew 18:10)*

NOTE TO PARENTS: There is a Jewish tradition that angels look like the person to whom they are assigned.

Q 316:
Are there angels in this room with us?

A: Angels aren't everywhere, so we shouldn't expect them to be with us at every moment, the way God is. But angels *may* be in the room with you right now. Angels *can* be with us without our knowing about it. In the Bible story about Balaam (Numbers 22:21-41), Balaam didn't know there was an angel with him until God allowed him to see the angel. Angels are invisible spirits, so we never know exactly where they are.

KEY VERSES: *As Balaam and two servants were riding along, Balaam's donkey suddenly saw the angel of the LORD standing in the road. (Numbers 22:22-23)*

Q 317:
Do angels stay in the car or fly beside?

A: God watches over us, using angels as his servants. If God wants an angel to be with you in the car, that is where the angel will be. If God wants the angel to be outside the car and moving along at sixty-five miles per hour, that's where the angel will be. Angels go wherever God tells them to go.

KEY VERSES: *I look up to the mountains— does my help come from there? My help comes from the LORD, who made the heavens and the earth! (Psalm 121:1-2)*

Q 318:
Do angels sin?

A: We don't know if angels can sin anymore. Human beings sin because they have a desire to sin. That is because after Adam and Eve disobeyed God in the Garden of Eden, every person ever born has been born a sinner. Angels are not like human beings, and they don't have a desire to sin. So it is not natural for angels to disobey God.

The Bible hints that they may be able to do wrong. Satan was once an angel who was thrown out of heaven because he wanted to take God's place. And other angels sinned then by following Satan. But can other angels sin now? We don't know. We know only that heaven cannot have any sin in it; if it did, it would not be perfect.

KEY VERSES: *If God cannot trust his own angels and has charged some of them with folly, how much less will he trust those made of clay! (Job 4:18-19)*

Q 319:

Can an angel be your friend and tell you that he is your angel?

A: In the Bible, we learn that God wants to be good friends with people. He doesn't give that job to angels. God called Abraham his friend. God spoke to Moses in the way that a man would speak to a friend. That's what he wants with us, too. God's angels do his work, but they don't try to become friends with us because the one looking for our friendship is God. If God has given you an angel, you won't see that angel or talk to him.

KEY VERSE: *I no longer call you servants, because a master doesn't confide in his servants. Now you are my friends, since I have told you everything the Father told me. (John 15:15)*

Q 320:

Do angels just appear for an instant one minute and then disappear?

A: Angels are not ghosts, gods, or superheroes. They serve God and always follow his directions, so they go wherever he says and appear however he tells them to. They appear to us the way they need to appear to do God's work. In the Bible we sometimes read of angels coming and going quickly, but they never did it to show off. In fact, usually no one saw them appear or disappear.

KEY VERSE: *Suddenly, the angel was joined by a vast host of others—the armies of heaven—praising God. (Luke 2:13)*

NOTE TO PARENTS: Some children may ask this question because they think they may have seen an angel, and they want to know if it is possible. Others may ask this because of the way angels are pictured in movies and television shows. Emphasize the fact that the only reliable source for our information about angels is the Bible.

Q 321:

Can an angel be a person to us like a real person?

A: Sometimes angels have made themselves look like humans and have appeared to people. That's how they appeared to Abraham one day. Abraham was sitting outside his tent when three men walked up and greeted him. As far as he knew, they were men, perhaps travelers looking for a place to stay. But in fact, they were angels. That's why the Bible urges us to be kind and neighborly to visitors. You never know when a visitor might be an angel. It is possible that you have met an angel and did not know it. But don't go looking for angels. Angels almost always stay invisible.

KEY VERSE: *Don't forget to show hospitality to strangers, for some who have done this have entertained angels without realizing it! (Hebrews 13:2)*

Bad Angels

Q 322:
What is evil?

A: *Evil* is another word for what is bad or sinful. Evil is anything that goes against God and displeases him. This includes a selfish attitude, bad actions, and ignoring God. Evil entered the world when Adam and Eve sinned in the Garden of Eden. You can read that story in the book of Genesis in the Bible. Ever since then, humans have been born wanting to do what is wrong. That's called our "sinful nature." So evil in the world comes from sinful human beings doing what comes naturally. Evil also comes directly from Satan. He is the enemy of God. The devil tries to get people to turn against God and disobey him. The good news is that we can overcome evil in ourself and in the world by giving our life to Jesus. God is far greater than Satan.

KEY VERSE: *Keep away from every kind of evil. (1 Thessalonians 5:22)*

Q 323:
Who is the devil?

A: The devil is also called Satan. The word *devil* means "liar" or "enemy." Satan used to be an angel. But he wanted to be like God, so he fought against God. God kicked him out of heaven. Ever since then, Satan has worked on earth, trying to defeat God and God's people. He is God's enemy. But God is far stronger than Satan. In the end, Satan will be thrown into hell and suffer forever.

KEY VERSE: *When people keep on sinning, it shows they belong to the Devil, who has been sinning since the beginning. But the Son of God came to destroy these works of the Devil. (1 John 3:8)*

Q 324:
Why is the devil after us?

A: Satan is God's enemy, so he is against anyone who is on God's side. Satan is jealous of our friendship with God—he can't stand it when we spend time with the Lord. And he wants to stop us from obeying God and from doing good. The devil hates God, so he hates us because we love God.

KEY VERSE: *Humble yourselves before God. Resist the Devil, and he will flee from you. (James 4:7)*

Q 325:

Does the devil have claws?

A: The devil can take many forms. When he tempted Adam and Eve, he was a serpent. But remember, Satan is an angel and once was an angel of light. So he probably doesn't look like the funny costumes we see at Halloween (all red, with horns and a pitchfork). Instead, the devil usually tries to look like something good and beautiful. Remember, Satan is the father of lies, so he is usually trying to trick us. He'll say that we don't deserve to be God's children and that we are not forgiven. But always remember that God is much stronger than Satan (it's not even a close contest), and God can keep us safe from Satan.

KEY VERSE: *Even Satan can disguise himself as an angel of light. (2 Corinthians 11:14)*

NOTE TO PARENTS: When children hear about Satan, they may wonder if he can hurt them physically. Of course that's possible, but Satan's attacks are usually much more subtle and focused on keeping people far from God. Usually he tries to get us to center our life around anything but God and to ignore God's commands. Explain to your child that God beats the devil every time and that we can beat Satan too (resist his temptations) if we stay close to God. This means doing what God says, relying on him, and talking to him about everything in our life.

Q 326:

What are demons?

A: Like the devil, demons are bad angels. They followed Satan when he turned against God. Demons are spiritual beings who work and fight against God. Demons are Satan's helpers. There is only one devil, but there are thousands of demons. They are all over the world, trying to keep people from following Christ and obeying God. But God is more powerful than all the demons and the devil put together. God will keep us safe from demons as we trust in him. At the end of time, all demons will be thrown into the lake of fire with the devil.

KEY VERSE: *The King will turn to those on the left and say, "Away with you, you cursed ones, into the eternal fire prepared for the Devil and his demons!" (Matthew 25:41)*

NOTE TO PARENTS: Here are some verses showing that demons are active in the world: Mark 5:9-13; Luke 4:41 and 11:15; Revelation 18:2.

Q 327:

Are demons red with horns and long tails?

A: Sometimes cartoons and Halloween costumes show the devil and demons as red creatures with horns and long tails. But that idea of what Satan looks like came out of someone's imagination, not from the Bible. The devil is a bad angel, and angels don't have physical bodies, so no one knows what Satan looks like. Like other angels, the devil can take different forms if he wants to. But he's not a red-clothed lizard with a pitchfork. He's a real being, living in the spiritual realm.

Satan is God's enemy, but Satan is not as powerful as God. When Satan was created, he was good. But he later rebelled against God and was kicked out of heaven. Jesus called him "a liar and the father of lies." The Bible says he is an "angel of light." So we see that Satan can be very tricky—he tries to make bad look good. His main way of doing this is to lie to us and accuse us, not scare us with the way he looks.

KEY VERSE: *I remind you of the angels who did not stay within the limits of authority God gave them but left the place where they belonged. God has kept them chained in prisons of darkness, waiting for the day of judgment. (Jude 1:6)*

NOTE TO PARENTS: Kids have the idea that the devil is God's equal, like a villain in a superhero cartoon. But the devil is no match for God. God is infinite and all-powerful, while Satan is a created being with limited power.

Q 328:

Will I ever get a demon?

A: It's easy to get the idea from watching television and hearing kids talk that demons can take over people's lives whenever they want. But that's not true. It is true that some people have demons in them. But demons can only enter people who let them and who are not close to God. And never forget, God is much more powerful than Satan or any of the demons. He can protect us.

KEY VERSES: *When the seventy-two disciples returned, they joyfully reported to him, "Lord, even the demons obey us when we use your name!" "Yes," he told them, "I saw Satan falling from heaven as a flash of lightning! And I have given you authority over all the power of the enemy, and you can walk among snakes and scorpions and crush them. Nothing will injure you. But don't rejoice just because evil spirits obey you; rejoice because your names are registered as citizens of heaven." (Luke 10:17-20)*

Q 329:

Why did God make Satan if God knew Satan would make sin?

A: God created all people and all angels with the ability to choose to obey him. God knew that some would choose to obey and some would choose to disobey. Still he created them because he knew it was a good thing to do. God makes everything good, and that includes people and angels who had the choice of whether or not to serve God. Also, Satan did not invent sin, but he tries to get people to choose it. God has allowed Satan to have freedom now, but in the end God will defeat Satan and punish him.

KEY VERSE: *"Yes," [Jesus] told them, "I saw Satan falling from heaven as a flash of lightning!" (Luke 10:18)*

Q 330:

Does the devil have power like God does?

A: The devil has great powers, but he is not even close to being as powerful as God. Satan can perform fake miracles, lie, accuse, twist the truth, tempt, and trick people into doing what is wrong. But he also has many limits: He cannot be everywhere at the same time; he cannot create anything; he is not all-powerful; he cannot read your mind; and he has no power over Jesus.

KEY VERSES: *[Jesus said,] "Dear friends, don't be afraid of those who want to kill you. They can only kill the body; they cannot do any more to you. But I'll tell you whom to fear. Fear God, who has the power to kill people and then throw them into hell." (Luke 12:4-5)*

NOTE TO PARENTS: You can assure your child that the devil has no power over Jesus (John 14:30). That's just one reason it's so great to be Jesus' friend.

Q 331:

What mean things does Satan do to people?

A:

Satan does *not* get to do whatever he wants to do to people. The main thing he does is get us to hurt ourselves and others. Lots of people think that Satan only tempts people to do bad stuff. He does tempt us, but the worst thing he does is lie to us. Satan hates God and does not want us to believe what God says. He wants us to sin. He wants us to believe what is false. He wants us to believe that we are no good. Satan lies to us about our worth and about what really matters so we'll hurt ourselves. The way to see Satan's lies is to know the truth that's in the Bible, God's Word.

KEY VERSE: *Be careful! Watch out for attacks from the Devil, your great enemy. He prowls around like a roaring lion, looking for some victim to devour. (1 Peter 5:8)*

NOTE TO PARENTS: Some children have heard of demon possession and wonder if it can happen to them. They may ask a question like this as a veiled way of asking the more frightening one. But the devil has no power over Jesus. If we have Jesus in our hearts, Satan won't be able to do whatever he wants to with us or make us do anything we don't want to do.

Q 332:

How come the devil wants us to be bad?

A:

Satan's main purpose is to make us part of his kingdom, not just to make us bad. The devil would be quite happy if you lived a good life but never did anything for Jesus. He doesn't want you to serve God. He wants to hurt your faith in God, to make you doubt God's love and goodness. One of the ways he does that is to tempt you to do bad things. If Satan had his way, Christians would just sit around, doing nothing good and telling no one about Jesus.

KEY VERSES: *Perhaps God will change those people's hearts, and they will believe the truth. Then they will come to their senses and escape from the Devil's trap. For they have been held captive by him to do whatever he wants. (2 Timothy 2:25-26)*

NOTE TO PARENTS: Satan's main job is to lie to people, to get non-Christians to stay away from God, and to prevent Christians from serving God. He tries to get us to sin so that we will be alienated from fellowship with God. He plants doubts and tries to convince us that we're not God's children.

Q 333:
Are Satan and Jesus still at war?

A: Jesus and Satan are definitely enemies at war, but Jesus will win. (By the way, when Jesus says to love your enemies, he's not talking about loving the devil. He's talking about loving people.) The devil will do everything in his power to try to stop people from believing in Jesus and living for Jesus. But we don't have to be afraid of Satan because God protects his people against Satan's power. Jesus never loses.

KEY VERSES: *Put on all of God's armor so that you will be able to stand firm against all strategies and tricks of the Devil. For we are not fighting against people made of flesh and blood, but against the evil rulers and authorities of the unseen world, against those mighty powers of darkness who rule this world, and against wicked spirits in the heavenly realms. (Ephesians 6:11-12)*

Q 334:
Will God forgive Satan?

A: God will never forgive Satan because Satan hates God and doesn't want to be forgiven. He doesn't want to have a relationship with God or to live in God's presence. He wants to take God's place. But God has already told us what will happen to Satan—he will be punished by being thrown in the lake of fire (hell), where he will suffer forever for his rebellion.

KEY VERSE: *Then the Devil, who betrayed them, was thrown into the lake of fire that burns with sulfur, joining the beast and the false prophet. There they will be tormented day and night forever and ever. (Revelation 20:10)*

NOTE TO PARENTS: Many people confuse niceness with God's love. They think that a loving God should be nice to everyone, even Satan. But a loving God does not love evil.

Q 335:
Can an evil spirit stop you from going to heaven?

A: If a person has given his or her life to Christ, nothing can stop that person from going to heaven. The only thing the devil can do is invent lies that sound like truth and then hope people believe them. Satan can't send you to hell or keep you from going to heaven, no matter what he does.

KEY VERSES: *I am convinced that nothing can ever separate us from his love. Death can't, and life can't. The angels can't, and the demons can't. Our fears for today, our worries about tomorrow, and even the powers of hell can't keep God's love away. Whether we are high above the sky or in the deepest ocean, nothing in all creation will ever be able to separate us from the love of God that is revealed in Christ Jesus our Lord. (Romans 8:38-39)*

Angels in the Bible

Q 336:
Why was there an angel and a fiery sword guarding the entrance to the Garden of Eden?

A: An angel stood at the entrance to the Garden of Eden to keep Adam and Eve from going back in. God had sent them out of the Garden because they had sinned. Because they disobeyed God, they would never be allowed to live in Eden again.

KEY VERSE: *After banishing them from the garden, the* LORD *God stationed mighty angelic beings to the east of Eden. And a flaming sword flashed back and forth, guarding the way to the tree of life. (Genesis 3:24)*

Q 337:
Why do some angels look like real people?

A: The word *angel* means "messenger," and God sometimes sends these messengers to take messages to people. The Bible describes them as bringing these messages while in the form of human beings. God can send angels to encourage a person, comfort someone, or merely to deliver news. If angels always appeared as blazing towers of fire, they would scare people away. Sometimes God wants angels to frighten people. But at other times he wants his messengers to hide their true identity as angels for a while; then they appear as people.

KEY VERSE: *[Abraham] suddenly noticed three men standing nearby. He got up and ran to meet them, welcoming them by bowing low to the ground. (Genesis 18:2)*

Q 338:
Who was the angel of the Lord?

A: The Bible mentions the angel of the Lord many times. In the desert, when Moses saw the bush that was burning but wasn't burning up, it was the angel of the Lord who spoke to him out of it. Who was this who spoke? Some people think it was a special appearance of God and not actually an angel. But usually the phrase "angel of the Lord" is just a good way to describe an angel. It probably does not refer to one specific angel.

KEY VERSE: *The angel of the* LORD *appeared to him and said, "Mighty hero, the* LORD *is with you!" (Judges 6:12)*

NOTE TO PARENTS: It is important to help your child focus on God, not on angels. The message sender and the message are most important, not the messengers.

Q 339:

Why are some people scared of angels?

A: In the Bible, we read that some people became frightened when angels appeared to them. They were scared because they were amazed at the power and glory of the angels. God is great and holy and awesome, and sometimes angels appear with a lot of light and noise. That can be quite scary. Also, remember that most people have never seen an angel. So when one appears, it is quite normal to be surprised and fearful. Many times when angels appeared, they had to tell the people they visited not to be afraid. God sends angels to us to help us, so we don't need to be afraid of them.

KEY VERSE: *Then the angel of the* LORD *touched the meat and bread with the staff in his hand, and fire flamed up from the rock and consumed all he had brought. And the angel of the* LORD *disappeared. (Judges 6:21)*

Q 340:

Why do some angels have four faces?

A: When the Bible describes angels as having four faces, it is not giving us a picture of what angels actually look like (like a photograph). Remember, angels don't have physical bodies, so they don't have faces the way people do. When a prophet saw an angel with four faces, God was telling him that angels have many abilities—that angels show us several things about God, that they can see in any direction, and that they can serve God in any way needed at any time.

KEY VERSE: *Each of the four cherubim had four faces—the first was the face of an ox, the second was a human face, the third was the face of a lion, and the fourth was the face of an eagle. (Ezekiel 10:14)*

Q 341:

Why did an angel come to Mary?

A: An angel came to Mary to tell her God's message—God wanted Mary to know that she would be the mother of Jesus, God's Son. When Mary heard the news, she was frightened, but she was also very happy. More than anything, she wanted to obey God. And she felt very honored to be Jesus' mother.

KEY VERSES: *In the sixth month of Elizabeth's pregnancy, God sent the angel Gabriel to Nazareth, a village in Galilee, to a virgin named Mary. (Luke 1:26-27)*

NOTE TO PARENTS: This is a good time to let your children know that God is able to show them his plan for their lives. God's plan probably won't be announced by an angel, but God will tell it to them when they seek him.

Q 342:

Why do angels light up and get bright?

A: When the angels came to tell about Jesus' birth, they glowed brightly. But angels don't always appear that way. When angels appeared to Abraham, for example, he thought they were ordinary men and offered them an evening meal (see Genesis 18:1-5). Angels may become bright to reflect God and his glory, or just whenever it is necessary, such as at night (which was when the angels appeared to the shepherds). As God's messengers, it's only fitting that they would light up and get bright because that's how it is in heaven, where they stand with God: "And the city has no need of sun or moon, for the glory of God illuminates the city, and the Lamb is its light" (Revelation 21:23).

KEY VERSE: *Suddenly, an angel of the Lord appeared among them, and the radiance of the Lord's glory surrounded them. They were terribly frightened. (Luke 2:9)*

NOTE TO PARENTS: People have many ideas about angels. Some think angels made regular appearances to biblical folks; in fact, they rarely did. Some think of angels as men with wings, yet many accounts don't mention wings. Some people speak of guardian angels, but the Bible describes angels as God's messengers, not our guardians. And some think too much of angels; Samson's parents tried to worship an angel and were told not to, and Hebrews 1 reminds us that Christ is superior to any angel. Your children may have different ideas about angels. Remember to look to God's Word for the truth.

Q 343:

Why didn't an angel take Jesus off the cross?

A: It was God's will for Jesus to die on the cross. Jesus could have called on thousands of angels to rescue him, but he did not do that because he was dying for us, taking the punishment for our sins. If angels had stepped in and rescued Jesus, he would not have died, and then we would not be forgiven. Jesus' disciple Peter tried to stop Jesus from being arrested, but Jesus told him not to do that because it was God's plan for him to die.

Just before Jesus died, he cried out, "My God, my God, why have you forsaken me?" meaning that God had left him totally alone. No one was there to help him or comfort him, not even the angels. This was part of his suffering for our sins.

KEY VERSES: *[Jesus said,] "Don't you realize that I could ask my Father for thousands of angels to protect us, and he would send them instantly? But if I did, how would the Scriptures be fulfilled that describe what must happen now?" (Matthew 26:53-54)*

Heaven

Q 344:
What is heaven like?

A: The Bible uses some wonderful pictures to tell us what heaven is like. In our world, we think that gold is important because it's so valuable. But in heaven, the streets will be gold—we'll *walk* on it. The best way to picture heaven is to imagine the most exciting and fun place that you've ever been to. Heaven will be like that only much, much better. Jesus told his followers that he was leaving earth to go to heaven to prepare a place for them. He has a special place for us where there is no crying or sadness, and we will be filled with joy.

KEY VERSES: *The throne of God and of the Lamb will be there, and his servants will worship him. And they will see his face. . . . And there will be no night there—no need for lamps or sun— for the Lord God will shine on them. And they will reign forever and ever.* (Revelation 22:3-5)

Q 345:
If we went high enough in the sky, would we find heaven?

A: No one but God knows exactly where heaven is. But the best way we can describe its location is to say it is "up." If we rode a spaceship up, way out into space, we would not find heaven—it can't be seen or found by people. Only God can take us there. And that's what he does, after we die, if we have trusted in Jesus as our Savior.

KEY VERSES: *It was not long after he said this that he was taken up into the sky while they were watching, and he disappeared into a cloud. As they were straining their eyes to see him, two white-robed men suddenly stood there among them. They said, "Men of Galilee, why are you standing here staring at the sky? Jesus has been taken away from you into heaven. And someday, just as you saw him go, he will return!" (Acts 1:9-11)*

Q 346:
Why did God make heaven?

A: God has only one use for heaven, and that is to share it with us. God is everywhere. When we talk about heaven, we are really talking about where God lives. We think of heaven as a place because that's how we describe going to be with God. But remember, God isn't just in one place—he's everywhere!

In the Bible, the word *heaven* can refer to several places: (1) the home or place of God; (2) the new Jerusalem; or (3) "the heavens," or sky. Just before Jesus left the earth, he said he would go and prepare a place for us, a place where we can live with him. Someday he will come back and set it all up for us—he will destroy this world and create a new one. That new world will be for all those who love him. That's the heaven that God will make for all believers to live in forever.

KEY VERSES: *[Jesus said,] "There are many rooms in my Father's home, and I am going to prepare a place for you. If this were not so, I would tell you plainly. When everything is ready, I will come and get you, so that you will always be with me where I am." (John 14:2-3)*

NOTE TO PARENTS: Heaven is one of the Christian's great hopes. It is God's guarantee that the evil, injustice, and cruelty of life here on earth will end and be put right. People without hope in Christ can feel overwhelmed by fear of the future, but Christians need not be afraid. Share this hope with your child.

Q 347:
Is Jesus the only way to heaven?

A: Yes, Jesus is the only way to heaven. He said, "No one can come to the Father except through me." Just as the only right answer to 2+2 is 4, Jesus is the only answer to our need for forgiveness. He is the only one who has the right to take away our sins since he died for us. He is the only one who has the power to take them away since he is God. And he is the only one who can be perfectly fair to every single person, from babies never born to the most wicked person who ever lived, since he is just and merciful. Since Jesus has offered a clear way to heaven, why would anyone look for any other way?

KEY VERSE: *Jesus told him, "I am the way, the truth, and the life. No one can come to the Father except through me." (John 14:6)*

NOTE TO PARENTS: A question like this usually means that other children were discussing their beliefs with your child. Take this time to reassure your child that belief in Christ is the only way to heaven, and take some time to pray with your child for his or her friends.

Q 348:
Are all people nice in heaven?

A: All the people in heaven are nice because everyone there loves God and loves one another. No one will hurt anyone or be mean to anyone in heaven. There will be no crying or pain. There will be no pushing or shoving or name-calling in heaven. The Bible says that in heaven we will know God like he knows us. When we know and understand God and his love, we won't want to hurt anyone ever again.

KEY VERSES: *Don't you know that those who do wrong will have no share in the Kingdom of God? Don't fool yourselves. Those who indulge in sexual sin, who are idol worshipers, adulterers, male prostitutes, homosexuals, thieves, greedy people, drunkards, abusers, and swindlers— none of these will have a share in the Kingdom of God. (1 Corinthians 6:9-10)*

NOTE TO PARENTS: Be careful not to give the impression that being nice gets you into heaven. While all people of God should be kind, not all kind people are people of God. Also, the question behind the question here may involve fear of others—the child wants assurance that in heaven no one will hurt him or her. You can assure your child that there are no bullies in heaven. Heaven is the safest, most wonderful place ever made.

Q 349:
Can you fall out of heaven?

A: People cannot fall out of heaven any more than they can fall out of their own front yard. You may have seen pictures or cartoons that show heaven as a place up in the sky or in the clouds. We don't know where heaven is; we only know that God and Jesus are there. Someday God will make a new earth and a new city called the new Jerusalem, where all his people will live forever. That place will be perfect for us—no dangerous streets, no diseases to catch, nothing to worry about at all. In heaven, you will never hear anyone say, "Be careful!" because you won't have any dangers to be careful about.

KEY VERSE: *I heard a loud shout from the throne, saying, "Look, the home of God is now among his people! He will live with them, and they will be his people. God himself will be with them."(Revelation 21:3)*

NOTE TO PARENTS: This question comes up when children confuse heaven with a physical location, usually one that is up in the sky. They are not able to imagine a spiritual—as opposed to physical—reality, so they can't imagine heaven *not* being a place. They naturally think of heaven as being up because that's where we put it in our descriptions of it.

Q 350:

Is heaven all made up of clouds?

A: Sometimes cartoons and movies show funny pictures of angels standing in clouds. But heaven is not made up of clouds. The Bible does say that clouds surround God's throne, that Jesus was caught up in the clouds, and that when Jesus returns he will come in the clouds. But those are word pictures. They don't mean that heaven is made up of rain clouds. Heaven is God's presence. It's a spiritual place. It's a world invisible to us now but very real just the same.

KEY VERSE: *Then I saw the Son of Man sitting on a white cloud. He had a gold crown on his head and a sharp sickle in his hand. (Revelation 14:14)*

NOTE TO PARENTS: Children pick up a lot of wrong ideas about heaven from cartoons and other popular tales. If you're not sure how to explain what's wrong with a false idea, it's better to say "I don't know how to explain it" than to fall back on a popular fantasy. Sit down with them and read Revelation 21–22 together so they can see what the Bible says about heaven and the new Jerusalem.

Q 351:

Why is heaven so shiny?

A: Heaven shines with the brightness of the glory of God. God is perfect, holy, 100 percent good. Because of that, God shines with light. Many descriptions of heaven mention light and gold because of God's glory.

KEY VERSE: *The one sitting on the throne was as brilliant as gemstones—jasper and carnelian. And the glow of an emerald circled his throne like a rainbow. (Revelation 4:3)*

Q 352:

Are the streets in heaven real gold or just painted with gold?

A: All of heaven is real—none of it is fake. When we get there, it will be the most real, beautiful place we have ever seen. Will even the gold be real? The Bible says that the streets will be paved with gold. This may just be a way of saying that it's a great place to be, like saying "It must be a million degrees out here" to describe a really hot day. Or it may refer to real gold streets running through town. It's hard to know *exactly* what heaven will be like because we really can't understand it now.

Imagine a frog trying to explain life on land to a tadpole. All the descriptions would sound bad—you can't swim, there's no water, etc. The frog can't really tell the tadpole what life on land is like. Only when the tadpole becomes a frog can the tadpole understand. Only when we get to heaven will we know what it will be like. But one thing is for sure: Nothing will be fake!

KEY VERSE: *The twelve gates were made of pearls—each gate from a single pearl! And the main street was pure gold, as clear as glass. (Revelation 21:21)*

Q 353:

Does God have angels watching over heaven so demons can't get in?

A: God will let no evil at all into heaven—no sin, no hurting, no demons. Life in heaven will be *safe*. In fact, heaven is the safest place anywhere—perfectly safe all the time. No one in heaven is afraid of anything, and no one there ever gets hurt.

KEY VERSES: *All the nations will bring their glory and honor into the city. Nothing evil will be allowed to enter. (Revelation 21:26-27)*

NOTE TO PARENTS: Every child craves safety and fears danger. A safe place is a happy place, and conversely, a dangerous place isn't. In order to be happy, a child needs to feel safe. A question like this one, therefore, applies a child's test of happiness to heaven: If it isn't safe, then it can't be happy. You can reassure your child that no place is safer than heaven.

Q 354:

Where did God live before heaven was made?

A: God has always lived in heaven because heaven is the place where God is. God has made a place for us where he is—so that is heaven for us. Wherever God is, there is heaven.

KEY VERSE: *Pray like this: Our Father in heaven, may your name be honored. (Matthew 6:9)*

NOTE TO PARENTS: Sometimes a child's question comes from a faulty assumption about God. You can use questions like this to explain how God is different from us.

Q 355:

Does Jesus live with God in heaven, or does he live by himself?

A: When Jesus left the earth, he went to heaven to live with God the Father. That's where he is right now. He sits at the Father's right hand, the place of highest honor. The Bible says he talks to God about us (1 John 2:1).

KEY VERSE: *[Jesus said,] "Now I am departing the world; I am leaving them behind and coming to you. Holy Father, keep them and care for them—all those you have given me—so that they will be united just as we are."(John 17:11)*

Q 356:

Why can't we go to heaven and just see it and then come back?

A: This question is like asking, "Can I become a teenager and then come back to my age right now?" It's impossible because you have to *grow* into your teens; you can't simply jump there and back. In the same way, heaven is more than a place you can visit. It's a time at the end of life, and God has to make us ready to go there. In fact, we have to change in order to go there. We know that heaven exists because God has told us so in his Word, the Bible. And Jesus promised to "prepare a place" so that we can live with him forever (John 14:2). Once we get there, we won't want to come back.

KEY VERSE: *All that I know now is partial and incomplete, but [when the end comes] I will know everything completely, just as God knows me now. (1 Corinthians 13:12)*

Q 357:

How long does it take to get to heaven from here?

A: It happens in an instant. It's like opening your eyes—you're suddenly there. That's because heaven isn't a faraway place but is the place where God is. He just takes you there. The Bible says that when Jesus comes back, he will change us "in the blinking of an eye."

KEY VERSE: *It will happen in a moment, in the blinking of an eye, when the last trumpet is blown. For when the trumpet sounds, the Christians who have died will be raised with transformed bodies. And then we who are living will be transformed so that we will never die. (1 Corinthians 15:52)*

Q 358:

What if I don't want to leave my friends and family to go to heaven?

A: It's OK to not want to go to heaven right now. God has given you a place to enjoy right here and now—your home and your family and friends. You don't have to go to heaven right away.

But heaven will be a happy place, not a lonely or a sad place. Once you're in heaven you won't feel afraid of it—you will be glad that you are there. And if your family and friends know Jesus, too, you all will be in heaven together. You will be together with your family again.

KEY VERSE: *Our aim is to please him always, whether we are here in this body or away from this body. (2 Corinthians 5:9)*

NOTE TO PARENTS: Don't be appalled if your child says he or she is afraid of heaven or doesn't want to go. Some kids fear going to heaven because it seems faraway and mysterious. All they can imagine is being taken away from their families and going to a cold and impersonal place where they don't know anyone. Assure your child that heaven is a warm and happy place.

When People Die

Q 359:
Does God put down a ladder to bring us to heaven?

A: God takes us to heaven as soon as we die— immediately. God doesn't need a ladder or an airplane or anything else; we will just be there with him. The Bible says that Jesus is preparing a place for us. Through faith in him, we can have forgiveness of sins. Then, when it comes time for God to take us to heaven, he will do it— will take us to live with him in his home forever.

KEY VERSE: *We are always confident, even though we know that as long as we live in these bodies we are not at home with the Lord. . . . We would rather be away from these bodies, for then we will be at home with the Lord. (2 Corinthians 5:6, 8)*

NOTE TO PARENTS: This question can mean two things: (1) What method does God use to transport us to heaven? and (2) How can a person be forgiven and go to heaven? Make sure you know which question your child means. In Jesus' story about the rich man and Lazarus (Luke 16:22), he mentioned that the angels carried Lazarus to heaven. Angels may be involved in the process.

Q 360:
When I die, will I become an angel?

A: Angels are spiritual beings created by God. They are different from human beings. You are a spiritual being, too. In other words, you have a soul and will live forever and can know God. But you are also a physical being. You live on earth and have a physical body. When you die, you will leave your physical body behind and will be given a glorified or perfect body in heaven. We don't know exactly what our glorified bodies will be like, but we know that people in heaven will be able to recognize us. One thing is for sure, we don't become angels when we die. In fact, angels will serve us in heaven. Wow!

KEY VERSE: *Don't you realize that we Christians will judge angels? So you should surely be able to resolve ordinary disagreements here on earth. (1 Corinthians 6:3)*

NOTE TO PARENTS: According to Matthew 26:53 and other passages, there are thousands of angels.

Q 361:
Why do people die?

A: People die because of sin. When God created the first human beings, they weren't supposed to die. They would never grow old or wear out. But then they disobeyed God, and sin and death entered the world. From that point on, every person born has been born a sinner into a sinful world. With sin came death, and so plants, animals, and people started to die. *Every* person has to die. But people can live eternally in heaven with God if they trust in Christ and ask God to forgive their sins. In heaven we aren't broken anymore. There is no sickness or pain or dying there.

KEY VERSES: *The LORD God gave him this warning: "You may freely eat any fruit in the garden except fruit from the tree of the knowledge of good and evil. If you eat of its fruit, you will surely die." (Genesis 2:16-17)*

NOTE TO PARENTS: This question often comes up when a relative or a pet dies. It is a good question and an important one for you to answer because it creates a "teachable moment." Answering it will probably lead to several more questions about salvation, eternal life, and heaven, so be prepared!

Q 362:
Does your body stay in the grave when you go to heaven?

A: The body you have here on earth is a physical, imperfect, short-term holding place for your soul. It's not made to last. When it's dead, it will decay. The real you is your soul, not your body. But in heaven you will be given a new body, a body that will last forever. This is known as the resurrection. The physical body will die, but the spiritual body will last forever. What happens to your body on earth or in the grave will not affect your eternal life in any way.

KEY VERSE: *You will not leave my soul among the dead or allow your godly one to rot in the grave. (Psalm 16:10)*

Q 363:

Will I go to heaven when I die?

A: Every person who trusts in Jesus gets to go to heaven. If you have asked Jesus to take away your sins, then you will go to heaven, too. That's God's promise. And nothing can take away God's promise of heaven. When you die as a Christian, you go straight to live with God—you don't need to be afraid of dying.

KEY VERSE: *[Jesus said,] "This is the will of God, that I should not lose even one of all those he has given me, but that I should raise them to eternal life at the last day." (John 6:39)*

NOTE TO PARENTS: Many children have a profound fear of death. They may have nightmares about it. But they may also hesitate to talk about it with you, so you may not hear them ask about it. Reassure them: Jesus defeated death. He made it possible for us to live forever in heaven. We don't need to fear death.

Q 364:

Is there any other place you can go to besides heaven or hell when you die?

A: You may have heard people talk about purgatory, limbo, or some other in-between place where people go after they die. But the Bible does not teach anything about a place like that. The Bible does teach, however, that death is the final cutoff point. People do not have a second chance after they die. There is no opportunity after death to undo the bad things a person did while alive. The Bible also makes it very clear that Christians immediately go to be with God after they die.

KEY VERSE: *Jesus replied, "I assure you, today you will be with me in paradise." (Luke 23:43)*

Q 365:

Can God take you to heaven if you're not dead yet?

A: God can do anything. He can take a person to heaven anytime he likes, even if that person has not died. And in fact, the Bible tells about two people who had that privilege: Enoch and Elijah. God took them directly to heaven before they died. The Bible also tells us that someday Jesus will come back and take all his people to heaven, even those who have not died yet.

KEY VERSE: *[Enoch] enjoyed a close relationship with God throughout his life. Then suddenly, he disappeared because God took him. (Genesis 5:24)*

Q 366:

Why are cemeteries so creepy?

A: Death is a scary thing because it is final. After a person dies, that person does not come back to earth ever again. It's not like going on a trip and then coming back. It's like going on a trip and *never* coming back.

Death also scares us because it can happen so suddenly. One second the person is here, awake and talking. Then he or she is dead, unable to talk or live with us ever again.

That's why cemeteries are so creepy. No one wants to die, and cemeteries are where dead bodies are buried. Also, television and movies show cemeteries as places where ghosts and other spooky things hang out. Because most people fear death, a cemetery can be a scary place. But Christians don't have to be afraid of death because they know that they will go to heaven when they die and that scary things are just made up by people who make movies and TV shows.

KEY VERSES: *I live in eager expectation and hope that I will never do anything that causes me shame, but that I will always be bold for Christ, as I have been in the past, and that my life will always honor Christ, whether I live or I die. For to me, living is for Christ, and dying is even better. (Philippians 1:20-21)*

NOTE TO PARENTS: Help your children develop a healthy attitude about death. Say positive things as you pass a cemetery; don't jokingly say things that foster a fear of death.

Q 367:

Why did God take Grandpa to heaven?

A: We don't like to think about this fact, but it is true—eventually every person has to die. Sometimes people die when they are young, through accidents, diseases, or other tragedies. But even the healthiest person will die someday. As we get older, our bodies get weaker and weaker and then finally wear out.

No one wants a grandfather or grandmother to die, but that's part of God's plan right now: We get old and our bodies die. Certainly it is better to be with God in heaven than to be on earth. If our grandparents believe in Jesus, then someday we will see them again.

KEY VERSE: *The LORD's loved ones are precious to him; it grieves him when they die. (Psalm 116:15)*

Q 368:

How can Jesus resurrect bodies that have been burnt to ashes?

A: God will have no trouble finding everyone's molecules. He created people in the first place, so why wouldn't he be able to put them back together? It doesn't matter what happens to a person's body—God can put anyone back together. Whether the person's body was burned, separated for organ donations, or decayed in the ground, God will make it new and immortal. The earth and sea will give up their dead, and God will resurrect us despite the fact that we "returned to dust."

KEY VERSES: *Since we believe that Jesus died and was raised to life again, we also believe that when Jesus comes, God will bring back with Jesus all the Christians who have died. . . . For the Lord himself will come down from heaven with a commanding shout, with the call of the archangel, and with the trumpet call of God. First, all the Christians who have died will rise from their graves. Then, together with them, we who are still alive and remain on the earth will be caught up in the clouds to meet the Lord in the air and remain with him forever.* (1 Thessalonians 4:14, 16-17)

Q 369:

Why do people believe in reincarnation?

A: Reincarnation is the belief that people come back to life after they die. They never really die once and for all but keep coming back as something else or as someone else. This belief says that people come back to earth as different creatures after they die.

Some people believe in reincarnation because their religion, such as Hinduism or Buddhism, teaches it. Some believe in reincarnation because they want to believe that they will get a second chance on earth to be better people. But the Bible does not teach reincarnation. The Bible teaches that we have one life and then we face judgment.

KEY VERSE: *It is destined that each person dies only once and after that comes judgment.* (Hebrews 9:27)

NOTE TO PARENTS: Some children misinterpret the term *born again* to mean reincarnation. You can explain that being born again means to be born into God's family, not to come back as a different person later. Being born again happens when we trust in Jesus Christ as Savior. It's not reincarnation.

Q 370:
What's a casket?

A: A casket is a metal or wooden box in which a dead body is placed. Usually a casket is buried in the ground in a cemetery. Putting a body in a casket is a very old custom and is a way of showing respect for the dead person. Also, it is part of the custom of mourning the person's death.

KEY VERSES: *The Hittites replied to Abraham, "Certainly, for you are an honored prince among us. It will be a privilege to have you choose the finest of our tombs so you can bury her there." (Genesis 23:5-6)*

Q 371:
Why do people cry at funerals?

A: People cry at funerals because they are very sad. They miss the person who has died. Even when people know that their family member or friend is now in heaven with Jesus, they cry because they miss their loved one. The purpose of funerals is to say good-bye to the dead person, to show respect for the person and his or her family, to cry and be sad, and to remember what the person meant to everyone.

KEY VERSES: *Then Jesus wept. The people who were standing nearby said, "See how much he loved him." (John 11:35-36)*

Q 372:
Why do they put stones on people's graves?

A: A gravestone or metal plate on a grave marks the place where the person's body is buried. After a person has died, friends and family will sometimes go to the cemetery, put flowers on the grave, and think about that person. The stone helps them find the grave. They can go there and remember the person instead of forgetting. Just think what it would be like if a family member was buried and no one marked where the grave was.

KEY VERSE: *[Moses] was buried in a valley near Beth-peor in Moab, but to this day no one knows the exact place. (Deuteronomy 34:6)*

Q 373:

Why do we give flowers to people after they have died?

A: Many people bring flowers to funerals, wakes, and gravesides. It looks as though they are giving something to someone who can't enjoy the gift. Why would they do that? It is to show respect and to show that they miss the person. It's like saying, "I wish you were still here. I love you. I miss you." Also, flowers remind us of life. Most important, people give flowers to honor the person and the family of the person who has died. Flowers on a casket or on a grave say, "This person was important to me."

KEY VERSE: *When others are happy, be happy with them. If they are sad, share their sorrow.* *(Romans 12:15)*

Q 374:

If I die when I'm a kid, will I miss out on doing fun things on earth?

A: When people die, their life on earth ends. That's true no matter how young or old a person is when he or she dies. But do these people miss their "fun" on earth? Are they up in heaven being sad about all the fun things they didn't get to do? Not at all! Living in the presence of God is the most enjoyable thing a person can do. It is what we were created for.

Don't worry—God has a wonderful plan for your life here on earth. Enjoy the life God has given you. You won't be sorry you went to heaven when the time comes for you to go!

KEY VERSES: *I'm torn between two desires: Sometimes I want to live, and sometimes I long to go and be with Christ. That would be far better for me, but it is better for you that I live.* *(Philippians 1:23-24)*

Living in Heaven

Q 375:
Will I be able to play games in heaven?

A: Heaven will be more exciting than you could possibly imagine. Will that mean playing lots of games? Probably not—you can get bored with games, and life in heaven will *never* be boring. You will never get tired of what you're doing there. The Bible says that you will always be happy in heaven. If you think games are fun, you should see what's coming next—it will be *much* better than playing games all the time.

It's OK if you don't understand this. Trying to understand life in heaven is like trying to understand how fun an amusement park will be before you get there. How can you really know what to expect? You can't. All you can do is hear the descriptions ("It's great! It's wonderful! You can ride on the Super Collosal Machine!"). Until you go, you won't *really* be able to get excited about it. But once you're there, *wow!*

KEY VERSE: *Now we see things imperfectly as in a poor mirror, but then we will see everything with perfect clarity. All that I know now is partial and incomplete, but then I will know everything completely, just as God knows me now. (1 Corinthians 13:12)*

NOTE TO PARENTS: The tadpole analogy (see Question 380) is useful for questions about boredom in heaven.

Q 376:
Is there a McDonald's in heaven?

A: No. In heaven, we won't need people to work to make us food. Our bodies will be different. They will be "glorified," or perfect, bodies. We don't know if we will eat there or what kind of food we will need. God will make sure that we have everything we need. Heaven will be fun. It will be great!

KEY VERSES: *Still they stood there doubting, filled with joy and wonder. Then he asked them, "Do you have anything here to eat?" They gave him a piece of broiled fish, and he ate it as they watched. (Luke 24:41-43)*

NOTE TO PARENTS: Children are concerned about food. Food is important to them, and they don't want to be hungry. Curiosity about what they will be eating in heaven may underlie questions like these.

Q 377:

Will there be toys in heaven?

A: We like toys because we have such fun with them. But we can get tired of toys, too. For example, you don't play with your baby toys anymore. That's because you outgrew them and got tired of them. God will have just the right kind of toys for you in heaven. You will enjoy heaven even more than your favorite toys.

KEY VERSE: *It's like this: When I was a child, I spoke and thought and reasoned as a child does. But when I grew up, I put away childish things. (1 Corinthians 13:11)*

Q 378:

Will my pet go to heaven when it dies?

A: We don't know what happens to animals when they die, but God does, and we know his plan is good. Sometimes we may get the idea that animals think and understand as we do. But God created animals different from people. Animals don't have souls or think as we do, so they can't enjoy God the way we can. Here on earth, pets are fun to play with and animals are interesting to watch. Only God knows if pets will join us in heaven.

KEY VERSES: *God made the wild animals according to their kinds, the livestock according to their kinds, and all the creatures that move along the ground according to their kinds. And God saw that it was good. Then God said, "Let us make man in our image, in our likeness, and let them rule over the fish of the sea and the birds of the air, over the livestock, over all the earth, and over all the creatures that move along the ground." So God created man in his own image, in the image of God he created him; male and female he created them. (Genesis 1:25-27)*

NOTE TO PARENTS: This question may be a way of testing the reality of heaven. A child's world is tied to his or her pet, and the death of a pet naturally raises the question of what happens to it afterward. But if you're not sure how to answer, don't be afraid of saying you don't know. The answer may not be as important as helping your child deal with losing a pet. When we get to heaven, God will give us everything we need to be filled with unspeakable joy.

Q 379:

Will I have my same name in heaven?

A: When we get to heaven, we will see our friends and family members who have died and gone there before us. They will recognize us, and we will know them. The Bible says that when we trust Christ as Savior, our names are written in the "Book of Life." That's God's list of who gets into heaven.

KEY VERSE: *All who are victorious will be clothed in white. I will never erase their names from the Book of Life, but I will announce before my Father and his angels that they are mine. (Revelation 3:5)*

185

Q 380:

In heaven, we don't just sing and worship all day, do we?

A: In heaven, we will be happy all the time. Heaven will be a place made just for us. We read in the Bible about angels singing and praising God day and night, and we can't imagine doing that all the time. But remember that they are singing because they are *glad*. They aren't bored, tired, or old. They are expressing happiness and joy. God is the happiest person in the universe, and living in heaven means being there with him doing the same thing. Life with God is happy, joyful, and cool.

Imagine that you're a tadpole. All your life you've lived only in the water. You know that someday you'll become a frog and you'll get to live on land. But until you become a frog, you will have no idea what life on land is like. And if anyone tries to explain it to you, it won't sound very appealing because there's no water and you can't swim. That's the way it is with heaven. Until we get to heaven, it will be hard for us to understand what's so great about it. But once we're there, we'll be perfect and we'll have new bodies, and that will make all the difference.

KEY VERSES: *You have turned my mourning into joyful dancing. You have taken away my clothes of mourning and clothed me with joy, that I might sing praises to you and not be silent. O Lord my God, I will give you thanks forever! (Psalm 30:11-12)*

NOTE TO PARENTS: Children can understand singing for joy by thinking of songs they sing when they're happy or celebrating. What they feel when singing those songs is like what they will feel in heaven—only better!

Q 381:

What will I do up there with no friends?

A: If your friends believe in Jesus, they will be in heaven with you, and you will have a *great* time together. Jesus is preparing a place for us; he won't keep us apart from each other. And we'll make new friends in heaven, too. If you aren't sure whether your friends will go to heaven, tell them about Jesus. If they put their faith in Christ, too, you will all be there together.

You don't have to worry—heaven *won't* be boring. Remember, God created butterflies, sunsets, electrical storms, mountains, the Grand Canyon, and all of nature. He will give us so much fun, beauty, and joy in heaven that we can hardly imagine it now.

KEY VERSE: *[Jesus said,] "Father, I want these whom you've given me to be with me, so they can see my glory. You gave me the glory because you loved me even before the world began! (John 17:24)*

Q 382:

Will I still have feelings in heaven?

A: Yes! People in heaven have lots of feelings—all good ones. People in heaven are filled with joy! You will be busy smiling, whistling, and singing for joy. When you are not doing that, you will be kicking your heels and jumping. Occasional high fives will interrupt the joviality. The timing will be perfect, and you'll love it. You will be happy because you will be with God and because all sin, death, and sadness will be gone forever. And think of the joy when you see your family and friends. Heaven will be a place of great joy and gladness—great feelings all around.

KEY VERSE: *You have shown me the way of life, and you will give me wonderful joy in your presence. (Acts 2:28)*

Q 383:

Can we still have birthdays in heaven?

A: The great thing about birthdays is the parties. In heaven, we won't grow old, but we will have lots of parties. The biggest party will be the celebration of "the wedding feast of the Lamb," when we celebrate our new life in heaven with Jesus. It will be ten times more fun than any birthday you've ever had.

The things we enjoy here on earth are like appetizers. They give us only a taste of what heaven will be like. The things you enjoy here on earth will only be better and greater in the presence of God.

KEY VERSE: *The angel said, "Write this: Blessed are those who are invited to the wedding feast of the Lamb." And he added, "These are true words that come from God." (Revelation 19:9)*

NOTE TO PARENTS: Heaven lacks a lot of the things that kids enjoy—toys, television, and games. This confuses many kids because they think they need these things to be happy. They don't realize that enjoyment of kid things depends on their being kids. In heaven they won't be kids anymore—they'll be perfect, so they'll enjoy different things. What will make us happy in heaven will match who we will be *then,* and that's something we can't see very well right now (1 Corinthians 13:12).

Q 384:

Will you see your great-great-grandparents in heaven?

A: All people who have ever believed in Jesus, no matter how long ago, will be in heaven. If your great-great-grandparents believed in Jesus, they will be there. Even though you have never met your great-great-grandparents, you will be able to meet them there. But not every person who ever lived has believed, so not every person will be there.

KEY VERSE: *God has reserved a priceless inheritance for his children. It is kept in heaven for you, pure and undefiled, beyond the reach of change and decay. (1 Peter 1:4)*

NOTE TO PARENTS: This kind of question could mean, "In heaven, will we see all people who have ever lived?" The answer is, "No, only those who have trusted in Christ as Savior." Or it could mean that your child is curious about past relatives whom he or she has never met. If great-great-grandparents and others were believers, this would be a great time to tell about your family's heritage of faith.

Q 385:

Will we look like we do now in heaven?

A: No one knows *exactly* what we will look like in heaven, but the Bible makes it clear that we will have new bodies—resurrected and perfect bodies. We will be different, but we surely won't be strangers to each other. We will be able to recognize each other and enjoy each other's company, just as we do here on earth—except it will be better because we'll never fight!

KEY VERSE: *He will take these weak mortal bodies of ours and change them into glorious bodies like his own, using the same mighty power that he will use to conquer everything, everywhere. (Philippians 3:21)*

Q 386:

When we go to heaven, will we get snarls in our hair?

A: Nope. Heaven is a place of happiness and joy—a place of no pain. We won't have irritations and frustrations. Also, we'll have new, "glorified" bodies. Our hair won't be the kind that snarls.

KEY VERSE: *Our earthly bodies, which die and decay, will be different when they are resurrected, for they will never die. (1 Corinthians 15:42)*

Q 387:

Will people have scars in heaven?

A: In heaven, everyone will have new bodies, and no one will feel any pain. There will be no physical or mental disabilities. Everybody will be able to sing, think, talk, run, and play . . . without growing tired. People may have scars, but they won't look bad.

KEY VERSE: *Our bodies now disappoint us, but when they are raised, they will be full of glory. They are weak now, but when they are raised, they will be full of power. (1 Corinthians 15:43)*

NOTE TO PARENTS: The pattern for heaven should be our pattern, too: to affirm people as they are, not reject them for being different or "imperfect."

Q 388:

Will we eat in heaven?

A: We will be *able* to eat in heaven, but we won't *have* to eat to live, as we do on earth. Jesus said he would eat with his people there. But no one in heaven will ever go hungry.

KEY VERSE: *In Jerusalem, the LORD Almighty will spread a wonderful feast for everyone around the world. It will be a delicious feast of good food, with clear, well-aged wine and choice beef. (Isaiah 25:6)*

Q 389:

Will we wear clothes in heaven?

A: The Bible says that people will wear clothes in heaven—dazzling white robes. But people won't wear clothes for the same reasons that they wear them here. On earth, people wear clothes to protect them from bad weather, to cover their nakedness, and to impress other people. We won't need clothes to protect us from the cold because it won't be cold. We won't need raincoats because it won't be stormy. And we won't need special designer clothes because we won't need to show off.

KEY VERSE: *Blessed are those who wash their robes so they can enter through the gates of the city and eat the fruit from the tree of life. (Revelation 22:14)*

Q 390:
Do babies stay in heaven until they are born?

A: Whenever God creates a person, he creates a new soul, a new person who never existed before. Babies do not live in heaven waiting to be born here on earth. The Bible teaches that God forms each one of us inside our mother's womb. Every baby—even one that is not yet born—is one of God's precious creations!

KEY VERSE: *You made all the delicate, inner parts of my body and knit me together in my mother's womb. (Psalm 139:13)*

Q 391:
Do people walk in heaven, or do they fly to where they need to be?

A: We don't know for sure how people get around in heaven. The Bible does say that angels fly, but it never says that people have wings or that they fly around, not even in heaven. Usually descriptions of people in heaven talk about them standing or walking.

KEY VERSES: *These are the ones coming out of the great tribulation. They washed their robes in the blood of the Lamb and made them white. That is why they are standing in front of the throne of God, serving him day and night. (Revelation 7:14-15)*

Q 392:
Does Jesus come into your house in heaven for a visit?

A: Jesus always visits those who let him in. On earth, Jesus often visited his friends Mary, Martha, and Lazarus. In his early ministry, he went to a friend's wedding. And just before Jesus went to the cross, he told his disciples that he would eat and drink with them in heaven. Jesus will visit all of his friends in heaven, including you. Just think—we will finally get to see him face-to-face!

KEY VERSE: *[Jesus said,] "Mark my words—I will not drink wine again until the day I drink it new with you in my Father's Kingdom." (Matthew 26:29)*

NOTE TO PARENTS: Above all else, God seeks a relationship with us. That is why he created us, that is why he sent his Son to die for us, and that is why he is preparing a place for us. Remind your child that *being with us* matters very much to God—now, as well as in heaven.

Q 393:

What would happen if I accidentally swore in heaven?

A: You will *never* accidentally swear in heaven because no one in heaven can sin. You cannot do wrong in God's presence. Jesus will make all of his people perfect, like himself, so you won't *want* to sin. Messing up is one thing you'll never have to worry about again.

KEY VERSE: *Yes, dear friends, we are already God's children, and we can't even imagine what we will be like when Christ returns. But we do know that when he comes we will be like him, for we will see him as he really is. (1 John 3:2)*

NOTE TO PARENTS: The real concern here may be that your children do not feel they are good enough to get into heaven. Assure them that if they believe in Jesus as their Savior, they will go to heaven. Also, as they pray and trust God to help them, they will become more like Jesus.

Q 394:

Do you pray in heaven or just talk to God face-to-face?

A: We will be able to talk to God face-to-face. (Moses talked with God face-to-face on earth, but that was unusual.) Remember, God wants to be our friend. Right now we are separated a little, and we have to pray to talk to God. But that relationship will be made perfect in heaven. Finally we will be able to go right up to God and talk to him, just as we have always wanted to do. In heaven, we will see God just as he is.

KEY VERSE: *Now we see things imperfectly as in a poor mirror, but then we will see everything with perfect clarity. All that I know now is partial and incomplete, but then I will know everything completely, just as God knows me now. (1 Corinthians 13:12)*

Q 395:

Will we live with angels in heaven?

A: We will live with God and the angels. But the angels will not be equal to us there. The angels are God's messengers, his servants. Part of the angels' job is to help us here on earth. Our friends and family in heaven will be the people we have known here on earth and other Christians who have died. Remember, angels aren't people; they're God's servants.

KEY VERSE: *You have come to Mount Zion, to the city of the living God, the heavenly Jerusalem, and to thousands of angels in joyful assembly. (Hebrews 12:22)*

Q 396:
Will God be with me all the time in heaven?

A: Yes! In heaven, you will get to go right up to God and talk to him. God will be with you all the time, and you will be with him. God will be your friend, and you will be his. Getting to be with God will be one of heaven's greatest joys.

KEY VERSE: *I heard a loud shout from the throne, saying, "Look, the home of God is now among his people! He will live with them, and they will be his people. God himself will be with them." (Revelation 21:3)*

Q 397:
Will there be a Bible "Hall of Fame" in heaven?

A: Some people think that heaven is just like earth, with shopping malls, schools, athletic stadiums, and airports. But heaven is very different from earth. The focus in heaven is on God, not people. We will praise and worship God because no one's fame can compare with his.

People *will* be honored in heaven, however. The Bible says that believers will receive rewards for their good deeds. The greatest reward, of course, is just getting there. God gives salvation—a free gift made possible by Jesus' death on the cross—to all who put their faith in Christ. He will give other rewards to every believer who does good deeds for God on earth. Everyone's service will be rewarded.

KEY VERSE: *[Jesus said,] "See, I am coming soon, and my reward is with me, to repay all according to their deeds." (Revelation 22:12)*

NOTE TO PARENTS: It's easy to confuse rewards for good service with salvation by works. We receive our salvation by faith, not good deeds!

Q 398:
Can we see people from the Bible in heaven?

A: Everyone who has ever trusted in Christ for salvation will be in heaven, and that includes all the Bible people who ever believed. You will get to know them, too. They can be your new friends!

KEY VERSE: *God had far better things in mind for us that would also benefit them, for they can't receive the prize at the end of the race until we finish the race. (Hebrews 11:40)*

NOTE TO PARENTS: When reading Bible stories, remind your children that the stories are true and that the Bible heroes are living now with God. This should help to make the stories more real.

Q 399:

Is there church in heaven?

A: In heaven, we won't have churches like the ones we have on earth because everyone in heaven will be a believer in Christ, and all of us will be together in God's presence. So we will be able to talk, laugh, pray, and have fun together all the time. We won't need church buildings either. We will see Jesus in person, so we will be able to worship him all the time, not just an hour a week. There will also be angels in heaven worshiping with us. We don't know exactly what worship will be like, but it won't include announcements, the offering, Bible reading, and a sermon. It will be pure joy. Think about it—we will be able to talk directly to Moses, David, Paul, and all the other faithful and famous servants of God!

KEY VERSE: *We are looking forward to the new heavens and new earth he has promised, a world where everyone is right with God. (2 Peter 3:13)*

NOTE TO PARENTS: Be careful of telling kids that in heaven we get to worship God all the time. They may think that they'll be singing hymn after hymn and listening to sermon after sermon for all eternity. Be sure to explain that heaven will be fun and exciting—better than Disney World, Nintendo, or any party they can imagine.

Q 400:

Will I have a bedroom up in heaven?

A: Jesus told his disciples that where his Father lived there were many homes. But we don't know exactly what that place or "house" will be like. In heaven, we will have what the Bible calls glorified bodies. In other words, our bodies will be different from what they are now. We will be able to recognize others, but we won't need food or sleep. We won't have bedrooms in heaven like the ones we have here; instead, we'll have very special places, each one prepared for us by Jesus. And we won't have to worry about the weather—the temperature will always be perfect. We won't even have to be concerned about what to wear—God will give us clothes. Heaven is a wonderful place, filled with joy, love, and happiness!

KEY VERSE: *[Jesus said,] "There are many rooms in my Father's home, and I am going to prepare a place for you. If this were not so, I would tell you plainly." (John 14:2)*

NOTE TO PARENTS: Children always have questions about heaven. The questions listed above are good and indicate that they are thinking in terms of *things* and *personal security.* Let them know that heaven is a place of massive joy—they will like being there more than anywhere else. We don't know what will happen in heaven—only that it will be wonderful!

Questions
Kids Ask

Right and
Wrong

5

Right and Wrong, Right?

Q 401:

How can people find out what is right and wrong?

A: We can know what is right by knowing God. God is perfect and always right, so everything good matches what God is like. For example, we know it is right to be loving and kind because God is love. Everything that is wrong goes against what God is like. We can learn what God is like by reading his Word, the Bible. The Bible helps us know how to be like God and act as he does. God has given us rules and guidance for how to live. Those are also in the Bible. When we read rules such as the Ten Commandments, we know how God wants us to act.

KEY VERSE: *Be careful to obey all my commands so that all will go well with you and your children, because you will be doing what pleases the LORD your God. (Deuteronomy 12:28)*

NOTE TO PARENTS: A child may use this question as an excuse to disobey you or to be disrespectful to teachers and others in authority. "How do you *know* that such and such is wrong?" God determines what is right and wrong, but he also tells children to honor and obey their parents and to respect the authorities. Encourage your children to trust God and his Word because he wants the best for us.

Q 402:

Why do people do wrong when they know that it's wrong?

A: People do wrong because of their sinful nature. Many, many years ago, God created the first man and woman, Adam and Eve. But soon afterward, Adam and Eve committed the first sin—they disobeyed God. You can read about it in Genesis 3:1-24. Before then, the world was perfect, with no sin, evil, or wrongdoing. But when Adam and Eve disobeyed God, sin entered the world, and ever since then everyone has been born with a sinful nature. In other words, people find it *natural* to do what is wrong; they find it easy to choose to do wrong. This is a weakness that all people have. Sometimes people will do something even when they know it is wrong because they are afraid of what others will say if they do right. They might feel pressured by friends to do wrong. They might have a bad habit. It's not that everything they do is wrong; they can do good and make right choices, too. But they find it easy to make the wrong choices. People still have the same choice today that Adam and Eve had. We can trust God and follow his way, or we can decide for ourselves what is right and wrong and do it our own way, the wrong way.

KEY VERSE: *When Adam sinned, sin entered the entire human race. Adam's sin brought death, so death spread to everyone, for everyone sinned. (Romans 5:12)*

NOTE TO PARENTS: Give hope that your child *can* do right; the fact that there is sin doesn't mean a person *has* to do wrong. This may be the time to explain that Jesus came to die for us and that through faith in him we can be free from the power of sin in our lives.

Q 403:

Why is it wrong to be bad?

A: It is wrong to be bad because God created us to do good. Think about your bicycle. It was made for riding, for helping you go from one place to another faster and easier than walking. If you tried to use your bike to scrape snow off the sidewalk or to ride across a lake, it wouldn't work—and it would mess up your bike, too. That's not what your bike was made for. In the same way, God designed us to do what is good and right to bring honor to him. When we do bad things, we do what we were not created to do. God created everything; he knows what works and what doesn't, and he knows what will make us happy and what will hurt us. And he loves us! If we trust him, we will do things his way.

KEY VERSE: *For we are God's masterpiece. He has created us anew in Christ Jesus, so that we can do the good things he planned for us long ago. (Ephesians 2:10)*

NOTE TO PARENTS: It may be helpful to save the word *wrong* for moral issues. You could avoid saying, for example, that it's wrong to wear stripes with polka dots. Unusual habits or choice of clothing may invite criticism from peers, but it's not wrong in the sense of being morally wrong. This makes a clear distinction between wrongdoing and bad taste.

Q 404:

How did God decide what was wrong and what was right?

A: God didn't have a meeting with the angels and announce that some actions were right and some actions were wrong. He is perfect and right. God's very nature is good, and whatever he does is right. And anything that is against God's nature is wrong. God's rules in the Bible tell us what God is like.

Remember also that God tells us what is right and wrong because he loves us. His rules protect us and guide us. It's like our telling a baby not to touch a hot stove. We want to keep the baby from getting hurt. We make the rule because we love the baby. God tells us what to do for the same reason. He wants to take care of us, to make us joyful, and to help us live.

KEY VERSE: *[Jesus said,] "You are to be perfect, even as your Father in heaven is perfect." (Matthew 5:48)*

NOTE TO PARENTS: You can often explain the usefulness of rules by drawing examples from the rules that adults "force" on very young children. For example, we don't let babies play in the toilet, break things, or toddle into the street because we love them and want to protect them. Even more important, babies *don't understand* these rules. They just have to obey them. Even a four- or five-year-old can understand that all of God's rules, in a similar way, come out of his love and care for us—even if we don't always understand how.

Q 405:

Are things always either right or wrong?

A: Not every choice we make is either *right* or *wrong.* Sometimes we just like certain things more than others—such as ice cream flavors. If you like strawberry, it isn't right or wrong—it's just something you like. Or you might have two toys to play with, and you choose one over the other. Both would be all right, but you chose one. At other times, we have to choose between what is *good,* what is *better,* and what is *best.* None of those choices would be bad or wrong, but we would be wise to choose what is best. In choices like those, parents and other wise people can give us good advice. Some choices are either right or wrong, but not *all* choices are.

KEY VERSES: *You say, "I am allowed to do anything"—but not everything is helpful. You say, "I am allowed to do anything"—but not everything is beneficial. Don't think only of your own good. Think of other Christians and what is best for them. (1 Corinthians 10:23-24)*

NOTE TO PARENTS: Again, be careful about how you use the word *wrong.* An absolute moral wrong, such as stealing, doesn't have the same "wrongness" as a matter of etiquette, such as what to say to a hostess about the food. Absolute right or wrong is that which is right or wrong for all people, at all times, in all places.

Q 406:

It's a free country–why do we have to pay tolls?

A: Living in a "free country" means that our highest laws guarantee our right to say and do certain things, not that our country doesn't cost us anything. For example, we have freedom of speech, freedom of the press, and freedom of religion. That means we can say, publish, and worship pretty much whatever we want. But we don't have total freedom because our country needs laws and rules so that everything will run smoothly. That is, the freedom we do have works because we have limits on it. Governments need money for paying leaders, police officers, firefighters, teachers, and other workers, and for building and repairing things like bridges and roads. The citizens provide this money by paying taxes and tolls. The laws of a country are not the same as God's laws, but God tells us to respect the government and to obey its laws. So we pay tolls, wear seat belts, stop at red traffic lights, and follow the speed limits.

KEY VERSES: *For the Lord's sake, accept all authority—the king as head of state, and the officials he has appointed. For the king has sent them to punish all who do wrong and to honor those who do right. (1 Peter 2:13-14)*

NOTE TO PARENTS: You can explain to your child that God wants us to obey the government because he established it. The rules that the government makes are meant to keep us safe.

Q 407:

Why shouldn't we take drugs?

A: Prescription drugs (medicine) are OK to take. In fact, doctors give those to us to help make us well when we're sick. We must carefully obey the doctor's instructions about when to take them and how much to take so the drugs can help us. Taking drugs in the wrong way can be very bad for us. That's why there are laws about them.

Drugs that can hurt us are against the law. Some people use these drugs because it makes them feel good for a little while. But often they get hooked, and the drugs take over their lives. They affect people's brains so that they can't think right, and they can even kill people.

We shouldn't let anything we put into our bodies control us, whether it's food, drink, drugs, alcohol, or any other chemical. Only God should be in control of our lives. And God wants us to take care of our bodies—bad drugs destroy our bodies. Stay far away from all illegal drugs.

KEY VERSE: *Don't be drunk with wine, because that will ruin your life. Instead, let the Holy Spirit fill and control you. (Ephesians 5:18)*

Q 408:

If the law says something is right but God says it's wrong, who's right?

A: The Bible tells us to obey the government. But when a government law goes against what God wants us to do, we should obey God instead of the government. God is in charge of the government and not the other way around. For example, if the government passed a law making it illegal to pray, we should break the law and pray anyway. The same would be true about worshiping God, reading the Bible, and telling others about Christ. And if the government were to make it OK to lie and steal, we still shouldn't do those things because they go against God's law. God created and rules the universe. No one can have higher authority than God. So we must always obey him first.

KEY VERSE: *Peter and the apostles replied, "We must obey God rather than human authority." (Acts 5:29)*

NOTE TO PARENTS: This could be a good opportunity to explain to your child that God is the ultimate authority on what is right. His standards are right for all people, all times, all places—whether the government agrees or not.

Q 409:

What are morals?

A: Morals are standards for right and wrong living. Morals are rules that we follow for doing one thing and not another. Different people live by many different sets of morals—what they think is best or fair or right. But only what God says about these things is right for all people everywhere all the time. God has only one set of morals that he wants everyone to follow. A person who lives by God's morals doesn't steal because that's God's standard, not just because the person doesn't like to steal.

KEY VERSE: *Don't you know that those who do wrong will have no share in the Kingdom of God? (1 Corinthians 6:9)*

NOTE TO PARENTS: It may be difficult to explain the difference between a nice person and a moral person. A nice person is concerned about what *other people* think and doesn't want to hurt other people's feelings. A moral person is concerned about what *God* thinks and wants to follow God's rules for thinking, talking, and doing what is right all the time.

Q 410:

How can I tell right from wrong?

A: Anything that goes against what God is like is wrong. We can discover what God is like by reading his Word, the Bible. The Bible also tells us what God wants us to do. So we can tell right from wrong by asking: Will this disobey a law that God has given us? (For example, "no stealing," "no lying," "love your neighbor," or "honor your father and mother.") Anything that breaks one of God's laws is wrong.

If we are faced with a choice that God hasn't given us a law about (or if we don't know where to find it in the Bible), we can ask: Will doing this go against my conscience? We can also ask: Will it hurt someone? If the answer is yes to either question, then most likely we should not do it.

Another question to ask is: Why am I doing this? If it's only because of pressure from friends or because of fear, then it may not be right. This is when we must carefully consider the choice that we have to make. We must think about what we know about God, pray for wisdom, and make the *best* choice we can.

KEY VERSE: *A good person produces good deeds from a good heart, and an evil person produces evil deeds from an evil heart. Whatever is in your heart determines what you say. (Luke 6:45)*

NOTE TO PARENTS: We need to *cultivate character* in our children and not just give them rules for behavior since most of our moral acts come from our tendencies and habits. We should teach our children the principles behind the precepts and ultimately point them to the person who embodies them, God himself. That is how our children will learn to tell right from wrong.

Q 411:

What are God's rules for right and wrong?

A: God has given us his Word, the Bible, which tells us about him and how he wants us to live. So we must do our best to obey what God tells us in his Word. Jesus said that the most important rule (called a commandment) is "'Love the Lord your God with all your heart, all your soul, and all your mind.' This is the first and greatest commandment. A second is equally important: 'Love your neighbor as yourself'" (Matthew 22:37-39). We should love God first and then other people. If we do that, we will do what is right.

Also, God wants us to develop a desire for the best, not just second-best. Some activities may not be wrong but aren't best for us. We should do what is *best* and not settle for anything less. Making right, moral choices means not just saying no to bad actions but also saying yes to what is good and helpful.

KEY VERSES: *Jesus replied, "'You must love the Lord your God with all your heart, all your soul, and all your mind.' This is the first and greatest commandment. A second is equally important: 'Love your neighbor as yourself.'"(Matthew 22:37-39)*

NOTE TO PARENTS: A child may think that being good means just avoiding the bad. Help your child to see that being good means making a positive choice to please God in everything we do. And we seek to do so because we know that God seeks our best.

Q 412:

When I ask a question, why do you always tell me what the Bible says?

A: The Bible is God's Word. When we read it, we learn what God is like and how he wants us to live in this world. Think of the Bible as an instruction book, like the one for the family car. If we do what the book says, the car will run right. If something goes wrong, we can read the book and find out how to fix it. The Bible is God's instruction book for our lives. We need to read and study it so that we will run right and so God can fix things that go wrong with us. It's not enough just to read the Bible; we also must do what it says.

KEY VERSE: *All Scripture is inspired by God and is useful to teach us what is true and to make us realize what is wrong in our lives. It straightens us out and teaches us to do what is right. (2 Timothy 3:16)*

NOTE TO PARENTS: One of the most powerful ways to help your child learn right from wrong is to read a Bible verse together that deals with a specific moral issue (such as honesty or lying) and then talk about how this might affect your own family life. For example, you could read Ephesians 4:25 and then call to mind the last time your child spoke the truth when it was difficult to do so. Perhaps you asked your child, "What are you doing?" and your child spoke honestly, despite being afraid of getting into trouble. This will reinforce the moral principle as well as its importance.

Q 413:

Why do some white and black people hate each other?

A: Hate is another problem caused by sin in the world. People get angry and hate others for many reasons. They may be upset over something a person said or did—they may feel insulted or hurt. They may be bitter about what a person's relatives did in the past. But hate is wrong. God tells us to love, not hate. If someone hurts us, we should forgive that person and try to fix the relationship.

Some people hate others for very silly reasons. They may not like another person's religion, nationality, neighborhood, school, or skin color. For a long time, many white people have hated black people just because they are black. And many black people have hated white people just because they are white. And people have been mean and cruel to other kinds of people, too, such as Hispanics, and Japanese or Irish people.

That is not God's way. God's way is for all kinds of people to live together, to work together, and to worship together. We should show love and respect to all people, no matter how different they are from us.

KEY VERSE: *There is no longer Jew or Gentile, slave or free, male or female. For you are all Christians—you are one in Christ Jesus. (Galatians 3:28)*

NOTE TO PARENTS: Watch your own words and actions. Go out of your way to have positive relationships with people who differ from you. Show your child by word and example how to treat all people with equal respect.

Q 414:

If I see someone who is poor, do I have to give that person money?

A: There are a lot of poor people in the world. Many people beg for money so that they can buy food. It makes us sad to see people beg, and we wish we could help everybody. Sometimes we walk by many people who are asking for money. Obviously we can't give money to every poor person. If we did that, we would run out of money very soon and be poor ourselves. But we can and should help *some* poor people. We can help people in the neighborhood by working around their homes and giving them food. We can give money to our churches and Christian organizations to help poor people in our community and around the world. We can give our time at a local mission. God wants us to be loving and kind to people. He wants us to show his love to widows, prisoners, the poor, and the hungry. When we help poor people, we are acting like Jesus.

KEY VERSE: *There will always be some among you who are poor. That is why I am commanding you to share your resources freely with the poor and with other Israelites in need. (Deuteronomy 15:11)*

NOTE TO PARENTS: There are small ways you can foster a sharing attitude at home. Also, you can find ways to give as a family. You can donate clothes, furniture, time, or other resources to ministries that serve the poor. And when you have things that are useful and in good condition that you no longer need, don't sell the good stuff and give away junk; that's convenience, not compassion.

Q 415:

Is it wrong to spread rumors?

A: A rumor (or gossip) is a story about someone or something that everybody talks about without really knowing whether it's true or not. Sometimes rumors are totally false, but they are spread because somebody got the wrong information. Sometimes rumors are deliberate lies, spread to hurt someone. Sometimes rumors are partially true, but they don't tell the whole story. Even if a story started out to be true, after a few people tell it, it usually gets changed and is only partly true. Rumors almost always do much more harm than good.

If you hear a bad story about someone, don't just pass it on. First, try to find out whether it is true or not. If you find out that the story is true, you have two good choices: (1) You can drop it and forget the whole thing, or (2) you can talk to the person that the story is about and try to help. God wants us to be loving and kind to others. Passing along gossip, spreading rumors, is not loving or kind.

KEY VERSE: *A troublemaker plants seeds of strife; gossip separates the best of friends. (Proverbs 16:28)*

NOTE TO PARENTS: Remember that your child learns from the way you talk about others. Make an effort not to confuse facts with guesses in your discussions about other people.

Q 416:

Is it a sin if you're not sure if something is wrong but you still go along with it?

A: It is not necessarily a sin to do something that we don't know is right or wrong. We can't know everything, and we shouldn't assume that everything we don't know about is wrong. On the other hand, if you have doubts and think it *might* be wrong, you'd better make sure before doing it. Put off doing it; then read the Bible and ask Mom or Dad. Remember, you should choose what is best, not just avoid what is wrong.

KEY VERSE: *But if people have doubts about whether they should eat something, they shouldn't eat it. They would be condemned for not acting in faith before God. If you do anything you believe is not right, you are sinning. (Romans 14:23)*

NOTE TO PARENTS: This touches on the issue of peer pressure. Kids don't always know what is right and wrong. They really don't. Whenever your kids report that they avoided doing something that they weren't quite sure about, affirm them. This may also be a good time to explain the Four Cs: Consider the choice, Compare our attitudes and actions to God, Commit to God's ways, and Count on God's protection and provision.

Q 417:

What is a conscience?

A: God has built into us a way of helping us tell right from wrong. We call this inner voice our *conscience,* and we need to learn to listen to it. It's a feeling inside about something we are thinking about doing. If what we are thinking about doing is not right, then our conscience can make us feel bad about it and give us the sense that we should not do it. Our conscience can also tell us when we *should* do something. When it does that, we get a strong sense that we should do what we're thinking about. God gave us our conscience to help us decide what to do. So it's important for us to listen to our conscience.

If we don't listen to our conscience, pretty soon we get into the habit of ignoring it. After a while we won't hear it at all. That can lead to trouble. Listen carefully to your conscience.

KEY VERSE: *Because of this, I always try to maintain a clear conscience before God and everyone else. (Acts 24:16)*

NOTE TO PARENTS: Be careful not to associate the conscience only with guilty feelings. The best decisions for what is right and good come out of a firm conviction and desire to do right, not out of a desire to silence a guilty conscience. When discussing the conscience with kids, emphasize the *positive* role it can have. The more we read and study God's Word, the more our conscience can help us choose to do right.

Q 418:

Is it all right to laugh at dirty jokes?

A: Some jokes are funny but not good. We should avoid laughing at dirty jokes. A "dirty" joke uses foul words or talks about sex in a wrong way, just to get a laugh. It is called a dirty joke, even by people who don't know God, because it's bad. Jokes that make fun of other people, their race, skin color, religion, and so forth are also bad. Why? Because God is holy and pure and he wants us to be pure. Being like him is the key to living the way he meant us to live. Telling or listening to dirty jokes fills our mind with wrong thoughts and may cause others to feel bad.

If you are near someone who is telling jokes that are bad, go away from that person. You don't want to listen to the jokes, and you don't want to encourage the person who is telling them. There are plenty of good, clean jokes. Listen to those, tell those, and have fun!

KEY VERSE: *Obscene stories, foolish talk, and coarse jokes—these are not for you. Instead, let there be thankfulness to God. (Ephesians 5:4)*

NOTE TO PARENTS: It is amazing what we will compromise because something makes us laugh. Be careful not to repeat or laugh at dirty jokes. Humor is not trivial. And to a child, laughter represents approval.

Q 419:

Do I have to let little kids in my room to play when I have special stuff?

A: Maybe. God is loving and kind, so he wants us to be loving and kind, too, not stingy and selfish. If friends, brothers or sisters, or small children want to play with your toys, you should let them if it's safe and OK with their parents. Sometimes we act as if our toys, clothes, and other belongings are more important than our friends and family. But it's good to take turns and to let other people enjoy our "special stuff." When we do that, people will be able to see that we are different from people who don't love Jesus.

On the other hand, God wants us to be responsible, too. Although God is loving and kind, he would not give us something that would hurt us. You don't have to let little kids do whatever they want with your things, especially if your special stuff is fragile or too hard for little kids to use right. Everybody should take good care of their things, and everyone should respect everyone else's things. Try to let other kids have a turn with your stuff whenever you can, and when you can't, be kind about it and make sure you have a good reason.

KEY VERSES: *Love is patient and kind. Love is not jealous or boastful or proud or rude. Loves does not demand its own way. Love is not irritable, and it keeps no record of when it has been wronged. (1 Corinthians 13:4-5)*

NOTE TO PARENTS: This touches on the issue of sharing. Place the emphasis on *taking turns* rather than on *sharing*; children will more easily understand what you're asking them to do.

Q 420:

Is it OK to tell people to shut up if they are being jerks?

A: When someone does something annoying or wrong, we don't have to like it. But we shouldn't do something bad to them in return. God wants us to be loving and kind to others. So the rule is to be respectful, not bossy or rude. If the person will listen to your opinion, say something, but say it kindly. Sometimes it's *good* to tell friends that they're not being nice or that they are being mean. You don't have to like someone else's cruelty, but you don't have to respond just like they do, either.

God knows that it's best for us when we do things his way. Responding to cruelty with kindness makes friends of people. But when we respond to cruelty with cruelty, we just feed the conflict and make more conflict. So the best way to make someone stop annoying you is to be nice to the person, not mean.

KEY VERSE: *A gentle answer turns away wrath, but harsh words stir up anger. (Proverbs 15:1)*

NOTE TO PARENTS: Don't let kids say cruel and unkind things to each other or to you. It's simply a matter of respecting others not to say shut up or other disrespectful words to people. Instead, show them how to discuss the concerns they have with each other without attacking. Help them solve problems instead of fighting over them.

Q 421:

Is it OK to slam the door when you're mad?

A: No, because the Bible says that we should have self-control. That means God wants us to control our emotions, not let them control us. Emotions are good, and it is good to understand what we are feeling. In other words, if we are angry, we shouldn't pretend we aren't. But we should also think about why we are angry, talk to God and others about it, and work at changing what caused the anger. And we have to be careful about how we express our anger—yelling, screaming, calling names, hitting, and slamming doors can hurt other people, making the situation worse. If you are polite, people will be more likely to listen and pay attention to your concerns.

KEY VERSE: *It is better to be patient than powerful; it is better to have self-control than to conquer a city. (Proverbs 16:32)*

NOTE TO PARENTS: Handling anger well takes practice. You can help your child learn this valuable skill in several ways: (1) If a question about anger comes up, talk together about alternatives to slamming doors, shouting, or stomping around. Ask, "What else could you do to let me know you're upset?" (2) The next time your child gets angry enough to slam a door, encourage him or her to tell you about it ("I'm angry because . . .") and be sure to listen patiently. (3) Whenever *you* are angry, set an example that your child can see and copy.

Q 422:

If you say Jesus when you're mad, isn't that like praying?

A: No. It is one thing to talk to God. It is another to say his name as a swear word because you got hurt or angry.

Sometimes the same word can have different meanings. When and how we say a word can help tell what we mean by it. For example, a person might smile and say, "That's great!" with a happy tone of voice. But another person could frown and mutter angrily, "That's great!" The same words would have very different meanings.

It's the same with God's name. When people use *God, Jesus,* or *Christ* in a sentence, when and how they say those words can tell us what they mean. We pray and worship using God's name. In Sunday school classes we talk a lot about Jesus. And we talk about Christ with our friends. Those are good ways to use God's name. But some people say his name in anger, in frustration, or just in passing. That's called swearing or using God's name "in vain." That's not OK. God says it's wrong.

We love God and want to please him. We love Jesus and thank him for dying on the cross for us. So we should only say *God, Jesus,* or *Christ* when we are being serious about God, praising him, or praying to him. We shouldn't even say "My God!" or "Oh, Lord!" when we're surprised. Treat God with respect. Honor his name. This will show others that you love and respect God, and that will affect them.

KEY VERSE: *[God said,] "Do not misuse the name of the LORD your God. The LORD will not let you go unpunished if you misuse his name." (Exodus 20:7)*

Q 423:

Is it all right to throw rocks at someone who threw rocks at you?

A: It is not right to do something bad to someone just because that person did something bad to us. The Bible calls that "returning evil for evil," and Jesus says it is wrong. The Bible also tells us that we shouldn't try to get back at people who hurt us. We do not have the right to punish people for the things they do wrong. Instead, we should talk about the situation with God and leave it with him. It's all right to protect ourselves, but it's not OK to get even.

This may seem unfair. But actually, only God knows how to judge fairly—we don't. By refusing to return evil for evil, we let God take care of making things right. And God is perfect in all his judgments.

Just because someone else is sinning doesn't give us the excuse to sin. We should always try to obey God and do what is right. God's way is always best. Getting back at others usually doesn't solve the problem; it just makes things worse.

KEY VERSES: *[Jesus said,] "You have heard that the law of Moses says, 'If an eye is injured, injure the eye of the person who did it. If a tooth gets knocked out, knock out the tooth of the person who did it.' But I say, don't resist an evil person! If you are slapped on the right cheek, turn the other, too." (Matthew 5:38-39)*

Q 424:

Is it all right to say bad things if there is no one there to hear you?

A: If something is wrong, then it is wrong even if no one else ever finds out about it. So swearing, lying, and saying bad things about others are wrong, even if our parents, friends, neighbors, and everyone else can't hear. God knows what's going on; he sees and hears everything.

That's why a true test of your character comes whenever you think no one else is watching or listening. If you really believe that swearing is wrong, you won't do it, period. You won't look for opportunities to do it when no one is around to catch you. Work hard at speaking and *thinking* what is good and right, even when no one else is around, because that's what really matters. Even what you think counts; God knows our every thought.

And if anyone ever does find out what you said in private, they will know that you can be trusted. Live every moment as a service to God.

KEY VERSE: *Don't use foul or abusive language. Let everything you say be good and helpful, so that your words will be an encouragement to those who hear them. (Ephesians 4:29)*

NOTE TO PARENTS: Kids often think that if a deed doesn't hurt anybody, it's OK. But wrong actions always hurt someone in some way *in the long run*. The damage may be indirect or take time to become obvious, such as when chronic lying destroys trust in a family. But in the end, everything we do has an effect on others.

Q 425:

Is thinking something bad the same as doing it or saying it?

CLEANSING POOL

A: No. Hating someone and wishing that person were dead are both terrible, but hating only affects the person who is thinking the bad thoughts. He or she would make the situation much worse by actually killing the other person. The same is true with stealing, lying, and other bad thoughts. As wrong as it is to think bad thoughts, it's even worse to do them or say them.

But our thoughts *are* important, because we often end up doing what we keep thinking about. Suppose your mother told you not to eat any cookies before dinner. But you see the cookies on the counter and keep thinking about how good they would taste, especially with a glass of cold milk. If you keep thinking about this, the desire to eat those cookies will probably grow and grow until eventually you might disobey your mom and take some. To keep from acting on bad thoughts, you should move on and think about something else.

God knows what we are thinking, and he wants us to fill our minds with good thoughts, not bad ones.

KEY VERSE: *O Jerusalem, cleanse your hearts that you may be saved. How long will you harbor your evil thoughts? (Jeremiah 4:14)*

NOTE TO PARENTS: At some point most children become concerned about being punished by God for their bad thoughts. Let your child know that it's not wrong to have a bad thought, but it is wrong to *keep on* thinking about it instead of thinking about something else. Make sure your child understands *why* it's wrong to dwell on bad thoughts: Our thoughts grow into desires and actions.

Q 426:

Why do people litter?

A: Some people litter because it's a habit. Others just don't really care. No matter why people litter, it is against the law and hurts the environment. Littering shows a lack of respect for others and their property, and it makes everything look ugly. Christians should respect other people, other people's property, God's creation, and the law. So we should not litter.

KEY VERSE: *The LORD God took the man and put him in the Garden of Eden to work it and take care of it. (Genesis 2:15)*

NOTE TO PARENTS: Kids often have the mentality that "I didn't make the mess so I don't have to clean it up." We need to teach our kids to take responsibility for the environment. If you see litter, pick it up. Keep some kind of bag for trash in your car. Set an example for your child in this area.

Truth or Consequences

Q 427:

Why does God have rules?

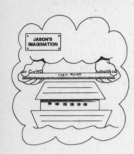

A: God has rules to protect us and to help us. In one way, God's rules are like a wall that protects us from danger. The wall stops us from going any further than we should and getting into trouble. Although we don't always know what is on the other side of the wall, God does, and he loves us so much that he wants to keep us away from it.

God also has rules to help us grow and become all that he wants us to be. Think of feeding a baby. The baby may not like the food—the way it looks, tastes, and feels—but we know that he or she needs to eat good food in order to be healthy and to grow. Like the baby, we don't know everything we need, but God does. In order to help us, he tells us what to do.

God loves us more than anyone else does, and he knows what is best for us. His rules are for our benefit. That's why we need to trust him and obey him.

KEY VERSES: *Until faith in Christ was shown to us as the way of becoming right with God, we were guarded by the law. We were kept in protective custody, so to speak, until we could put our faith in the coming Savior. Let me put it another way. The law was our guardian and teacher to lead us until Christ came. So now, through faith in Christ, we are made right with God. (Galatians 3:23-24)*

Q 428:

Why doesn't God want us to have fun?

A: If people think or say that God doesn't want us to have fun, they don't know the truth about God. He *does* want us to have fun. Jesus was happy, and he told people that they would find joy by following him. Also, God tells us in the Bible that heaven is a place of nonstop joy.

Doing what is wrong (sinning) can be fun, but the fun doesn't last, and it leads to bad consequences. It's like eating something that tastes good but that makes you sick later. The main reason we shouldn't sin is that God tells us not to, and we need to trust him. God knows us better than anyone else does. His fun and joy and happiness are the greatest! And they last forever!

Nobody can have more fun than people who know God. You don't have to sin to have fun.

KEY VERSE: *I have told you this so that you will be filled with my joy. Yes, your joy will overflow! (John 15:11)*

NOTE TO PARENTS: Be careful not to imply that people who sin *aren't* having fun. Kids know better, from observation and from their own experience! Emphasize the fact that God's way is the best way for us, even though another way may seem better. Also, make the distinction between immediate pleasure and a joyful, healthy life.

Q 429:

Is God sad when I do something wrong?

A: God is very sad when we do bad things. In fact, he is more upset and grieved over the sins of the world than anyone else. God is sad because he sees how much sin hurts us and others. But God realizes that we are growing and we make mistakes sometimes. He keeps on encouraging us. He loves us so much that he will not give up on us.

KEY VERSE: *Do not bring sorrow to God's Holy Spirit by the way you live. Remember, he is the one who has identified you as his own, guaranteeing that you will be saved on the day of redemption. (Ephesians 4:30)*

NOTE TO PARENTS: Some parents use this truth to get children to behave. But many children, especially younger ones, already feel guilty about their wrongdoing and will be oversensitive to the idea that they have hurt God's feelings. Instead, tell them that God loves them, is helping them to be good, and is very pleased when they do the *right* thing!

Q 430:

How do you get permission to go to heaven?

A: There is only one way to get to heaven, and that is through Jesus Christ. Only people who trust in Jesus go to heaven. We can place our trust in Jesus by praying to God and telling him:

1. We are sorry for our sins—for disobeying him and living only for ourselves;
2. We believe that Jesus, his only Son, came to earth and died on the cross, in our place, to take the punishment for our sin, and that he rose again from the dead; and
3. We want his Holy Spirit to live inside us and guide us.

   The Bible says that whoever does this and means it becomes a new person, a child of God. And all of God's children will go to be with him in heaven when they die.

KEY VERSE: *[Jesus said,] "God so loved the world that he gave his only Son, so that everyone who believes in him will not perish but have eternal life." (John 3:16)*

NOTE TO PARENTS: Leading your son or daughter to Christ can arise quite easily out of discussions about right and wrong. Be ready for it by knowing what to say when a child asks a question such as this one.

Q 431:

If you swear and you're a Christian, do you still go to heaven?

A: If we have given our lives to Christ, we will go to heaven, even if we occasionally do something bad (such as swear). But our relationship with God will affect the way we live. People will be able to see a difference in our lives because we are Christians. Yes, we can do bad things and still go to heaven, but why would we want to? God wants only the very best for us, and sinning hurts us.

Heaven is a place where everyone does good all the time. That's because heaven is perfect and God is there. People who love God love doing good. If we love God, we will want to please him, and we will trust that he knows what's best for us.

KEY VERSE: *Now is the time to get rid of anger, rage, malicious behavior, slander, and dirty language. (Colossians 3:8)*

NOTE TO PARENTS: This question will usually arise out of what kids hear from *adults*, not just their peers. If you hear your child using swear words, take the opportunity to explain that it is wrong and why it is wrong. Also keep in mind that what you model pulls a lot of weight. If you swear, so will your kids.

Q 432:

Why do I feel bad when I do something wrong?

A: When we do something wrong, we may feel bad because it hurts others. Or we may feel frustrated because we didn't do what was best. Also, we may feel guilty because we have let God down.

God wants us to do right, so he built a warning system in us to alert us when we are about to do something wrong. That warning system is called a *conscience*. If we get too close to a fire, the heat warns us to move away before we get hurt. Our conscience warns us that doing bad things will hurt us if we do them.

KEY VERSES: *I am no longer sorry that I sent that letter to you, though I was sorry for a time, for I know that it was painful to you for a little while. Now I am glad I sent it, not because it hurt you, but because the pain caused you to have remorse and change your ways. It was the kind of sorrow God wants his people to have, so you were not harmed by us in any way. For God can use sorrow in our lives to help us turn away from sin and seek salvation. We will never regret that kind of sorrow. But sorrow without repentance is the kind that results in death. (2 Corinthians 7:8-10)*

NOTE TO PARENTS: There's a difference between guilt feelings and a true sense of wrong. Some children are supersensitive and feel guilty about almost everything they do. If that describes your child, help him or her understand the depth of God's love and forgiveness.

Q 433:

What does God want me to do when I do something wrong?

A: The first thing we should do is to pray and admit to God what we have done. We should tell him that we are sorry and that we want him to help us not to do it again. Also, we should ask God to help us learn from the experience. Admitting our sins to God brings us back close to him. Remember, God wants to protect us and to provide all we need for living. So we should stay close to him and talk with him about everything. Try praying when you first think of doing something wrong. God can help you avoid or get out of trouble.

If our sin has hurt others, we should talk to them, too, saying we're sorry and asking for their forgiveness.

KEY VERSE: *If we confess our sins to him, he is faithful and just to forgive us and to cleanse us from every wrong. (1 John 1:9)*

NOTE TO PARENTS: If your child comes to you with a confession, see it as a teachable moment—help the child see what can be learned from it. Be gentle, loving, and forgiving; otherwise the child may be unwilling to come to you again. Often children are strapped with guilt. If so, consider rituals that can help free them from it, such as writing down their sins on a piece of paper, talking with God about them, and then tearing up the paper together.

Telling the Truth

Q 434:

Is it all right to tell a lie once in a while?

A: We should always tell the truth because God always tells the truth. Would it be all right to touch a hot stove every once in a while? If you did, you would burn yourself every time. It is never right to lie, not even once in a while. God tells us to tell the truth because he is truth.

Lying also gets us into trouble. Usually one lie leads to another. It's so much simpler to tell the truth than to have to remember the lies we have told so that we can keep them covered up. And lying makes it hard for others to trust us. But people who are honest are free and joyful.

KEY VERSE: *[Jesus said,] "God is Spirit, so those who worship him must worship in spirit and in truth." (John 4:24)*

NOTE TO PARENTS: Your example is going to make a big difference here. How do you represent the truth? How you represent the truth will guide them more than the answer you provide to a question about lying. When you catch children lying, find out why they lied, point out the mistake in their reasoning, and show why the truth would work better.

Q 435:

Is it all right to lie if you are embarrassed or scared?

A: No. Lying is wrong because God is truth and because he has told us not to lie. Telling the truth can be difficult at times, especially when we might get embarrassed or punished for doing so. But we should do what is right even when it's not easy. Doing it God's way is better in the long run.

Actually, although lying is common, people want others to be truthful with them. If you tell the truth when it's hard, people will think, *Wow!* They will really respect you. They will come to trust you and learn that you are a dependable person. They may even look to you for advice and leadership. Get into the habit of telling the truth. Very few people will stop being your friend just because you tell the truth. Your friends, classmates, relatives, and neighbors want to be able to trust what you say. The truth helps you; lies get you into even more trouble.

KEY VERSES: *He never sinned, and he never deceived anyone. He did not retaliate when he was insulted. When he suffered, he did not threaten to get even. He left his case in the hands of God, who always judges fairly. (1 Peter 2:22-23)*

NOTE TO PARENTS: Children sometimes face embarrassing situations in school—situations that tempt them to lie to save face or to improve their image. At times like that, encourage them to trust in God and in his protection.

Q 436:

What if I told a lie and didn't know it was a lie–is it still a lie?

A: To pass on information that you *think* is true but really isn't, is *not* lying. But what you say can be wrong and can hurt somebody. That's why it is so important to check out the facts to see if something is true, especially if the information sounds fishy or you're not very sure. Suppose you heard from a friend that the school concert would begin at 8:00, but it really is going to begin at 7:30. It would be good to find out for sure before telling your parents about the concert. Just think how they would feel if they showed up half an hour late.

Beware of talking too much. Being slow to speak will help you avoid getting into trouble with your words. It's to your own benefit for people to know that they can rely on what you say. And if you are afraid that you lied without knowing it, tell God about it. He will forgive you.

KEY VERSE: *My dear brothers and sisters, be quick to listen, slow to speak, and slow to get angry. (James 1:19)*

NOTE TO PARENTS: Help your children learn to say "I don't know" or "I'm not sure" if they don't have all the facts. For example, "I'm not sure, but I think it starts at 8:00" is better than "It starts at 8:00." Tell your children that it's OK not to be certain. Then they will be less likely to pass on incorrect information to you or others.

Q 437:

Is it OK for Mom and Dad to lie to you about your Christmas presents?

A: God wants us always to be truthful. But that doesn't mean that we have to answer every question that people ask us, nor does it mean that we have to tell them everything we know. If you ask your parents, "What did you get me for Christmas?" or "Did you get me a bike for Christmas?" they can say something like: "I'm not going to tell you because I want you to be surprised."

Be careful not to make excuses for lying. Don't lie and then make up a reason for doing it. When it comes to giving gifts, there are ways to surprise people and make them feel special without lying to them.

KEY VERSE: *Most of all, my brothers and sisters, never take an oath, by heaven or earth or anything else. Just say a simple yes or no, so that you will not sin and be condemned for it. (James 5:12)*

NOTE TO PARENTS: Children often don't make allowances for "socially acceptable" lies the way some adults do. And that's good! Make it a household rule always to speak the truth. Your commitment to truth telling will have the benefit of developing honesty in your child.

Q 438:

If I break something that belongs to someone else but fix it, do I have to tell what I did?

A: How would *you* feel if a friend broke something of yours and didn't tell you, even though your friend fixed it? You probably wouldn't like it, especially if you found out later. Treating another person the way you want to be treated is called the Golden Rule. Jesus taught that this is the way we should always act.

Telling the person what you did is both telling the truth and showing that you respect that person. If you break something that belongs to someone else, it *is* important to fix it or to pay to have it fixed. But you should let the person know what you did and not try to hide it.

When you do that, people will know you are responsible, and they will let you borrow other things and trust you more. But if you try to hide it and they find out, they won't trust you anymore.

KEY VERSE: *[Jesus said,] "Do for others what you would like them to do for you. This is a summary of all that is taught in the law and the prophets." (Matthew 7:12)*

NOTE TO PARENTS: Many children lie for reasons that are related to self-doubt and insecurity. They lie to show off or because of fear—fear of being thought less of, fear of failure (they lie to seem to have succeeded), fear of not being accepted, and fear of getting punished. Help your child to see that God can protect us from these fears when we respect others and their property. If you get a gratuitous confession of wrongdoing, accept it lovingly, with gentleness. This will encourage your child to tell the truth instead of being afraid of punishment.

Q 439:

Do all people lie?

A: All people sin, and one of the most common sins is lying. In fact, some people don't know the difference between truth and lies because they lie so much. Some are so confused that they think a lie is the truth. But not all people lie. Lying is a choice.

Sometimes people say something that is not true because they don't know all the facts; that's not the same as lying. For example, they might say, "Jimmy is in the backyard," when actually he came inside a few minutes ago. It's good to check the facts to make sure that what you say is correct. Watch out for saying something before you're sure it's true.

People who want to do things God's way make a decision not to lie because they want to obey God. Jesus never lied. If we do lie, we must ask God for forgiveness, admit our lie to the people involved, and try not to do it again.

KEY VERSE: *All have sinned; all fall short of God's glorious standard. (Romans 3:23)*

NOTE TO PARENTS: It's confusing for children when they hear something that later turns out to be false information and think that they have been lied to. Instead of knowingly telling a lie, however, the person may simply have been passing on misinformation. Use this fact of life to warn your children against accusing someone of being a liar, and encourage them to be careful about what they themselves say. For example, they could say, "I'm not sure, but I *think* . . ."

Q 440:

Is it wrong to tell someone your parents are home when they're not?

A: Telling someone that your parents are home when they aren't is a lie, and God tells us not to lie. If we tell this kind of lie, we will find it easier to lie about other things.

But that doesn't mean you have to answer every question that a stranger on the phone asks you. If you are home alone, you probably shouldn't tell people on the phone that your parents aren't home. Instead, you could say something like: "They can't come to the phone right now," or, "They are not available," or, "Please let me take a message, and they will get right back to you." Talk with your mom or dad about what you can say without lying.

KEY VERSE: *An honest witness tells the truth; a false witness tells lies. (Proverbs 12:17)*

NOTE TO PARENTS: Telling the truth doesn't mean telling everything you know about something. Telling everything you know may be more than the person could understand or may simply not be appropriate. Help your child understand that you can withhold information without lying. You can say, "I can't tell you," or, "I'm not going to tell you," or, "I can't explain it right now." Just because you want them to withhold certain facts doesn't mean they have to say something false. Help kids learn the difference between handling information wisely and lying.

Q 441:

Is it OK to lie, knowing you will tell the truth later?

A: One of the most common excuses for lying is, "I was going to tell the truth later." That may sound all right, but usually it is just another lie.

This often happens when people are joking around. They make up a story for the sake of making people laugh. It's OK to joke and to kid around, but it's not OK to lie. Be careful not to make an excuse for lying by saying, "It was just a joke," or, "I was going to tell the truth later." If you do, after a while people won't know when you're telling the truth and when you're not, and they might stop trusting you.

The second most important thing in life is our relationships with others, and one of the most important parts of a good relationship is trust. No joke is more important than that.

KEY VERSES: *Just as damaging as a mad man shooting a lethal weapon is someone who lies to a friend and then says, "I was only joking." (Proverbs 26:18-19)*

NOTE TO PARENTS: Parents tend to justify lies by saying, "This person can't handle the truth." If you want to keep some truths or pieces of the truth from kids, then say the parts that you *can* tell, or say nothing. Sometimes parents make up lies to motivate kids to do certain undesirable things ("Eat your bread crusts because they'll make your hair curly"). Think of good ways to motivate without resorting to lies.

Q 442:

Is it OK to lie to keep a friend from getting hurt?

A: We don't have to lie to keep our friends from getting hurt. We can think of better ways. For example, depending on the situation, we can get the help of an adult who knows the friend and cares about him or her, or we can say to the friend, "I'm not going to tell you because I don't want you to get hurt." There are many other ways to help a friend besides lying.

God loves you and wants you to be truthful. So he won't force you to lie or put you in a situation where you have to lie. Look for other ways to respond.

Remember that God's way is always the best. You may think that lying will keep someone from getting hurt, but actually it will just make the situation worse.

KEY VERSE: *Remember that the temptations that come into your life are no different from what others experience. And God is faithful. He will keep the temptation from becoming so strong that you can't stand up against it. When you are tempted, he will show you a way out so that you will not give in to it. (1 Corinthians 10:13)*

NOTE TO PARENTS: Beware of talking about hypothetical situations. If your child asks you this kind of question, try to determine what real situation is behind it. Then, together, you can think of a way to help the friend and your child stay out of trouble.

Q 443:

What should you do if someone lies to you?

A: How you respond to a lie depends on who it affects. A friend might lie and say, "I shot twenty free throws in a row without missing." That kind of lie doesn't need any response (in fact, saying nothing is probably best). But if a class partner shows up to give a report with you and says, "I'm all ready" and isn't, that will affect both of you and the class. Or if someone lies to an adult about a situation you were involved in, that will affect both of you and possibly others. In cases like that, you need to respond in some way.

In other words, you can ignore some made-up stories or exaggerations. At other times, however, you should tell the person telling the lie that what he or she is saying just isn't true. This is important when the lie will hurt someone, such as making up a bad story about someone at school, cheating in class, or telling something that isn't true to get money from someone or to get that person to do something wrong.

With very serious lies, you should tell an adult. In these situations, someone could get in big trouble or get hurt badly.

KEY VERSE: *Dear brothers and sisters, if another Christian is overcome by some sin, you who are godly should gently and humbly help that person back onto the right path. And be careful not to fall into the same temptation yourself. (Galatians 6:1)*

Q 444:

Is it OK to keep secrets from your friends?

A: Most of the time it is all right to keep secrets. Telling the truth doesn't mean that we have to tell *everything* we know to everyone who asks. Sometimes secrets can be fun, like with birthday presents or other pleasant surprises. Sometimes secrets are important because it's better for you not to give out certain information to just anyone.

We should *not* keep something a secret if it means that someone will get hurt or get into serious trouble. For example, a boy might say that he is going to beat up another kid, or a girl might say that she's going to steal something from a store. In those cases, we should tell someone who can help—perhaps a parent, a teacher, a coach, a youth leader, or a school counselor.

Be careful not to promise to keep a secret before you hear what it is. Whether you tell or not should depend on what the secret is.

KEY VERSE: *A gossip tells secrets, so don't hang around with someone who talks too much.* (Proverbs 20:19)

NOTE TO PARENTS: Encourage your child to tell you if they hear something from a friend that will hurt someone or lead to serious trouble. Let your child know that telling secrets to people who can help in those situations is part of being a good friend. On the other hand, don't encourage "tattling." A tattletale runs and tells adults insignificant things in order to get what they want out of a problem that they could have resolved themselves.

Q 445:

Should I tell the truth to someone even if they won't like it?

A: You should strive to tell the truth, even if it hurts, but never just to be cruel. Here are a few examples to help you decide how to do that.

Sometimes the truth hurts, but we still need to say it. Imagine that a friend asks you to a party. You can't go, but you don't want to hurt your friend's feelings. So you say yes, or you don't say anything and let her think you will be there. Even though your friend will feel bad that you can't come to the party, it would be much better to tell her the truth right away.

Another time you need to tell the unpleasant truth is when a friend is getting into trouble. That friend might be starting to hang around with bad kids. Being a good friend means telling your friend the truth. That friend may not like what you have to say, but it's the truth, and he or she needs to hear it from you.

Being honest and truthful, however, does *not* give us permission to be cruel. Remember, God is loving and kind. So we shouldn't tell people things that will hurt their feelings just because those things are true. It would be cruel, for example, to tell someone, "You have a big nose," or, "You don't play basketball very well," or, "Your house sure needs to be painted," or, "Your clothes are old and worn out."

KEY VERSE: *Instead, we will hold to the truth in love, becoming more and more in every way like Christ, who is the head of his body, the church. (Ephesians 4:15)*

Q 446:

If you don't like something a person wears and they ask you if you like it, are you supposed to tell them the truth?

A: We are not supposed to lie, but that doesn't mean that we have to be mean or hurtful about what we say. We need to learn *tact*. Tact is telling the truth in a nice way, even if it's hard for the other person to take. For example, suppose you think a person's new coat is ugly. You don't have to say, "I *hate* that ugly coat!" You can think of something good about it, like, "It looks nice and warm." Practice saying what you think in ways that respect people's feelings.

KEY VERSE: *Let everything you say be good and helpful, so that your words will be an encouragement to those who hear them. (Ephesians 4:29)*

NOTE TO PARENTS: This may be the time to explain the difference between lying and being tactful. *Lying* is an attempt to deceive or to trick someone. *Tact* is an attempt to be kind in the delivery of a truth that may offend someone. Also, teach your child not to go to the other extreme: Flattery is equally wrong—and can be itself a form of lying. We should never lie just because it will make someone feel good. Rather, we should always deliver the truth in a loving way.

Q 447:

If lying is a sin, why did some people in the Bible tell lies?

A: It is true that the Bible has stories about people who told lies, but the huge majority of Bible people told the truth. God never says in the Bible that lying is right. Some people in the Bible chose to lie, but God didn't say they were good for doing that. God is truth, and he wants us to tell the truth. Honesty is very important for families, neighborhoods, cities, schools, companies, and friendships. Honesty protects us from danger and helps us to be happier people. Be someone who always tells the truth because that's how God is.

KEY VERSE: *Put away all falsehood and "tell your neighbor the truth" because we belong to each other. (Ephesians 4:25)*

NOTE TO PARENTS: One of the reasons for the stories in the Bible is so we can learn from the examples, both good and bad, of the people in them. Some of their choices set good examples, and some set bad ones. We shouldn't follow every example in the Bible. The fact that Samson lied doesn't mean we should. Whenever you read Bible stories about such people, ask, "What did this person do that was right?" and, "What did this person do that was wrong?"

School Days and TV Daze

Q 448:

Why is it wrong to do something if all the other kids do it?

A: If something is wrong, it's wrong, no matter how many people do it. Suppose a group of your friends started throwing stones through windows in the neighborhood. Would it be OK just because everyone did it? Of course not! It would be wrong whether *one* person or *everyone in school* did it. You can be sure that the police and the homeowners would say it was wrong!

If a lot of kids swear, cheat, lie, do drugs, drink, smoke, disobey their parents, shoplift, or do something else that is wrong, don't think that you have to do it, too. You should do what is right, even if you are the only one. That's what God wants.

If the group you hang around with does things that are wrong and pressures you to join them, find another group. Get away from kids who are always tempting you to do wrong.

KEY VERSES: *With the Lord's authority let me say this: Live no longer as the ungodly do, for they are hopelessly confused. Their closed minds are full of darkness; they are far away from the life of God because they have shut their minds and hardened their hearts against him. They don't care anymore about right and wrong, and they have given themselves over to immoral ways. Their lives are filled with all kinds of impurity and greed. (Ephesians 4:17-19)*

NOTE TO PARENTS: Peer pressure on kids can be quite strong. As your child grows older, you can help combat peer pressure by spending time together one-on-one and together as a family.

Q 449:

Should I tell on other kids?

A: If a law will be broken or someone will be hurt, yes. God puts adults in positions of authority to protect you and others against wrongdoing. If those adults don't know about a problem, they can't provide that protection. Tell a parent, teacher, coach, counselor, police officer, or another concerned adult if someone is stealing, doing drugs, selling drugs, drinking, planning to break the law, talking about committing suicide, or talking about hurting someone. There's nothing wrong with telling on other kids at times like that.

But there *is* something wrong with "telling on" kids you don't like just to get them in trouble. Remember, you aren't a parent, teacher, principal, or police officer. Also, if you tell on someone and that person gets into trouble, don't brag and make a big deal about what you did. God's purpose for us is to serve him and help others—that's the reason for telling in the first place—so bragging is out of place.

KEY VERSE: *Take no part in the worthless deeds of evil and darkness; instead, rebuke and expose them. (Ephesians 5:11)*

NOTE TO PARENTS: The issue of tattling on other kids is very real—kids hate tattlers so much that some parents encourage their kids not to tell on anybody at any time, fearing that they will lose friends. But it's important for kids to report wrongdoing—it's a basic part of being a responsible friend and citizen. Teach your child to enforce the rules out of a desire to help others respond properly to God rather than appearing morally superior.

Q 450:

Is it wrong to watch music videos?

A: It's not wrong to watch television, listen to the radio, watch videos, or listen to music. But God wants us to be wise about what we put into our minds. A lot of the stuff on TV, in movies, in videos, and on talk radio is not good. In fact, often the people on them use bad language, do bad things, and make it look as if sinning is the right thing to do. That's a lie. We know that God wants us to do what is right, not wrong. He doesn't want us to disobey him. So we should be very careful about what we watch and listen to. Many music videos are not good. Seeing and hearing bad videos is like eating garbage. It's bad for us, won't help us grow, and will make us sick. Instead, we should fill our minds with pictures, words, and thoughts that honor God.

KEY VERSE: *And now, dear brothers and sisters, let me say one more thing as I close this letter. Fix your thoughts on what is true and honorable and right. Think about things that are pure and lovely and admirable. Think about things that are excellent and worthy of praise. (Philippians 4:8)*

NOTE TO PARENTS: Beware of making a sweeping statement against music videos. Some Christian musicians make music videos. Beware of making sweeping statements against anything in youth culture. As you and your children confront new challenges, learn to compare them to God's standards.

Q 451:

Why do some people make music with bad words?

A: Some music writers and performers have no hope and don't love God, so they write and sing angry and hateful songs. Other music has bad words because the writers and singers want to shock the listeners, to get their attention. Because these musicians don't love God, they think it's all right to use shocking language. Much of the time, however, music has bad words because the writers, singers, producers, and stores want to make money. Unfortunately, that kind of music sells, so they keep making the bad songs.

Don't buy music that has swearing or a false message about life. If a bad song comes on the radio, change the station. Don't fill your mind with garbage.

KEY VERSES: *People who long to be rich fall into temptation and are trapped by many foolish and harmful desires that plunge them into ruin and destruction. For the love of money is at the root of all kinds of evil. And some people, craving money, have wandered from the faith and pierced themselves with many sorrows. (1 Timothy 6:9-10)*

NOTE TO PARENTS: Music itself isn't bad. It's a good thing that some people corrupt. Help your children find music they can enjoy listening to that doesn't violate God's standards.

Q 452:

Is it OK to listen to bad music groups if you don't listen to the words?

A: Trying to listen to bad songs without hearing the words would be like trying to watch a video with your eyes closed. It can't be done. Even if you aren't concentrating on the words, you still hear them and they affect your thoughts. Also, imagine what others would think of you if they saw and heard you listening to music that *they* know is bad. They probably would wonder what kind of Christian you were. Also, buying and listening to music supports the musicians who perform it, and you don't want to support the bad groups.

But not all music is bad! Many songs are fun to listen to, and they have good words. Fill your mind with what is good—do everything to the glory of God. Trust that the things God approves are the best for you. He loves you!

KEY VERSE: *Whatever you eat or drink or whatever you do, you must do all for the glory of God. (1 Corinthians 10:31)*

NOTE TO PARENTS: Music matters a great deal to most older kids and to their relationships. It's OK to limit what your children can listen to, but it will be more effective to steer kids instead of blocking them. In other words, when you say that they can't listen to a certain group, suggest alternatives. Don't give them the impression that the only good music is the stuff that *you* listen to (or listened to when you were their age).

Q 453:

Why don't you let us watch certain TV shows?

A: Many TV programs show people saying and doing things that go against God and what he says. Many of the people who make television shows aren't Christians. They don't know God and will often make programs that are not good for us to watch. Some shows even encourage us to do wrong things. We should always try to do what is right. So it is good to turn off the set or change the channel when a bad show comes on. We should guard our hearts because what we put into our hearts will show up in our lives (Proverbs 4:23).

KEY VERSE: *And now, dear brothers and sisters, let me say one more thing as I close this letter. Fix your thoughts on what is true and honorable and right. Think about things that are pure and lovely and admirable. Think about things that are excellent and worthy of praise. (Philippians 4:8)*

NOTE TO PARENTS: This is the kind of question that touches on the fundamental issue of *what we are here for.* We are here to learn to love, to learn to trust, to live with God beside us, and to show God's love to others—not to seek immediate personal pleasure. Help your children to see the bigger picture to help them make good choices in individual areas of life.

Q 454:
On TV, why do people who aren't married live together?

A: Many of the people who make TV shows don't know God, and they don't care about what God wants. They don't understand that his way is the way that works best. Some television programs try to show that marriage isn't important. But God created marriage, and he says that it *is* important and that it's the right way for a man and a woman to live together.

KEY VERSE: *Yes, they knew God, but they wouldn't worship him as God or even give him thanks. And they began to think up foolish ideas of what God was like. The result was that their minds became dark and confused. (Romans 1:21)*

NOTE TO PARENTS: Monitor your family's TV viewing. If you see an inappropriate scene in a program or an advertisement, talk about it with your child. Discuss why it's wrong and what the Bible says about sex.

Q 455:
What if one parent says you can watch a certain movie, and then the other one says you can't?

A: If one parent tells you no, then accept that as your answer and don't go looking for permission from your other parent. Some kids go back and forth between parents until one gives in and says OK. That's wrong because it dishonors what the first parent said. If Mom or Dad says you can't do something (like watch a certain movie), you may nicely ask why. That will help you understand the reason for the no. But don't argue, complain, or whine about it. Instead, say thank you and obey. God wants us to honor and obey our parents. He told us that in his Word.

Why does God want children to obey their parents? Because that's how God keeps kids safe and gives them what they need to grow up. Obeying and honoring your parents will help you learn the things you need to live a happy and productive life.

KEY VERSES: *My son, obey your father's commands, and don't neglect your mother's teaching. Keep their words always in your heart. Tie them around your neck. (Proverbs 6:20-21)*

NOTE TO PARENTS: It's very important for parents to support each other when kids come to one parent with a request designed to undo what the other said. Make it a policy to enforce the first answer as the final answer unless you both agree to change your mind.

Q 456:

Is it wrong to leave your homework till the last minute so that you can watch TV?

A: School is important because that's where we learn important information that can help us live in this world. Homework is an important part of school. Teachers give homework to help students learn what is being taught in class. Remember, God wants us to do our best at everything we do—that includes school. TV is all right (if we watch good programs), but school is more important.

To get the most out of school, do your homework first, and do the best you can at it. Family jobs and responsibilities should come before play and entertainment. Then, if you have time, you can take time for playing, watching TV, and other activities. You will often enjoy your relaxation, entertainment, and playtime more after you have completed your responsibilities!

KEY VERSES: *Take a lesson from the ants, you lazybones. Learn from their ways and be wise! Even though they have no prince, governor, or ruler to make them work, they labor hard all summer, gathering food for the winter. (Proverbs 6:6-8)*

NOTE TO PARENTS: You can use this kind of question as an opportunity to talk about *responsibility* and the satisfaction of a job well done. Everyone has "jobs" to do, and some of them just aren't fun! But we can choose our attitude in every situation, and we can choose to take pleasure in the responsibilities God has given us. Encourage your child not to see work as a drag but to do it as a service to God and to take pleasure in it.

Q 457:

Why do people say things that aren't true about the stuff they sell on commercials?

A: Companies make commercials to try to get people to buy their products. Some companies don't care what they say, even if it's not true. They just want to get people to buy their stuff. All commercials try to make the product look good. So they may not lie, but they may give an impression that isn't true. For example, a TV ad may show a group of kids having great fun playing a game. We really don't know whether the game is fun—the kids on TV are actors who were paid to look as if they were having fun. We are led to believe that it would make us happy to play the game.

When you see or hear an advertisement, look and listen carefully. Also, don't get into the habit of wanting everything that looks good on TV. You probably don't need it, and it may not be as good as it looks anyway.

KEY VERSE: *Don't let anyone lead you astray with empty philosophy and high-sounding nonsense that come from human thinking and from the evil powers of this world, and not from Christ. (Colossians 2:8)*

NOTE TO PARENTS: Some kids don't know that commercials can create false impressions because they don't have the benefit of experience that you have. You can turn commercials into an educational experience by pointing out how they may be misleading the audience. Perhaps you have a story of how an ad had this effect on you.

Getting Along with Your Family

Q 458:

Why do I have to obey my parents?

A: The most important reason for children to obey their parents is that God said to. God knows that children need protection and guidance, and parents are the best ones to provide that. Parents take care of their children, give them food and other things they need, and teach them how to know right from wrong. Living God's way means listening to him and doing what he says, and that includes obeying Mom and Dad. Obeying your parents is the best way for you to learn and grow now and to have a better life in the future.

KEY VERSES: *Children, obey your parents because you belong to the Lord, for this is the right thing to do. "Honor your father and mother." This is the first of the Ten Commandments that ends with a promise. And this is the promise: If you honor your father and mother, "you will live a long life, full of blessing." (Ephesians 6:1-3)*

NOTE TO PARENTS: Don't use authority to justify different standards for yourself unless you have a very good reason beyond just the fact that "you're in charge." On the other hand, don't be surprised if your child resists your rules because kids *will* protest their parents' decisions no matter how loving and wise they are. To minimize the hassles, always have a good reason for the rules you enforce.

Q 459:

Is it wrong to put my fingers in my ears so I can't hear my parents?

A: Some children think that if they can't hear their parents, they don't have to do what their parents tell them. But God tells us to *honor* our parents, not just obey them. That means treating them with respect. When we respect our parents, we look at them when they talk to us, and we listen carefully to what they say—we *don't* try to plug our ears or ignore them. It also means having a good attitude and not talking back. Listening to your parents doesn't just make them feel good—it's for *your* good. God loves you and wants the best for you.

KEY VERSE: *Honor your father and mother. Then you will live a long, full life in the land the LORD your God will give you. (Exodus 20:12)*

NOTE TO PARENTS: Don't fall into the trap of yelling to get a child's attention. Often obedience comes more easily if you explain *why* they are to obey, as well as what you want them to do.

Q 460:

Is it OK to beg for things from your parents?

A: It is OK to *ask* your parents for things, but it's not OK to beg. For example, you could ask for a special treat, Christmas presents, or permission to go to a friend's house or stay up late. You should ask politely and explain your reasons. But if they say no, you should accept their answer with a good attitude. Don't beg. That is, don't ask over and over and over to try to get them to give you what they really don't want to give you. Don't try to wear them down.

The key is simply to respect your parents. They gave their answer because they thought it was best for you. If you wear them down, you may get what you want and then regret it later. God gave you parents to protect you and provide for you. If you talk them into going against their first answer, you step outside that protection. Respect and obey your mom and dad.

KEY VERSE: *Even when you do ask, you don't get it because your whole motive is wrong—you want only what will give you pleasure. (James 4:3)*

NOTE TO PARENTS: Don't let a child wear you down with nagging. (More to the point, don't allow the child to nag!) And when your child does push or beg, don't give in unless you have a good reason. Also, affirm your children every time they make a polite request, respond the right way to your answers, and have a positive attitude. Finally, always think about your answer before giving it. If the answer could be or should be yes, but you say no for convenience, you'll probably change your mind when your child nags you. And that will encourage nagging with every *no!*

Q 461:

Why is it wrong to complain when my mom asks me to do something?

A: Remember, the Bible tells us to honor our parents. This means being polite, having a good attitude, and showing them respect, even when we disagree with them. If you don't agree with your parents, you can tell them how you feel without complaining or hurting them with words. Also, think about how much they do for you. That will help you have a thankful attitude rather than a complaining one. People who complain a lot don't have many friends, are usually unhappy, and often have miserable lives. And the more they complain, the worse it gets! You can choose to be content and to make the best of every situation.

KEY VERSES: *In everything you do, stay away from complaining and arguing, so that no one can speak a word of blame against you. (Philippians 2:14-15)*

NOTE TO PARENTS: Explain to your child: "You don't have to like it; you just have to do it." If your child calmly and respectfully explains his or her objections, affirm the good attitude and consider the objections carefully.

Q 462:

If my parents are arguing, is it OK to tell them to stop?

A: Sometimes parents disagree, and they need to talk it out. Just because a husband and wife argue doesn't mean they are having serious problems. Even people who love each other deeply will disagree from time to time. Disagreeing isn't wrong, and arguing doesn't mean the people hate each other. Also, it is not your job as a child to see that your parents don't argue. You can tell them how you feel, but don't try to tell them what to do. Pray for your parents if they are arguing. Ask God to help them get along and to give them wisdom for their conversation.

However, if the arguing leads to yelling, screaming, swearing, or hitting, you may have to tell another adult who can help your mom and dad. Your pastor would be a good choice.

KEY VERSE: *Yanking a dog's ears is as foolish as interfering in someone else's argument.* (Proverbs 26:17)

NOTE TO PARENTS: Hearing parents argue can be very hard for a child. You and your spouse will disagree and argue from time to time. But be careful about how you argue, especially in front of your children. Fight fairly; that is, don't swear, call the other person names, or use privileged information against him or her. Instead, calm down, lower your voice, acknowledge the other person's position, state your position, and propose a solution. Demonstrate to your children that differences can be resolved peacefully and lovingly.

Q 463:

Is it OK to tell secrets to parents?

A: Yes. It is wonderful to have someone you can trust. Mothers and fathers who love their children want to help them every way they can. There is no better person with whom you can share a secret. So it's OK to tell *your own* secrets to your parents. Just be sure to tell them that it's a secret and that you don't want them to tell anybody—then they'll know not to tell. Some children have secrets that they keep from their parents. That is not God's way. How can your parents help you and teach you and take care of you if you don't trust them and talk to them? If someone says you can't tell your parents something, tell them not to tell you, either.

KEY VERSE: *A gossip tells secrets, so don't hang around with someone who talks too much.* (Proverbs 20:19)

NOTE TO PARENTS: Children need someone with whom they can share their fears, dreams, and secrets. Your children should always feel confident that they can tell you everything that is on their mind. Guard that information carefully and lovingly. Don't use the information against them, don't belittle what they have shared, and don't betray their trust. Use this opportunity to affirm your children for being honest and for trusting you.

Q 464:

Is it OK to hit my brother back if he hit me first?

A: No, that would be taking revenge. In the Bible, God says that vengeance, or revenge, belongs to him. And he has delegated the authority to settle fights to the human authorities—police, teachers, and (for brothers and sisters who fight) parents. It's not right to hit back.

God also wants us to love, not hate. If we say we love him but hate people, then we don't really love him. That's because if we can't love someone in our own family, whom we can see, we can't possibly love God, whom we cannot see. That's why Jesus told us to be kind and to respond with love, even when someone hits us.

So if your brother (or sister) hits you, respond by being nice. If he or she continues to be mean, tell your parents and let them take care of it. God wants you to learn how to get along with people. Sometimes that can be very difficult at home. But if you can learn to love and to be kind to your family members, you probably will be able to get along with almost anyone else.

KEY VERSE: *Never pay back evil for evil to anyone. Do things in such a way that everyone can see you are honorable. (Romans 12:17)*

NOTE TO PARENTS: One of your challenges as a parent involves teaching kids to talk out their differences rather than fight. You can use a question like this one to emphasize the importance of being a peacemaker. Don't allow your kids to fight, or that is how they will learn to solve problems. Instead, encourage them to talk through their differences, and they will gain valuable skills in working through all sorts of conflicts.

Q 465:

Is it OK to bug my sister?

A: God wants us to be kind and considerate; respectful, not mean. Sometimes we may be having fun teasing or tickling each other, but we should stop if the person asks us to. We should not be cruel.

Sometimes we may bug other people by accident. In other words, we may do something that bothers people or makes them angry with us, and we don't even know it. As soon as we find out, we should stop doing it. That would be kind and considerate.

It's easy for brothers and sisters to get on each other's nerves. That's because they spend so much time together and because what one person does affects other people in a family. We need to work hard to make our families places of love and kindness.

KEY VERSE: *Let us not become conceited, or irritate one another, or be jealous of one another. (Galatians 5:26)*

NOTE TO PARENTS: When your children are bothering one another, remember to teach both children the correct response. The person doing the bothering should stop when asked and apologize. But the person being bothered should also try to be more patient.

Q 466:

Is kissing wrong?

A: Kissing isn't wrong. Many family members kiss each other. In some countries, friends kiss each other on the cheek when they say hello. And husbands and wives also often kiss each other. Kissing is one way that people can show love and affection to the people who are important to them.

KEY VERSES: *Then [Jesus] turned to the woman and said to Simon, "Look at this woman kneeling here. When I entered your home, you didn't offer me water to wash the dust from my feet, but she has washed them with her tears and wiped them with her hair. You didn't give me a kiss of greeting, but she has kissed my feet again and again from the time I first came in."* (Luke 7:44-45)

NOTE TO PARENTS: Many children try to copy what they see on TV, where kissing happens often. They may be confused and think that kissing is the cool way to express love (or "like") to someone. That's why a boy will sneak up on a girl, kiss her on the cheek, and run away. When young children ask about kissing, take time to explain its proper place and purpose.

Q 467:

Is it OK to drive my dad's car for four seconds?

A: If you drive a car on a public street and don't have a driver's license, you are breaking the law. If you drive a car on private property (for example, a driveway) and don't have a driver's license, you are being very foolish. This is true no matter how long you drive the car—four seconds or four hours. A car is a huge machine with a lot of power. It can be very dangerous to you and to others. That's why people have to be trained to drive and why they have to pass a driving test to get a license.

KEY VERSE: *[Joshua said,] "Be strong! Be very careful to follow all the instructions written in the Book of the Law of Moses. Do not deviate from them in any way." (Joshua 23:6)*

NOTE TO PARENTS: This kind of question may arise out of a child's judgment that it's OK to obey only the letter of the law. Also, some kids will try to see whether a rule can be broken under *any* circumstances at all so that they can then expand the rule-breaking into further territory. If it's OK to drive the car for four seconds, isn't it OK to drive it for eight seconds?

Q 468:

Do I really have to eat my vegetables, or are my parents just making sure I clean my plate?

A: God has said that children must obey their parents. So even if you don't like the taste of some food, you should eat it if your parents tell you to. Parents serve vegetables and tell children to eat them because vegetables help build strong bodies. The Bible tells us that we should take care of our bodies because that's where God lives and because God wants to use us. We should do what we can to stay healthy. That means eating good food, including vegetables.

KEY VERSES: *You do not belong to yourself, for God bought you with a high price. So you must honor God with your body. (1 Corinthians 6:19-20)*

NOTE TO PARENTS: Make good and healthy rules for eating and be very consistent in enforcing them. This brings peace and minimizes arguing because your child knows where the boundaries are. Be careful not to make too big a deal about food rules, though; eating should be a pleasant experience.

Q 469:

Why do I have to do chores?

A: Three reasons: (1) Good families work together. (2) Good family members want to help the family. (3) Doing chores is a way of taking responsibility, which is a part of growing up.

When children are very young, the parents do most of the work around the house. As children get older, they begin to help out as they are able. Many families assign special jobs, or "chores," to each person in the family. This way, everyone in the family can help make sure that everything in the house runs smoothly and the work gets done. Chores can include setting the table, cleaning and dusting, cutting the grass, shoveling the snow, washing clothes, washing windows, cooking meals, and even fixing the car—depending on the age and ability of the person.

When your parents give you chores to do, think of it as a compliment and an opportunity. They know you can handle the job. And you can be a helpful member of the family.

Remember, your parents aren't just trying to get you to do their work for them. They are preparing you for life. If you can learn now to be diligent and helpful, it will save you a lot of trouble when you grow up.

KEY VERSE: *Those who won't care for their own relatives, especially those living in the same household, have denied what we believe. Such people are worse than unbelievers. (1 Timothy 5:8)*

Q 470:

Why do I have to brush my teeth?

A: If your parents tell you to brush your teeth, then you should do it. God wants children to obey their parents. But there's another reason for brushing your teeth. You see, each person is a very special creation of our loving God. He has given us bodies to live in and to use for serving him. It is our job to take care of our bodies and to use them well. This means eating the right food, getting enough sleep, watching our weight, exercising, dressing warmly in cold weather, and not hurting ourselves with drugs, alcohol, and tobacco. It also means brushing our teeth and keeping ourselves clean.

It wouldn't be a sin if an adult didn't brush his teeth one day. It *would* be a sin, however, if he didn't take care of his teeth and let them get decayed. It's not a sin to eat candy. But it would be sinful if a person only ate candy and destroyed her health. God wants us to take care of our bodies.

KEY VERSE: *Don't you know that your body is the temple of the Holy Spirit, who lives in you and was given to you by God? (1 Corinthians 6:19)*

NOTE TO PARENTS: Be careful not to make conflicts over hygiene too big an issue. In fact, a wise parent will make it enjoyable. For example, you can tape a fun note to the toothbrush every night or offer to play a game as a family when everyone finishes brushing.

Q 471:

Why is it not good to talk to strangers?

A: Sadly, there are a lot of bad people in the world. Some of these people want to do bad things to children. That's why children are told not to talk to strangers. God does not have a rule against it in the Bible, so it's not wrong in that way. But God has said to obey your parents, so it would be wrong to disobey your mom or dad if they told you not to talk to adults you don't know. Even if your parents haven't said anything, it would be *wise* to stay away from strangers. Of course, some "strangers" are good people, and some may even need help. But still it is a good rule to stay away from adults you don't know.

So it's not *wrong* to talk to a stranger, it just could be dangerous. That's why your parents tell you not to do it. They don't want you to put yourself in a place where a stranger who is a bad person could hurt you. If a stranger asks you for help or you see someone in trouble, get your mom or dad or another adult that you know. Don't try to help by yourself.

KEY VERSE: *First, I want to remind you that in the last days there will be scoffers who will laugh at the truth and do every evil thing they desire. (2 Peter 3:3)*

NOTE TO PARENTS: One way to help your child learn how to talk to strangers is to role-play. This can give the child the opportunity to practice what to say and do *before* a scary situation arises. Also, explain that in the proper context and situations God requires us to be kind to new people we meet.

Q 472:

Can I do whatever I want when I'm older?

A: Some kids think that when they grow up they will be able to do anything they want. And it may appear that some adults live that way. But that's not true. All our lives we will have rules and laws to obey. When God gave the Ten Commandments, he gave them to all people, of all ages, for all time. No one outgrows the need to follow God's ways. We should always obey God.

That's one of the reasons God tells us to obey our parents. Doing what they say helps us learn to obey those in authority over us later in life. It also helps us want to do what's right.

KEY VERSE: *Don't let anyone think less of you because you are young. Be an example to all believers in what you teach, in the way you live, in your love, your faith, and your purity. (1 Timothy 4:12)*

NOTE TO PARENTS: The question behind the question here may be about double standards. If parents do something they forbid kids to do, it will appear to the children that adults can do whatever they want. Don't use your age to justify wrong behavior.

Fair and Square

Q 473:

Is it OK to say you tagged someone in tag when you really didn't?

A: Saying that you tagged someone in a game when you didn't would be lying. God says that lying is wrong. Actually, cheating is always lying and always wrong, even in a fun game like tag. Rules make a game fun. If there were no rules, then no one would know how to play, and you wouldn't know who won or lost. Think of how silly it would be if, in tag, everyone tagged everyone else all the time. It wouldn't be any fun and certainly wouldn't be tag. In a good game, all the players follow the rules. Breaking the rules ruins the game.

This is more important than most people realize. The Bible says that if you are true and honest in "small matters," you will be true and honest in important ones. If you cheat in simple games, you may make cheating a habit in your life. Be honest in everything you do, even playing tag.

KEY VERSE: *[Jesus said,] "Unless you are faithful in small matters, you won't be faithful in large ones. If you cheat even a little, you won't be honest with greater responsibilities." (Luke 16:10)*

NOTE TO PARENTS: Encourage your children to take the smallest opportunities to be honest and fair. This will make it easier to be honest whenever a harder situation comes along, and it will make it easier for others to trust them in other matters.

Q 474:

Is it OK to cheat at a game when the game is called "Cheat" and that's what you're supposed to do?

A: It is too bad that this game is called "Cheat" because it gives the idea that cheating is all right. Cheating is wrong because it's lying. When you are playing a game, no matter what it is called, you should play by the rules of the game. A game might call for players to make up stories about themselves, then people try to see which stories are true and which ones are false. That's not lying because it's a game and everyone knows that the stories are made up. Even in a game like that, you should play by the rules. Games with funny rules can be fun. For example, you and your friends might want to make up new rules for a game of baseball in the snow. As long as everyone understands the rules and follows them, you can have a fun game. It will be different from regular baseball, but that's OK because everyone will be playing by the new rules.

You don't have to play every game. Some games are bad and can cause harm. Some games might make you do something that is wrong or something you know your parents would not approve of. In other words, play by the rules of every game unless it breaks God's rules!

KEY VERSE: *The LORD hates cheating, but he delights in honesty. (Proverbs 11:1)*

NOTE TO PARENTS: As a practical matter, make sure everyone understands the rules when you're playing a game. That way you can head off arguments about cheating.

Q 475:

Why is it wrong to look at someone's spelling test and write the words down?

A: When you look at a person's test or copy from another person's homework, you are not being honest. God commands us to be honest because he is truthful, and whenever our behavior is not like God's, we are wrong. When you look at someone else's answers on a test and then put the answers on your test, you are telling the teacher that you knew the right answer when you didn't. That is cheating—and lying. When you copy a friend's homework and turn it in, you are telling your teacher that you did the work by yourself when you didn't. That is cheating—and lying.

Remember that every time you lie or cheat you hurt youself in the long run. You are hurting yourself because you aren't learning what you need to learn, and someday you will regret it.

KEY VERSES: *Be sure to do what you should, for then you will enjoy the personal satisfaction of having done your work well, and you won't need to compare yourself to anyone else. For we are each responsible for our own conduct. (Galatians 6:4-5)*

NOTE TO PARENTS: When a question like this arises, you can remind your child of the reasons for going to school and how cheating on a test undermines that purpose.

Q 476:

What's so bad about cheating in sports?

A: Cheating in sports is bad because it deceives others and ruins the game. Sometimes on TV or even in school, it can seem as if winning a game is the most important thing in the world. We forget that it's only a game. We let winning become too important. But nothing is so important that we should cheat to get it because God wants us to be honest, truthful, and fair in *all* that we do.

That's also why we should play clean. Some people think that playing dirty (hurting others in a game) is OK as long as it doesn't break any rules. But Christians should respect others as well as obey the rules.

Remember, the best reason to play sports is to improve our skills and physical condition and to learn about teamwork and how to win *and* lose. When we play any sport, we should do our best, play fair and clean, and enjoy the game. That's much more important than winning or losing.

KEY VERSES: *Cry out for insight and understanding. . . . Then you will understand what is right, just, and fair, and you will know how to find the right course of action every time. (Proverbs 2:3, 9)*

NOTE TO PARENTS: Some parents put tremendous pressure on kids to succeed in sports. Don't lose perspective. If you put too much pressure on your children, you may unknowingly encourage them to cheat, thinking that winning matters more to you than playing well.

Q 477:

Is it cheating when you let the other team win when their team wasn't playing that well?

A: No. Cheating is when you break the rules in order to gain an advantage. You can play differently without breaking the rules. There are times when you might want to play easier to give another person or team a chance in a game. If you do, just be up front about it.

But don't do it to make fun of them. If teams are very uneven and you know that one will slaughter the other, you may want to adjust the rules or change the teams to make it more even and thus more fun. Remember, what matters to God is that we treat each other with respect and love, not that we win.

KEY VERSES: *When the Holy Spirit controls our lives, he will produce this kind of fruit in us: love, joy, peace, patience, kindness, goodness, faithfulness, gentleness, and self-control. Here there is no conflict with the law. (Galatians 5:22-23)*

NOTE TO PARENTS: Sometimes parents wonder whether they should go easy when playing games with their kids and let the children win. If children lose all the time, they will grow discouraged and quit. You could say, "I'll go easy on you to help you get the hang of it." And if it bothers your child that you let him or her win, promise to play harder next time—and do so. You'll both enjoy the challenge and have some fun. It's appropriate to give them some challenge— that's how they learn and grow.

Q 478:

If I cheated and I won, do I have to tell?

A: You shouldn't cheat in the first place. But if you did cheat, you should admit what you have done and make it right, whether you win or lose. In a game that's very important to you, you will feel the temptation to win at any cost. That's when you might think about cheating to gain an advantage. Just remember that winning is not the most important thing—doing what God wants is.

When you do something wrong and realize it, the best response is to confess. First, talk to God about what you have done. Then tell the other team or individual, and ask for forgiveness. You also may need to tell your parents.

Of course, telling afterward doesn't make the cheating right. In fact, you may have to pay back or give back what you took through cheating. Don't think you can cheat and then laugh about it later. God wants you to become an honest person.

KEY VERSE: *Confess your sins to each other and pray for each other so that you may be healed. (James 5:16)*

NOTE TO PARENTS: This will be hard for kids. The typical response will be that they were just joking. But God doesn't want us to break his rules even temporarily. Help your child understand that if a person cheats and is caught, no one will believe that he or she was going to tell later, no matter what that person says about having innocent motives.

Q 479:

When you're playing a game, is it OK to fool the other players?

A: In any game, it is all right to fool the other players if that's part of the game and doesn't break the rules. For example, in basketball a good player will fake a shot to fool the person guarding him or her. Or the player might pretend to go one direction and then go the other way. A good soccer player may fake a pass and then shoot instead. A good quarterback in football will pretend to hand off the ball to a halfback. All of these fakes are important parts of the sports—and within the bounds of the rules.

The important thing is to play fair and clean, within the rules. It would *not* be OK, for example, for a soccer player to fake a kick to the ball in order to kick another player. That would be cheating.

KEY VERSE: *Whatever you eat or drink or whatever you do, you must do all for the glory of God. (1 Corinthians 10:31)*

NOTE TO PARENTS: There is a difference between fooling others within the rules of the game and breaking the rules of the game in order to gain an unfair advantage. Be aware that some coaches will encourage players to fake an injury or be unnecessarily rough. The problem with that advice is that it bends or breaks the rules, not that it fools the other team.

Q 480:

Why do people cheat just to win a stupid game?

A: Some people cheat in sports or in a game because winning means too much to them. They have to win at everything. Maybe they like the feeling of power and control. Perhaps they like the attention that the winner receives. Maybe they really think they are better people because they win. They may even be desperate for respect and think people will only like them if they win. People who cheat don't understand that God loves them whether they win or lose.

God wants us to work hard at whatever we do and to do it well. If we are not very good at something and want to be able to do better, then we should practice more and try harder. If we cheat to win, we are taking a short cut, and we will have to keep on cheating in order to win.

Remember, when you play a game, play fair, play clean, and play by the rules. God wants you to do your best and to be honest. And whether you win or lose, you should be a good sport.

KEY VERSES: *Jealousy and selfishness are not God's kind of wisdom. Such things are earthly, unspiritual, and motivated by the Devil. For wherever there is jealousy and selfish ambition, there you will find disorder and every kind of evil. (James 3:15-16)*

NOTE TO PARENTS: Affirm the character of kids who don't always brag about winning. You can illustrate this by talking about a favorite athlete who focuses on excelling rather than on bending the rules to win a game. Many people justify their cheating by saying, "I'm not the only one. Other people do it." Kids may do this, too. But that doesn't make it right.

Q 481:

What should I do if someone cheats me?

A: If you are playing a sport like soccer and someone on the other team does something like kick the ball when it's out of bounds, let the referee deal with it. Don't call the player a cheater or argue with the referee. Be careful about saying that someone cheated you just because you lost a game. Maybe you lost fair and square.

If you are playing a game that has no referees, like a board game, and someone continues to cheat, you can tell the person that he or she is not playing fairly. Be sure to keep your cool and explain that cheating is wrong and that the game isn't fun when people cheat. If the person doesn't listen or continues to cheat, you don't have to keep playing.

If an adult cheats you out of money at a store, you should tell your parents and let them deal with it.

Sometimes, no one can help. Then it might be better just to accept the wrong and trust God to work it out OK.

KEY VERSE: *Don't make accusations against someone who hasn't wronged you. (Proverbs 3:30)*

NOTE TO PARENTS: If your children are complaining about someone who cheats, encourage them to pray for that person. Ask that God will show that person why cheating is wrong and why it doesn't help.

What's Yours Isn't Mine

Q 482:

Why is it wrong to steal things?

A: God is honest and true. Taking what doesn't belong to you goes against God's nature. That is why stealing is wrong. God wants us to give to others, to help them, and to trust him to provide what we need.

Sometimes people steal because they want something (such as a bike, a tape player, or money) so badly that they will do anything to get it. Some people steal because they feel desperate. People who steal show that they don't trust God very much. God loves us and will never allow us to get into a situation where we have to steal something. He will provide what we need.

When you steal, you hurt God and yourself as much as you hurt the other person. You ignore and miss out on God's provision, get a bad reputation, and make other people feel like stealing from you. So you see, God really has our best interests in mind when he tells us not to steal.

KEY VERSE: *Do not steal. (Exodus 20:15)*

Q 483:

Is it OK to steal something back from someone who stole it from you?

A: No. Stealing is always wrong. Be careful about accusing people of stealing. You may *think* someone stole something from you when he or she really didn't. If you are pretty sure that someone stole something from you, politely ask the person about the item. Perhaps you are wrong and the person only has something that *looks* like yours. If you go and take it back, you may end up taking something that really doesn't belong to you. Then *you* will be guilty of stealing!

If someone actually did take something from you, it's better to ask the person about it than to make an accusation of stealing, even if the item has your name on it. You could say something like: "I see you found my pen. Thank you for finding it." Always assume the best of the other person's motives.

If you catch someone stealing from you or you know that this person has been stealing from a lot of kids, first talk to the person about it. If that doesn't seem to help, then talk to an adult—a parent or teacher—about the problem.

KEY VERSES: *Never pay back evil for evil to anyone. Do things in such a way that everyone can see you are honorable. Do your part to live in peace with everyone, as much as possible. (Romans 12:17-18)*

NOTE TO PARENTS: Handling a suspicion of stealing this way places the emphasis where it should be—on making friends instead of hurting people and making enemies.

Q 484:

Is it OK to keep a toy that belongs to someone else if they don't ask for it back?

A: No. Stealing is taking something that doesn't belong to you. One type of stealing happens when a person borrows something from someone else but doesn't give it back. We know that stealing is wrong, all kinds of stealing, because God has told us not to steal. And if God has said it's wrong, then doing it will end up hurting us and others. Stealing is wrong and ends up hurting us even if no one finds out about it. Remember, God knows.

If a friend gives you something to keep, then that gift is yours. It would not be stealing to keep it—you don't have to give it back. But if someone loans you something or gives you something to use for a while, then you need to give it back when the time is up or when you are finished— even if the person doesn't ask for it or has forgotten about it. The same is true if you find something that belongs to someone else. You should give it to the person—that would be the honest thing to do.

God gives us the command not to steal. He does this to help us and to protect us from the penalties of stealing and the reputation of being a thief. Besides, isn't that the way you would want to be treated? Wouldn't you want your toy or book or ball returned, even if you had forgotten about it?

KEY VERSE: *[Jesus said,] "Do for others as you would like them to do for you."(Luke 6:31)*

Q 485:

Would it be wrong if your friends told you something was for free, so you took it, and then you found out later it wasn't really free?

A: Wrongdoing is always wrong, even if we don't know it when we do it! Have you ever gone someplace you weren't supposed to go, said something you weren't supposed to say, or taken something you weren't supposed to take—without knowing you weren't supposed to? Everyone has at one time or another. Sometimes we don't find out until later that what we did was wrong. But when we find out, then what should we do? That's what really matters. We might have to ask for forgiveness or take something back. We certainly shouldn't do it again, now that we know better. For example, if friends said that something was free so you took it and then later you found out it wasn't free, you should take it back or pay for it. That would be the honest thing to do. Keeping it would be wrong.

Sometimes we just need to use common sense. For example, things in a store are hardly ever free. So if someone says they are, we should make sure by asking someone who works at the store. We shouldn't go along with *everything* our friends say. But we should go along with *everything* God says.

KEY VERSE: *You seem to believe whatever anyone tells you, even if they preach about a different Jesus than the one we preach, or a different Spirit than the one you received, or a different kind of gospel than the one you believed. (2 Corinthians 11:4)*

Q 486:

If it's wrong to steal, why do they call it "stealing bases" in baseball?

A: It's not really stealing; that's just the word they use to describe that kind of play. "Stealing bases" is part of the game of baseball. Baseball has other words that can be confusing, too: Batters are "walked" by the pitcher, some batters "sacrifice," the game is played on a "diamond," and the fourth base is called "home plate." Every game has its own special words and rules. To play any game the right way, it is important to know the rules and to understand what the special words mean. So "stealing" in baseball isn't the same as stealing in life. If someone really did *steal* second base, that person would pick the base up off the field and take it home. And that would be wrong!

KEY VERSE: *Young man, it's wonderful to be young! Enjoy every minute of it. Do everything you want to do; take it all in. But remember that you must give an account to God for everything you do. (Ecclesiastes 11:9)*

NOTE TO PARENTS: Be aware that kids sometimes don't understand the different meanings that a term can have. Encourage them to use words carefully because what we say has great power.

Q 487:

Is it wrong to copy computer games?

A: If a computer game is copyrighted, yes. What does *copyright* mean? It means that the person (or company) who created it is the only one with the right to copy it. People who write books, songs, magazine articles, and computer software often copyright their work so that other people can't sell or misuse it. The law says that anyone who *does* take or sell someone else's copyrighted work is guilty of stealing.

With stealing, usually we think of taking an object (money, a toy, a pencil, a hat, a ball, etc.) that belongs to someone else. But you can also steal information. When someone writes a song, the song belongs to that person. When someone writes a book, the book belongs to that person. Other people can have copies of the song or book if they *buy* them. Or someone could borrow another person's copy of the song or book. But it would be wrong just to *take* them—which is what happens when you make your own copies.

Remember, even if everybody does something wrong, it is still wrong because it still goes against God's nature.

KEY VERSE: *If you are a thief, stop stealing. Begin using your hands for honest work, and then give generously to others in need. (Ephesians 4:28)*

NOTE TO PARENTS: Don't accept bootleg copies of software or music for your kids, and don't make illegal copies for your own use. If you're unsure of what you can do with a particular program, check the license agreement that came with it.

Q 488:

Is it wrong to keep money that you find on the street?

A:

An honest person makes an honest effort to return things to their rightful owners, even when no one knows about it. With a wallet, the person could look for a name inside and contact the owner. With a large amount of money, the person could put up a sign or tell the police about it. Where the money is found is also important. Money found on a classroom floor was probably lost by someone in the class. Money found in a store was probably lost by someone who had just been in the store. In those cases, the person who found the money should tell the teacher or tell the store cashier. That would be the honest thing to do. The important thing is to do for the person who lost the money exactly what you would want them to do for you.

Sometimes it will be impossible to find the owner of the money. For example, you would probably never find the rightful owner of money found on the street or a dollar blowing across a field. But don't make excuses for keeping what doesn't belong to you—try to find the owner if you can.

KEY VERSES: *Jesus replied, "'You must love the Lord your God with all your heart, all your soul, and all your mind.' This is the first and greatest commandment. A second is equally important: 'Love your neighbor as yourself.'" (Matthew 22:37-39)*

NOTE TO PARENTS: Kids have their own saying for this scenario: "Finders keepers, losers weepers." Tell your kids that God's greatest commandment gives us a different standard—one that respects people and looks out for their best interests.

Q 489:

Is it stealing if a poor person takes food?

A:

Yes. No matter what a person steals or why, it is still stealing.

The Bible says a lot about poor people. God's people, the nation of Israel, were supposed to help the poor. And hungry people were allowed to gather leftover grain from the fields (called gleaning). But the poor were never told that they were allowed to steal food.

There are many poor and hungry people in the world. We should do whatever we can to help them (sending food, donating money to relief organizations) so they won't be tempted to steal food.

KEY VERSES: *O God, I beg two favors from you before I die. First, help me never to tell a lie. Second, give me neither poverty nor riches! Give me just enough to satisfy my needs. For if I grow rich, I may deny you and say, "Who is the LORD?" And if I am too poor, I may steal and thus insult God's holy name. (Proverbs 30:7-9)*

NOTE TO PARENTS: When your child asks a question like this, it's a great opportunity for you as a family to begin to support a relief agency or sponsor a child or family. It is also a good opportunity to pray together that God will meet your own family's daily needs and thank him for doing so.

Q 490:

Is it stealing to borrow someone else's stuff without asking?

A: It sure can be. Borrowing anything from anybody without asking doesn't show much respect for the owner. What if the owner needed it right away or had promised it to someone else? It always is best to ask permission to borrow something, even if it belongs to a good friend and you have used it before.

If the person has told you something like, "Use it anytime you want," and he or she isn't around to ask, that's different. You can go ahead and borrow it and leave a note. You want the person to know that it wasn't stolen and that *you* borrowed it. Asking permission and leaving notes show respect for your friend. Don't ever steal something and then make the excuse that you were "just borrowing it." Stealing is wrong, and so is lying. Be an honest person who respects others and their property.

KEY VERSE: *Do not steal your neighbor's property by moving the ancient boundary markers set up by your ancestors. (Proverbs 22:28)*

NOTE TO PARENTS: Siblings often fight over toys when they're young and over each other's clothes when they're older. This is an opportunity to teach children how to share and be generous. Kids don't learn this naturally; they need you to teach them.

Q 491:

What if someone is shoplifting and it is your friend—what do you do?

A: If you know that your friend is going to steal something or is trying to do so, you should point out that stealing is wrong and he or she shouldn't do it. If your friend doesn't want to listen to you, you should walk away, leave the store or wherever you are, and go home right away. Being with a person who is breaking the law can get you into trouble, too, because it is a crime not to report a crime. Tell your parents as soon as you get home.

KEY VERSES: *My dear brothers and sisters, if anyone among you wanders away from the truth and is brought back again, you can be sure that the one who brings that person back will save that sinner from death and bring about the forgiveness of many sins. (James 5:19-20)*

NOTE TO PARENTS: Help your child know how to pick friends and when it's time to stop being friends with someone. We want our kids to be positive influences, but there comes a time when they need to dissociate themselves from troublemakers.

Q 492:

What if you find something that doesn't belong to you and you can't find who it belongs to—is that stealing?

A: Finding something that doesn't belong to you isn't stealing, but you should try to find the owner if you can. How hard you try should match the value of what you find. A penny or nickel is worth very little; you don't need to put an ad in the paper to find the person who lost it. But an album of wedding pictures, a box of jewelry, or a wallet is worth a great deal. You should make a far greater effort to find the owner of such valuable items. Often your mom or dad will know exactly how to look for this person. If you find something at school, you can take it to the lost and found. Never use the statement "I just found it and can't see anybody around" as an excuse to call something yours.

KEY VERSES: *"If you see your neighbor's ox or sheep wandering away, don't pretend not to see it. Take it back to its owner. If it does not belong to someone nearby or you don't know who the owner is, keep it until the owner comes looking for it; then return it. Do the same if you find your neighbor's donkey, clothing, or anything else your neighbor loses. Don't pretend you did not see it."* (Deuteronomy 22:1-3)

NOTE TO PARENTS: Give examples of when you did this or when it was done to you and how you felt. You might also mention to your children that people will look with favor upon those who make an attempt to return something.

Questions
Kids Ask

Money Matters

6

Money Doesn't Grow on Trees

Q 493:

Where does money come from, God or people?

A: The Bible says that in the very beginning, God created the heavens and the earth (Genesis 1:1) and that everything was made by him (John 1:3). So everything there is came from God. The sun, moon, oceans, trees, animals, sky, and land all came from him. The Bible also says, "Whatever is good and perfect comes to us from God above" (James 1:17). But this doesn't mean that God makes every little thing in the world himself. Instead, he expects people to use the materials he has given them to make things like bread, cars, toys, medicine, houses, clothes, and money. God made the world and people, and he makes it all work right. You might say that money comes *from* God *through* people. But God doesn't make money—*people* print money and mint coins. God enables people to earn and use it.

God makes it possible for people to earn money. He made people. He made their skills. He made the bosses. He controls the world.

KEY VERSE: *It is a good thing to receive wealth from God and the good health to enjoy it. To enjoy your work and accept your lot in life—that is indeed a gift from God. (Ecclesiastes 5:19)*

NOTE TO PARENTS: This question assumes money comes *either* from God or from people. Emphasize the important role of both by thanking God for what you have and for the people through whom it comes.

Q 494:

Why is there such a thing as money?

A: People use money to trade one thing for another. Think about when you go to the store. If you want to get something in the store, how would you do that without money? You would have to trade something for what you want in the store, and the store would have to want what you have to trade. That might get very complicated. That's why there is money—it's something that everyone can use for trade.

KEY VERSE: *The king replied to Araunah, "No, I insist on buying it, for I cannot present burnt offerings to the LORD my God that have cost me nothing." So David paid him fifty pieces of silver for the threshing floor and the oxen. (2 Samuel 24:24)*

Q 495:

Why don't people just trade for what they need?

A: Long ago (and in some places even today) people traded *things* with each other instead of using money. They traded food they grew, animals they raised, things they made, and so forth. For example, someone might trade some grain for a table. Or someone might trade a cow for shoes and clothes. But this only worked if each of the traders wanted what the other had to trade. If you had only a model airplane to trade and no one else wanted it, you wouldn't be able to get what you needed. Money makes trading easier because everybody can use it. If you trade money for a new model airplane, the person who sold it to you can use the money to trade for a baseball glove. Money makes trading easy.

KEY VERSE: *Joseph collected all the money in Egypt and Canaan in exchange for grain, and he brought the money to Pharaoh's treasure-house. (Genesis 47:14)*

Q 496:

When was money invented?

A: Money was invented many thousands of years ago. We know that early Egyptian civilizations traded precious minerals, for example. In Old Testament times, people traded gold and silver by its weight rather than using coins. By New Testament times, people throughout the Roman Empire used coins to buy and sell.

KEY VERSES: *So they left Egypt and traveled north into the Negev—Abram with his wife and Lot and all that they owned, for Abram was very rich in livestock, silver, and gold. (Genesis 13:1-2)*

Q 497:

Why are those little pieces of paper worth so much?

A: It may seem strange that a little piece of paper, like a dollar bill, is worth so much. Actually, the paper itself isn't worth very much at all. The paper of a one-dollar bill is worth less than a penny. But the one-dollar bill has worth because the government says it does. It is worth 100 pennies.

The federal government says how much each special piece of paper is worth. And only the government can print money. If you drew your own money on paper, it wouldn't be worth anything, even if you said it was.

KEY VERSES: *[Jesus said,] "Here, show me the Roman coin used for the tax." When they handed him the coin, he asked, "Whose picture and title are stamped on it?" "Caesar's," they replied. "Well, then," he said, "give to Caesar what belongs to him. But everything that belongs to God must be given to God." (Matthew 22:19-21)*

Q 498:

Why are there all different kinds of money?

A: One reason is that each country makes its own money. Other differences come from different denominations of money. In Old Testament times, people used a unit of money called the *shekel*. Coins and bills are made with different values so money will be easy to manage. If the only kind of money were the penny, you would have to carry bags and bags of pennies to buy groceries.

Some people have a lot of fun collecting different kinds of money. They make a hobby of collecting coins and bills from all over the world and from different times in history.

KEY VERSES: *The LORD said to Moses, "If any of the people sin by unintentionally defiling the LORD's sacred property, they must bring to the LORD a ram from the flock as their guilt offering. The animal must have no physical defects, and it must be of the proper value in silver as measured by the standard sanctuary shekel." (Leviticus 5:14-15)*

NOTE TO PARENTS: If your child shows a lot of interest in this, you could start a collection of different types of money from different countries. You could even use the money as a way of studying those countries' cultures.

Q 499:

Where does the money go when you buy what you want?

A: When you give money to a store owner or a salesperson, that person puts it in a safe place, such as a drawer, a safe, or a bank. Later the store owner can use the money to pay the employees and to pay for things he or she wants. The employees then go out and buy things that they want. And the store owners who get those dollars do the same thing with the money they get.

Let's say you give Mr. Jones a dollar to buy a toy you want. Later, Mr. Jones uses that dollar to buy a stamp at the post office. Then the postal clerk gives the dollar to Mrs. Smith as change. Mrs. Smith goes home and gives her son the dollar for his allowance. The money just keeps going from person to person!

KEY VERSE: *When she told the man of God what had happened, he said to her, "Now sell the olive oil and pay your debts, and there will be enough money left over to support you and your sons." (2 Kings 4:7)*

NOTE TO PARENTS: It's not immediately obvious where money goes when you buy something, so this is a logical question. Just try to explain that it simply changes hands. One person gives it to another.

Q 500:

Why isn't a dollar worth a dollar anymore?

A: When people say that a dollar isn't worth a dollar anymore, they mean that a dollar doesn't buy as much in a store as it used to. Let's say that ten years ago a dollar bought ten chocolate-chip cookies. But today when you go to the store you only get seven cookies for your dollar. You would be getting less for your money than you used to.

This happens for many reasons, but it's a little like a circle of dominoes. The store owner, the baker, the chocolate-chip maker, and the cocoa-bean farmer are all dominoes in the circle. If a hurricane wipes out part of the cocoa-bean crop, the cocoa-bean farmer has to raise his prices. The chocolate-chip maker has to pay more for cocoa, so he then has to raise *his* prices. The baker has to pay more for chocolate chips, so he has to raise *his* prices. And the store owner has to pay more for cookies, so he has to raise *his* prices. It is not always that simple, but that's one reason prices go up.

Don't worry about it, though. No matter what a dollar is worth, God is in control, and we can trust him to take care of us.

KEY VERSE: *The LORD will not let the godly starve to death, but he refuses to satisfy the craving of the wicked. (Proverbs 10:3)*

You Can Bank on It

Q 501:

Why do we put our money in the bank when we have to keep going back there to get it?

A: The main reason that people put money in banks is for safety. At home you can lose your money or someone can steal it. But it is very difficult to steal from a bank.

It's also easier to keep your money in a bank than to keep it all in your house or in your pocket. Banks are safe and easy to use.

Banks also pay you a little bit when you save your money there. That's called interest.

KEY VERSES: *The master replied, "You wicked and lazy servant! You think I'm a hard man, do you, harvesting crops I didn't plant and gathering crops I didn't cultivate? Well, you should at least have put my money into the bank so I could have some interest." (Matthew 25:26-27)*

NOTE TO PARENTS: Children who are old enough to have their own bank accounts are still years away from being able to get to their money without your help. It's a good idea to let them keep enough of their spending money at home that they are not frustrated by this.

Q 502:

How much money are we supposed to put in the bank?

A: You don't *have* to put any money in the bank. The Bible doesn't tell us that people have to put their money in banks. But putting money in the bank is a good idea.

When you put money in the bank, you are saving it for later. You should decide first what it is you want to save for. Maybe you want to save up for a special toy, a campout with the youth group, or college. Once you know what you're saving for, you can figure out how much money you need to put in the bank each week or each month so you will have enough for what you want when the time comes.

KEY VERSES: *[Jesus said,] "Their master returned from his trip and called them to give an account of how they had used his money. The servant to whom he had entrusted the five bags of gold said, 'Sir, you gave me five bags of gold to invest, and I have doubled the amount.' The master was full of praise. 'Well done, my good and faithful servant. You have been faithful in handling this small amount, so now I will give you many more responsibilities. Let's celebrate together!'" (Matthew 25:19-21)*

NOTE TO PARENTS: Take this sort of question as an opportunity to talk about budgeting. Children should have savings goals and work toward them, even if the goals are small. Help your child identify these goals, write them down, and save up little by little. This will illustrate the wisdom of saving money, the reasons for saving, and the power of *choice*.

Q 503:

Why do we have to put money in the bank when we have our own piggy banks?

A: A bank lets you do a lot more with your money than just store it. If someone has money in the bank, he or she can write checks, get small amounts of money out as it is needed, and pay bills from the money in the bank.

A bank has other benefits too. It pays you a little bit for keeping your money, it keeps the money safe, and it can hold as much as you'll ever get. It's fun to put money in a piggy bank. But sooner or later you'll want to have a bank account.

KEY VERSE: *Guard these treasures well until you present them, without an ounce lost, to the leading priests, the Levites, and the leaders of Israel at the storerooms of the LORD's Temple in Jerusalem. (Ezra 8:29)*

NOTE TO PARENTS: A young child has no idea how much money passes through an adult's checking account, so a child might think, If I can keep my money in a piggy bank, why can't you? Explain to your children that you have to keep track of much more money than they do. You might even want to show your children your monthly budget and your plan to meet all your commitments. You can also point out the bank systems that help you do this.

Q 504:

What does the bank do with everyone's money?

A: They put some of it in a vault and loan a lot of it to others. They don't need to keep everyone's money in a separate place. And they don't even need to keep all of it in the vault. They just need to have enough to give to anyone who comes to get some of his or her money out. The bank keeps track of everybody's money through its computer system.

A bank is a business that makes money by loaning money to others. Here's how it works. A lot of people put money in the bank. Then the bank loans some of the money to other people. For example, most people who want to buy a house borrow money from a bank. The people who borrow the money pay it back plus a little more. The extra that they pay is called interest. The more loans the bank makes, the more people pay interest, and the more money the bank makes.

KEY VERSES: *Do not charge interest on the loans you make to a fellow Israelite, whether it is money, food, or anything else that may be loaned with interest. You may charge interest to foreigners, but not to Israelites, so the LORD your God may bless you in everything you do in the land you are about to enter and occupy. (Deuteronomy 23:19-20)*

Q 505:

What happens to my money if the bank gets robbed?

A: Don't worry about your money in the bank. It's safe. Very few banks get robbed, and most bank robbers get caught. The few thieves who get away get very little money. Also, the money in the bank is insured. The government guarantees that even if someone stole all the money in the bank, you would still get yours back.

KEY VERSES: *[Jesus said,] "Don't store up treasures here on earth, where they can be eaten by moths and get rusty, and where thieves break in and steal. Store your treasures in heaven, where they will never become moth-eaten or rusty and where they will be safe from thieves." (Matthew 6:19-20)*

NOTE TO PARENTS: Children tend to believe horror stories, especially stories about bank robberies. Assure your child that a bank is a safe place to put money. Because of tight security, many bank robbers take a very small percentage of the money actually in the bank. Also remind your child that our ultimate trust is in God, not the bank. In 1929, those who trusted in American banks *did* suffer losses, but God did not abandon his people.

Q 506:

Why do banks give interest?

A: Interest is a small payment you get for putting your money in the bank. The bank wants you to let it keep your money so it can loan the money to others. To get you to do this, the bank pays you a little bit for leaving your money there. The bank pays you interest.

Why does the bank want to loan money to others? So it can make money. The people who borrow money from the bank have to pay interest on their loans. The more the bank has to loan, the more interest payments it can collect.

It's OK for a bank to charge interest because that's how it makes money. But we should not treat our family and friends that way. In Old Testament times, God did not allow his people to charge each other interest. They were to loan money without charging for it.

KEY VERSE: *Do not charge your relatives interest on anything you lend them, whether money or food. (Leviticus 25:37)*

NOTE TO PARENTS: You can demonstrate the way interest works by giving your child money to buy candy. Pretend you are a bank and are loaning the money to him. He will have to pay it all back plus a penny if he pays you tomorrow, a nickel if he pays in a week, and so on. Whoever the money belongs to gets to collect the interest.

Q 507:

What are accounts?

A: An account is a place to put your money in a bank. The money is set aside just for you. An account is like a piggy bank or an envelope with your name on it at the bank. It's a way for the bank to keep track of your money.

Your parents, friends, and many other people also have money in the bank. The bank keeps track of each person's money by using accounts. If three of your friends gave you some money to keep for them, you could keep it in three separate places. Another way would be to write on a piece of paper how much each person had given to you. Then you could put all the money in one place. That's how accounts work at a bank. All the money is put together, but the bank has a record of how much of *your* money they have.

KEY VERSE: *They gave Hilkiah the high priest the money that had been collected by the Levites who served as gatekeepers at the Temple of God. The gifts were brought by people from Manasseh, Ephraim, and from all the remnant of Israel, as well as from all Judah, Benjamin, and the people of Jerusalem. (2 Chronicles 34:9)*

NOTE TO PARENTS: You can explain that a bank account is like a piggy bank at home, except that the bank pays you and can hold a lot more. You might even get out the Monopoly money and play "bank." You can illustrate a lot and have fun as well.

Q 508:

How can we buy things with a check instead of money?

A: A check is a set of instructions to the bank to pay money from a person's account to someone else. If you look closely at a check you will see the words *Pay to the order of* and then a blank line. This line is a message to the bank; it means, "When the person named on this line asks for the amount of money written on this check, go ahead and pay the person, and take the money from my account." There is a place for the person who wrote the check to sign it to show that the check is real.

Checks are more convenient than cash. A check allows you to pay someone without having to go to the bank or carry a lot of money with you.

Checks are also safer than cash. If you lose cash, anyone can use it. But a check can only be cashed by the person you wrote it to. That's why people send checks—not cash—through the mail.

KEY VERSES: *[Nehemiah] also said to the king, "If it please Your Majesty, give me letters to the governors of the province west of the Euphrates River, instructing them to let me travel safely through their territories on my way to Judah. And please send a letter to Asaph, the manager of the king's forest, instructing him to give me timber. I will need it to make beams for the gates of the Temple fortress, for the city walls, and for a house for myself." And the king granted these requests, because the gracious hand of God was on me. (Nehemiah 2:7-8)*

NOTE TO PARENTS: Write a check the next time you give your child money. Then take your child to the bank to cash it.

Q 509:

How does a check bounce?

A: The word *bounce* describes what happens when a person writes a check for more money than he or she has in the bank. A check is a set of instructions to the bank that says, "Pay this amount of money to the person named on this check." If there's not enough money in the account, the bank won't follow the instructions. It won't cash the check. The bank says, "This person doesn't have enough money to cover this check" and returns the check. It "bounces" back.

A check is a promise. Just as we should always keep our spoken promises, so we should always make sure we have enough money in the bank to cover the checks we write. It is dishonest to write a check when we know we don't have enough money to cover it.

KEY VERSES: *[Jesus said,] "Who would begin construction of a building without first getting estimates and then checking to see if there is enough money to pay the bills? Otherwise, you might complete only the foundation before running out of funds. And then how everyone would laugh at you! They would say, 'There's the person who started that building and ran out of money before it was finished!'"(Luke 14:28-30)*

Q 510:

Where does all the money in the bank machines come from?

A: Bank workers put it there. About once a week they open the machines (called automatic teller machines, or ATMs) and put the money in. They get the money from the bank's safe. The bank workers put enough into the machines so whoever needs to get some from their account can do so.

KEY VERSES: *Joash gave instructions for a chest to be made and set outside the gate leading to the Temple of the LORD. Then a proclamation was sent throughout Judah and Jerusalem, telling the people to bring to the LORD the tax that Moses, the servant of God, had required of the Israelites in the wilderness. This pleased all the leaders and the people, and they gladly brought their money and filled the chest with it. (2 Chronicles 24:8-10)*

NOTE TO PARENTS: Younger children often get the impression from watching adults use automatic teller machines that you can get money whenever you want and get as much as you want. Explain that using an ATM is like getting money out of your piggy bank. You are getting out money that you had put in earlier. Older children can benefit from having and using an ATM card. It can be very convenient for them and for you, and it can give them practice managing their own money.

In God We Trust

Q 511:
Is it all right to pray to God for money?

A: Yes, it is fine and good to pray to God about money and to ask him for money. The Bible tells Christians to "pray about everything" (Philippians 4:6), that "whatever is good and perfect comes to us from God" (James 1:17), and that "the reason you don't have what you want is that you don't ask God for it" (James 4:2). God *wants* you to know this, and there is no better person to ask than God whenever you need anything, including money. You *should* ask God for the money you need.

Just think carefully about what you want the money for. God promises to provide what we need. But Jesus warned against greed and love for money. God won't give you money to get something just because you want it badly.

KEY VERSE: *This same God who takes care of me will supply all your needs from his glorious riches, which have been given to us in Christ Jesus. (Philippians 4:19)*

NOTE TO PARENTS: Whenever you pray for money as a family, thank God for the jobs, gifts, and other sources of income he has already provided. Remember to show your thankfulness even when you need more.

Q 512:
How do I trust God for money?

A: First, pray. Tell God what you need, what you would like, and how you feel. But also tell him that you trust him to take care of you and to do what is best for you. Then put your mind at ease and do not worry. God promises to provide for his people. He also tells us to be content with what we have. You can be sure that God is doing what is best for you.

KEY VERSE: *[Jesus said,] "Don't be troubled. You trust God, now trust in me." (John 14:1)*

NOTE TO PARENTS: You can demonstrate trust with this simple exercise: Give your child five dollars. Tell him or her that you will need that money to buy groceries later. Emphasize that you are *trusting* him or her to keep the money safe and give it to you when you need it. This is the same way we should trust God, believing that he will provide for us when we need something and not worrying about our future.

Q 513:

Why doesn't God just give us money when we need it?

A: God does give us money when we need it. God always meets our needs. But sometimes we don't see God's provision for what it is. God usually provides for us through jobs, people, and other ordinary means. Even though we don't think of these as "miracles," they still come from God.

God wants you to plan, to work, to be responsible, and to use well what he's already given to you. When you need something, God may want you to use something that you already have instead. Or he may want you to make something yourself instead of buying a new one. Or he may ask you to get along without whatever you think you need.

There is a difference between *need* and *want*. People often want a lot of things they don't really need. Your basic needs are a little bit of food, a few clothes, and someplace to sleep. Most of us have much, much more than we truly *need*.

You also should realize that God lets people experience the results of their own choices—including their choices about spending money. He doesn't rescue his people from every mistake they make. If you make lots of bad choices with your money, you will suffer lots of bad consequences.

KEY VERSES: *"My thoughts are completely different from yours," says the LORD. "And my ways are far beyond anything you could imagine. For just as the heavens are higher than the earth, so are my ways higher than your ways and my thoughts higher than your thoughts." (Isaiah 55:8-9)*

Q 514:

Why are some people rich?

A: People become rich for many different reasons. Some people are rich because they were born into rich families. Others become rich by working hard, saving, and investing wisely. A few get their money as gifts or by winning contests. Some people get their money illegally—they cheat others and commit crimes.

But some people who seem rich have lots of nice things but no money. They're so far in debt that they may never get out. They're not really rich; they just *look* that way.

Remember that "rich" and "poor" are just labels. Many people who live in poor countries would say that *everyone* in the United States is rich. They would say *you* are rich. Why? Because compared to them, you are. You have a lot more than they have.

You are truly rich only when you are content with what you have. If you have enough for your needs and enough to give some away, you can be content. Be glad just to love and serve God. Then you will be the richest person in town.

KEY VERSE: *[David prayed,] "Riches and honor come from you alone, for you rule over everything. Power and might are in your hand, and it is at your discretion that people are made great and given strength." (1 Chronicles 29:12)*

Q 515:

Do billionaires still need to trust God for money they need?

A: *Everybody* needs to trust God for money, even billionaires. The Bible tells about a man named Job who lost all his wealth in one day. At the time, Job was one of the richest men alive.

No one has any money except what God lets them have. Billionaires get all their money from God, just as you do. God could take the money away in a second, just as he could give you a billion dollars in a second.

KEY VERSES: *This is what the LORD says: "Let not the wise man gloat in his wisdom, or the mighty man in his might, or the rich man in his riches. Let them boast in this alone: that they truly know me and understand that I am the LORD who is just and righteous, whose love is unfailing, and that I delight in these things. I, the LORD, have spoken!" (Jeremiah 9:23-24)*

NOTE TO PARENTS: If you talk or joke about wanting to be rich, your kids will get the impression that rich people are truly happier than the rest of us. But the reality is that rich people have more to worry about—much more (see Ecclesiastes 5:12). Remind your kids that *every* person should trust God for his or her needs, even billionaires. The key to happiness is loving God, not having more money.

Q 516:

Why doesn't God take rich people's money and give it to the poor people?

A: God wants more than to just end poverty. He wants us to love each other as much as he loves us. Just imagine how awful it would be if everyone had plenty of money and no kindness. Money alone will not make anybody happy. But if everyone would obey God and love one another, we would be better people *and* happier.

That is why God has chosen to use his people to help others instead of just making everyone rich. He wants us to learn to be kind, generous, and wise. He wants people to love and help each other.

KEY VERSE: *Yes, you will be enriched so that you can give even more generously. And when we take your gifts to those who need them, they will break out in thanksgiving to God. (2 Corinthians 9:11)*

NOTE TO PARENTS: It is important for children to understand that we are God's hands and feet in this world.

Q 517:

How do poor people get poor?

A: Most people become poor by being born into poor families. In fact, many people in the world are born in a poor country where almost everyone is poor. It's not their fault that they are poor.

There are many other reasons for poverty too. Some people are born with a physical or mental handicap, or they are injured in an accident or in war, and they find it very hard to get a good job. Some are poor because they have been cheated by other people. And some people become poor because they made bad choices.

No matter what makes someone poor, we must try to help. God is kind to us even though we make bad choices and mistakes. So we should be kind to others, even if we think it's their own fault that they are poor.

KEY VERSE: *A poor person's farm may produce much food, but injustice sweeps it all away. (Proverbs 13:23)*

NOTE TO PARENTS: Never tell a child that poor people are always to blame for their own poverty, or that people always become poor because of wrongdoing. People become poor for many reasons, and misfortune and injustice are responsible for a lot of poverty (see Amos 8:4-7). Our duty as Christians is to help those who hurt.

Q 518:

Why doesn't the government just print more money in factories and give it to the poor?

A: Some governments have tried to print more money and give it to the poor. It did not work because very soon the money was worth very little.

Money is not just printed paper. It gets its value from something else. In our country, money gets its value from all the goods and services that people make. Each dollar means that someone somewhere did one dollar's worth of work. The more work we (the whole country) do, the more money we have. The less work we do, the less money we have.

The best way to help poor people get more money is to help them get jobs. That way they get paid while they also create more valuable goods and services.

KEY VERSE: *Hard workers have plenty of food; playing around brings poverty. (Proverbs 28:19)*

Q 519:

Why didn't God give us money right away when my dad lost his job?

A: We don't always know why God does what he does. But we know that he loves us and has a plan for us, even for the hard times.

Sometimes God is working out something that we don't know about yet. Maybe it's even better than what we wanted or had before. God can use times like this to teach us to trust him more. As we trust him more, he can trust us with more.

Losing a job can be very painful and difficult. The person without a job wonders what he or she will do and where the money will come from. If your dad has lost his job, pitch in with any money you can. Say encouraging words to him. Donate your allowance. Do odd jobs for neighbors to earn more money if you can. Ask God to provide what you need, and trust him to do so.

KEY VERSE: *[God says,] "Trust me in your times of trouble, and I will rescue you, and you will give me glory." (Psalm 50:15)*

NOTE TO PARENTS: This question is difficult to answer when a family member has lost a job and needy dependents don't know what the future holds. But it is very important to avoid blaming God or anyone else. Pull together, help each other, and readjust your expectations of needs and wants. Take the experience as an opportunity to show your children what it means to live by faith.

Q 520:

Why does God sometimes wait until the last minute to supply our needs?

A: It may seem as though God waits until the last minute to supply your needs, but remember that God has a timetable that you can't see. He has a plan for you. Nothing can stop that plan, not even a shortage of money. God may wait because he wants you to trust him more. God always remembers you and hears your prayers. And he never runs out of anything.

Sometimes people wait till the last minute to pray. Instead, we should be praying to God all the time about our needs. We can trust him to take care of us.

KEY VERSES: *[Moses said,] "For forty years I led you through the wilderness, yet your clothes and sandals did not wear out. You had no bread or wine or other strong drink, but he gave you food so you would know that he is the LORD your God." (Deuteronomy 29:5-6)*

NOTE TO PARENTS: This question can arise when a child hears about God providing for someone in the nick of time, such as right before a rent check is due. Remind your family that God provides for us day after day. Moses pointed out to the Israelites that God had prevented their sandals and clothes from wearing out for forty years (Deuteronomy 29:5). Just like the Israelites, we sometimes forget that God is providing for us all the time. Thank God for all he has given so far.

Q 521:

If God owns everything, why doesn't he keep it all in heaven?

A: God owns everything because he is the Lord of all. But he created all good things for *us* to use and enjoy. He didn't create things just so he could keep them all or even because he needed them. He mainly wants *us* to use them and to use them wisely so we will be happy.

Remember that God is spirit. He doesn't need money, toys, food, or other things. What would he do with all our stuff? He would rather give it to us so we can learn to be responsible and use it in his service.

KEY VERSES: *[God says,] "All the animals of the forest are mine, and I own the cattle on a thousand hills. Every bird of the mountains and all the animals of the field belong to me."* (Psalm 50:10-11)

NOTE TO PARENTS: Always tie ownership of things to stewardship of those things. Having a pet means feeding and taking care of it. Having a toy means using it properly and putting it away when you're done. Reward your children whenever they show good stewardship by being more willing to grant their next request. And be sure to say why you're so willing.

Q 522:

If God owns everything, why do people sell stuff like it is their own and charge however much they want for it?

A: God owns everything because he created everything and is in charge of everything. But God trusts people with things and money. He makes people managers of the things they have. God has given you your toys, for example. Those toys are yours to take care of. As part of that responsibility, you may decide one day that you are too old for them and want to sell them or give them away. If your parents say it's OK, you can sell those things and use the money for other things. Just remember to set fair prices.

KEY VERSE: *[David prayed,] "Who am I, and who are my people, that we could give anything to you? Everything we have has come from you, and we give you only what you have already given us!"* (1 Chronicles 29:14)

NOTE TO PARENTS: Helping your children clean up and sell old things and then allowing them to use that money to buy something they want can teach them a lot about the benefit of taking care of the things they manage.

Q 523:

Why did Jesus talk about money when he didn't have very much?

A: We don't know how much money Jesus had. We know that he didn't own a home and that he had few possessions. But we also know that he had everything he needed. The Bible doesn't say that Jesus or the disciples lived in poverty. Luke 8:3 tells us that some women gave money to support Jesus and his disciples. Judas was in charge of the money bag.

Jesus talked about money because he wanted to teach us how to use it right. He knew that we would love money and be tempted to be greedy. And he knew that the love of money leads to all kinds of evil. How we feel about money and how we use it matter a great deal.

KEY VERSES: *Among them were Mary Magdalene, from whom he had cast out seven demons; Joanna, the wife of Chuza, Herod's business manager; Susanna; and many others who were contributing from their own resources to support Jesus and his disciples. (Luke 8:2-3)*

NOTE TO PARENTS: Be careful not to idealize poverty or imply that being like Jesus means going hungry. If you sense that your child is afraid of being poor "like Jesus," reassure him or her that Jesus was not poverty-stricken. He had everything he needed. God met all his needs, and God will meet ours, too.

Q 524:

Did Jesus ever have problems with money?

A: If you mean "Did Jesus have trouble paying his bills?", the answer is no. God provided all Jesus needed. Jesus never lived in poverty. People gave money to him and to the disciples so they could spend most of their time telling people about God's good news. Jesus had enough money for all his bills.

If you mean "Did Jesus ever spend money foolishly?", again the answer is no. Judas once accused Jesus of misusing money, but the truth was that Judas had been stealing from Jesus (John 12:1-6).

KEY VERSES: *Jesus said, ". . . Open the mouth of the first fish you catch, and you will find a coin. Take the coin and pay the tax for both of us." (Matthew 17:26-27)*

NOTE TO PARENTS: A question like this naturally follows a child's struggle to understand exactly how Jesus was human. Make a distinction between needing money, which Jesus did—and mishandling money, which Jesus didn't. Taxes are a good example. Jesus had to pay them just like everyone else. He did not try to avoid his duty to pay taxes or squander his money and become unable to pay them.

Q 525:

Is money one of the most important things in life?

A: Money is both very important and not at all important. Money makes it possible for us to pay bills and buy food and other things we need. Money also helps us support God's work in the world. We can use money to help feed hungry people, clothe poor people, and share the good news about Jesus with people all over the world. We need money to do these things.

Money is not the *most* important thing in life, however. The most important thing in life is our relationship with God. Only God can forgive our sins, and only God can teach us how to live. The people God has put in our lives are also much more important than money. Money can't buy you a new mom or dad, good friends, good health, or good neighbors. Money can't buy you any of the things that matter most in life.

So put God at the top of your list. Then put your family and friends. Then put everyone else God created. And then put money underneath all of those. Use money to serve people, not the other way around.

KEY VERSES: *Being wise is as good as being rich; in fact, it is better. Wisdom or money can get you almost anything, but it's important to know that only wisdom can save your life. (Ecclesiastes 7:11-12)*

Q 526:

If salvation is free, why do we have to buy a Bible?

A: We pay for Bibles because it costs money to produce them. The publishers that publish them, the printers that print them, and the stores that sell them all need to be able to pay their workers. God tells us to pay what we owe (Leviticus 19:13), and the price we pay for a Bible pays the workers' wages.

The Bible is God's Word. It's reasonable to pay for something so important.

Salvation, on the other hand, comes from God and *is* free, but it has nothing to do with money. God says that the penalty for sin is death. If you sin, you must die. That means that you will be separated from God forever. God sent his only Son, Jesus, to die on the cross in our place. Because Jesus did not sin, he did not have to die. But he chose to die in our place. If we ask God to forgive our sins and accept that Jesus died in our place, God will forgive us. We will become his children. So salvation is *free* for us because we do not have to pay the penalty for our sins. Jesus paid it.

KEY VERSES: *If you confess with your mouth that Jesus is Lord and believe in your heart that God raised him from the dead, you will be saved. For it is by believing in your heart that you are made right with God, and it is by confessing with your mouth that you are saved. (Romans 10:9-10)*

Living and Giving

Q 527:

What is tithing?

A: *Tithe* is a word used in the Bible. It means "a tenth." In Old Testament times, God commanded the Israelites to give to the priests a tithe of all they produced. They gave sheep, grain, cows, and so forth. These tithes were like income for the priests, enabling them to work full-time leading the people in worship and taking care of God's house. Sometimes people gave even more to say thank you to God for all the good things he had provided. Their giving showed that they trusted God to supply their needs.

Many Christians use the word *tithe* to describe the giving they do. Usually they mean that they give back to God a portion of their income. Sometimes they give a tenth (10 percent); sometimes they give less or more. When we give gladly, we show that we trust God to take care of us.

KEY VERSE: *[God said,] "Should people cheat God? Yet you have cheated me! But you ask, 'What do you mean? When did we ever cheat you?' You have cheated me of the tithes and offerings due to me." (Malachi 3:8)*

NOTE TO PARENTS: Some parents require that their kids tithe; they want their children to develop this important habit early in life. Other parents are reluctant to require it; they want their children to give willingly. One way to handle this is by requiring your children to give, telling them about tithing and what you do, and letting them decide how much they want to give. Whatever the amount, help them set aside a portion for God every time they earn money.

Q 528:

Why do I have to give money to church?

A: It is part of God's plan for Christians to give money to the church so the church can do God's work and help others learn how to follow him. Like families and businesses, churches have bills to pay—electric bills, phone bills, water bills, and many other expenses. Churches also have to pay salaries to the pastors and secretaries. The church's money pays for ministries such as Sunday school, missions, and special events. Churches don't sell tickets for the worship services or sell products, so they get their money from people in the congregation who give freely.

God's people have always given money to those who lead in worship and service to God. Abraham did it. The Israelites did it. Jesus did it. The apostles did it. Everyone who loves God does it. They know it is a lot of work to lead God's people, so they pitch in and help pay for it.

KEY VERSE: *For I can testify that they gave not only what they could afford but far more. And they did it of their own free will. (2 Corinthians 8:3)*

NOTE TO PARENTS: Help your kids understand that the church is a community. It is a group of people who all share a relationship with Christ, much like a family. And like a family, every person should pitch in and help make it work.

Q 529:

How much should a person give to the church?

A: Christians are free to give as much as they want to the church. But many like to start with 10 percent of their income. That's their tithe. Those who are able should give even more to other people and ministries that serve God.

Just be careful not to brag about your giving. Jesus scolded the Pharisees for boasting about what they gave (Matthew 23:23). He said, "When you give to someone, don't tell your left hand what your right hand is doing. Give your gifts in secret, and your Father, who knows all secrets, will reward you" (Matthew 6:3-4).

Some people need to ask a different question: Why am I not giving anything to the church? Some people can't bring themselves to give 10 percent but start smaller and pray that God will help them increase their giving. It's better to give *something* than to wait until you have enough to give a lot.

KEY VERSE: *You must each make up your own mind as to how much you should give. Don't give reluctantly or in response to pressure. For God loves the person who gives cheerfully. (2 Corinthians 9:7)*

NOTE TO PARENTS: Children can be very generous givers. They will often give money to people whom they like just to show their affection or give everything they have on a wave of good feeling. If your child wants to give extra, talk about it. Ask whether the gift matches the need. Explore other ways of giving besides handing over cash. You don't need to protect them from every mistake—they'll learn from the experience—but you can give them guidance.

Q 530:

Why do some people keep all their money to themselves instead of giving some to God?

A: It is true that some people do not give any money to the church. Some of them haven't learned to trust God yet—they are afraid to let go of their money. They are growing in their faith and are just learning to trust him. Some don't know that they have a responsibility to give. Some are just greedy. If you know of someone like this, pray that they will learn to trust in God instead of their money.

But be careful not to spy on others and try to figure out who is a good giver and who isn't. You can never really know how much people give or whether it's a little or a lot in God's sight. Jesus once told about a poor widow who gave only two small coins (Mark 12:41-44). Jesus said she gave more than the rich people did because she gave all she had. Set a good example yourself and let God teach everyone else how to give.

KEY VERSE: *If you are really eager to give, it isn't important how much you are able to give. God wants you to give what you have, not what you don't have. (2 Corinthians 8:12)*

NOTE TO PARENTS: This question gives you a good opportunity to expand your child's idea of giving to include other kinds of selflessness. Whenever your child shares a toy, defers to someone else's choice of video, or lets someone else get the bigger dessert, affirm your child for giving.

Q 531:

Where does the money I give to church go?

A: It goes to the church's bank account, where it stays until the church treasurer writes checks to pay all the church's expenses. The church has to pay for the building, heat, light, phone, postage, Sunday school supplies, pastors' salaries, staff salaries, missions, and other ministries and expenses.

A gift to God's people is a gift to God. Give because you are thankful for all God has given you, and he will take care of you.

KEY VERSES: *Don't you know that those who work in the Temple get their meals from the food brought to the Temple as offerings? And those who serve at the altar get a share of the sacrificial offerings. In the same way, the Lord gave orders that those who preach the Good News should be supported by those who benefit from it. (1 Corinthians 9:13-14)*

NOTE TO PARENTS: Most kids never see where their offerings go or what becomes of them. It's OK for them to wonder. Explain as much as you can how your church uses its money. Name programs that your kids know, point to staff who receive salaries from the church, and mention missionaries they've heard of before.

Q 532:

How does God get the money that I give to him?

A: When people say that they are giving money to God, they mean that they are giving it to the church, to a missionary, to the poor, or to other people *in service to God.* In other words, they give money *to* people *in obedience to* God or *in God's name.* And they are giving it for a specific purpose: to help God's people. You don't give money directly to God. He doesn't reach down with a hand and take it from you or from a special spot where you put it. Instead, you give money to people in God's name and for God's work.

This is exactly the way God wants it. We show our love for God by loving others (1 John 2:9-11; 4:20-21).

KEY VERSES: *Then these righteous ones will reply, "Lord, when did we ever see you hungry and feed you? Or thirsty and give you something to drink? Or a stranger and show you hospitality? Or naked and give you clothing? When did we ever see you sick or in prison, and visit you?" And the King will tell them, "I assure you, when you did it to one of the least of these my brothers and sisters, you were doing it to me!" (Matthew 25:37-40)*

NOTE TO PARENTS: Take a question like this as an opportunity to explain the different ways giving supports God's work—through church, through other ministries, and in other countries.

Q 533:

Do we have to give money to poor people?

A: Christians have the responsibility to help people who have needs, including poor people. One reason for this is that God cares about people in need, and we should all try to be like God.

You can help the poor in many ways. For example, you can give food to a community food pantry or soup kitchen, serve meals at a rescue mission, give money to programs that help poor children, or give money to organizations that help the poor.

Remember, everything you have came from God's goodness and kindness to you. He wants you to treat others the way he treats you.

KEY VERSE: *[God said,] "If any of your Israelite relatives fall into poverty and cannot support themselves, support them as you would a resident foreigner and allow them to live with you."(Leviticus 25:35)*

NOTE TO PARENTS: This can be a difficult issue for kids because they lack the discernment to judge the merits of every giving opportunity. Fear of strangers, a sense of fairness, and knowledge that Christians should give all point them in different directions. Try to do some charitable giving as a family so you can provide guided practice.

Q 534:

Is it wrong to see poor people on the street and not give them any money?

A: No. God doesn't expect you to give money to *everyone* who asks. If you did, you would soon run out of money entirely. But it would also be wrong to never give anybody anything.

There are many poor people who desperately need money, food, and clothes. It is good that you feel compassion for them and want to give. But you can help them in many ways besides just giving money. You can also give to food pantries, support international organizations that serve in very poor countries, or give clothing and other good used things to places in your community that help the poor.

Not everyone who asks for money really needs your help. Some pretend to be poor to get money. Some are lazy and beg instead of going to work. You have to use good judgment. Your parents can help you know when to give, and you can pray for wisdom. It is best to give to people you know and whose needs you know to be real.

KEY VERSES: *[Moses said,] "If there are any poor people in your towns when you arrive in the land the LORD your God is giving you, do not be hard-hearted or tightfisted toward them. Instead, be generous and lend them whatever they need."(Deuteronomy 15:7-8)*

Q 535:

Where does all the money from fountains and wishing wells go?

A: Some people think that if they wish for something when they throw a coin into a fountain or a wishing well, they'll get their wish. That's just not true. It's superstition. Fountains and magic don't control anything—God does.

The good news is that many people who have fountains and wishing wells on their property collect the money and give it to charities. That's a good way to use the money.

It's fun to throw change into a fountain or a wishing well. But if you do, don't bother to make a wish. Instead, pray for the people who will benefit from the money.

KEY VERSE: *Many sorrows come to the wicked, but unfailing love surrounds those who trust the Lord. (Psalm 32:10)*

NOTE TO PARENTS: If you allow your children to throw money into fountains, remind them that it's just a game. Don't propagate the superstition that their wish will get some power from throwing money into the water. God is Lord of all (Psalm 33:18-19).

A Penny Saved

Q 536:

What is the reason for learning to save money?

Jason for President in 2044

A: It is important to save money because you will need the money in the future for things that you don't need now. For example, you may want to buy something that costs a lot, you may want to buy a special gift for a friend, you may have an emergency and need money quickly, or you may want to go to college. People who don't save for these things have to borrow money to pay for them. But then they have to pay back the loan *plus* interest. It's better to save up for what you will need so that when you need the money it's there.

KEY VERSES: *Take a lesson from the ants, you lazybones. Learn from their ways and be wise! Even though they have no prince, governor, or ruler to make them work, they labor hard all summer, gathering food for the winter. (Proverbs 6:6-8)*

NOTE TO PARENTS: Help your kids divide the money they get into three parts: some to give to the Lord, some for savings, and some to spend. (One possible plan would be 10 percent giving, 40 percent saving, and 50 percent spending.) This way they are not frustrated by saving because they have some immediate spending money. Then help them set a short-term goal for saving. Make sure it's something they really want. This will help them begin to realize the power to purchase the things they want because they have saved for them.

Q 537:

What should we know about saving money?

A: Here are seven important facts about saving money:

1. God wants us to do it because he knows we need to.
2. It's important because it's part of God's plan for meeting our needs.
3. It's difficult now but will reward us later.
4. It takes planning and work but less effort than getting out of debt.
5. Responsible people do it because they know they will need it someday.
6. It should be done for a specific purpose so you know when to use the money you have saved.
7. Most people are not good at it.

Try to have a purpose for all your saving. It will be easier to set aside some money each week if you have a goal in mind. For example, you may want to save for a special trip or for college.

KEY VERSE: *The wise have wealth and luxury, but fools spend whatever they get. (Proverbs 21:20)*

NOTE TO PARENTS: If your child doesn't appreciate the reasons for saving money, give him or her some practice. Start small and work up to more challenging goals. First have your child save up for something that costs only two allowances. As time goes by, set bigger goals. Eventually your child will build a habit of purposeful saving.

Q 538:

What is the quickest way to save money?

A: The easiest and quickest way to save money is to set some aside *every time* you get some. You may want to begin by putting some in a jar. Then when you get a few dollars, you can put it in the bank.

Some people don't save because they think they can't save enough to make it worthwhile. But it may surprise you how much you end up saving when you save a little out of every bit that comes in.

Remember these things about saving:

- Have a *purpose* for your saving and write it down. Example: "I want to buy _____."
- Have a *plan*. Example: "I will set aside half of my allowance and any other money I get."
- Have a *procedure*. Example: "Put the cash in a jar every week and take it to the bank once a month." Or "Write down new total each time I put in some money."

KEY VERSE: *Those who love pleasure become poor; wine and luxury are not the way to riches. (Proverbs 21:17)*

NOTE TO PARENTS: Whenever your child wants to save up for something, ask him or her to describe the purpose, plan, and procedure for the project. (If you have preschoolers or early grade-school kids, use the words *why, when,* and *how.*) Write down the goal with the amount that's needed and put it with his or her savings where it will serve as a reminder.

Q 539:

If I put money in a savings account, can I get it back?

A: Oh, yes! The bank is just a holding place for your money. It's like a big piggy bank. Later, when you need it, you will be able to get your money back. To get money from your savings account, just go to the bank with Mom or Dad and fill out a withdrawal slip. The teller will give you the money, and the computer will keep track of how much you took out. The money is yours, and you can always get it.

Remember, the purpose of a savings account is to save for the future. Try not to take money out until you've reached your goal.

Do not get too attached to your money, though. God doesn't want us to trust in our savings. He wants us to trust in *him.* God will help you save, and he will take care of you no matter what. Remember that God—not money, banks, or anything else here on earth—is your provider. Place your trust in God.

KEY VERSE: *If your wealth increases, don't make it the center of your life. (Psalm 62:10)*

NOTE TO PARENTS: The first time your child opens a savings account, you might want to go back to the bank together after a few days and take some money out just for practice. Also, once he or she has set a savings goal, help your child stick to it.

Q 540:

Is it selfish to save money?

A: Saving money *can* be selfish, but it doesn't have to be. We need to plan ahead and save for future needs, so we need to save. If we don't, we are being foolish. But we also need to give. We need to trust God to meet our needs. If we try to save *all* our money and never share any of it, we aren't trusting God, we're trusting in our money. That's called hoarding, and God doesn't like it. Saving should always meet a future need. It should not just make us richer.

Most selfish people show their selfishness by spending all their money on themselves, not by saving it.

KEY VERSE: *Don't be selfish; don't live to make a good impression on others. Be humble, thinking of others as better than yourself. (Philippians 2:3)*

NOTE TO PARENTS: Emphasize that saving is good if it is for a good purpose, such as providing for some future need. It is bad if it's just for hoarding. Help your child set goals for saving. Don't let him or her continue to save without a goal.

Q 541:

Why do some people hide their money?

A: Most people who hide money do so because they don't want their money to be stolen. The world has many bad people who look for ways to take other people's money. So people on a trip may hide their money in their motel room or suitcase. And just about everyone keeps some money in their wallet or purse when they walk around town. A good steward is careful with his or her money.

People who hide large amounts of money usually don't trust the banks. They think their money will be safer if they hide it in their house or in the ground. But we should not be so afraid that we bury our money. God will take care of us even if something happens to our money.

Some people even hide money because they got it illegally. They know that if someone finds them with it, they will get in trouble. But in the end they will be found out anyway. They can't run from God forever.

KEY VERSES: *The servant with the one bag of gold came and said, "Sir, I know you are a hard man, harvesting crops you didn't plant and gathering crops you didn't cultivate. I was afraid I would lose your money, so I hid it in the earth and here it is." (Matthew 25:24-25)*

NOTE TO PARENTS: Explain to your child that hiding small amounts of money is fine, but large amounts should be placed in the bank. It is a safer place to keep money, and the money will earn interest.

Q 542:

Is the stock market a place where you buy animals?

A: Sometimes animals are called "stock" or "livestock" by people who raise them. But the stock market is a place where people trade companies, not animals. Anyone who buys stock in a company becomes part owner of that company. They can sell their stock to other people if they want to. Meanwhile, the company gets to spend the money on supplies, equipment, and workers that help the company grow.

Buying stock is one way to save for the future. The shares of a company are worth money. If a company does well, its stock price will go up. People who own the stock can sell it at the higher price. But if the company does not do well, the price will go down. People who sell their stock at the lower price will lose money. That's why it's unwise to put all your savings in stock.

KEY VERSE: *The servant who received the five bags of gold began immediately to invest the money and soon doubled it. (Matthew 25:16)*

NOTE TO PARENTS: If you invest in the stock market, show your children what you are doing and how you do it. Let them see the results as well. If they are really interested, let them buy a small part of your share. Then when you sell or when they want to sell, return their money plus their earnings or minus their losses. (Don't shelter them from losses. They need to learn both sides.)

Q 543:

How can retired people go on trips if they don't have a job?

A: Retired people can go on vacation trips because they saved their money when they were working. They put some in the bank and probably invested some more. And they started when they were young, like you.

In order to go on trips when you don't have a job, you have to save up for a long time. You have to start when you're young. That is why saving is so important. One day, you too will want to retire.

KEY VERSES: *The LORD also instructed Moses, "This is the rule the Levites must follow: They must begin serving in the Tabernacle at the age of twenty-five, and they must retire at the age of fifty." (Numbers 8:23-25)*

NOTE TO PARENTS: This is a good time to have a live example of the benefits of saving. Ask your retired relatives to tell your child how they saved for retirement. You could even illustrate this way: If you invest fifty cents every week at 8 percent interest, starting when you're eight years old, you would have $25,798.86 (before taxes) by the time you're sixty-five.

Q 544:

How much do investments cost?

A: An investment is something you buy so you can sell it later at a higher price. Investments, like stocks, have all different prices. Some cost more than others. Most investments cost more than children can pay. That's why most kids have their money in bank savings accounts, not in stocks or other investments like that.

Some people say you can get rich quickly or easily by buying their investment. The Bible warns us to stay away from those kinds of tricks. God's plan is that we trust him and that we let our money grow bit by bit. Greed causes us to listen to get-rich-quick ideas because we want more quickly. But trying to do it this way usually results in a loss, not a gain.

KEY VERSE: *Don't begin until you count the cost. For who would begin construction of a building without first getting estimates and then checking to see if there is enough money to pay the bills? (Luke 14:28)*

NOTE TO PARENTS: This topic is only hypothetical to kids who have no investments in the traditional sense, but it is a good way to talk about *value*. An investment pays you something back. The most expensive investment is one that never pays anything. The next time your child wants to buy something, encourage him or her to ask, "What am I getting for my money?"

Gotta Have It

Q 545:

Why do parents sometimes not let kids buy what we want, even when we have enough money for it?

A: Usually parents stop their children from buying everything they want because they love their children.

Sometimes you want something that isn't good for you. Your parents know this and forbid it. When you were a baby, you may have wanted to drink drain cleaner because the bottle was colorful. You didn't know any better, and you thought it would be good. Your parents stopped you because they knew the drain cleaner would hurt you.

Your parents also want you to learn discipline so you can control your desires. You can't buy *everything*, because if you did, you would soon run out of money.

You can buy a lot of things with your money, but that doesn't mean you should buy all of them. You have to make choices—to buy some things and not others. Your parents are trying to help you learn these skills.

KEY VERSE: *Only a fool despises a parent's discipline; whoever learns from correction is wise. (Proverbs 15:5)*

NOTE TO PARENTS: Strike a balance between boundaries and freedom. Let your children spend their spending money however they want to. Let them set their own saving goals. Then establish the rule that if it's their idea, they pay, and if it's your idea, you pay. This gives them enough control to buy what they want but restrains them to using their money, not yours. And it really cuts down on the "gimmes."

Q 546:

Why can't I have all the things I want?

A: There are at least three reasons: First, you don't ask God for them. Second, you ask God for them, but you want them only for yourself, so he says no. Third, they cost too much or are bad for you, so your parents say no. God wants you to love him, help others, give to his work, and be content. Money gets in the way of all that. You can't spend all day, every day shopping and also love God, help others, give to his work, and be content. Sooner or later you have to stop being selfish.

You don't need all the things you want anyway. And think about this: If you got everything you wanted, what would you do with all that stuff?

KEY VERSE: *Then [Jesus] said, "Beware! Don't be greedy for what you don't have. Real life is not measured by how much we own."(Luke 12:15)*

NOTE TO PARENTS: Most kids pressure parents to buy things they want. Do not let your kids nag you into buying things. They will survive without them. Don't let kids convince you that they can't be happy without that special something. What people want most—a loving family and loyal friends—can never be bought. Learning to do without is one of the most powerful skills you can teach your children.

Q 547:

Why do people fight over money?

A: One reason is greed. Some people want more money than they have, and they want it so much that they fight to get it. They are being selfish.

Another reason is that families just have to work out an agreement. Sometimes families argue about money because husbands and wives need to agree on how they are going to manage and spend their money. They should not fight about it, but it does take time to work out a plan, and they may not agree at first.

Always remember that people are more important than money. Talk over your money problems rather than fight about them. But if you can't agree, it's usually better to let someone else have his or her way than to lose a friend because of a fight over money.

KEY VERSE: *Greed causes fighting; trusting the Lord leads to prosperity. (Proverbs 28:25)*

NOTE TO PARENTS: This question highlights the importance of contentment. People fight over money because they want what they don't have. Whenever a question like this comes up, remind your child that it's better to be content than to have more money.

Q 548:

Why do people want more money if they already have lots of it?

A: Greed makes people want more and more and more. They feel as if they never have enough, even though they really do. Greedy people become so worried about money that they think about it all the time. Greedy people are never satisfied, never content. God wants us to be satisfied and to find our contentment in him.

Sometimes people want more money for good reasons. They want to do something for God's kingdom or for other people, such as giving to those who have lost their homes or spreading the message of Jesus.

KEY VERSE: *Those who love money will never have enough. How absurd to think that wealth brings true happiness! (Ecclesiastes 5:10)*

NOTE TO PARENTS: A question like this may arise when news of professional athletes' contract negotiations hits the front page. It's a fair question, one that occurs to many adults as well as kids. Rather than condemn rich people, use the opportunity to point out that an addiction to money hurts. Greed and selfishness are terrible forces in a person's life, making otherwise nice people act cruel, unfair, and even criminal.

Q 549:

Is buying a lottery ticket the same as gambling?

A: Yes. Gambling is when you buy a chance to win a big amount of money with a small amount of money, so buying a lottery ticket is the same as gambling.

The difference between gambling and investing is that in investing you are buying a product—a piece of a company or a bond, for example. In gambling, you are just buying a "chance." And your chances of winning are very poor. In fact, the only way you can win is if a lot of other people lose. That's not a good or wise way to use money.

It's fun to play games and it's fun to win a prize, but don't let it turn into gambling. A game becomes gambling when you try to win a large amount with a small amount. Your whole reason should be to have fun, not to get rich.

KEY VERSE: *[Jesus said,] "Yes, a person is a fool to store up earthly wealth but not have a rich relationship with God." (Luke 12:21)*

Q 550:

Why do people play the lottery if they probably won't win?

A: People gamble and play the lottery because they *hope* to win. They imagine winning, and they imagine how much it would enable them to buy. They think that having a lot of money would solve all their problems. Meanwhile, the cost of one lottery ticket is very low, so people figure they aren't losing much.

Playing the lottery is a foolish thing to do. It plays right into our love of money, which Jesus warned us against. Many people who win millions in lotteries end up worse off than they were before. They spend all the money and have more problems than ever. That's because having lots of money doesn't solve your money problems. You need only to manage your money according to God's principles to have enough.

Being rich and having more can actually make your life worse. You have a lot more to manage and a lot more to lose. Loving God and others and receiving their love in return are the keys to happiness, not more things or more money.

KEY VERSE: *Wealth from get-rich-quick schemes quickly disappears; wealth from hard work grows. (Proverbs 13:11)*

NOTE TO PARENTS: The lottery plays directly into a love of money. For the person who doesn't love money, the lottery has no attraction.

Q 551:

Does money make people bad?

THE EVILS OF MONEY

HELP MY ANTI-MONEY CAMPAIGN! GIVE GENEROUSLY!

A: Money itself isn't bad, and money itself doesn't make people bad. But the *love* of money is and does. When people love money, they become greedy and do all sorts of bad things to get and keep money. God wants us to use money to help hurting people. When we hurt and use people so *we* can get money, we've got it wrong.

KEY VERSE: *The love of money is at the root of all kinds of evil. And some people, craving money, have wandered from the faith and pierced themselves with many sorrows. (1 Timothy 6:10)*

NOTE TO PARENTS: Try not to paint a one-sided picture of money's goodness or badness. It is true that money is a snare and a temptation to selfishness. We have to resist its negative influence; this is one reason for giving. But rich Christians have used their money to finance ministries and good works. Encourage your kids to be honest in their business dealings, pay what they owe, be generous, and use money in God's service. Using money the right way helps us keep it in perspective.

Q 552:

Why can't my parents just get a loan instead of waiting for payday?

A: Your parents probably could get a loan. But if they did, they would have to pay the loan back plus interest. Getting a loan doesn't really solve the problem of needing money. It just postpones the problem and makes it a little worse.

We need to learn to be patient. Usually we don't need to buy what we think we need right now. Usually we can wait a little while. It's better to wait and not borrow the money than to borrow money and buy something right now because you'll pay more if you borrow the money.

This is why it is best to be patient. Besides, if you wait, you may get a better deal!

KEY VERSE: *This same God who takes care of me will supply all your needs from his glorious riches, which have been given to us in Christ Jesus. (Philippians 4:19)*

NOTE TO PARENTS: Your children will remember how you handled lean times long after those times have passed. Set the pattern now. If you are strapped for money, pray as a family about it, entrust yourselves to God, and look for ways other than a quick loan to weather the storm. Do without if you can. If doing without hurts, comfort each other. Take this opportunity to point out how God has met your needs and to express confidence that he will keep on doing so, as he has promised (Philippians 4:19).

Q 553:

If people keep buying lots of things, won't they run out of money?

A: Yes. No one, not even the richest person in the world, has an unlimited supply of money. Anyone who keeps spending will run out of money sooner or later.

Some people act like they have a lot of money by borrowing a lot. They keep buying new things and buying new things and buying new things. They always seem to get whatever they want. But most of them don't really have that much money. They're just borrowing lots of it. Meanwhile, they keep having to pay more and more interest. And they pay so much for this debt that they aren't putting any money into savings. Then when they need money for college or another important expense, they don't have it.

You make a lot of *choices* about your money. Choose how much money you want to spend *before* you spend it. Make sure you set some aside for giving, saving, and paying for things you *have* to buy. Then have fun spending the rest, *and stop when it's gone.*

KEY VERSE: *Those who love pleasure become poor; wine and luxury are not the way to riches. (Proverbs 21:17)*

NOTE TO PARENTS: This question usually arises when neighbor kids have more toys than your kids, when your kids *think* the neighbor kids have more, or when a neighbor spends money conspicuously. Exodus 20:17 reminds us that we must not be jealous of how others spend their money. We need to be content with what we have.

Q 554:

Why do people spend money they don't have?

A: Some people do it because they can't say no to their wants. They haven't learned how to save money and wait. They have to have everything right away.

Pride is another reason. Many people think that happiness is related to how rich they are. They think that having something will make them popular. Or they believe that everyone will think they are rich if they have a new car, a new suit, or a big TV. So they buy it even if they can't afford it.

Some people spend money when they feel bad. They have no joy so they go buy something to try to make themselves feel better. But when the bills come in, they feel worse.

Try to control your spending. Overspending leads to lots of problems and makes it impossible for you to give.

KEY VERSE: *Enjoy what you have rather than desiring what you don't have. Just dreaming about nice things is meaningless; it is like chasing the wind. (Ecclesiastes 6:9)*

NOTE TO PARENTS: Be careful about telling a child that things don't make us happy. Things *do* make us happy. That is why we crave them. But things can get lost, broken, or stolen. Remind your child that nothing can take God away. No matter what happens to our things, God will always be there for us, working out his plan (Romans 8:38-39).

Q 555:
What are taxes?

A: Taxes are money given to the government by the citizens of a country. It's the main way most governments get money. They use the money to run the country and provide all the services the government provides. The elected officials in the government decide how much tax people have to give. People pay income taxes (a tax on their paycheck), property taxes (a tax on the value of their house), sales taxes (a tax on items they buy), and many other kinds of taxes. The Bible tells us that we should not try to cheat the government out of taxes we owe.

KEY VERSE: *Pay your taxes, too, for these same reasons. For government workers need to be paid so they can keep on doing the work God intended them to do. (Romans 13:6)*

Q 556:
What does the government do with all the taxes we pay?

A: The national government collects taxes to pay for services that they provide—highways, bridges, courtrooms, judges, military personnel, assistance for the poor, national parks, and so forth. Local governments collect taxes to pay for the services that they provide—police protection, libraries, public health, fire protection, schools, and so forth. The government uses money from taxes to provide things that all the taxpaying citizens need and want.

KEY VERSE: *A just king gives stability to his nation, but one who demands bribes destroys it. (Proverbs 29:4)*

NOTE TO PARENTS: List some of the services that taxes pay for, such as schools, libraries, streets, sewers, soldiers, sailors, police officers, and firefighters. Then pray together and thank God for these people and institutions.

Q 557:
Why is there so much tax on prices?

A: Every kind of tax pays for government services. Many local governments charge sales taxes. The amount of this tax differs from place to place. Some people think it's high because they forget that these taxes pay for a lot of the things they use every day. If you and your friends were going to buy a pizza together, it would be right for each person to pay his or her share. When you pay sales taxes, you are paying for your share of roads, schools, libraries, police officers, firefighters, and things like that. Taxes ensure that everyone in a town, city, or country pays for the things they all use.

KEY VERSES: *Each year Solomon received about twenty-five tons of gold. This did not include the additional revenue he received from merchants and traders, all the kings of Arabia, and the governors of the land. (1 Kings 10:14-15)*

Q 558:

Why should you pay property taxes if you already own your house?

A: One kind of tax that local governments charge is property tax. Property taxes are paid by people who own property. Every person who owns land or buildings pays a certain amount of tax every year. The amount they pay depends on the value of their land or building. The owners of some buildings, such as churches, schools, post offices, and so forth, do not have to pay taxes. They are "tax-exempt."

The government uses property taxes to pay for things that landowners and building owners need. These include water lines, sewer service, roads, streetlights, and things like that. Even if your house is paid for, you still need these services every year. That's why you have to pay property taxes each year. It's just another way for the government to collect money from its citizens to help pay for important public services.

KEY VERSE: *[Jesus] said, "Give to Caesar [the Roman emperor] what belongs to him. But everything that belongs to God must be given to God." (Matthew 22:21)*

NOTE TO PARENTS: It is easy for people to forget that they are part of a community that depends on the cooperation of all its members. The services provided by property taxes benefit everyone.

Q 559:

Why do people get bored with something they just bought?

A: People get bored quickly with something new that they just bought because they thought it would be better than it is. They may have believed the commercials that said the product would be exciting, but it really wasn't. When they finally got the product, it wasn't what they thought it would be. For example, they may have seen a game that looked like fun for the whole family to play. But what looked good on TV really wasn't very good at all.

Some people expect a product to do more than it can. A girl might think that a special dress will make her popular. Or a boy might think that a certain brand of basketball shoes will make him a better player. Then they discover the truth.

Many people "impulse buy." They go into a store not planning to buy anything, but then they see something they want and change their mind. They didn't plan to buy it, but it looked good in the store. Then later they wonder why they ever bought this thing that they don't need.

KEY VERSE: *Then [Jesus] said, "Beware! Don't be greedy for what you don't have. Real life is not measured by how much we own." (Luke 12:15)*

Q 560:

Why do people waste their money on dumb things?

A: Some purchases really are dumb, but people make them because at the time they think they need whatever they buy. They may waste their money because they believe the advertisements. Maybe they want to have what their friends have. Or maybe they just don't value their money and don't mind throwing it away.

But be careful about calling someone's decision dumb. Sometimes what may seem dumb to you is really smart. Remember, you don't know the other person's situation in life or his or her needs. So don't judge others for what they buy. They may think that you waste your money on some of the things you buy. It's easy to criticize someone else's spending.

KEY VERSE: *[Jesus said,] "Stop judging others, and you will not be judged. Stop criticizing others, or it will all come back on you. If you forgive others, you will be forgiven." (Luke 6:37)*

NOTE TO PARENTS: Try not to criticize how others spend their money. It is an unhealthy habit that cultivates the wrong type of attitudes about other people. And if you do it, so will your kids.

Give Me Some Credit

Q 561:
Are credit cards good or bad?

A: They're both. Credit cards are good because they provide a very easy way to buy things. People can buy things they want without having to carry cash or a checkbook. People can also buy things over the phone and through the mail using credit cards. Some credit cards can be used in bank machines and can be used for borrowing money from a bank.

But credit cards can be bad because they make it easy for people to buy things that they can't afford or should not buy. In fact, many people use credit cards to spend *much* more than they should. When you spend too much and can't pay the whole bill, the credit card company lets you make a small payment and charges you a lot of interest on what you don't pay. Misusing credit cards has put many people deeply in debt.

The right way to use a credit card is to use it only for things you have planned and budgeted to buy. Then you know you can pay the whole amount when the bill comes.

KEY VERSE: *Just as the rich rule the poor, so the borrower is servant to the lender. (Proverbs 22:7)*

NOTE TO PARENTS: If you have a credit card bill with a finance charge on it, show it to your child. Explain that this charge is the extra money you have to pay for using a credit card and not paying the bill in full right away.

Q 562:
How do credit cards work?

A: A credit card lets you borrow money from a bank whenever you want to buy something. The bank gives you the card and says you can borrow a certain amount of money. When you want to buy something with the credit card, the salesclerk checks to make sure that you have permission to borrow that much money. The clerk also makes sure you are using your *own* card and not someone else's. If everything checks out OK, the *bank,* not you, pays for the item. The bank loans you the money. The salesclerk lets you take home what you wanted to buy.

A little while later, a bill for the amount you borrowed comes in the mail. You have to pay this bill right away. If you don't, the bank charges you extra money called interest. This is how most people get in trouble with credit cards. They borrow more than they can pay back. Then the interest payments get higher and higher. Sometimes people borrow so much that they can't possibly pay it back. Wise people borrow only as much as they know they can pay back.

KEY VERSES: *Do not co-sign another person's note or put up a guarantee for someone else's loan. If you can't pay it, even your bed will be snatched from under you. (Proverbs 22:26-27)*

NOTE TO PARENTS: To many kids, credit cards give the appearance that you can get something without paying. It's important to explain that you *do* have to pay.

Q 563:

Why can't I have my own credit card?

A: It is against the law for children to have their own credit cards. That's because children don't have regular jobs, and most children don't have much money. How would they pay the bills without any money?

Children can have debit cards, though. Debit cards are just as easy to use as credit cards. You can buy anything, anywhere, anytime. But the money comes right out of your bank account instead of a loan from the bank. You never borrow any money because you spend only what is in your account. You still need to be responsible and spend only the amount you planned to spend. If you are responsible with your budget and your saving and spending, perhaps your parents will let you have a debit card.

KEY VERSE: *"Well done!" the king exclaimed. "You are a trustworthy servant. You have been faithful with the little I entrusted to you, so you will be governor of ten cities as your reward."* *(Luke 19:17)*

NOTE TO PARENTS: Emphasize the tie between responsibility and privilege. The person who can spend a little money wisely will be given more money to manage later. You can encourage your child to handle money wisely by affirming and rewarding wise use of his or her allowance.

Q 564:

What happens if a person doesn't pay a credit card bill?

A: A person who doesn't pay a credit card bill on time is charged interest. Sometimes the bank will charge extra penalty fees too. If someone goes for a long time without paying off a credit card bill, the small bill will turn into a huge one.

People who don't pay *anything* on their credit card bills get in big trouble with their bank. Not paying credit card bills goes on a person's credit record. It shows that the person cannot be trusted with money. That will hurt the person if he or she ever wants to get a loan from a bank.

It also displeases God. God wants us to always be honest and do what we say we are going to do. When we don't pay the bills we agreed to pay, we are being dishonest. It is important that we borrow money only if we know we can pay it back.

JASON'S IMAGINATION

KEY VERSE: *The wicked borrow and never repay, but the godly are generous givers.* *(Psalm 37:21)*

NOTE TO PARENTS: Explain the difference between credit and debt. *Credit* is when someone is willing to lend you a certain amount of money. Credit is good to have. It shows that others trust you. When we use credit for convenience and within our budget, it is a good thing. *Debt* is when you owe money to someone else. Debt is not wrong, but it can cause problems and therefore should be avoided as much as possible.

Q 565:

Is it wrong to borrow money?

A: It is not a *sin* to borrow money; it's just not very smart. God gave rules to the Israelites for loaning money to each other, so obviously it was OK for them to do it. You can find those rules in the Bible (Deuteronomy 15:1-11; 23:19-20; 24:10-13).

Although it isn't wrong, borrowing money is not the best thing to do. Borrowing money from a bank will cost you interest charges. Borrowing money from a friend may cost you a friendship. That's because you may forget or be unable to pay back your friend, and he or she may get mad.

Sometimes borrowing money is necessary, such as when someone wants to buy a house. But a lot of people borrow in order to buy things they really don't need. If you really want something, try to save up for it first. If you can't save up for it, maybe you need to get along without it.

KEY VERSE: *A prudent person foresees the danger ahead and takes precautions; the simpleton goes blindly on and suffers the consequences. (Proverbs 22:3)*

NOTE TO PARENTS: Be willing to give your children *credit:* If you are out together and they want to buy something but have not brought their spending money, buy it for them and have them pay you back when you get home. But avoid *lending* them money against future income since borrowing is a foolish habit to develop. (Save the word *wrong* for issues such as lying and cheating. Borrowing is not wrong; it's just not the ideal way to buy things.)

Q 566:

Why do people have to pay interest on money they borrow?

A: People have to pay interest only if they agree to do so when they borrow the money. All credit cards come with a contract that tells exactly how much the user of the card has to pay. When people borrow money from a bank, they sign an agreement that explains how much interest they will pay. Banks charge interest on loans and credit cards because that's how they make money. Paying interest to a bank is like paying rent. You want to use the money for a while, so you pay the bank for that privilege.

When God gave the Law to the Israelites, he told them not to charge each other interest for loans. Today many people will loan money to relatives and close friends without charging interest to help them in an emergency.

KEY VERSES: *If any of your Israelite relatives fall into poverty and cannot support themselves, support them as you would a resident foreigner and allow them to live with you. Do not demand an advance or charge interest on the money you lend them. Instead, show your fear of God by letting them live with you as your relatives. Remember, do not charge your relatives interest on anything you lend them, whether money or food. (Leviticus 25:35-37)*

Q 567:

What is a mortgage?

A: A mortgage is an agreement to pay back a loan that is secured with a piece of property. The agreement says that the borrower will pay back the loan over a certain period of time and at a certain rate of interest. It also says that the bank can take possession of the property and sell it if the borrower does not pay back the loan as agreed.

This is how most people buy a house. Houses cost a lot of money. Most people do not have enough money to pay for a house all at once, so they borrow the money from a bank. The agreement between the home buyer and the bank is the mortgage.

Most people repay their home loans by paying a little each month. Then after fifteen to thirty years, the whole loan is paid back, the mortgage is canceled, and the house is paid for.

KEY VERSE: *The man fell down before the king and begged him, "Oh, sir, be patient with me, and I will pay it all." (Matthew 18:26)*

Q 568:

Why are there bills to pay?

A: A bill is simply a charge for something you bought or used but haven't paid for yet. Most people get bills for water, electricity, telephone service, gas, magazines, and things like that. Because your family used gas for the water heater, electricity for the lights, and water to drink, you have to pay for them.

KEY VERSE: *Do not cheat or rob anyone. Always pay your hired workers promptly. (Leviticus 19:13)*

NOTE TO PARENTS: This question often arises when bills become the focus of attention, such as when they come in the mail or when a parent blames them for making money tight. Simply explain what bills are and how the family benefits from the things they buy—the water you drink, the electricity that keeps the refrigerator going and the lights on, the house and furnace that keep you warm, and the book bag you bought last week to carry your books. In other words, help your children appreciate the value of paying the bills rather than seeing them only as impediments to getting what they want.

Q 569:

What if I don't have enough money to pay my bills?

A: It is very important to pay your bills. Paying what you owe is part of being honest and trustworthy. If for some reason you lose your money or run out of money, you need to work out a plan for paying what you owe. Your plan should involve getting more money and spending less. You may have to sell some of what you own. You will also need to talk to the people whom you owe and see if they will let you pay little by little. See if you can work out a way to pay them each a small amount every week or month until the bills are all paid off.

This is not a good situation to be in. If you learn to budget, save, tithe, and spend wisely, you may never have to go through it. That is why it is important to follow God's guidelines. God knows how things work best, and his way is always best.

KEY VERSES: *When the people of Egypt and Canaan ran out of money, they came to Joseph crying again for food. The next year they came again and said, "Our money is gone, and our livestock are yours. We have nothing left but our bodies and land. Why should we die before your very eyes? Buy us and our land in exchange for food; we will then become servants to Pharaoh." (Genesis 47:15, 18-19)*

Q 570:

Should I borrow money from the bank or from my friends?

A: It's better not to borrow at all. Save your own money until you have enough for what you need. Or pray for a way to earn extra money and look for work you can do. If you must borrow for some emergency, make sure you sign a written agreement, even if the money comes from a friend. Then pay it back as soon as you can.

But try not to borrow from friends. It could easily lead to arguments, and Proverbs makes it clear that arguments can separate close friends. It's better not to put your friends under this kind of pressure.

If a friend wants to borrow from you, it is best just to give it as a gift. Or if you do make a loan, think of it as a gift. That way you will never worry about whether it gets paid back. If someone does not pay you back, forgive the person right away and forget it.

KEY VERSE: *Do not charge interest on the loans you make to a fellow Israelite, whether it is money, food, or anything else that may be loaned with interest. (Deuteronomy 23:19)*

NOTE TO PARENTS: Tell your kids not to borrow money from friends. Good friends are hard to find and even harder to replace; losing them over a money-related squabble is not worth it.

From Allowance to Paycheck

Q 571:
Why do some kids get their allowance free and others have to earn it?

A: Every family is different. In some families, children have to do jobs around the house to earn their allowances. In other families, children receive money just for being part of the family. Some don't get any allowance at all. It's all up to the parents.

Be careful about comparing your parents and family with others. God has given your mother and father the responsibility of rearing you, not your friends. And your friends' parents are not in charge of you.

What really matters is how you deal with your own situation. God wants you to learn to manage your money wisely. He also wants you to be a good worker and learn how to be a valuable member of a team. Whether the two are tied together doesn't matter as much as what you need to learn from them.

KEY VERSE: *Work brings profit, but mere talk leads to poverty! (Proverbs 14:23)*

NOTE TO PARENTS: Try not to tie allowances to chores. Doing so gives children the impression that they should be paid for all work, even cleaning up after themselves. Give them both chores and an allowance because they are part of the family.

Q 572:
Why do some kids get huge allowances and others don't get any?

A: Allowances vary a lot among kids for many different reasons. Some families have lots of money, and others have very little. Some parents have no money left after paying the bills, so their children get no allowance—the money just isn't there.

Remember also that some parents give their children money in other ways besides allowances. They may give money for doing special work around the house. Or some parents may give their kids a large amount of money and let them buy all their own clothes.

Every family is different—different personalities and different situations. In fact, no other family is exactly like yours. Thank God for your family and make the most of it. God will always supply what you need.

KEY VERSE: *Fix your thoughts on what is true and honorable and right. Think about things that are pure and lovely and admirable. Think about things that are excellent and worthy of praise. (Philippians 4:8)*

NOTE TO PARENTS: It is important that your children get money of their own through one means or another so they can begin to learn how to handle money wisely.

Q 573:

How come I don't get enough allowance to buy anything?

A: You can always buy *something* with the money you have, even if it's very little. You may think you don't have enough money to buy anything when you look at your allowance, but just because you can't buy *expensive* things doesn't mean you can't buy *anything*.

Some people want to buy just about everything they see, so they never have enough money. Don't be like that. Instead, learn to be content with what you have. If there is something you want and your parents agree that you can have it, save your money until you have enough to buy it. Be patient. You can also ask God for opportunities to earn extra money.

KEY VERSE: *I know how to live on almost nothing or with everything. I have learned the secret of living in every situation, whether it is with a full stomach or empty, with plenty or little. (Philippians 4:12)*

NOTE TO PARENTS: When your kids feel that they can't buy the things they really want, teach them to ask God for the things they want and to save diligently. It's best not to increase allowances or buy them what they want all the time.

Q 574:

Why do kids get less money than adults?

A: The more you can do, the more you can earn. Adults earn more than kids because they can do more. They get paid for the *skills* they have learned. The older they get, the better they are at doing their work, and the more they get paid for it. And the more skill their job takes, the more they get paid.

For example, repairing a car, being a doctor, keeping financial records, closing a sale, and writing a book are all difficult jobs. They take a lot of skill. Only people who have been trained and have the experience can do them well. And those people are paid well for the work they do.

Also, many adult jobs carry great responsibility. A person who runs a store has to take care of all the workers, all the products in the store, and the building. That's a lot of responsibility. People are paid according to how much *responsibility* they have.

Be glad you don't have to earn as much as an adult. Adults make more money than kids, but they also have many more bills and many more responsibilities.

As time goes on, you will learn how to do many jobs through skills, training, and experience. Eventually you will get to serve God in a job that uses your abilities. Your responsibilities and your income will increase bit by bit as you continue to get more training and experience. *Then* you will be able to think about getting more money and things.

KEY VERSE: *Do you see any truly competent workers? They will serve kings rather than ordinary people. (Proverbs 22:29)*

Q 575:

How are kids supposed to earn money?

A: Kids can earn money by doing work for their parents and neighbors. Maybe you can clean up the yard, wash dishes, wash the car, or run errands. Most adults like to pay kids for doing those kinds of jobs.

You can also start your own business. Make something that you can sell, or provide a service such as gardening, lawn care, or delivery. Ask your parents and God for ideas and for good opportunities.

If you really want to earn money, do every job well and always do more than is expected of you. Think about what you're doing, keep going until you're done, and never complain.

KEY VERSES: *Work hard and cheerfully at whatever you do, as though you were working for the Lord rather than for people. Remember that the Lord will give you an inheritance as your reward, and the Master you are serving is Christ. (Colossians 3:23-24)*

NOTE TO PARENTS: Giving children small jobs to do is a good way to introduce them to work. Make a job list and post jobs that need to be done and how much you are willing to pay for each. Let your children know they can pick jobs off the list once their regular chores are done. Give clear instructions, show the child what to do, and make sure he or she understands what you expect to find when it is done. Don't forget to give praise for a job well done.

Q 576:

Where does the money that bosses pay come from?

A: Every company sells something. Bosses get money from the people who buy a company's products or services. The money that comes from these sales pays the workers—all of them, from the bosses to the people who work for the bosses. It works like this: If you owned a field of pumpkins, you could sell the pumpkins for $10 each. So if you had 100 pumpkins, you would have $1,000 if you sold them all. Out of that money, you would pay your workers—the people who helped pick and sell the pumpkins. You would have to plan well in order to have enough money to be fair to your workers, to pay your other expenses, and to make a profit. That's how companies work.

KEY VERSE: *At that time, Egyptian chariots delivered to Jerusalem could be purchased for 600 pieces of silver, and horses could be bought for 150 pieces of silver. Many of these were then resold to the kings of the Hittites and the kings of Aram. (1 Kings 10:29)*

NOTE TO PARENTS: You can help your children start a small business of their own. Help them plan their costs, sale price, and profits. Whether your children ever go into business for themselves or not, this will help them learn how a business works.

Q 577:
What does minimum wage mean?

A: The minimum wage is the smallest amount that a business is allowed to pay a person for one hour of work. The government decides that amount. It's a law.

When God gave the Law to the Israelites, he told them to pay their workers fairly. That's what it means when it says, "Do not keep an ox from eating as it treads out the grain" (Deuteronomy 25:4). A good boss pays his or her workers fairly.

KEY VERSE: *The Scripture says, "Do not keep an ox from eating as it treads out the grain." And in another place, "Those who work deserve their pay!" (1 Timothy 5:18)*

NOTE TO PARENTS: When you are paying your children to do jobs, make sure you pay them fairly, in keeping with the jobs and their skill levels. Paying them too much can give them unrealistic expectations that they will carry with them into the workforce. Paying them too little can discourage them.

Q 578:
Should people stay at a good-paying job that they don't like?

A: Whether or not a person should stay in a yucky job depends on the person and the job. What matters most is doing what God wants. When you become an adult and have a family, God will want you to take care of them. You will need to work so you can pay for food, clothes, housing, and other bills. You may have to stay in a job you don't like so you can do this.

That doesn't mean that you *must* have a job you don't like. God loves you and has a plan for your life. If you follow his guidance and do what he says, he will lead you to a good job and make you content. He doesn't want you to be miserable.

No one has a job that he or she enjoys in *every way, all the time*. Every job is hard—and maybe even yucky!—sometimes. That is why it is important to learn to be content.

Pray now about your future job. Give your life to God's service. Ask God to guide you in your education. Trust God to help you find work that suits how he made you. Life on earth will never be perfect, and you may not always have a fun job. But if you do what God wants you to do, do your duty to your family, and be content with what you have, God will take care of you.

KEY VERSE: *"For I know the plans I have for you," says the LORD. "They are plans for good and not for disaster, to give you a future and a hope." (Jeremiah 29:11)*

Q 579:

What should people do if they do not get paid enough at their job?

A: The first thing these people should do is ask God to provide for them. Then they can ask the boss for overtime, do some extra part-time work, or look for another job that pays better.

But it's important to realize that many people *think* they do not get paid enough when they really do. Every month, their bills seem to grow, and they don't know how they can pay everyone. The real problem is that they spend too much. Even people who make a *lot* of money can have this problem. They need to budget their money and control their spending better.

Some people don't make very much but still manage to pay all their bills. They have learned to budget their money and control their spending so they never spend more than they earn.

No matter how much you get paid, a lot depends on what you do with your money. You can often have enough if you budget your money and spend less than you earn.

KEY VERSE: *Work brings profit, but mere talk leads to poverty! (Proverbs 14:23)*

NOTE TO PARENTS: Live within your means and help your children do the same. It's the same principle with $5 as it is with $5,000.

Q 580:

Why do athletes get paid so much money to do something that's fun?

A: In In this country, people enjoy professional sports so much that basketball, football, baseball, hockey, golf, and other sports have become big businesses. Millions of people pay a lot of money for tickets to the games. Television networks pay millions of dollars for the right to show games. Sports fans spend countless dollars on shirts, caps, and other things. So sports stars ask for big salaries, and they usually get them.

But it's not all fun. To be excellent in a sport takes years of hard work and training. Many professional athletes suffer many cuts, bruises, and broken bones.

It doesn't seem right that athletes get paid so much for playing a game, especially when teachers and ministers do more important work and get paid much less. But life isn't always fair. Often the world has things backwards.

KEY VERSE: *I have observed something else in this world of ours. The fastest runner doesn't always win the race, and the strongest warrior doesn't always win the battle. The wise are often poor, and the skillful are not necessarily wealthy. And those who are educated don't always lead successful lives. It is all decided by chance, by being at the right place at the right time. (Ecclesiastes 9:11)*

NOTE TO PARENTS: Point out to your child that athletes got where they are by *working hard*. They practiced day after day for years before they became professionals, and they keep on practicing. They practice whether or not they feel like it.

Q 581:

How will I know what I want to do when I grow up?

A: It is good to think about what you want to do when you grow up. God has made you good at doing certain things. He has given you talents, interests, and abilities. As you get older, you will learn more and more about your abilities. Your parents and other people who know you well will help you uncover and develop your talents.

But don't wait for them to tell you what to do. Whenever you get interested in something or do well in something, keep working at it. Find out more about it. Ask questions about it. Read books about it. Take an extra class. Ask God to guide you and keep learning.

God has a plan for your life. He created you and loves you. He knows exactly what you will be best at and enjoy most and where you fit in his plan. Keep asking God to direct you, and he will do it.

KEY VERSE: *If you need wisdom—if you want to know what God wants you to do—ask him, and he will gladly tell you. He will not resent your asking. (James 1:5)*

NOTE TO PARENTS: Avoid telling kids that they should pursue a certain career for the money or because of some ambition of your own. Children need to seek God and pursue his plan for their lives even if it does not follow in a parent's footsteps or make up for a parent's lost opportunity.

When the Budget Won't Budge

Q 582:

What is budgeting?

A: A budget is a plan for how to use your money. If you knew you would be receiving $10, for example, you might decide ahead of time to put aside $1 for church and $2 in your savings account in the bank. You might also decide to put $4 in your jar to use in two weeks for a church camping trip. The final $3 you might decide to carry with you to spend on snacks. That plan would be your budget.

It's a good idea to write down your budget so you always know how to divide your money. Start with at least three categories: tithe, savings, and spending money. Then you can add others as your needs change. You could include one, like in the example above, for an upcoming church camping trip.

A budget is also a good way of tracking your spending. After you have spent the money, you can compare what you did to how you planned to spend it. That helps you plan better in the future.

KEY VERSE: *Good planning and hard work lead to prosperity, but hasty shortcuts lead to poverty. (Proverbs 21:5)*

NOTE TO PARENTS: The best time for children to practice managing money is when they are young. And one of the best ways to give them practice is to give them an allowance. Help your child set up a budget that makes sense for him or her.

Q 583:

Why do people have to budget their money?

A: People should budget their money so they will have enough for all the bills they must pay. Everyone has big bills that come due in the future. It is good to write them down as a reminder so you won't be surprised when they come. The budget tells you how much to set aside each week or month so that you will have the money to pay the bills when they come.

Every day brings opportunities to spend money— opportunities to buy something that you didn't plan for. A budget helps you know whether or not you can afford it.

You don't *have* to budget your money. You can just go and spend it. But if you do, you will probably run out of money too soon. Then you will not have enough for the things you need, and you will never get to spend your money on the things you really want. Everyone should have a plan for how to spend his or her money.

KEY VERSE: *A prudent person foresees the danger ahead and takes precautions; the simpleton goes blindly on and suffers the consequences. (Proverbs 22:3)*

NOTE TO PARENTS: To illustrate the need for budgeting, sit down one evening with your child and list all the things he or she would like to have. Then write down what each item would cost, total them, and compare this with how much he or she has to spend over the next month. The only way to keep from running out of money is to look at this list and plan!

Q 584:

Why can't parents afford a lot of things?

A: Parents can't afford to spend money on certain things because they have chosen to spend their money on other things. All people have bills to pay with a limited amount of money. And all people have to make choices about how they will spend that money. When your parents say they can't afford to buy something you want, it's probably because it is not in their budget, not because they don't have any money.

That may sound unfair, but it's really wise planning. People should say no to some things so they can have enough for the things they need and want most.

If the thing you need is really important, ask your parents nicely if they will include it in their budget as soon as they can. If it's something you just want badly, put it into *your* budget. Then you can start earning money and saving for it.

KEY VERSE: *Those who love pleasure become poor; wine and luxury are not the way to riches.* *(Proverbs 21:17)*

NOTE TO PARENTS: If your child is old enough, show him or her your budget. Explain that this is what you *must* spend money on and that this is why you sometimes say, "We can't afford that"—it's another way of saying, "We need the money for other things" (food, clothes, an upcoming vacation or birthday party, a home repair, savings for college, and so on).

Q 585:

Why do some people spend every cent they get right away?

A: Some people spend all their money right away because they have no self-control. They have no discipline or patience. They can't wait even though they should. They don't save money because they convince themselves that they have to buy things they don't really need.

This is not good. God wants his people to be self-controlled so they will use well what he has given them. God also wants people to take care of each other. It would be wrong for parents to spend all their money on themselves and forget about the children or the house payment. It would be wrong for Christians to spend all their money on themselves and neglect the church. It would be wrong for the boss to spend all the company's money on himself and not pay the workers.

We need to control our spending, not let our spending control us.

KEY VERSE: *The wise have wealth and luxury, but fools spend whatever they get.* *(Proverbs 21:20)*

NOTE TO PARENTS: If your children overspend, do not bail them out by giving or lending them more money. Let them learn the truth: Overspending hurts.

Q 586:
Why do people spend their money on little things and not on the important things?

A: Some people waste their money because they are foolish. They don't care about what really matters, so they spend money on worthless things. They don't love God or don't know what is important to him. Some don't think about the future enough.

Some people simply never make a plan for how to spend their money. They just spend until the money is gone. They may want important things, but they can't get them because they have no plan.

Others only *seem* to spend money on things that are not important. These people are just different from you, not foolish. What is unimportant to you is important to them.

Be careful not to judge others who spend differently. Not every small item is unimportant. It may be that what others buy is important after all—just not important to you.

KEY VERSE: *So be careful not to jump to conclusions before the Lord returns as to whether or not someone is faithful. When the Lord comes, he will bring our deepest secrets to light and will reveal our private motives. And then God will give to everyone whatever praise is due. (1 Corinthians 4:5)*

NOTE TO PARENTS: Be careful about judging how your neighbor spends his or her money. But you can explain to your child that some purchases are more foolish than others.

Q 587:
Why is it that when I want to buy something I am always short of cash?

A: If you want to buy something but don't have enough money, you probably decided to buy it at the last minute, before you had time to save money for it. It's OK to buy small things that way as long as you have enough spending money. But if it costs more, you need to plan and save to buy it. So you aren't really short of cash; you just can't buy everything right away. That's why we need to learn to save.

Sometimes you save up for something, but it costs more than you thought it would. Check on the price of what you want to buy before you go to the store. That way you will know whether you have enough money. Remember also that you have to pay tax on just about everything. You have to add tax to the price before you can buy it.

KEY VERSE: *Wise people think before they act; fools don't and even brag about it! (Proverbs 13:16)*

NOTE TO PARENTS: If your child really wants something but doesn't have enough spending money, resist the temptation to make up the difference or loan the money. Help your child wait until he or she has saved the money. Children need to learn to plan their purchases and stay on budget.

Q 588:

Does God get angry when I spend my money foolishly?

A: Does he rant and rave? No. But God does want us to be wise, and he's sad when we are foolish.

Think of it this way: God is your biggest fan. More than anyone else, he wants you to win. That's why he cares about how you take care of your money. If you keep wasting it and ignoring wise advice from everybody all the time, *of course* he will be sad because things won't go as well for you.

KEY VERSE: *Do not bring sorrow to God's Holy Spirit by the way you live. Remember, he is the one who has identified you as his own, guaranteeing that you will be saved on the day of redemption. (Ephesians 4:30)*

NOTE TO PARENTS: Don't use fear of angering God as a tool for getting your child to behave. Emphasize God's care for your child, not his punishment. Meanwhile, demonstrate what you mean by controlling your own anger when your child makes a foolish money decision. Give your child room for making mistakes without blowing your top.

Q 589:

How do I know what is wise to spend my money on?

A: The Bible explains that it is important to give to the church and to help people in need, to pay bills that you promised to pay, and to buy things that you need. It is always wise to spend money that way.

It is also wise to use your money for the most important things first and the least important things last. Here they are in order: (1) Giving to the church. (2) Paying for commitments you made. (3) Taking care of your needs. (4) Saving. (5) Spending for things you would like. If you want to spend money on something you would like, make sure you have done the other four things first.

It is also wise to get a good deal. Never buy something just because it looks good, just because you saw it advertised on TV, or just because your friends have it. Buy things that are good quality and have a reasonable price.

Whenever you want to buy something, ask, *Do I really need it?* If you're unsure, ask God for wisdom, and wait awhile before deciding. Ask your parents because God gives them wisdom too.

KEY VERSE: *If you need wisdom—if you want to know what God wants you to do—ask him, and he will gladly tell you. He will not resent your asking. (James 1:5)*

NOTE TO PARENTS: You may need to explain the difference between *necessities* and *luxuries*. You may also want to go over a list of priorities you use for evaluating purchases: Is it something I need? Will it last? Have I shopped for the best price? Should I save the money instead and get something of better value later?

Honesty Is the Best Policy

Q 590:

Would it be right to keep the money if someone paid too much?

A: No. Suppose you sold something to a friend, and the friend paid you too much by mistake. You should give back the extra money. That's just being honest and fair. And isn't that the way you would want to be treated? You should be truthful and honest with people—just the way you want them to be truthful and honest with you.

Also, you shouldn't cheat people by charging them too much for something. God told his people not to take advantage of each other, and he had harsh words for people who broke this rule. Some people say, "If the person doesn't notice, then it's his own fault." But that's not God's way. God wants us to look out for each other. If we are dishonest or mean, people soon find out and then they don't want to be with us or do business with us. Doing things God's way is always best.

KEY VERSE: *A person who gets ahead by oppressing the poor or by showering gifts on the rich will end in poverty. (Proverbs 22:16)*

NOTE TO PARENTS: Encourage your children to be honest by demonstrating honesty in your own dealings with other people.

Q 591:

What should a person do if the bank machine doesn't give the right amount of money?

A: If you ever get too much money from a bank machine, you should take it to the bank and explain to a teller what happened. If the machine is not near a bank, you should call the bank that owns the machine and tell them what happened. Try to give the money to whomever it belongs.

The same goes for other machines that handle money. If a pop or candy machine gives you an extra quarter, you should return the money to the people who own the machine. Machines do make mistakes, and we should try to make sure no one gets cheated as a result. God's rewards for honesty will always be greater than the money you could get from being greedy or dishonest.

KEY VERSE: *No accounting was required from the construction supervisors, because they were honest and faithful workers. (2 Kings 12:15)*

NOTE TO PARENTS: Whenever you get someone else's money by mistake, try to return it to its rightful owner. Going back to a store to return extra change or to return extra money from a vending machine can make a lasting impression on a child.

Q 592:

What if the waiter gives me a kid's meal free because he thinks I'm younger than I really am?

A: It is important to do what is right even if it costs you money. So if you get a children's price for a meal or a ticket and you are older than a "child," you should tell the truth. Tell the waiter, waitress, ticket seller, or whoever is in charge how old you really are. You can't put a price on honesty.

Remember that God is looking after you. He will meet all your needs and take good care of you if you do things his way. God's way is to be honest. It shows that you trust him.

KEY VERSE: *Love does not demand its own way. . . . It is never glad about injustice but rejoices whenever the truth wins out. (1 Corinthians 13:5-6)*

Q 593:

Is it really finders keepers?

A: The old saying "Finders keepers, losers weepers!" is an excuse for making no effort to return something that belongs to someone else. People usually say this when they are the finders, not the losers.

If you find something valuable, make an effort to find the owner. If you were to find a bag full of money in a parking lot, you should take it to a police station. If you find a wallet, look for a name inside and let the owner come and get it from you. If you find a ten-dollar bill in a classroom, take it to the teacher. If you find a basketball on the playground, take it to the principal. For some items, you may even want to put a note in the local paper.

On the other hand, don't worry about finding the owner of a nickel that you find in the street. It's not that valuable, and finding the owner would be practically impossible. You can keep it.

KEY VERSE: *[Jesus said,] "Do for others as you would like them to do for you." (Luke 6:31)*

Q 594:

If I try to pay my friend back and he forgot I borrowed some money, is it wrong to keep it?

A: If you owe somebody money, you should pay that person back, even if he or she has forgotten about the debt. You should do what is right, even if no one else knows or cares. God knows. Think about how you would feel if someone paid you back after you had forgotten. It would be a wonderful surprise, and you would think very highly of your friend.

This is the best kind of friend to have—one who looks out for you and helps you, even when he or she doesn't have to. If you are that kind of friend, you will have lots of loyal friends.

Remember, though, it's best not to borrow money. Then you never have to worry about paying your friend back.

KEY VERSE: *Do not steal. Do not cheat one another. Do not lie. (Leviticus 19:11)*

Q 595:

Why do some people trust me and lend me money?

A: People usually lend money to those whom they trust. They have watched you and have come to believe in your honesty. They know you are honest because they have seen you (1) do what is right and (2) do what you say you will do.

It is good to be known as an honest person. If you do what is right and do what you say you will do, you will be known as an honest person.

KEY VERSE: *A false witness will be cut off, but an attentive witness will be allowed to speak. (Proverbs 21:28)*

NOTE TO PARENTS: Affirm any child for being honest. Honesty is a genuine treasure in its own right.

Q 596:

Why do some salesclerks steal money from the cash register?

A: The good news is that most salesclerks are honest and trustworthy. Otherwise they wouldn't have gotten their job in the first place. There aren't many salesclerks who steal money from cash registers.

Salesclerks who *do* steal are greedy. When they see the money in the cash register, they can't resist the temptation to steal. They give in. People who do this may try to justify what they have done by thinking that it's OK because they don't get paid very much or that the store will never miss it. But the truth is that the money is not theirs. If the boss finds out, they will lose their job.

These people don't realize that they are hurting themselves. You get more problems from dishonest money than you do from no money at all.

KEY VERSES: *Slaves must obey their masters and do their best to please them. They must not talk back or steal, but they must show themselves to be entirely trustworthy and good. Then they will make the teaching about God our Savior attractive in every way. (Titus 2:9-10)*

Q 597:

Is it OK to use Canadian coins in American vending machines?

A: Many vending machines have a sign that says "No foreign coins." Money from other countries may get jammed in the machine. But even if the coins work, they may not be worth the same amount. So putting foreign coins in the machine would cheat the owner of the machine. That would be wrong.

Do not look for ways to "save money" by being dishonest. Instead, be honest all the time and trust God to take care of you. God owns everything. He can help you with the extra few cents you think you would gain from cheating the vending machine.

KEY VERSE: *The Lord despises double standards of every kind. (Proverbs 20:10)*

Questions Kids Ask

Friends and School

7

Making Friends

Q 598:

How do I make friends?

A: The first step is to look for places where you might find friends. Actually, potential friends are everywhere—in your neighborhood, at school, on your sports team, and at church. You probably already know a lot of kids who could become very good friends.

The best way to make friends is to be friendly. In other words, you should be the kind of person that others will like to have as a friend. Think about what you like in a friend, and be that kind of person to others. This probably will mean showing interest in other people and being a good listener—all of us want friends who will listen carefully to what we say and take us seriously. To have a friend, be a friend!

KEY VERSE: *[Jesus said,] "Do for others what you would like them to do for you. This is a summary of all that is taught in the law and the prophets." (Matthew 7:12)*

NOTE TO PARENTS: If your children ask how to make friends, use this opportunity to teach social skills. Try to find out what's behind the question. Perhaps, as their social circles widen, your children may be worried about losing friends. Or they may be feeling lonely. Start by reassuring them that having trouble making friends is a problem that can be solved. They just need to learn how to do it.

Q 599:

When you're making friends, how do you know what to say?

A: The best way to start a conversation with someone is to ask questions about that person. You can look for visible clues on the person to help you know what to ask. For example, if the person is wearing a hat or shirt of a professional sports team, you could ask about the team. If someone is holding a book, you could ask what it's about. It's important to ask people questions about themselves. Talk about them, not just about yourself. Also, look for ways to compliment people. If you hear about a good grade or honor that someone received, you could say, "Good going!" or "Great job!" If someone did well in a concert, you could say something like, "I really enjoyed your solo." Look for ways to give sincere compliments. Try to make others feel good about themselves.

KEY VERSE: *Kind words are like honey—sweet to the soul and healthy for the body. (Proverbs 16:24)*

NOTE TO PARENTS: You can teach your children how to begin conversations by role-playing with them. This will be fun and will give them valuable practice. Also, be sure to model the above advice in your own relationships with your children and with others.

Q 600:

I want to have nice friends, but how do I know if kids are nice?

A: You can get an idea of what a person is like by reputation, especially if the reputation is good. For example, if you hear from a lot of people that someone is nice, that's probably a good sign that the person really *is* nice. Sometimes, however, a person's reputation is not always accurate. For example, someone may say that a boy is stuck-up when, instead, he is only shy. Be careful not to judge kids before you know them—give them a chance.

The best way to know if kids are nice is to get to know them yourself. Start talking with them. The Bible teaches that a person's words show what is in that person's heart. If people talk about bad things, swear, or tell dirty jokes, that is a sign of what they are really like. Watch kids in action with others. Pretty soon you will know if they're nice or not.

KEY VERSE: *Many will say they are loyal friends, but who can find one who is really faithful?* (Proverbs 20:6)

NOTE TO PARENTS: Have fun with this one. Look at magazine pictures and ask your kids what they think the people in the pictures are like. Then you can discuss how looks often deceive and how important it is to get to know a person. You may need to help your children identify the types of words and actions that show whether or not someone is nice. Since kids these days are used to hearing bad or unkind words, they may say something like, "Oh, he talks like that, but he's really a nice person." Help your children recognize words as a gauge to a person's heart.

Q 601:

Where can I find some friends?

A: Potential friends are everywhere, usually pretty close by. One of the best places to look for friends is in a group or activity. If you play soccer or sing in choir, for example, you probably will find friends there. Or someone who sits near you in class might turn out to be a good friend. Also consider your church and neighborhood. You might look for someone who needs a friend just as you do. Maybe there's a new family in your neighborhood or church with a child your age. Or maybe you've seen a new student in school. People like that need friends. Perhaps you can be a friend to them.

KEY VERSE: *Anyone who fears you is my friend—anyone who obeys your commandments.* (Psalm 119:63)

NOTE TO PARENTS: Help your children enlarge their friendship circles; plug them in to positive groups. For example, church offers many opportunities for social activities—Bible clubs, choirs, and so on. In addition, you can help by opening your house to other children. Make your home a place where kids want to be.

Q 602:

What should I do if I'm scared to go up to someone and say, "Hi, do you want to be my friend?"

A: You don't have to do that. In fact, that's not a very good way to make friends. That question really puts people on the spot, and they don't know how to answer. It's better to go slower and work at getting to know a person. You can do this by asking them questions about themselves. Let friendship happen; don't force it.

KEY VERSE: *Love each other with genuine affection, and take delight in honoring each other.* (Romans 12:10)

NOTE TO PARENTS: This is another good place to role-play or practice. You can also tell your children how *you* make friends.

Q 603:

Why can't I have everyone as a friend?

A: There are too many kids and not enough time for you to be a good friend to everyone. Actually, there are many different kinds of friendships. Some friends who are very close will be your very good friends. Some kids, however, you will just know by name; they are called acquaintances. Even if you don't know someone's name, you can be friendly to that person. It's good to like everybody and be friendly, but don't expect everyone to like you the same way and to be a really close friend. Friendship takes time. It takes a lot of talking with someone to know someone well. Be friendly with everyone, but work at having a few very close friends. Keep in mind that even Jesus, who loved everyone, had just three very special friends.

KEY VERSE: *Jesus took Peter, James, and John to the top of a mountain. No one else was there.* (Mark 9:2)

NOTE TO PARENTS: Children who ask this question may feel insecure, realizing that not everyone wants to be their friend. Explain the various levels of friendship (acquaintance, friend, close friend, very close friend, etc.), and give examples from your life of friends at each level. Some children will easily develop a few close friendships and tend not to socialize beyond them. Others will easily have many friends, but they may not be close friends. Both casual acquaintances and close friends are helpful and bring happiness to our lives. It's natural to lean one way or the other, but we should help our children develop in both areas.

Q 604:

Why do some kids not want to have friends?

A: They may be shy. Or they may be afraid. It can be scary to meet new people if you don't know how. They may be new to the school or neighborhood. And some kids just like to do things by themselves instead of with others. They may have had bad experiences with other kids rejecting them or making fun of them. If this has happened, they may not want to try again. It may seem that some don't want to have friends, but perhaps you just don't know them very well. Maybe you can be a friend to them.

KEY VERSE: *[Jesus said,] "The time is coming—in fact, it is already here—when you will be scattered, each one going his own way, leaving me alone. Yet I am not alone because the Father is with me."(John 16:32)*

NOTE TO PARENTS: Maybe your children have been rebuffed in their attempts to befriend other kids. If this is the case, encourage them to continue to be friendly toward those kids but to look for closer friends elsewhere.

Q 605:

How should I treat kids who are different?

A: Kids differ in many ways. They may be different races, come from different cultures, or be different sizes. Some children may be mentally or physically challenged. People in a school or neighborhood may even speak different languages. It's never right to make fun of people or ignore them because of those differences. Just because kids are different doesn't mean that they are wrong or to be feared. Think about this: It's God who made the different races and gave people the ability to do things differently. Even if people have different ideas about God, he still wants us to be kind and to respect others. No matter how different kids are, God wants us to treat them in the way we would like to be treated.

KEY VERSE: *The woman was surprised, for Jews refuse to have anything to do with Samaritans. She said to Jesus, "You are a Jew, and I am a Samaritan woman. Why are you asking me for a drink?" (John 4:9)*

NOTE TO PARENTS: Schools and communities vary. Some are homogenous; others are diverse. Every school will have children who are quite different from the others. So be prepared for this question. Also, help your children enjoy and experience the diversity in your community. Take them out for ethnic food. Point out good things in other cultures. Take them to visit special-needs patients in a hospital. The more you help your children experience the differences, the more comfortable they will be with them.

Q 606:

Why do parents not like your friends just because they have green hair or something?

A: Parents want the best for their children. They know that friends have a big influence. So when they see green hair, they may be surprised or shocked and not know what to think. They know that having green hair may be one way kids express themselves or get attention. But it may also be their way of rebelling against their parents. Your mom and dad probably won't assume that you will want to have green hair too, but they may think that you will pick up your friend's bad attitude. It's not the clothes or hair that your parents don't like; it's what they think the clothes mean to that person. What kind of impression do you give other parents by the way *you* look or act?

KEY VERSE: *Don't copy the behavior and customs of this world, but let God transform you into a new person by changing the way you think. (Romans 12:2)*

NOTE TO PARENTS: It's important to get to know your kids' friends. Be careful not to judge them simply by their appearance. Invite the friends to your house. If you notice bad language, bad attitudes, or other negative tendencies, discuss those with your children. Don't make a big issue about appearance unless it becomes evident that it's an outward sign of an inward problem.

Q 607:

Why don't parents just let you pick your own friends?

A: Most parents try to let their children choose their own friends, but some of the choices may not seem very good. Your parents usually know more about your friends' families than you do, and they want you to hang around good and positive moms, dads, brothers, and sisters in other families. Talk this over with your parents. God gave you your parents for a reason. They know you well. Your parents can help you find good friends.

KEY VERSE: *Listen, my child, to what your father teaches you. Don't neglect your mother's teaching. (Proverbs 1:8)*

NOTE TO PARENTS: Don't be afraid to be involved in helping your children find the right friends. Don't choose for them, but give them guidance. If they really want to befriend someone who is not a good choice for a close friend, that child can still be an acquaintance whom they see from time to time.

Q 608:

If I'm supposed to love everybody, why am I supposed to stay away from certain kids?

A: God wants us to be loving and kind to everyone, but that doesn't mean we have to be a close friend to everyone. Some people can be bad influences on us. If we spend too much time with them, we can find ourselves doing what we shouldn't do and getting into trouble.

It is good to want to be a good influence on others. So you can try to be friendly to kids whom others think are bad. But if *they* begin to influence *you,* you will need to back off. Think about where you play with them and what you do. Try bringing them to your house to play or inviting them to church. Your closest friends should be those who help you become a better person—those who have the same attitudes about serving God as you have. Try to be close to kids who love God and want to serve him.

Talk with your parents about this problem. And if they tell you to stay away from certain kids, do what they say. Picking good friends is one way parents can really help you.

KEY VERSE: *Whoever walks with the wise will become wise; whoever walks with fools will suffer harm. (Proverbs 13:20)*

NOTE TO PARENTS: Friends can have a powerful influence on kids. It's important for you to monitor your child's friendships and affirm positive relationships that your child has formed.

Q 609:

Sometimes when I hang around with my friends, they do something bad. What should I do?

A: If the kids you are with begin to talk about or plan something that is not right, tell them not to do it, firmly but nicely. Don't yell or get angry—just explain that what they are doing is wrong. You can suggest doing something else. If that doesn't work, you should leave. If those kids don't want to be friends anymore or if they continue to do things that are wrong, then they aren't very good friends or the type of friends to have. When something like this happens, be sure to discuss it with your parents.

KEY VERSE: *Put away all falsehood and "tell your neighbor the truth."(Ephesians 4:25)*

NOTE TO PARENTS: Let your children know that they can talk to you about things like this. Tell them you won't assume that they're bad, too, and you are happy to know that they want to do what's right. When they do come to you, emphasize what they did right more than how bad their friends are. Seeking your advice demonstrates the maturity your children have to make the right friendship decisions on their own, with a little guidance from you.

Q 610:

What should I do when my old friends don't like my new friends?

I'D LIKE YOU TO MEET MY NEW FRIEND, LEROY.

A: You can't control other people's feelings, so you can't make one person like someone else. Maybe your old friends don't know your new friends— you can help them get acquainted. If one group of friends criticizes the other, you can stick up for those who are being criticized. That's the sign of a real friend. Don't let yourself be drawn into rejecting one group of friends for another—it's all right to have more than one group of friends. You can have friends at church, friends at school, friends who are relatives, and friends in your neighborhood.

KEY VERSES: *When Peter arrived back in Jerusalem, some of the Jewish believers criticized him. "You entered the home of Gentiles and even ate with them!" they said. (Acts 11:2-3)*

NOTE TO PARENTS: Friendships change, and that can be tough for children. It's painful to see relationships fade, whatever the reasons. Changes often occur when new children move into a neighborhood. Even greater changes will take place when your children enter middle school and when they begin high school. Encourage your children to learn now not to give in to pressure to reject new friends. Give them suggestions for ways to be friendly to both old and new friends.

Being a Good Friend

Q 611:

What's the difference between being best friends and just being friends?

A: "Best friends" is a way of saying "very close friends." The difference between "very close friends" and others is that you spend a lot of time with very close friends and you can talk to them about lots of things. Very close friends stick with you when you are having problems or are in a bad mood. You can have a lot of friends, but you'll probably have just a few very close friends. You should be careful about the kinds of kids you choose as your very close friends. They should want to please God and do what is right—like you do. It's hard to be close friends with kids if you and they don't see life the same way.

KEY VERSE: *After David had finished talking with Saul, he met Jonathan, the king's son. There was an immediate bond of love between them, and they became the best of friends. (1 Samuel 18:1)*

NOTE TO PARENTS: Someone may be one of your children's best friends one week and then somebody else's best friend the next. Be available to give advice and support whenever you discover that your children are negotiating friendships. Encourage them to invite Christian friends over, and try to say yes to activities or outings that involve these children. You can be more sparing with other approvals, but don't always say no. And be sure to always explain your reasoning.

Q 612:

Can you have more than one best friend?

A: God wants us to be loving and kind to all people. If you are doing that, you probably will know many kids who like you and want to be your friend. Friends are great, and it's fun to have a lot of them. You can have many good friends, and you don't have to put them in order of who's best. You may have one or two friends who are closer than all the others. But be careful about saying that one person is your *very best* friend. That may make the others feel bad. And don't say that one person is your "best friend" just to make another friend angry or jealous or because you want to exclude the other person.

You can have a favorite food, but you don't *have* to have a best friend. You can be the best kind of friend to many people.

KEY VERSE: *Whenever we have the opportunity, we should do good to everyone, especially to our Christian brothers and sisters. (Galatians 6:10)*

NOTE TO PARENTS: Encourage your children to be loyal friends, respectful of others' feelings and preferences. Caution them about describing any of their friends as "best friends" if they have other friends who may feel hurt by not having that title. Encourage them to concentrate on *being* a best friend rather than on *getting* a best friend. Everything the Bible says about loving others applies to friendship.

Q 613:

My friend's parents are getting a divorce. What can I do?

HERE'S MY WALKIE-TALKIE. I JUST PUT FRESH BATTERIES IN IT. CALL ME WHENEVER YOU NEED A FRIEND.

A: Be a good friend—listen to your friend and give your support. Pray for your friend and his or her parents. Remember, you can't do anything about the parents' relationship with each other. They will have to work that out. You probably don't know much about what has been going on in your friend's family, and that's OK. Being a friend means just being there to talk, listen, and care. Right now your friend really needs you.

KEY VERSE: *I would speak in a way that helps you. I would try to take away your grief.* (Job 16:5)

NOTE TO PARENTS: When divorce happens to other families, your children may wonder if it will happen to *your* family. Assure them of your commitment to Christ and to each other, explaining that you intend to remain married—they don't have to worry.

Q 614:

Why do friends get mad at you when you tell the truth?

A: Truth hurts, especially when someone points out something wrong in our life. Sometimes telling the truth to friends can make them feel very uncomfortable. But just because something is true doesn't mean you have to say it. In fact, sometimes you might think that you're "telling the truth" when you're really just bragging. For example, you may find yourself saying something like, "I'm a better singer than you are." Don't do that—don't compare yourself to others. Instead, look for truthful ways to compliment your friends.

You should be sensitive to others' feelings. There's a right time and a wrong time to speak the truth. If you have an important and possibly painful message, wait to tell your friend in private instead of in front of everyone. Also, the *way* you say something means as much as *what* you say. Always remember to be kind and gentle.

KEY VERSE: *Instead, we will hold to the truth in love, becoming more and more in every way like Christ, who is the head of his body, the church.* (Ephesians 4:15)

NOTE TO PARENTS: This is a good opportunity to explain tact and the loving use of truth versus the hurtful use of truth. Hurtful truths usually are said during an argument. Help your children understand that it's all right to disagree with someone, but we need to disagree agreeably and lovingly.

Q 615:

Is it wrong to stop telling my friends about Jesus even when they won't listen?

A: It is good that you want to tell your friends about Jesus, but it is also good to respect them as people. Sometimes your friends won't seem interested. And sometimes, they may tell you that they don't want to talk about it anymore. When that happens, you need to respect their wishes and stop talking a lot about it. This doesn't mean that they won't learn about Jesus from you. You can always share about what God is doing in your life. And, most important of all, you can live like a Christian. Your friends will notice that you are loving and kind and that you don't do bad things. They will see Jesus in you.

KEY VERSES: *[Jesus said,] "Don't hide your light under a basket! Instead, put it on a stand and let it shine for all. In the same way, let your good deeds shine out for all to see, so that everyone will praise your heavenly Father." (Matthew 5:15-16)*

NOTE TO PARENTS: Teach your children how to share their faith, but don't put pressure on them to witness. God wants us to live out our faith and to share experiences as well as the facts. You can pray together with your children for opportunities to tell people about Jesus.

Q 616:

When you are talking with people, how do you know that they are actually listening to you?

A: People who listen carefully to you look at you when you are talking—they don't look at the TV or other people. Also, they usually will comment on what you are saying. If you want to make sure that someone is listening, ask a question from time to time about what you have been saying. You could ask, for example, "What do you think?" If someone says, "What?" or "Huh?", you know that the person has not been listening.

Everyone likes to talk to people who know how to listen. Here are three steps to being a good listener: (1) LOOK—stop what you are doing and look at the person who is talking to you. Give that person all of your attention. (2) LISTEN—concentrate on what the person is saying and try to understand. Don't interrupt. (3) RESPOND—say something related to what the person has been talking about. Comment or ask a question; don't just grunt and change the topic.

What kind of listener are you?

KEY VERSES: *My child, listen to me and treasure my instructions. Tune your ears to wisdom, and concentrate on understanding. (Proverbs 2:1-2)*

NOTE TO PARENTS: Consider how well you listen to your children. When you talk with them, be sure to look at them and not interrupt. Then comment on what they are saying. Give them your full attention. Be a good example by following the points mentioned above.

Q 617:

Why do friends talk behind your back?

A: Every person is sinful, so everyone does things that are wrong. Sometimes we even harm the people we love. It hurts when friends do that to each other, but it happens.

Most kids who say bad things about others don't realize that it's wrong and hurtful. They have never learned that they are not only hurting others, they are also hurting themselves by pushing friends away. Some kids give in to pressure from others and go along with what has been said, even if it's about a friend. Many times kids will repeat things they've heard about someone without talking to the person to see if those things are true. This is known as gossiping. Spreading rumors can really hurt people. The Bible says gossiping is wrong—it hurts people and breaks up friendships.

KEY VERSE: *I am afraid that when I come to visit you I won't like what I find, and then you won't like my response. I am afraid that I will find quarreling, jealousy, outbursts of anger, selfishness, backstabbing, gossip, conceit, and disorderly behavior. (2 Corinthians 12:20)*

NOTE TO PARENTS: What kind of example do you set? Be careful not to gossip. A good time to teach your children the difference between gossiping and reporting facts is when they tell you about some trouble between them and another child. Teach your children how to report facts without making judgments.

Q 618:

Why won't my friend let me play with his stuff?

A: Your friend may be afraid that his stuff will be broken or misused. Maybe someone recently played with one of his toys and broke it. Remember, the stuff belongs to your friend, so respect his wishes. If you want to play with your friend's things, ask him and promise to take good care of them. If he lets you, show him how careful you can be. If he says no, don't keep asking. Let it go.

KEY VERSE: *Show respect for everyone. Love your Christian brothers and sisters. Fear God. (1 Peter 2:17)*

NOTE TO PARENTS: Explain to your children that although people are more important than possessions, misusing someone's property can destroy a relationship. The key is to respect the friend. Showing respect to a friend involves respecting that person's property. On the other hand, encourage your children to be willing to share their things. "I'm afraid they might break it." can be an excuse for selfishness.

Q 619:

Why can't I go over to my best friend's house very often?

A: If your parents are saying that you can't go over to your friend's house very often, ask them why. Maybe they don't know your friend very well. You can fix that by having your friend come to your house. If your friend doesn't invite you very often, maybe it's because the parents won't allow it. They may have several reasons, so don't blame your friend. Perhaps your friend is busy with other activities and doesn't have much free time.

Of course, it may be that you want to go over to your friend's house every day. If that's the case, your parents probably don't want you to "wear out your welcome."

KEY VERSE: *Don't visit your neighbors too often, or you will wear out your welcome. (Proverbs 25:17)*

NOTE TO PARENTS: Teach your children some of the guidelines for moderate and mutually fair hospitality. Double-check your children's knowledge and performance of good manners. Remind them that polite, courteous, and helpful people are pleasant to be around and usually get invited back.

Q 620:

Why don't my parents let me go to special places with my friends?

A: What are some places that are special to you? The movie theater? The mall? An arcade? An ice cream shop? Sometimes a certain place may seem special, but your parents know that bad things can happen there. They will want to know if any adults will be present if you go there, because even a safe place can become dangerous quickly. Because your parents love you, they want to protect you so you won't get hurt or get into trouble. This means they probably won't let you go to many places by yourself or just with your friends. When your parents do let you go to special places, be extra careful to be responsible and obedient. Your parents will probably allow you to do more as they see you becoming more responsible.

KEY VERSE: *Obey your spiritual leaders and do what they say. Their work is to watch over your souls, and they know they are accountable to God. Give them reason to do this joyfully and not with sorrow. That would certainly not be for your benefit. (Hebrews 13:17)*

NOTE TO PARENTS: As spiritual leaders for our children, sometimes we can be overprotective. Eventually, however, we have to let them go. This process begins when children are young. Show them that you love and trust them by allowing them to venture out to select places with their friends. But make sure that these places are safe and supervised or chaperoned by responsible adults.

Q 621:

Why should we always have to rescue our friends when they get in trouble?

A: God says that we should help those who are in trouble, even our *enemies*. That's what it means to love, and it's how we can show others God's love. You can help your friends when they are in trouble. That's being a very good friend to them. However, there's a limit to what you can do—parents and other adults may need to help. You shouldn't lie for friends or make excuses for them. Sometimes letting friends learn to solve their own problems is the best thing to do.

KEY VERSE: *The greatest love is shown when people lay down their lives for their friends.* (John 15:13)

NOTE TO PARENTS: It's good for your children to learn how to help others, but don't be afraid to step in when friends seem to be taking advantage of your children's goodwill. Kids want to help their friends and will automatically try to defend and protect a child who is in trouble for doing something wrong. Help your children understand that at times they need to rescue their friends, but at other times it is better to let those kids experience the consequences of their actions.

Q 622:

What should I do if my friend turns on a show that I'm not allowed to watch?

A: You can explain that you're not allowed to watch that show and ask your friend to change the channel. If that doesn't work, you can excuse yourself and go to another room or even go home, telling your friend in a nice way how you feel. You can explain why your parents don't want you to watch that show. This may help your friend make wiser choices when it comes to watching television. You may also want to explain that your parents will get very upset if they find out—it's just not worth the risk. Then you can suggest something else to do.

KEY VERSES: *I will refuse to look at anything vile and vulgar. I hate all crooked dealings; I will have nothing to do with them. I will reject perverse ideas and stay away from every evil.* (Psalm 101:3-4)

NOTE TO PARENTS: Regulating your children's TV watching is easier said than done. Talk about specific TV shows and videos with your children. Let them know your expectations and reasons. Also assure them that at *any age* and at *any time* they can call you if a situation gets out of hand, and you will come pick them up.

Q 623:

If some of my friends are doing something that I think is bad, should I tell my parents?

A: Yes. It is good to be able to share with your parents what is going on in your life, especially the things that bother you. It is also good to ask for their advice on what to do in certain situations. And if kids are doing something that will hurt themselves or someone else, then definitely tell your parents. They will know what to do to help.

Don't forget, though, that you yourself can speak with your friends about what they're doing. When you tell your parents, you can tell about what your friends are doing; then explain what *you* are going to do. Don't expect Mom or Dad to jump in every time and come to your rescue.

And finally, don't just tell about the bad things that kids are doing. Tell your mom and dad about the good that your friends do, too.

KEY VERSE: *Take no part in the worthless deeds of evil and darkness; instead, rebuke and expose them. (Ephesians 5:11)*

NOTE TO PARENTS: Value honesty. Don't overreact if kids tell you about things that surprise you. (Otherwise they may be less likely to share in the future.)

Handling Friendship Difficulties

Q 624:

Why do friends let each other down?

A: Sometimes we expect too much from our friends; then we feel let down when they don't come through for us. Some of our friends may be having a bad day and are working on their own problems. At those times your friends will find it difficult to help you. At other times your friends may not even be aware of your problems. They may not know that they have let you down. It's all right to express your disappointment and explain to them how you feel. When you talk to your friends in a nice way about how you feel, it will help you and them learn how to be better friends.

KEY VERSE: *The godly give good advice to their friends; the wicked lead them astray.* *(Proverbs 12:26)*

NOTE TO PARENTS: This provides a good opportunity to explain that friendships have ups and downs. That's normal. It's also a good time to encourage your children to have several good friends and not just one best friend.

Q 625:

If a friend asks me to keep a promise and it's something wrong, should I do it?

A: You don't have to keep a promise if someone will be hurt by it. If your friend says something like, "I'm going to tell you something, but you have to promise not to tell anyone else," you can say, "I can't promise to do that if what you are going to tell me is wrong." Let your friend know that you can't make any promise that goes against your promise to God to obey him. It's better to let your friend know up front what promises you will keep. Then, when you do promise something, be sure to keep your promise.

KEY VERSE: *Peter and the apostles replied, "We must obey God rather than human authority."* *(Acts 5:29)*

NOTE TO PARENTS: You can model appropriate keeping of promises with your children. Be sure to keep the secrets they share whenever you can. Let your children know, however, that if someone will be hurt, you won't keep quiet.

Q 626:

Why can't my best friend stay here with me and not move away?

A: It hurts when friends leave. It hurts your friend even more because, although you are losing one person, your friend is leaving almost everyone familiar. Your friend's family probably had a good reason for moving; for example, a parent may have received a promotion or a new job. Perhaps you can get your friend's new address and continue your friendship as pen pals or e-mail pals. Many families who move away from a city come back to visit. If you stay in touch, you will know when your friend is coming and possibly be able to get together.

Someday *you* might have to move. One of the facts of life is that situations don't stay the same, so it's important to learn how to deal with change.

KEY VERSES: *When he had finished speaking, he knelt and prayed with them. They wept aloud as they embraced him in farewell, sad most of all because he had said that they would never see him again. Then they accompanied him down to the ship. (Acts 20:36-38)*

NOTE TO PARENTS: Because society has become very mobile, some of your children's friends will probably move away. Instead of focusing on the losses, help your children learn to value the friendships they have. Encourage your children to keep in touch with their long-distance friends through E-mail, phone calls, and letters. If your family will be moving, pray together about the new friendships that will be formed in your new neighborhood, church, and school.

Q 627:

Why would your friends expect you to lie for them?

A: Some people think that friends should do anything for them—even lie. But that's not part of friendship. More important than doing what your friends want or expect is doing what God wants. That's what you should consider first. Your relationship with God should be your most important friendship, and God says that lying is wrong.

KEY VERSE: *Do not steal. Do not cheat one another. Do not lie. (Leviticus 19:11)*

NOTE TO PARENTS: Help your children know that a lie is the "intent to deceive." It's intentionally keeping quiet about the truth. In other words, a lie is not limited to saying words that are untrue. Saying nothing or saying the right words in the wrong way can also be lying.

Q 628:

Why don't your friends like you just for who you are?

A: Usually they do. That's probably what caused you to become friends in the first place—they like who you are. At times, however, friends may want to change something about who you are that's different from who *they* are. They may want you to stop doing things that are different from what *they* do. One of the great parts of friendship is getting to know someone who is completely different from you. God didn't make any two people alike, so learn to appreciate how your friends are different.

KEY VERSES: *Just as our bodies have many parts and each part has a special function, so it is with Christ's body. We are all parts of his one body, and each of us has different work to do. And since we are all one body in Christ, we belong to each other, and each of us needs all the others. (Romans 12:4-5)*

NOTE TO PARENTS: Kids face pressure to conform. Help them be true to themselves without being weird. Encourage your children to accept constructive criticism and to change when their friends bring up something that they perhaps should change.

Q 629:

Why do you have to do whatever your friends want, or they get mad?

A: It's natural to want to have our own way, so your friends may get mad at you when you don't do something they want you to do. That's not the way friendship should work, however. Sometimes a compromise is the way for everyone to be happy. Other times it means taking turns doing what each friend wants. If friends always want things their way or if they get angry with you when you don't conform, talk with them about it. If your friends are pressuring you to do something that you aren't comfortable with or that is dangerous or wrong, then you probably should find a new set of friends.

KEY VERSES: *Keep away from angry, short-tempered people, or you will learn to be like them and endanger your soul. (Proverbs 22:24-25)*

NOTE TO PARENTS: Help your children think about times when it's appropriate to give in to others and times when it's important not to give in to them, even if they get angry.

Q 630:

Why can't friends just get along instead of fighting and arguing with each other?

A: You'd think that friends would get along great *all the time*. But conflicts happen because everyone has ups and downs; sometimes a person is just in a bad mood. No two people agree on everything all the time. In any disagreement, however, instead of fighting and arguing, the people should talk it through and work together to solve the problem. If your friends are always fighting and arguing, you can be a good example yourself and help them resolve the issue. And you can keep from following the bad example of your friends by spending more time with kids who are learning to get along with each other.

KEY VERSE: *Beginning a quarrel is like opening a floodgate, so drop the matter before a dispute breaks out. (Proverbs 17:14)*

NOTE TO PARENTS: A good place to teach children how to get along with others is at home as they deal with their brothers and sisters. Enabling your children to work out sibling conflicts takes time. But it's an important way for them to develop the skills they need to get along with each other and with their friends. When arguments occur, teach your children how to "fight fair." Let them know it is possible to disagree with someone without screaming, yelling, and calling them names.

Q 631:

Why do my friends break their promises to me?

A: Only God is perfect and will never break his promises. Most people who make promises intend to keep them, but they may forget. Or circumstances may change. For example, a friend may say that you can visit her anytime, but a baby brother arrives and the family limits the number of visitors for a while. Sometimes people make promises that are almost impossible to keep—like saying, "I will never get angry with you." If a friend breaks a promise to you, let that person know how you feel, but try to be forgiving and understanding. Ask God to help you make only promises that you can keep. Then do your best to keep those promises.

KEY VERSE: *It is better to say nothing than to promise something that you don't follow through on. (Ecclesiastes 5:5)*

NOTE TO PARENTS: When children discover the promise concept, they can overuse it to make pacts with their friends. Help your children understand that promises are important and that we should say what we mean and do what we say.

Q 632:

When one of my friends is picking on someone, what should I do?

A: Don't join in. Maybe you could change the subject or get your friend to do something else instead. If things get bad, remember that no one has the right to touch or hit another person if that person doesn't want them to. Adults who hit people can go to jail for their actions. It's against the law, and it's not the way God wants us to treat others. If your friend's actions involve pushing or hitting of any kind, tell him to stop. Then go tell an adult immediately.

KEY VERSE: *Dear friend, don't let this bad example influence you. Follow only what is good. (3 John 1:11)*

NOTE TO PARENTS: This is an answer that's easy to say but hard to do. Your child may need backup from you. With all the violence that children see on television and in movies, they may think that mild physical abuse is part of life. Respect for others begins at home. Teach your children to respect others' rights for safety. Never allow any touching with the intent to harm.

Q 633:

If my friends ignore me, should I ignore them?

A: No—we should do what is right toward others even if they do wrong to us. This is difficult, but God expects us to do what is right regardless of what others do. Over time, our friendliness may win the other kids over. Sometimes we should just overlook what people do to us, but we should not ignore them as people. Probably the best way to act toward someone who is ignoring you is the exact opposite. You can go right up to the person and say something like this: "I'm sorry if I have upset you. Can we talk about it?"

KEY VERSE: *Never pay back evil for evil to anyone. Do things in such a way that everyone can see you are honorable. (Romans 12:17)*

NOTE TO PARENTS: This issue can be a crisis for children. You may say, "Just ignore anyone who ignores you." But the hurt will still be there. Friendships change over time, and even the strongest ones experience stress. Talking with someone who doesn't want to talk is not a natural thing to do. However, if you can help your children through it a couple of times until they see positive results, they will develop it as a life habit.

Q 634:

Why do some people want to be friends one day and not the next?

A: Learning how to be a good friend takes time and effort. Your friends may not realize that the way they are behaving is wrong. Nicely talk with them about it and how it makes you feel. Explain that you would like to know you can count on your friends every day.

It is possible that some kids may *seem* like they're changing their mind about being friends, but they may just be having a bad day. Or they may be spending time that day with another friend. If that's the case, don't worry; they are still your friends.

KEY VERSE: *Never abandon a friend. (Proverbs 27:10)*

NOTE TO PARENTS: Sometimes children can be possessive about friendships and want to monopolize a person's time and attention. But that will suffocate any friendship. If you think that's happening, help your child understand the importance of developing other friendships as well.

Q 635:

What can I do when one of my best friends used to like me but now hates me?

A: First, try to find out what happened. Did you do something to hurt your friend's feelings? If you find out that you did, say that you're sorry. Pray about the situation and ask God for wisdom. Remember, however, that there just may not be a good reason— people change, and you may have lost a friend. Don't try to get even, and don't decide to dislike the person back. You can still be nice and pray for your old friend, but be sure to find other friends.

KEY VERSE: *My friends scorn me, but I pour out my tears to God. (Job 16:20)*

NOTE TO PARENTS: Children will often use the word *hate* when referring to a former friend. What they usually mean is that they are upset with the person. A number of things can spoil a friendship. When relationships sour, there's a tendency to try to "get even." Instead, encourage your children to see this as a good opportunity to become more like Jesus, showing kindness even when it's not returned.

Getting Along with Others

Q 636:

Is it OK to think that you are better than somebody else if you really are better?

A: Be careful not to fall into the trap of thinking of yourself as better. Who says you are better? Sometimes we believe that we are better than we are, and we become filled with pride. Be realistic about yourself, and humble, too. Remember that all of your abilities and talents are gifts from God. And all of us, even it we're good at something, need to depend on God. Remember that your relationship with God is most important.

There is nothing wrong with being glad that you did a good job at something—singing a solo, scoring points in a game, getting good grades, or being honest, for example. It's OK to feel good about yourself and to have confidence in what you do. You don't have to pretend that you aren't good or apologize for being good. But don't compare yourself to others or think of yourself as better than they are.

When someone pays you a compliment, say, "Thank you." Just remember that you may be a better basketball player, but that doesn't make you a better person.

KEY VERSE: *As God's messenger, I give each of you this warning: Be honest in your estimate of yourselves, measuring your value by how much faith God has given you. (Romans 12:3)*

NOTE TO PARENTS: Humility is a key part of developing healthy self-esteem. When your child feels down, offer affirmation. When your child feels inappropriate pride, remind him or her that all have sinned and fallen short of God's glory (Romans 3:23).

Q 637:

Why are some kids so messy?

A: Kids are different. Some are neat, some are messy, and some are in between. Also, every family is different; some keep their homes much neater than others. So a person who grows up in a messy home may tend to be messy. It's good to be tidy and organized, and hopefully your messy friends will learn this as they grow up. But we shouldn't expect everyone to have everything perfectly in order all the time. While a messy person can be frustrating for someone who is neat, we should remember that being neat is not the most important thing in life. If some people aren't as neat as we are, that doesn't mean that they're bad—just different.

KEY VERSE: *Are we not all children of the same Father? Are we not all created by the same God? (Malachi 2:10)*

NOTE TO PARENTS: It's easy to get into the habit of seeing others' weaknesses. This habit will frustrate us and divide friends. Help your children work on their own weaknesses and focus on others' strengths. This habit will mature them and strengthen their friendships.

Q 638:

Why do some kids get their own way when they cry and get angry?

A: Some adults give in when children cry, pout, whine, or throw tantrums. The adults let those children get what they want. Kids who have been treated that way think they can always get what they want by acting like that. But someday those actions won't work. Can you imagine adults falling to the floor in a store, crying loudly, and beating the floor just because the store didn't have what they wanted? It's much better to learn as children to talk things through, be cooperative, and not try to get our way all the time.

KEY VERSES: *So Samson's wife came to him in tears and said, "You don't love me; you hate me! You have given my people a riddle, but you haven't told me the answer." "I haven't even given the answer to my father or mother," he replied. "Why should I tell you?" So she cried whenever she was with him and kept it up for the rest of the celebration. At last, on the seventh day, he told her the answer because of her persistent nagging. Then she gave the answer to the young men. (Judges 14:16-17)*

NOTE TO PARENTS: If your children point out that some friends get *their* way by throwing tantrums, help your kids understand that every home is unique. You are doing your best before God to be a good parent to *your* family in *your* home. No one should worry about whether or not other families are different or better. Talk about the fact that when someone in your family is disappointed over something, everyone can get together to work out a happy alternative.

Q 639:

Why do some kids always try to be first?

A: They're selfish. And, by the way, that's part of the sinful, human nature. *All* people tend to be selfish. Only God can help us be unselfish and think of others—we have to depend on him. Kids who always try to be first may be trying to feel better about themselves. They may feel that they are important and valuable because they won a game or got to be first in line. But God says that each person is valuable and important to him, even those who come in last. When we know how much God loves and cares for us, we can let others go first.

KEY VERSE: *[Jesus said,] "Many who are first now will be last then; and those who are last now will be first then." (Matthew 20:16)*

NOTE TO PARENTS: We should encourage our children to do their best, and it's certainly not wrong to win a game or contest. The problem comes when winning becomes everything. In small matters, like lining up for the drinking fountain, help your children learn that God is happier when we don't try to be first all the time.

Q 640:

Should I stand up for myself around pushy kids?

A: Yes, tell them how you feel. Be firm, but don't yell and lose your cool. The Bible says that a gentle answer will help calm a situation. Staying cool and being as nice as you can is your best chance for a good outcome. Sometimes this won't work, and you'll be tempted to fight. But don't do it—walk away instead. If kids get pushy, tell an adult.

KEY VERSE: *A gentle answer turns away wrath, but harsh words stir up anger. (Proverbs 15:1)*

NOTE TO PARENTS: Many parents tell their children to stand up for themselves and push back. But the Bible says to honor others and to turn the other cheek. This doesn't mean that children should become doormats. They should stand up for their rights but do it respectfully. They shouldn't fight.

Q 641:

Why do some kids just have to talk in class? Why can't they wait until recess?

A: Some are not mature enough to wait. Babies can't wait for anything. They want to be changed or fed or moved *now!* As children get older, however, they learn to have patience and do things at the right time, not whenever they feel like it. They also learn that the whole world doesn't revolve around them and that other people have needs too. Some kids, however, take a little longer than they should to learn these lessons.

Some kids might talk in class because they're afraid they will forget what they have to say. You could suggest that they write a reminder note to themselves to talk about it at recess or between classes.

KEY VERSE: *Don't talk too much, for it fosters sin. Be sensible and turn off the flow! (Proverbs 10:19)*

NOTE TO PARENTS: If your children talk too much, encourage them to work on this. Discuss possible solutions with their teachers.

Q 642:

Why do kids wreck my things for no reason?

A: Some kids are careless, and they break things by accident. Some are stronger than they realize and may not know what they are doing. Of course, some may be mean and break your things to hurt you. Some have never learned to take care of other people's property. Let your friends know that you expect them to be careful with your things. You don't have to let kids play with your toys if you know those kids don't care how they handle your things. You don't have to let people into your room if you know they don't care if they mess it up. Be careful, however, not to overreact to a small incident or an accident. Sharing is an important part of friendship.

KEY VERSE: *Let everyone see that you are considerate in all you do. (Philippians 4:5)*

NOTE TO PARENTS: Some kids may be mean and cruel. You have to help your children draw the line between sharing and protecting their stuff from careless kids. Be careful what you teach about ownership. Teach your children to respect others' ownership but also to be willing to share what they own.

Q 643:

Why do some kids act tough?

A: Usually kids who act tough are trying hard to feel good about themselves. They want everyone to look up to them the way people look up to entertainment or sports celebrities. Tough kids might be nice if they would just start being themselves. And kids who act important would have a lot more friends if they didn't pretend to be better than everyone else. The best person to be is yourself. Then when people like you, you will know that they like you for who you are and not for a pretend image that you are trying to have.

KEY VERSE: *Live in harmony with each other. Don't try to act important, but enjoy the company of ordinary people. And don't think you know it all! (Romans 12:16)*

NOTE TO PARENTS: All kids need attention, and they need to feel good about themselves. We should look for ways to affirm our children, always being ready to give them positive feedback. Don't be afraid that this will make them act important. Instead, children who are confident that they are loved, accepted, and special to their families as well as to God find it much easier to act natural. They know it's OK to be themselves.

Q 644:

Why do some kids say bad things about others?

A: They think it's fun. They might be jealous of other kids or angry with them. They might be in competition with them. Or they may not have learned yet that it's unkind. Whatever the reason, it's not right to say bad things about people, to call them names, to spread rumors, or to make fun of others. Unfortunately, a lot of humor these days is based on making fun of someone. But laughing at someone is a cruel way to joke around. Don't do it. A good rule to follow is to make sure that everything you say about people will make them feel good. Pretend that they are present to hear what you're saying about them, even if they're not.

KEY VERSE: *They must not speak evil of anyone, and they must avoid quarreling. Instead, they should be gentle and show true humility to everyone. (Titus 3:2)*

NOTE TO PARENTS: Kids can be cruel to each other. Their cutting remarks often relate to a physical characteristic or other superficial attribute, such as clothing. In addition to helping your children see how unkind it is to put others down, encourage them to look beyond the superficial to the real person. Remember that your children are listening when you talk about others. Making cutting remarks and put-down jokes is a bad habit, and using sarcasm is a destructive disciplinary tool. Make your home a safe place where your children and their friends feel welcomed and affirmed. You may want to add "saying only kind things about people" to your list of family rules.

Q 645:

Why are some kids bullies?

A: They are very selfish and care more about themselves than others. Usually bullies are bigger and stronger than other kids and can take advantage of them. They have learned to get what they want by force. Bullies come in all ages. You can find them in many places in the grown-up world as well as on the playground. No one should get away with bullying others. If you see it or get bullied yourself, tell a teacher, the principal, or your parents right away.

KEY VERSES: *Goliath walked out toward David with his shield bearer ahead of him, sneering in contempt at this ruddy-faced boy. (1 Samuel 17:41-42)*

NOTE TO PARENTS: If your child is being bullied by someone at school, talk to the teacher. If it's someone in the neighborhood, talk to the parent. Your child does not have to endure cruelty from a bully.

Q 646:

Should I stick up for someone who's being bullied?

A: Yes, always stick up for the person who is being hurt, not the one doing the hurting. If there is a big, strong bully at your school or in your neighborhood, you may want to encourage your friends to stay together in a group to be safer. Be sure to tell an adult about the situation too. Let this person know if extra adult supervision is needed on your school playground. If kids don't feel safe walking home from school, parents may be able to take turns giving rides.

KEY VERSE: *I say to the rest of you, dear brothers and sisters, never get tired of doing good. (2 Thessalonians 3:13)*

NOTE TO PARENTS: Encourage your child to inform a caring adult about bully action. This could be a coach, a teacher, a parent, a principal, or another caring adult.

Q 647:

If you know a friend is going to do something wrong, should you try to stop the person?

A: Yes, definitely. First, try to talk your friend out of doing what is wrong. Explain that you care about him or her and that's why you want to help. Use your friendship to encourage this friend into doing what is right instead of wrong. If he or she won't listen, tell your parents. If you are present when your friend starts to do what is wrong, leave immediately.

KEY VERSE: *Don't think only about your own affairs, but be interested in others, too, and what they are doing. (Philippians 2:4)*

NOTE TO PARENTS: Two kids can handle many issues without outside help. On the other hand, a "wrong" may be destructive and involve dangerous actions such as drinking, experimenting with drugs, vandalism, or shoplifting. In those situations, adults should be involved as soon as possible. Help your children understand the difference.

Q 648:

What should I do when kids are mean to me?

A: This will be difficult, but you should be kind to them no matter how mean they are to you. Also, you should pray for them. That's what God expects his people to do. God's way always works out best. You may think that you'll feel better by getting even, but you won't. If you respond God's way, you'll feel better about yourself, and you may even help those kids change when they see your good example. If you have to, avoid them. Don't let their meanness get to you. If they threaten to hurt you physically, you should tell an adult right away.

KEY VERSES: *Do what the Scriptures say: "If your enemies are hungry, feed them. If they are thirsty, give them something to drink, and they will be ashamed of what they have done to you." Don't let evil get the best of you, but conquer evil by doing good. (Romans 12:20-21)*

NOTE TO PARENTS: Every child experiences unkind behavior. "Being mean" can involve anything from name-calling and taunting to hurting someone physically. Sometimes kids feel sad or even guilty about being mistreated and, therefore, won't mention it. So it's important that from time to time you ask your children how people are treating them at school and in the neighborhood.

Q 649:

Why is it so hard to love your enemies?

A: It is very difficult to love enemies because it's not natural. It's the opposite of how everyone around us seems to be behaving. When people hurt us, we want to get back at them because we are human. When people don't like us or act mean toward us, it's natural not to like them. But Jesus tells us to love our enemies, and he promises to give us the strength to do it. "Loving" enemies doesn't necessarily mean having warm feelings about them. It means acting in a loving way toward them, treating them the way Jesus would—praying for them, being kind to them, and so on.

KEY VERSE: *[Jesus said,] "But I say, love your enemies! Pray for those who persecute you!" (Matthew 5:44)*

NOTE TO PARENTS: Here's another place where you can be a positive example for your children. They are watching you. How do you react when people cut you off in traffic, yell at you, or accuse you falsely? Pray for God's help to respond in love.

Q 650:

How can I love my enemies?

A: By doing kind things for them, wishing them well, and praying for them. Loving your enemies also means forgiving them and not condemning them. It means that rather than fighting back or trying to hurt them, you treat them like a friend.

If you think that sounds hard to do, you're right! Enemies don't like us and are out to hurt us. They may push us, hit us, call us names, and try to get us into trouble. We don't have to like what they do to us. But with the help of God's Holy Spirit, we can love *them*. After all, that's what God did for us.

God can do anything—even change people. Who knows— today's enemies may turn out to be tomorrow's friends.

KEY VERSES: *[Jesus said,] "Love your enemies! Do good to them! Lend to them! And don't be concerned that they might not repay. Then your reward from heaven will be very great, and you will truly be acting as children of the Most High, for he is kind to the unthankful and to those who are wicked. You must be compassionate, just as your Father is compassionate. Stop judging others, and you will not be judged. Stop criticizing others, or it will all come back on you. If you forgive others, you will be forgiven." (Luke 6:35-37)*

NOTE TO PARENTS: Every conflict with others is an opportunity for us to learn how to love. Encourage your child to turn conflicts into opportunities to be friendly and loving toward others.

Q 651:

Is it wrong to hate people if they're nerds?

A: Yes. Some people are given names like *nerd* or *jerk* for no good reason. Instead of believing the bad things we hear about others, we should think the best of them and try to get to know them.

Even when we meet people who really are "jerks"— who say bad things and are mean to us—we should not *hate* them or be mean back to them. God wants us to be loving and kind to others. So we shouldn't hurt others or make fun of them.

KEY VERSE: *God created people in his own image; God patterned them after himself. (Genesis 1:27)*

NOTE TO PARENTS: This touches on the issue of prejudice. You need to teach your child to respect all people regardless of race, nationality, religion, or economic class. God created diversity among people; there is no need for us to judge some good and some bad. Set the example: Avoid saying negative or stereotypical things about groups or classes of people.

Q 652:

When kids tease me, is it OK to tease them back?

MAN! WHERE DID YOU GET SUCH WEIRD HAIR?

A: There's a difference between fun teasing and mean teasing. Sometimes kids say nonsensical things about each other, not meaning to hurt anyone's feelings. That's OK. When kids tease you in a mean way, however, don't tease them back. Try to ignore them if possible. Just stay quiet. This won't be easy because it's natural to want to say something back to hurt them. If you can, be kind to them. Jesus calls this "turning the other cheek." If a certain group of kids seems to tease you all the time, don't go near those kids. If they call you names, remind yourself that the names do not describe the real you. God knows you, and he says you're special.

KEY VERSE: *Don't repay evil for evil. Don't retaliate when people say unkind things about you. Instead, pay them back with a blessing. That is what God wants you to do, and he will bless you for it. (1 Peter 3:9)*

NOTE TO PARENTS: Words can hurt, can't they? They can hurt you, and they can hurt your children. Words can cut and wound deeper than "sticks and stones." Be prepared to heal some word wounds.

Q 653:

Why don't other kids ever do what I say?

A: Do you like to tell others what to do? Do you always want things your way? If that's the case, kids may start ignoring you. Or perhaps some kids don't know you well enough to listen to your suggestions. Your good friends who know you and like you will probably take your ideas and suggestions seriously if you're not too bossy.

Remember, though, no one *has* to do what you say or suggest. You need to learn how to present your ideas in a way that others will want to go along with you. If you support your friends when they have good suggestions, those kids will be a lot easier to convince when you have a good idea.

KEY VERSES: *The next day, as Moses was out visiting his people again, he saw two Hebrew men fighting. "What are you doing, hitting your neighbor like that?" Moses said to the one in the wrong. "Who do you think you are?" the man replied. "Who appointed you to be our prince and judge?" (Exodus 2:13-14)*

NOTE TO PARENTS: Children don't develop great social and communication skills automatically. They do, however, often act like their parents. Therefore, if your children talk too much or boss others around, they may have learned that at home. Model and teach good listening skills, and help your children learn how to explain their ideas and suggestions clearly.

Fitting In at School

Q 654:

Why do some kids dress so weird?

A: They may like to do it. Actually, their clothes may seem weird to you but not to them. Of course, some kids wear loud and different clothes to be noticed. They want to get a reaction, to get attention. Some kids whose clothes seem weird may be copying musicians or other celebrities who they think are cool. Others may look different just because they don't have enough money to dress in style. Remember not to judge people by the way they dress.

KEY VERSES: *[Jesus said,] "Everything [the Pharisees] do is for show. On their arms they wear extra wide prayer boxes with Scripture verses inside, and they wear extra long tassels on their robes. They enjoy the attention they get on the streets." (Matthew 23:5, 7)*

NOTE TO PARENTS: Remember, clothes don't make the person. This cuts both ways. A wonderful person may be dressed in weird clothes. Conversely, a rotten person can hide in the latest styles. It's easy to judge people by their appearance. Be careful to set a good example in this area.

Q 655:

Sometimes I'm afraid to go to school. What should I do?

A: Talk to your parents about your fears. They will help. If there's a specific reason why you are afraid, tell them about it. Teachers and school counselors can also help. You may want to go to school with a friend. This friend can encourage you, pray for you, and give you moral support. Also, you can ask Christian friends, such as your Sunday school teacher and pastor, to pray for you. They can pray also that God will take care of the situation that is causing you to be afraid.

KEY VERSE: *I am holding you by your right hand—I, the LORD your God. And I say to you, "Do not be afraid. I am here to help you." (Isaiah 41:13)*

NOTE TO PARENTS: Find out why your child is afraid. The first answer may not be the real reason. Instead of telling your son or daughter to be tough, take time to talk it through and find out what's really happening. A bully may be lurking. Kids may be making fun of your child's clothes or looks. Or your child may be afraid of failing. After determining the cause, you can pray about it together and work toward a solution.

Q 656:

Why do kids always want to dress according to different fads?

A: They want to fit in, to look like everyone else. Advertisers spend tons of money to make it seem as if everyone should wear certain clothes. Or a famous person might wear an outfit that looks good, and everyone starts buying a similar outfit. That's how fads get started. Soon it seems as though everyone is wearing the same styles and colors. But fads don't last very long. You don't have to dress in every new fad. Many clothing styles are classic and always seem to be in style. You can ask your parents to help you choose the right clothes to wear.

KEY VERSE: *Everything is so weary and tiresome! No matter how much we see, we are never satisfied. No matter how much we hear, we are not content. (Ecclesiastes 1:8)*

NOTE TO PARENTS: Let your children know that it's all right to wear the latest styles as long as they aren't too extreme. However, you'll want to point out that kids can be stylish without being faddish. Explain that fashion fads usually look pretty silly a few years later. To prove this point, find some pictures of fads from twenty years ago, or show photos of yourself as a kid.

Q 657:

What's so bad about wanting to wear clothes that are in style?

A: It's all right to wear nice clothes that are in style. We should take care of ourselves and try to look our best. But we shouldn't think that having the latest clothes will make us happy and help us make friends. And we should remember that wearing nice clothes doesn't make a person nice. It's what's on the inside of the person that really counts.

People who design and make new clothes are trying to make money. So they broadcast very clever ads on TV and radio to make people want to buy their clothes. They change the styles every season and say that everyone should wear the latest style. Often the most stylish clothes are also the most expensive.

Work with your parents to buy what you can afford. God wants us to be content with what we have, so don't think that you have nothing to wear because your clothes are not the very latest style. And God wants us to put him in first place in our lives, so don't make clothes and other things more important than he is.

KEY VERSES: *[Jesus said,] "Don't worry about having enough food or drink or clothing. Why be like the pagans who are so deeply concerned about these things? Your heavenly Father already knows all your needs, and he will give you all you need from day to day if you live for him and make the Kingdom of God your primary concern." (Matthew 6:31-33)*

Q 658:

Why does everybody want to do things that other people do?

A: Because they feel pressured. They want to fit in, be liked, and not be too different. They may be afraid that kids will make fun of them if they don't do what everyone else is doing. Sometimes we assume that a movie, TV show, or product is good because it's popular. We may think, *If so many people do that, it must be fun.* Or, *If so many people have seen that movie, it must be good.* That's OK as long as what's popular is pleasing to God. But no one has to feel pressured to do things that are wrong.

KEY VERSE: *I didn't want to do anything without your consent. And I didn't want you to help because you were forced to do it but because you wanted to. (Philemon 1:14)*

NOTE TO PARENTS: This is a good time in your children's lives to teach them the importance of knowing the difference between right and wrong, having an opinion, and acting on what you believe. Peer pressure will increase dramatically as children get older.

Q 659:

What should I do if other kids laugh at me for going to church?

A: You can ignore their laughter. If you get the chance, you can quietly explain that you go to church because you love God and because you enjoy church and want to be with your family and friends there. Someone who laughs at you for going to church may not know what church is, may have never been to church, and probably doesn't know what it means to love God and his Son, Jesus. That's someone for whom you can pray. You can even invite that person to go to church with you sometime, especially when your church has a fun night or other social activity.

KEY VERSE: *[Jesus said,] "God blesses you who are hated and excluded and mocked and cursed because you are identified with me, the Son of Man." (Luke 6:22)*

HA HA, GOODY TWO SHOES IS GOING TO CHURCH

NOTE TO PARENTS: Most children don't understand the differences among the various religions and denominations. It's important for them to learn how to accept children from all cultures and backgrounds. They also need to understand, however, that they can't accept all beliefs. Help your children learn what is unique about the Christian faith and about your particular denomination so they will know how to explain what they believe.

Q 660:

Why do you have to be good and obey in school?

A: School leaders and teachers have rules for how students should act in school so that the school will be safe and students will be able to learn. Just think of the confusion if all the kids did whatever they wanted whenever they wanted. No one would learn anything, except how to be rowdy. In class, for example, if everyone talked at the same time, no one would hear the teacher. And if kids were allowed to run, push, and shove in the hall, people would get hurt.

KEY VERSE: *Oh, why didn't I listen to my teachers? Why didn't I pay attention to those who gave me instruction? (Proverbs 5:13)*

NOTE TO PARENTS: Sometimes children can become overwhelmed by all the rules in school. They may even fear that they might break some rules by accident. Help them understand that the rules make sense and that most rules are easy to obey. Help your children understand the long-term benefits of applying themselves in school and doing well. Point out that obeying school leaders is one of the ways that we obey God, who has given us these leaders.

Q 661:

Why are some kids so big and other kids so small?

A: People come in all different shapes and sizes. Just look at adults. Some professional football players weigh over three hundred pounds, and some professional basketball players are well over seven feet tall! Most people, however, are much lighter and shorter than that. Kids come in different shapes and sizes too. They also grow at different rates. A girl might grow quickly and seem very tall compared to other kids. But in a few years other kids will begin growing and pass her in height. It can be frustrating to be very small or very tall right now, but eventually these things average out. Be patient. Size won't matter so much in the future when everyone has finished growing.

KEY VERSE: *The LORD said to Samuel, "Don't judge by his appearance or height, for I have rejected him. The LORD doesn't make decisions the way you do! People judge by outward appearance, but the LORD looks at a person's thoughts and intentions." (1 Samuel 16:7)*

NOTE TO PARENTS: Tell stories about when you were growing up and when you experienced your growth spurt.

Q 662:

What if I don't like the music that everyone else listens to?

A: You don't have to enjoy certain music just because others do. It's like with food. What if everyone else liked french fries, but fries made you sick to your stomach? Would you eat french fries? You wouldn't have to. In the same way, you will develop your own taste in music. It may be the same as others, but it doesn't have to be. Of course you should respect others' tastes too. Don't yell at them to "turn off that stupid music" just because you don't like it. Pay attention to the words, though. If you know they aren't pleasing to God, let your friends know you have no interest in listening.

KEY VERSES: *"Just as the mouth tastes good food, the ear tests the words it hears." So let us discern for ourselves what is right; let us learn together what is good.* (Job 34:3-4)

NOTE TO PARENTS: The fact is, at about nine or ten years of age, kids begin listening to the music styles that their peers seem to like. Beware of criticizing this music just because you don't appreciate it. Your children may interpret your criticisms as a put-down of their friends, not the music. On the other hand, be sure to point out specific problems you have with certain songs and stations (suggestive lyrics, depraved performers, dirty-talking DJs, and so on) and recommend alternatives. This is the ideal time to help your children learn to appreciate a wide variety of music. And remember that you probably can find a Christian artist for almost every music style.

Q 663:

I feel so stupid in some subjects. What can I do?

A: Some subjects are difficult to understand at first—not everyone gets everything right away. God made each person different, each with special gifts. It's normal that some subjects will be easier for you than others. But you can still conquer the ones that seem very difficult. In those classes, you can ask the teacher for help. Most teachers encourage their students to ask questions and to ask for help when they need it. Your parents will also be happy to help you. Subjects that are difficult will help you learn to think and to figure things out.

KEY VERSE: *If you need wisdom—if you want to know what God wants you to do—ask him, and he will gladly tell you.* (James 1:5)

NOTE TO PARENTS: Keep in mind that just because kids feel a subject is difficult doesn't mean they lack ability in that subject. Help your children understand that learning difficult material takes work. Do not use words such as *stupid* or *dumb*—never hint that your children don't have the mental capability to understand difficult subjects. Instead, challenge your children to do their best. Then give whatever help you're able to offer, find a tutor if needed, and look for ways to affirm your children's work.

Q 664:

Why do some kids swear?

A: Usually kids swear or curse because they are trying to act older or cool. Some kids live in homes where their parents swear a lot, so they hear the words every day. Or they may have seen movies or videos with a lot of swearing. That makes it easy for them to use swearwords when they talk, too. Swearing is a very bad habit to get into. In a certain group at school, it may seem as though swearing will make you accepted. But often people think that those who swear a lot are crude and not very smart. Swearing is *not* cool!

KEY VERSE: *Don't use foul or abusive language. Let everything you say be good and helpful, so that your words will be an encouragement to those who hear them. (Ephesians 4:29)*

NOTE TO PARENTS: Talk with your kids about swearing and why it's bad. Often kids will repeat a word that they have heard without having a clue about its meaning. When that happens at your house, be careful not to overreact. Instead, explain why the word is bad and help your children understand which words are swearwords and which ones aren't. If you have used swearwords yourself, apologize to your children. Ask them to pray with you, asking God to help you stop saying those kinds of words.

Q 665:

What should I say if someone makes fun of the Bible?

A: If a friend makes fun of the Bible, you can politely explain how you feel and ask that person to stop. Your friend may not know how special the Bible is to you. This might give you a good opportunity to explain that the Bible comes from God, who created the whole universe, and it's very important to you. You might be the first one to help this person understand that the message in the Bible is for everyone in the world. If your friend doesn't want to listen, it's best to let it pass and just pray for him or her.

KEY VERSES: *Even if you suffer for doing what is right, God will reward you for it. So don't be afraid and don't worry. Instead, you must worship Christ as Lord of your life. And if you are asked about your Christian hope, always be ready to explain it. (1 Peter 3:14-15)*

NOTE TO PARENTS: Talk with your family about the significance of the Scriptures. Be sure your children understand that no other book ever has been or ever will be inspired by God the way the Bible is. God shows us in his Word exactly who he is, how much he loves us, and how important it is for us to love him. This would be another ideal time to teach your children how to explain to others what they believe. See *Ready for Life* (Tyndale House Publishers) for devotions that will help you do this.

Dealing with the Desire to Be Popular

Q 666:

How does someone become popular?

A: The best way to become popular is to be a positive, helpful, nice person—someone that people enjoy being around. If that's the kind of person you are, kids who get to know you will like you for who you are. Eventually, lots of people will get to know you and like you. Whatever you do, however, don't pretend to be someone you aren't just to be liked by others. Be the kind of person God wants you to be, whether you become popular or not. In other words, be like Jesus!

KEY VERSE: *Be kind to each other, tenderhearted, forgiving one another, just as God through Christ has forgiven you. (Ephesians 4:32)*

NOTE TO PARENTS: Most groups of children develop a natural pecking order, with the most popular kids on top. Children are very aware of this order, and most would like to move up the order. Several factors determine this order—height, attractiveness, silliness, etc. Explain that it's nice to be liked, but a person doesn't have to be liked by everybody. Also, don't be afraid to give extra attention at home. This will go a long way in preventing your children from worrying about their position in any pecking order.

Q 667:

Is it OK to be popular?

A: Nothing is wrong with being popular if it's for the right reasons. Some kids are popular because they are kind and caring. Sometimes Christians are very unpopular, however, because they stand for what is right. They have to say things that people don't want to hear and do what is right even though just about everyone else is doing what is wrong. (The prophets in the Bible sure weren't very popular!) It's much more important to have God's approval than to be popular with people.

KEY VERSE: *Obviously, I'm not trying to be a people pleaser! No, I am trying to please God. If I were still trying to please people, I would not be Christ's servant. (Galatians 1:10)*

NOTE TO PARENTS: If your children want to become more popular, don't be concerned—that's normal and all right. They may be trying to figure out what to do to gain popularity. As you give advice about how to act at school, help your kids be aware of God's love for them as well as yours. Being assured of this love will help your children want to please God and please you, which will help fulfill their need to be popular.

Q 668:

Do you have to wear makeup or dress cool to make people like you?

A: Some advertisements, television shows, magazines, and movies make it seem that way, but it's not true. Attention and popularity based on makeup and clothes don't last very long. People should like you for who you are. It's good to be neat and to *look* nice, but it's more important to *be* nice. People are drawn to others who are gentle and loving.

KEY VERSES: *Don't be concerned about the outward beauty that depends on fancy hairstyles, expensive jewelry, or beautiful clothes. You should be known for the beauty that comes from within, the unfading beauty of a gentle and quiet spirit, which is so precious to God. (1 Peter 3:3-4)*

NOTE TO PARENTS: Although most young children are not very fashion conscious, many of their parents are. Thus children of all ages can be found dressed like the magazine ads. This puts other kids under pressure to get new clothes all the time. Don't get caught in that trap. You can dress your children nicely and in style without spending a bundle on designer clothes. Let your children know that it's all right to wear the latest fashions (as long as they're not too extreme), but it's vital to be the right kind of person in those clothes. Character, not clothes, makes the person.

Q 669:

How do you get someone to like you if you aren't as popular as everyone else?

A: You can't force people to like you or talk them into it. And you shouldn't do whatever they say just so they will be your friends. When you live for Jesus and let the Holy Spirit control your actions, people will like you for who you are. So the idea is to help people get to know the real you. You can be liked, even if you're not voted Most Popular. Outgoing, likable people are often very popular, but you can be likable even if you're quiet. A few good friends who enjoy doing the same things can be just as much fun as a big group of the most popular kids. God made each person special and unique, so we should value all people (ourself included) no matter how popular they are or aren't.

BE RIGHT WITH YOU MAX, MY MAN. JUST NEED TO ORDER A DOUBLE DE-CAF LATTE, AND TALK TO THE PRESIDENT OF MY FAN CLUB!

KEY VERSES: *When the Holy Spirit controls our lives, he will produce this kind of fruit in us: love, joy, peace, patience, kindness, goodness, faithfulness, gentleness, and self-control. (Galatians 5:22-23)*

NOTE TO PARENTS: As kids grow up, they become acquainted with the pecking order in the various groups to which they belong. (See the note with question 666.) Look for groups— church groups, community choirs, and certain sport teams—where the other kids are more likely to accept your children for who they are. Usually the tone for a group is set by a caring adult.

Q 670:

Why do kids think something is cool one day and stupid the next?

A: People change, so those kids may just have changed their minds. Think about times when you did the same thing. What was your favorite TV show last year? How about your favorite music group? Your favorites are probably different now. As kids grow up, they outgrow the things they liked a year or even a few months before. Also remember that fads change quickly. Something is "in" one day and "out" the next. That's a good reason for not getting too carried away trying to follow every fad that comes along.

KEY VERSE: *When I was a child, I spoke and thought and reasoned as a child does. But when I grew up, I put away childish things. (1 Corinthians 13:11)*

NOTE TO PARENTS: Children are susceptible to fads. Discuss the power of advertisements with your children—ads are the source of many fads. Have fun analyzing the advertisers' strategies and talking back to the TV together when one of those ads comes on. You can say, "Come on, I don't need that!" or "Who are you trying to fool?" or "No one will want one of those next month!"

Q 671:

Why do some kids all dress, talk, and act the same?

A: People like to belong, to be accepted as part of a group. Many times kids will cluster into groups of friends, almost like a club. Then those kids will dress alike, talk alike, and act alike. Maybe they're afraid of being singled out or laughed at, or maybe they're all together because they just like the same things. It's all right to be part of a group, but be careful not to become a clique (a group that thinks it's too good for anyone else). And don't allow any group to convince you to dress, talk, and act in a way you don't want to or that you know is wrong. Be committed to what you believe, and be confident about your own tastes.

KEY VERSES: *[Jesus said,] "If you love only those who love you, what good is that? Even corrupt tax collectors do that much. If you are kind only to your friends, how are you different from anyone else? Even pagans do that."(Matthew 5:46-47)*

NOTE TO PARENTS: Fitting in with peers can be a big deal to children. Try to accommodate your kids without going overboard. Let them know that it's all right to be like everyone else in a group as long as what they do doesn't keep them from pleasing God. Then encourage them to stay friends with others who aren't part of their group.

Q 672:

Should I get a cool nickname?

A: Nicknames are fun to have, especially if they make us sound good. But nicknames often come from others—the names describe how other people see us. It's not the same if we give them to ourselves. You don't need to have a good nickname to be a good person. If your friends give you a nickname that you like, however, let them know that it's OK for them to keep calling you by that name.

KEY VERSES: *These are the names of the twelve [Jesus] chose: Simon (he renamed him Peter), James and John (the sons of Zebedee, but Jesus nicknamed them "Sons of Thunder").* (Mark 3:16-17)

NOTE TO PARENTS: Unfortunately, kids can pin cruel or demeaning nicknames on their peers, so don't give your children's peers any ammunition by using unusual nicknames with your children in public. If you have a pet name or nickname for your child held over from earlier years ("precious," "bunny," "babycakes," "champ," and so on), make sure it won't turn out to be used in a derogatory way outside your home.

Q 673:

Do you have to be good at a sport to be popular?

A: Good athletes are popular because people enjoy sports and like winners. But all athletes aren't well liked, and you don't have to be athletic to be popular. Don't try to be something you're not. If you're in a sport, do your best and play hard and fair—enjoy yourself instead of worrying about what others think. If you're not good at sports, most likely you enjoy other kinds of activities. Be yourself, and let popularity take care of itself.

KEY VERSE: *Physical exercise has some value, but spiritual exercise is much more important, for it promises a reward in both this life and the next.* (1 Timothy 4:8)

NOTE TO PARENTS: Your children may suddenly become interested in sports or want to join a team because they want to be popular. Often kids will want to try a sport because other friends are playing. You may think that your children are doing it for the wrong reasons. That's all right. It may be a way to broaden their interests and skills. Sports will also help them develop social skills, such as teamwork.

Q 674:

If someone isn't popular, how come others think less of him or her as a person?

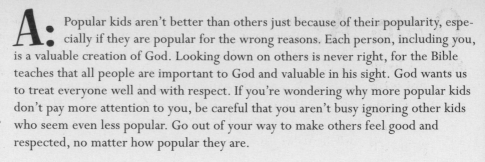

A: Popular kids aren't better than others just because of their popularity, especially if they are popular for the wrong reasons. Each person, including you, is a valuable creation of God. Looking down on others is never right, for the Bible teaches that all people are important to God and valuable in his sight. God wants us to treat everyone well and with respect. If you're wondering why more popular kids don't pay more attention to you, be careful that you aren't busy ignoring other kids who seem even less popular. Go out of your way to make others feel good and respected, no matter how popular they are.

KEY VERSES: *Then these righteous ones will reply, "Lord, when did we ever see you hungry and feed you? Or thirsty and give you something to drink? Or a stranger and show you hospitality? Or naked and give you clothing? When did we ever see you sick or in prison, and visit you?" And the King will tell them, "I assure you, when you did it to one of the least of these my brothers and sisters, you were doing it to me!" (Matthew 25:37-40)*

NOTE TO PARENTS: The real problem may be that your children believe that others think less of them. They may be experiencing rejection. When the social-life road at school becomes bumpy, the atmosphere at home becomes especially important. Spend one-on-one time with your children, for they may be the "brothers and sisters" for whom Jesus wants you to do things right now.

Q 675:

Why does my friend always want me to ask people what they think about her?

A: Your friend may be unsure and afraid. She may think that no one likes her, and perhaps she is afraid to talk directly to people. Try not to get caught in a situation like this. Instead, assure your friend that *you* like her—*you* think she's special. If you would like to help her get to know more people, invite her to a group activity at your church. Or invite another friend or two over to your house when you invite her. If your friend wants you to ask boys whether or not they like her, it's better not to get involved.

KEY VERSE: *Encourage each other. Live in harmony and peace. Then the God of love and peace will be with you. (2 Corinthians 13:11)*

NOTE TO PARENTS: As kids get older, it's natural for them to begin feeling concerned with what others think about them. Help your children learn to affirm their friends, to make their friends feel good about themselves. Make your home a safe place where the friends feel welcomed and accepted.

Q 676:

Should I hang out with popular people to become popular?

A: This may seem like the way to be popular, but that kind of popularity is pretty shallow and won't last very long. It's OK to be friends with the popular kids, but it's not OK to do whatever they say to be accepted by them. Instead, be the right kind of person, the kind that others will want to hang with. Be confident in the fact that God loves you. Remember that the Bible teaches us to think about the needs of others, not just our own. Spend some time and attention on kids who aren't very popular and help them feel good about themselves. You'll be amazed at how good *you* will feel when you make others feel good.

KEY VERSE: *Oh, that my actions would consistently reflect your principles! (Psalm 119:5)*

NOTE TO PARENTS: Physical, mental, and social maturity varies greatly among children. In addition, some kids within a grade can be as much as eleven months older than the others. If your children are less mature, they may want to hang around with more mature kids to become more popular. But this probably is not a good idea. Get to know your children's friends so you can determine the kind of influence these friends have on your children. Encourage friendships with kids at similar stages of development by offering to have them over even before your children ask.

Relating to Teachers

Q 677:

Why is it that some teachers are nice to other kids but mean to me?

A: Most teachers try to be fair and treat all their students the same. But here are three situations that can make it seem otherwise:

1. It's easy to be nice to students who listen carefully, try to learn, do their assignments on time, and stay out of trouble. And it's natural to *not* be attracted to kids who seem to have bad attitudes.
2. God gave people different personalities. Thus, although we should love everyone, we get along better with some than others. This is also true with teachers. You'll find that you will get along OK with some teachers and great with others.
3. Some kids get nervous wondering how a teacher feels about them. Therefore, they misinterpret some of the teacher's words or actions as being negative toward them.

    If you have problems with a certain teacher, pray about it; then do your best to cooperate and learn. That combination often works wonders.

KEY VERSES: *My child, never forget the things I have taught you. Store my commands in your heart. Then you will find favor with both God and people, and you will gain a good reputation. (Proverbs 3:1, 4)*

NOTE TO PARENTS: If your child complains that a teacher is mean, don't judge the teacher. Instead, talk it through with your child to see if together you can figure out the situation. If that doesn't work, talk to the teacher and get the other side of the story.

Q 678:

Why do some teachers let you get away with stuff while others give you trouble when you drop a pencil?

A: Some teachers are pretty relaxed, and others are more nervous and on edge. Some teachers have few rules in class, while others are more strict. One way is not better than the other. If your teacher is kind of nervous and strict, then be careful to act right and obey the rules. You can get along with any teacher if you try. Remember that even after you grow up, you'll always have to relate to different types of people. For example, you may have a boss who is strict. If you can get along with others, you'll have more opportunities to advance and succeed. If you can't, you may become frustrated and discouraged.

KEY VERSE: *[Jesus said,] "A student is not greater than the teacher. A servant is not greater than the master." (Matthew 10:24)*

NOTE TO PARENTS: Teachers who seem strict and keep their class under control are often more systematic and organized with their teaching methods. Kids who tend to be creative or people-oriented may complain about this type of teacher. But those types of students may benefit the most from this approach. Help your children understand that a strict teacher isn't necessarily mean—class discipline is more complicated than that.

Q 679:

Why do teachers make it easy for some kids to get good grades and hard for others?

A: It may seem as though teachers sometimes make it easier for some kids than others, but all teachers try to be fair. They really try to treat everyone the same. Also, most teachers are more concerned that their students try hard and do their best. They want kids to learn, not just get good grades. So they might push some students to work harder. Instead of worrying about others, make sure that *you* work hard and do *your* best.

KEY VERSE: *Brothers and sisters, we urge you to warn those who are lazy. Encourage those who are timid. Take tender care of those who are weak. Be patient with everyone. (1 Thessalonians 5:14)*

NOTE TO PARENTS: Teachers may push kids who they believe are not working up to their potential. In other words, one student may work hard just to understand the material and pass the class, while another may be coasting to an A. The teacher may push the A student harder to challenge that child. Let your children know that the teacher may be tougher on them because they are able to learn even more than they have been learning.

Q 680:

Why do teachers give so much homework?

A: Teachers give homework because they are trying to be *good* teachers and they want to help you learn. Doing assignments at home will remind you of what the teacher said in class and help you put it into practice. The school system was designed to include homework. It's not a punishment—homework is an important part of learning.

The best way to get the homework done is to start on it right away. Don't put off doing an assignment until the last minute. It's a good idea to do homework *first*, before watching TV, playing with friends, or talking on the phone. Even when you don't have assignments to do at home, you can review what you learned that day with your family.

KEY VERSE: *If you stop listening to instruction, my child, you have turned your back on knowledge. (Proverbs 19:27)*

NOTE TO PARENTS: Homework can be a blessing if it helps kids learn organizational skills and discipline. Help your children develop a daily schedule, and encourage them to do the work without your nagging. Too much homework may pile up on one night, especially if the schedule is already jammed. For example, one afternoon and evening schedule might include a music lesson, sports practice, and a Bible club meeting. When that happens, you will have to set priorities. Teachers, coaches, and church leaders will usually understand and work with you if you talk to them about your dilemma.

Q 681:

Why won't the teacher let me sit next to my friend?

A: Your teacher probably knows that you won't learn very much if you're seated next to your friend. Sometimes when friends sit next to each other, they talk or pass notes instead of paying attention. The purpose of school is to learn, and teachers want their students to learn without distractions. You can still play with your friends at recess or sit with them at lunch.

If you do get an opportunity to sit next to a friend, pay attention and don't talk or goof around. When your teacher sees that you and your friend are paying attention and learning, then there won't be any reason to separate the two of you.

KEY VERSE: *Work brings profit, but mere talk leads to poverty! (Proverbs 14:23)*

NOTE TO PARENTS: Help your kids understand that it's good to have friends, and you are glad that they have friends at school, but learning comes first. Explain to your children the importance of obeying the rules and not distracting others, no matter whom they are sitting beside. Who knows, they might end up sitting next to a friend someday!

Q 682:

Why do we have to respect teachers?

A: The Bible says that God expects his people to respect those in authority over them. That includes teachers. Also, for teachers to do their best, they need the respect of their students. If you respect your teachers, you'll be polite and kind to them, listen to them, and do what they say. Remember, the only one who benefits from your going to school and learning is you. If you don't cooperate, listen, and learn, you won't be hurting the teacher—you will be hurting yourself and your future.

KEY VERSE: *The authorities do not frighten people who are doing right, but they frighten those who do wrong. So do what they say, and you will get along well. (Romans 13:3)*

NOTE TO PARENTS: You may not always agree with your children's teachers, but let your kids know that you still respect these people. Teach your children that when you send them to school, you are extending your parental authority over them to their teachers and school administrators. So if they are disrespectful or disobedient to the school authorities, they are doing the same to you.

Q 683:

Why are some children suspended from school?

A: The purpose of school is to provide a safe environment where students learn the things they need to know as they grow up. Children who break rules related to weapons, drugs, fighting, and so on make it difficult for everyone else in the class to learn. Sometimes those kids have to be taken out of the classroom or even be suspended from school for everyone else's good. Hopefully their punishment will teach them not to threaten the safety of their classmates.

KEY VERSE: *Throw out the mocker, and fighting, quarrels, and insults will disappear. (Proverbs 22:10)*

NOTE TO PARENTS: Just a few years ago, suspension was very rare in elementary schools. Recently, however, because of the violence among younger children, every threat is taken seriously, and children are being suspended for saying things like "I'll kill you" or "I'll get you." Help your children understand that a suspension is very serious. Kids who have been suspended from school may have done something more serious than the rest of the class realizes.

Q 684:

Why do kids often take advantage of a substitute teacher?

A: Students think the substitute doesn't know them, the class procedures and rules, or what the kids have been studying. So some students think they can get away with things like being rude or not doing what the substitute says. If other kids ask you to join them in tricking the substitute, don't go along with them. Substitute teachers should be treated with respect, just the same as regular teachers. Besides, the substitute will probably leave a note for the regular teacher that tells how everyone acted in class!

KEY VERSE: *Give to everyone what you owe them. . . . And give respect and honor to all to whom it is due. (Romans 13:7)*

NOTE TO PARENTS: Even though giving a substitute teacher a hard time seems to be a time-honored tradition, we should let our children know that we expect them not to get involved.

Q 685:

Why don't teachers just get to the point instead of blabbing on and on about the subject?

A: Some kids find it more difficult to learn certain subjects than other kids. Good teachers take time to teach *all* the students in a class, not just the ones who understand the material right away. Sometimes teachers explain other material that is also important, adding facts and reasons for what they are teaching. Listen and pay attention—you may learn something!

KEY VERSE: *[The Levites] read from the Book of the Law of God and clearly explained the meaning of what was being read, helping the people understand each passage. (Nehemiah 8:8)*

NOTE TO PARENTS: In elementary school, teachers usually do not give long lectures. If your children ask this question, the problem may be that they do not feel challenged in class. Or it may be that one of your children has a learning disability or a different learning style and has difficulty understanding what is being taught. You may want to talk with the teacher about this. You could explain that you think your child might respond better to written instructions than to oral ones.

Q 686:

Why do my friends get fun teachers and I get mean ones?

A: Let's face it, some teachers are more fun than others. Everyone is different, and it takes all kinds of teachers to teach all kinds of kids. But no one is trying to make sure that you don't get any fun teachers. Take a good attitude to class and give your teachers a chance. You may find that they are more fun than you thought. Also, remember the "grass is greener" syndrome—other kids may think that *you* have the fun teachers.

KEY VERSE: *Indeed, the Teacher taught the plain truth, and he did so in an interesting way. (Ecclesiastes 12:10)*

NOTE TO PARENTS: Encourage your children to have a good attitude toward their teachers. Teachers who seem mean may just be trying to establish their authority in the classroom at the beginning of the year. A few weeks later, those teachers may loosen up if the class is under control.

Q 687:

Why doesn't the teacher ever choose my papers or pictures to put on the wall?

A: Teachers usually choose very good papers to display in class. *Very good* may mean the highest score on a test or homework. *Very good* may be a beautiful picture or project. But *very good* can also mean showing great improvement. The teacher may want to recognize a student who has made great progress in the class. Do your best. It's an honor to have your work displayed, but don't worry about it. Just because your paper didn't go on the wall doesn't mean it's not good. Doing your best is more important than having a paper displayed.

KEY VERSE: *Be sure to do what you should, for then you will enjoy the personal satisfaction of having done your work well, and you won't need to compare yourself to anyone else.* (Galatians 6:4)

NOTE TO PARENTS: Look for ways to affirm your children's work. Display their tests, homework assignments, and artwork on your refrigerator or wall, complimenting them for doing their best.

Q 688:

Why do some teachers have rules that don't even make sense?

A: Almost all rules have good reasons behind them. Sometimes, however, the reasons may not be obvious, so those rules may not make sense to you. It's all right to ask a teacher for the reasons, but be sure to ask nicely. It's important to have a good attitude in class. You should obey all rules whether you like them or not. If all the kids disobeyed the rules or just obeyed the rules they liked, no one would be able to learn anything.

KEY VERSE: *Help me understand the meaning of your commandments. (Psalm 119:27)*

NOTE TO PARENTS: Encourage and compliment your children for wanting to know the reasons behind rules. Let them know it's all right to ask questions like that. Be sure, however, that they really want answers and aren't just looking for an excuse to break a rule. When children understand the reason behind a rule and how people benefit from it, most of them usually have no problem following it.

Succeeding in Class

Q 689:

Why do we have to study subjects that we might not need to know when we grow up?

A: People may think that the only reason to study a subject in school is to learn something that they might need in a future job. But that's wrong. Some classes teach information and skills that students can build on. Some classes teach students how to think. Most of what you learn in the early grades of school, such as reading and math, will help you in many areas of your life. Also, you never know when God will use you and what you have learned to help others. It will be exciting to see how God will someday use what you're learning now.

KEY VERSE: *Teach the wise, and they will be wiser. Teach the righteous, and they will learn more. (Proverbs 9:9)*

NOTE TO PARENTS: Encourage your children to try to do well in *all* their subjects. Help them understand that the things they learn now will prepare them for many things, not just for a future job. For example, they may need to know how to follow recipes, teach Sunday school, plant a garden, etc. Because no one knows the future, no one can predict which subjects will or won't be of value.

Q 690:

If you have already studied something, such as addition, why do you have to keep studying it?

A: To get really good at anything, a person has to practice. This can mean doing the same drills, playing the same scales, or reviewing the same material over and over. It's true in sports and music, and it's true in math and other subjects. Also, the simple problems will lead to more complicated ones. You won't be able to move on to the more difficult problems if you haven't mastered the easy ones.

KEY VERSES: *Then you will understand what is right, just, and fair, and you will know how to find the right course of action every time. For wisdom will enter your heart, and knowledge will fill you with joy. (Proverbs 2:9-10)*

NOTE TO PARENTS: Textbooks and the curriculum of a school district are designed to review and reinforce previous learning. Usually the first part of each school year is spent reviewing facts and skills learned the year before. This may be boring for some children, but help yours to understand that it is necessary.

Q 691:

Why do some people find a subject hard, and others find it easy?

A: Some people do better in math. Others do better in reading and writing. Still others do better because they work harder than most students. They listen in class, ask questions, and do their homework. Some people may learn a certain subject right away because God gave them the ability to do so. People are good at different things. Isn't that great?

KEY VERSE: *God gave [Daniel, Shadrach, Meshach, and Abednego] an unusual aptitude for learning the literature and science of the time. And God gave Daniel special ability in understanding the meanings of visions and dreams. (Daniel 1:17)*

NOTE TO PARENTS: Explain to your children that just about everyone has to work hard at some subjects. It may be because of something as simple as life experience. For example, a kid who has moved often and has traveled a lot may know geography better than those who have lived in the same place all their lives.

Q 692:

Is it OK to stay up late on school nights if your friends do?

A: What your friends do does not determine what is wrong and right. Every family has its own rules. It is important for *you* to obey *your* parents. So if your parents tell you to go to bed at a certain time, do it, no matter what your friends do. God has given the responsibility of raising you to your parents, not to your friends.

Your parents have a good reason for not wanting you to stay up late on a school night: You will be sleepy the next day, so you won't do your best in school. Mom and Dad know that, so they insist that you get your rest. They know how important it is for you to do well in school.

Sometimes your parents may let you stay up late, like at a sleep-over at a friend's house on a weekend. So it wouldn't be *wrong* in that situation. But still it may not be the smartest thing to do, especially if you try to stay up all night. It's not good for you. Use your head and get the sleep you need.

KEY VERSE: *Don't copy the behavior and customs of this world, but let God transform you into a new person by changing the way you think. Then you will know what God wants you to do, and you will know how good and pleasing and perfect his will really is. (Romans 12:2)*

NOTE TO PARENTS: When your children start using the excuse, "But all my friends get to do that," remind them of the reason and the reward for doing the right thing. Encourage your children to set a good example and not to copy whatever others do.

Q 693:

How can I stop daydreaming and pay better attention in class?

A: It's easy to let your mind wander and daydream in class, especially when you don't find the subject very interesting. One way to concentrate and stop daydreaming is to take notes about what the teacher is saying, maybe even write down questions that come to mind. If this doesn't work, ask your teacher for suggestions about what you can do. Teachers like it when their students *want* to learn, and they will be happy to help.

KEY VERSE: *Commit everything you do to the LORD. Trust him, and he will help you. (Psalm 37:5)*

NOTE TO PARENTS: Some children struggle with this. It's difficult for them to stop daydreaming once they've started. If you think this is a problem for any of your children, you may want to schedule a teacher conference. If your kids know that the teacher will ask them at least one question at the end of each class, they may be motivated to break the habit.

Q 694:

Do you need to learn math only if you want to be a pilot or a construction worker?

A: You'd be surprised how math is used in life. People in all kinds of jobs use math every day, not just pilots and construction workers. Engineers, writers, homemakers, musicians, doctors, managers, and even professional athletes use math. Go figure. Even if you just wanted to paint a room in your house, you'd use math to figure out how much paint to buy. Almost everything you learn now will help you understand the things you need to know later, whatever you end up doing.

KEY VERSE: *Intelligent people are always open to new ideas. In fact, they look for them. (Proverbs 18:15)*

NOTE TO PARENTS: You can have fun with this by discussing a variety of occupations and showing how each one uses math. Explain how math is important on your job and in the rest of your life. For example, explain what you do when you balance your checkbook. (In *addition*, you can show how to *divide* the responsibilities at home by *multiplying* the factors involved in making your decisions!)

Q 695:

Why do we have to learn geography and history?

A: Geography helps you learn about the world and gives you information about your own country as well as other countries and their citizens. People travel more than ever these days. One day you might be able to visit some of the countries that you have studied. Wouldn't *that* be exciting! Because of the Internet, TV, and other communication tools, people all over the world seem closer. History is an important subject too. It teaches lessons from the past that we need to learn so we won't repeat the same mistakes that people made before.

KEY VERSE: *All these events happened to them as examples for us. They were written down to warn us, who live at the time when this age is drawing to a close. (1 Corinthians 10:11)*

NOTE TO PARENTS: One way to help your children see how these subjects are relevant is to talk about your ancestors, where they lived, and what was going on in the world in their time. Also, you might tell about a subject you didn't like when you were a kid but which turned out to be important in your life.

Q 696:

Why are grades so important?

A: Tests and grades help teachers check to see what students have learned. Grades also help students and their parents see how well the kids are doing at school. Use your grades as a tool to help you see where you need to work harder. Remember that grades don't make a person better or worse than anyone else. More important than grades is whether you're doing your best and learning the material.

KEY VERSE: *Work hard so God can approve you. Be a good worker, one who does not need to be ashamed and who correctly explains the word of truth. (2 Timothy 2:15).*

NOTE TO PARENTS: Some children need to be constantly held accountable for their grades, and they need encouragement to work harder. Other children get straight A's without even trying—these kids may need to be pushed to do extra work. Still other students may be obsessed with getting good grades and be devastated with a B. They might need encouragement to relax about the letter grade. Whatever categories your children fall into, make it clear to them that grades are a tool, not a goal.

Q 697:

Why do people cheat?

A: People cheat because they're lazy. They don't want to work hard to complete an assignment or do well on a test. Cheating is wrong because it's lying, and God tells us not to lie. People cheat in many areas, not just school. Some cheat in games— trying to win without following the rules. Some cheat with money, and others cheat by not being honest with their friends. People who fall into a pattern of cheating find it hard to stop. Kids who cheat in school keep themselves from learning. Then they have to cheat again. After a while, people who cheat lose confidence in themselves and their ability to learn anything. Don't be a cheater—you will cheat yourself.

KEY VERSE: *[Jesus said,] "Unless you are faithful in small matters, you won't be faithful in large ones. If you cheat even a little, you won't be honest with greater responsibilities."* (Luke 16:10)

NOTE TO PARENTS: It's easy for kids to get into the habit of cheating. If your children have been caught cheating, don't let them try to explain it away. And don't overlook an incident, rationalizing that it was a onetime occurrence. Also, don't think that one talk will solve the problem. Allow your children to experience punishment for cheating. Then return to the issue several times over the ensuing months until you are sure that they have learned their lesson and are determined to stop cheating.

Q 698:

How can I do better in spelling?

A: The way to improve in any subject is to study and practice. You can become a better speller by reviewing the assigned words many times. Get someone to help you by testing you on those words. Your parents will be happy to help. Reading more will also help you improve your spelling because you will see words spelled correctly in the books. If you are writing with a computer and using the spellchecker, stop and review the actual spelling when corrected. Ask your parents to look over your papers before you turn them in. If you keep working on this every time you write something, you will improve.

KEY VERSE: *Plans go wrong for lack of advice; many counselors bring success.* (Proverbs 15:22)

NOTE TO PARENTS: Don't berate your children about the difficulties of spelling. Some children learn to spell more easily than others. Kids need to develop a working command of the language, but it should be fun for them. Take time to review spelling words with your children, and help them find a review method that works for them.

Q 699:

The kids around me keep getting me into trouble. What can I do?

A: First, you can ignore the other kids. If you don't give them your attention, they probably will stop trying to get you to do what is wrong. If this doesn't work, ask the teacher to change your seat. To do your best in class, you need to be quiet and listen carefully to the teacher. Remember, no one can *make* you do something wrong or break the rules. Other kids can *pressure* you, but in the end *you* always make the decision. Decide that no matter what the kids around you do or how much they pressure you, you will do what is right. And you will do your best to focus on studying your lessons.

KEY VERSE: *Stay away from fools, for you won't find knowledge there. (Proverbs 14:7)*

NOTE TO PARENTS: The first challenge is to see if the trouble is being started by the other kids or by your child. Don't be afraid to ask the teacher to move your child to a different seat, no matter who is initiating the trouble. Help your child understand that the they-made-me-do-it excuse isn't valid. Children need to learn that they are responsible for their actions and that their parents will hold them to that responsibility. This knowledge will motivate them to stand their ground.

Q 700:

I want to get A's, but my friends say getting good grades is dumb. What should I do?

A: It's always important to do what is right and to do your best no matter what others think or say. Some kids make fun of getting good grades because they don't want to work hard to get those grades. Others may think that it's not cool to seem smart. They're wrong. It's really cool to do well in school. Doing well now will lead to doing well in high school and college, which will lead to doing well in adult life. Kids who think that it's not cool to get good marks may think that they are somehow cheating the system, but they are only cheating themselves.

KEY VERSE: *It is senseless to pay tuition to educate a fool who has no heart for wisdom. (Proverbs 17:16)*

NOTE TO PARENTS: This issue can be a problem for gifted students. Often, they get bad grades on purpose because they fear rejection from their peers. Parental support and friendship with other children who are interested in doing well in school can help to solve this problem. Sometimes peer groups will place a high value on doing *poorly* in school. This is why parental involvement is very important. Let your children know that you expect them to do their best, regardless of what others think or say. Of course your children don't have to broadcast or brag about their grades—encourage them not to do either of those things.

Q 701:

When kids miss a lot of school, how do they pass?

A: Anyone who misses a lot of school will have a tough time catching up on the work. Kids who are ill or out of town on a trip sometimes get help from a tutor. When there is a good reason for missing school, teachers will give parents the assignments. Then the kids can do their work at home and try to keep up with the class. Parents can also help by teaching their children themselves.

KEY VERSE: *Learn to be wise, and develop good judgment. (Proverbs 4:5)*

NOTE TO PARENTS: If this subject comes up, explain that just because kids are away from school doesn't mean that they aren't doing any schoolwork.

Q 702:

Why do we have to study computers?

A: Computers are becoming a very important part of society, and they are getting easier and easier to use. Almost every kind of store and business uses computers—from grocery stores to car-repair shops. By using computers people can keep on learning more and more about almost everything there is to know. So studying computers will become more and more important. There is no doubt that computers will be part of everyone's adult life. People who know how to use computers will get good jobs and will be able to help others.

KEY VERSE: *Wise people treasure knowledge, but the babbling of a fool invites trouble. (Proverbs 10:14)*

NOTE TO PARENTS: Most schools don't have enough computers for all kids to get enough practice on them. Your children might want more access, or you might want this for them. If you don't have a computer at home, let your child use one at the public library.

Choosing Activities

Q 703:

Why don't I have enough time to play?

I'VE DECIDED THAT I JUST DON'T HAVE ENOUGH PLAYTIME BOOKED INTO MY SCHEDULE. I'M AFRAID MY CHORES WILL HAVE TO GO.

A: Schedules get packed with activities, lessons, sports, and schoolwork. Sometimes it seems as if there's no time to play. If this is a problem for you, talk with your parents about it. After you have done your homework and activities, there should be some time to play. If your schedule is too full, you and your family can talk about the possibility of eliminating some activities.

KEY VERSE: *There is a time for everything, a season for every activity under heaven. (Ecclesiastes 3:1)*

NOTE TO PARENTS: These days, kids are busier than ever. When teachers give too much homework, coaches call too many practices, and parents want their children involved in too many activities, time for play may get squeezed out. But play is an important creative outlet for children and a good way for them to reduce their stress. Be careful not to make your children's schedules too full. And remember that play is important for adults too—try to schedule time each week to relax and play as a family.

Q 704:

Why don't we have gym class every day?

A: Each school has its own schedule. The schedule depends on many factors: the number of students, the classes that students are required to take, the number of teachers, the rooms available, etc. It would be fun to have gym every day, but that might not be possible in your school. After school or on weekends you may want to be part of a sports team, take swimming lessons, or do something else you enjoy. You can do these things with friends or family.

KEY VERSE: *Physical exercise has some value, but spiritual exercise is much more important, for it promises a reward in both this life and the next. (1 Timothy 4:8)*

NOTE TO PARENTS: This question may come from the fact that kids are full of energy and need a physical outlet. Organized sports and playing with friends can meet that need.

Q 705:

When you are home during the summer and nobody is around, what can you do to have some fun?

A: Use your imagination. You could plant a garden, collect rocks or insects, take pictures, or check out the neighborhood to find some new friends. You could go to the library to read magazines and books or use the computers. You could organize a garage sale. You could ask your parents how you might help around the house. Perhaps these suggestions will help you think of other fun ways to keep busy during the summer.

KEY VERSE: *So I recommend having fun, because there is nothing better for people to do in this world than to eat, drink, and enjoy life. That way they will experience some happiness along with all the hard work God gives them. (Ecclesiastes 8:15)*

NOTE TO PARENTS: When kids seem bored, some parents merely tell them to find something to do and may say something like "Only boring people get bored." It's better to make specific suggestions and to offer help in finding something fun to do around the house. Help your children think of ideas themselves by asking them questions and showing them how to go through a mental list of options.

Q 706:

My parents want me to play soccer, but I hate it. What should I do?

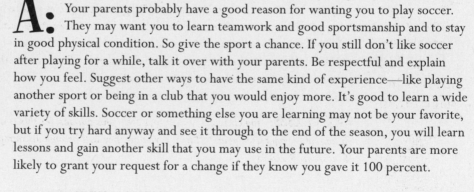

BUT JASON, WE'RE SURE YOU'LL GET A REAL KICK OUT OF IT.

GROAN

A: Your parents probably have a good reason for wanting you to play soccer. They may want you to learn teamwork and good sportsmanship and to stay in good physical condition. So give the sport a chance. If you still don't like soccer after playing for a while, talk it over with your parents. Be respectful and explain how you feel. Suggest other ways to have the same kind of experience—like playing another sport or being in a club that you would enjoy more. It's good to learn a wide variety of skills. Soccer or something else you are learning may not be your favorite, but if you try hard anyway and see it through to the end of the season, you will learn lessons and gain another skill that you may use in the future. Your parents are more likely to grant your request for a change if they know you gave it 100 percent.

KEY VERSES: *Children, obey your parents because you belong to the Lord, for this is the right thing to do. "Honor your father and mother." This is the first of the Ten Commandments that ends with a promise. And this is the promise: If you honor your father and mother, "you will live a long life, full of blessing." (Ephesians 6:1-3)*

NOTE TO PARENTS: It's not easy to know when to push kids into something and when to let them make the choice. Try thinking of several options that will meet your learning objectives for your children, and then let them choose. Don't give in the first time that your kids complain about an activity, but also avoid pushing them into something that they dislike intensely. Remember, you want to find ways to meet your children's needs, not yours.

Q 707:

I like playing the piano, but I hate practicing. Should I quit?

A: Getting good at anything takes practice. Practicing usually isn't fun, but it is necessary. Keep practicing—don't quit. When you get good enough to play music that you enjoy, you'll really have fun playing the piano. This works the same way in other areas of life. You've probably heard that practice makes perfect. This means that the more you practice, the better you will get.

KEY VERSE: *So don't get tired of doing what is good. Don't get discouraged and give up, for we will reap a harvest of blessing at the appropriate time. (Galatians 6:9)*

NOTE TO PARENTS: If your children like the piano but don't want to practice, this will give you the opportunity to teach personal discipline. If your kids hate the instrument, recitals, and practicing, however, you may need to find another way to expose them to music. They might prefer playing another instrument, or they may enjoy simply listening to CDs and attending concerts.

Q 708:

Why do my parents want me to be involved in so many things?

A: Your parents love you and want the best for you. They want you to have many experiences that will help you grow and be a more informed person. Because they don't know what you are going to be good at or what you're going to be interested in when you are older, they want you to try a lot of different activities now. You can learn a lot through music lessons, church choir, sports, and other activities outside of school. Everything you learn will help you enjoy life more. Be thankful that your parents are trying to help you learn as much as you can.

KEY VERSES: *You children must always obey your parents, for this is what pleases the Lord. Fathers, don't aggravate your children. If you do, they will become discouraged and quit trying. (Colossians 3:20-21)*

NOTE TO PARENTS: Children who ask this question may be feeling overwhelmed with their schedule. Being involved in too many activities can be dangerous for children because of the stress it creates. Children need time to relax and play even more than adults do. You may want to evaluate the number of activities and the kinds of activities you are expecting them to take part in.

Q 709:

Why does my coach care so much about winning? It's not fun anymore.

A: Sometimes winning becomes too important to people. In our society being number one seems to be most important. Coaches and parents can get caught up in this pressure. It's good to win, but it's also important to have fun playing a sport. If winning seems to be more important to your team than having fun, talk to your parents. Then they can talk with the coach. If nothing changes, you may want to ask your parents what they think about helping you get on a different team.

KEY VERSE: *So I saw that there is nothing better for people than to be happy in their work. That is why they are here! No one will bring them back from death to enjoy life in the future. (Ecclesiastes 3:22)*

NOTE TO PARENTS: The pressure of having to win at a young age usually is not good. If your children are competitive, this may not be a problem. But most children are more interested in playing than in winning. Exposure to a high-pressure coach may burn out your child's interest in that sport. Changing to a different team may be the best solution.

Q 710:

How can I get better at art?

A: If you have talent in art, you will get better at it in the same way you get better at anything else—by practice. To get better at art, you need to do a variety of art projects. Ask your parents if you can get some art supplies for your birthday or Christmas. Then find creative ways to use things your parents are throwing out, such as old magazines and cardboard boxes. Get some scrap paper and spend time drawing or designing. You might ask your Sunday school teacher to help you find an adult at church who is artistic and would be willing to give you lessons. You may also ask your parents if there are art classes in your community that you can take.

KEY VERSE: *[Jesus said,] "To those who use well what they are given, even more will be given, and they will have an abundance. But from those who are unfaithful, even what little they have will be taken away." (Matthew 25:29)*

NOTE TO PARENTS: When a child shows strong interest in art or music, Mom and Dad should look for ways to build on that interest and develop that talent. Outside of school, park districts and other community groups often provide classes and seminars where children—even the very young ones—can participate and further develop their skills.

Q 711:

I want to be with my friends. Why do we have to go to church so much?

A: Christians go to church to worship God, study the Bible, and be with other people who believe in Jesus. Church is a special place where you can learn more about God's love and how to please him. Churches also sponsor clubs and other children's activities. Remember, you can bring your friends to church. You can also make friends at church.

KEY VERSE: *I was glad when they said to me, "Let us go to the house of the LORD." (Psalm 122:1)*

NOTE TO PARENTS: Be sensible about thinking and then insisting that you and your family are to be at the church every time the doors are open. You may have to miss some activities and programs for the sake of your family. On the other hand, don't give the impression that regular church attendance is optional. Make worship and Christian education a regular part of your family life. Also do whatever you can to make church attendance pleasant, such as allowing plenty of time to get ready beforehand.

Questions Kids Ask

Our World

8

Cultures and Countries

Q 712:
Why do some countries have weird names?

A: Some names sound strange to you, but they sound fine in the countries that have them. Names have meaning inside their own cultures. For example, we might think that a name like Botswana or Bosnia-Herzegovina sounds weird because we don't live there and don't know what the name means. But in those countries, New York, Vancouver, Saskatchewan, and Alaska probably sound silly too.

KEY VERSE: *That area, too, was once considered the land of the Rephaites, though the Ammonites referred to them as Zamzummites. (Deuteronomy 2:20)*

Q 713:
Why do people in different countries have different customs than we do?

A: One reason is that many years ago there was very little communication among countries that were far apart. People living in Africa, for example, didn't know anything about people living in Asia, and people in Australia didn't know about people in America. The people in each country developed their own way of doing things without knowing how others around the world were doing them.

Another reason for many of the differences is climate. In places where the weather is always hot, people will dress and eat in ways that make sense in hot areas. Eskimos dress in furs and eat lots of fish because that's what they need to wear and that's what kind of food is available in their climate.

Always show respect for people who are not like you. It is a simple way to honor and learn to enjoy the marvelous variety of people and nations God has made.

KEY VERSE: *I try to find common ground with everyone so that I might bring them to Christ. (1 Corinthians 9:22)*

NOTE TO PARENTS: Be sure to distinguish between moral issues and cultural ones. It is wrong to steal or hate, no matter what your culture is. But differences in dress, food, language, music, special celebrations, and even the way a family operates are not wrong. Speak positively of these differences.

Q 714:

Do people keep their culture when they move to a different country?

A: At first they do. In fact, people who move from one country to another often try hard to keep the customs and traditions of their home country. But it is difficult to do because few of the people around them live the same way, and it takes a big group of people all living the same way to support a culture.

For example, if the people want to speak their native language, they have to talk with others who also speak their language. If they want to eat the food of their homeland, they need to know where they can buy the ingredients. If they celebrate the holidays they grew up with, they may be the only ones doing so.

In most families that move to another country or culture, this is a real struggle. People like that need all the hospitality and welcoming they can get from friends and neighbors.

KEY VERSES: *These righteous ones will reply, "Lord, when did we ever see you hungry and feed you? Or thirsty and give you something to drink? Or a stranger and show you hospitality? . . . And the King will tell them, "I assure you, when you did it to one of the least of these my brothers and sisters, you were doing it to me!" (Matthew 25:37-40)*

NOTE TO PARENTS: Some children who move from one country to another will treasure the habits and customs of the country they left. Other children will more readily adapt to the customs and habits of their new homeland. Usually this is a matter of personality and disposition. A parent should guide each child through the trauma of moving in the ways that are appropriate for that child. Be sensitive to the different types of personalities and how each person reacts to moving.

Q 715:

Why do people have to speak different languages?

A: It all started at a place called Babel in Babylonia, where Iraq is today. During the time of Adam and Eve and Noah, everyone in the world spoke the same language. But shortly after Noah and his family emerged from the ark, the people of the world gathered together to build a tower as a monument to their own greatness. They had completely forgotten about God. So God caused their language to divide into dialects. God changed the languages to confuse the people so they wouldn't finish building the Tower of Babel. People who spoke the same language stayed together, moved away, and settled in different areas all over the world. Ever since then, languages have been part of what makes countries different from each other. And even within countries, different ethnic groups often speak different languages.

KEY VERSES: *In that way, the LORD scattered them all over the earth; and that ended the building of the city. That is why the city was called Babel, because it was there that the LORD confused the people by giving them many languages, thus scattering them across the earth. (Genesis 11:8-9)*

Q 716:

Why do some families speak more than one language?

HAND ME THAT WARP FUSER. I NEED TO ENERGIZE THE SHIELD PODS BEFORE IVAN GETS THE FLUX CAPACITATOR ONLINE.

A: Some families live in parts of the world where all people speak more than one language. Many Europeans, especially those in small countries, are in this situation. People in Germany, for example, live quite close to people in France and England, and they will probably need to speak to English speakers and French speakers many times throughout their lives. So as they grow up, they learn to speak English and French as well as German. That's three languages right there.

Some people live in countries that have two or more official languages. Canada has two—English and French. Switzerland has three—French, German, and Italian. In countries like these, people usually speak the language most common to their area.

Some people live in cultures where they did not grow up. They have had to learn a new language so they can talk to the people in that land. This is what happens when people come to the United States from Mexico, for example, or when people move from North America to Switzerland.

Many missionaries need to learn another language so they can tell people about God in their own language.

KEY VERSE: *Then Eliakim son of Hilkiah, Shebna, and Joah said to the king's representative, "Please speak to us in Aramaic, for we understand it well. Don't speak in Hebrew, for the people on the wall will hear." (2 Kings 18:26)*

Q 717:

Why do people in other countries eat different food?

A: People choose what foods to eat for many reasons. Sometimes they eat the foods that they can get easily and that don't cost very much money. A rice farmer, for example, probably would eat a lot of rice. Some foods are very expensive because they have to be grown a long way away or because a certain food is very scarce.

Some foods are chosen because of culture and habit. In some countries, the people have learned to enjoy eating very spicy foods. In other countries, everyone likes fish. And in still other countries, people eat a lot of meat and potatoes. What people eat is a matter of tradition, habit, and personal taste.

KEY VERSES: *Every one of these depends on you to give them their food as they need it. When you supply it, they gather it. You open your hand to feed them, and they are satisfied. (Psalm 104:27-28)*

NOTE TO PARENTS: A fun way to help your children learn about and be more accepting of other cultures is to introduce them to different ethnic foods. Take them to an ethnic restaurant, make a meal from an ethnic cookbook, or invite a friend to show you how to make a favorite ethnic dish.

Q 718:

In other countries, why do people burp aloud after meals?

A: In some countries, burping aloud after a meal shows that you enjoyed the meal. In other countries, it is more polite to say something nice about the meal instead of burping. Different groups of people have different ways of life. It's a good idea to show respect for the people when you travel to another country. Find out which of your behaviors may offend others. That way you can try hard to avoid embarrassing yourself and your hosts.

KEY VERSES: *In those days it was the custom in Israel for anyone transferring a right of purchase to remove his sandal and hand it to the other party. This publicly validated the transaction. So the other family redeemer drew off his sandal as he said to Boaz, "You buy the land."* (Ruth 4:7-8)

Q 719:

Why are some countries rich and others poor?

A: Some countries are very rich and others very poor for many reasons. Wealthy countries often have many natural resources (such as oil, gold, rich fisheries, or tourist attractions) that bring them great wealth. They also have economic systems that reward people for making and selling goods and services; they attract buyers with the things they make and sell. And they have laws that protect people from being cheated.

Other countries don't have these things, and that makes them poor. Perhaps they don't have the natural resources that people want to buy. Or perhaps they have the resources, but the economic system makes it hard for people to sell them or for buyers to buy them. Also, some countries have been hurt by war, hurricanes, earthquakes, famines, or other tragedies.

It takes time and cooperation for a country to change from being poor to being rich. Everyone has to work together and support free trade. Everyone has to make rules and keep them. That is one of the ways God rewards people who abide by his laws—obeying the laws keeps things orderly. This is just another example of God's love at work. When we follow God's principles, life works better.

KEY VERSE: *Hard workers have plenty of food; playing around brings poverty.* (Proverbs 28:19)

Q 720:

Why is there a McDonald's in almost every country?

A: Some companies, like McDonald's and Coca-Cola, can be found in many places around the world because they have worked hard to sell their products in those places. They have hired people to set up factories, stores, or distributors in other countries. They have signed contracts with other companies to help them. These companies keep doing this until it seems they have products in almost every country.

Another reason is communication among people around the world. Television, E-mail, the Internet, long-distance telephone connections, and air travel allow people to know a lot about those who live a long way away from them. They learn about other people's customs, products, food, and stores. Some decide to open a branch store in a faraway town. Modern technology has made it easier than ever to do business all over the world.

KEY VERSE: *Judah and Israel traded for your wares, offering wheat from Minnith, early figs, honey, oil, and balm. (Ezekiel 27:17)*

Q 721:

I don't get it— why are people prejudiced?

A: The biggest reason for prejudice is fear of people who are different. People tend to fear what they don't know or understand, including other people or their customs. People also tend to think badly of people and customs that they don't understand. People become prejudiced when they believe false ideas about what others are like.

We do not need to fear variety in the way people cook, dress, and talk. We need to appreciate these differences and not judge or criticize people just because they do not do these things our way.

Some people also believe—wrongly—that certain kinds of people are better or more important than others. This is called *racism*. People who have this perspective don't realize that God created *all* people in his image. Every person who has ever been born is equally important and valuable. No one is better or deserving of superior treatment.

Jesus wants us to love and respect others, even if we don't know or understand them. We should not think badly of people just because we don't understand them. We should not be prejudiced.

KEY VERSE: *God does not show favoritism. (Romans 2:11)*

NOTE TO PARENTS: Children learn prejudice by watching others show it; few parents or others actively teach it. We need to be careful to not use prejudiced language, tell prejudiced jokes, or avoid people for prejudiced reasons.

Religion

Q 722:

Why do some people believe in ghosts?

A: A ghost is a disembodied spirit—the spirit of a person separated from the body. Some people believe in ghosts because they have heard about them on television shows, in movies, and in cartoons, and because many other people believe in ghosts. Some people believe in them because they have had strange experiences that they can't explain, and they figure that ghosts are the only answer.

The Bible gives no evidence that people come back to earth without their bodies. When you die, God takes your spirit from earth forever—believers into God's presence, unbelievers to a place of suffering. People do not come back as ghosts.

KEY VERSE: *It is destined that each person dies only once and after that comes judgment. (Hebrews 9:27)*

Q 723:

Why do they put horoscopes in the newspaper?

I DON'T HAVE ENOUGH NEWS FOR THE NEWSPAPER. WHAT WILL I DO?

A: Newspapers print horoscopes because many people want to read them. And people read horoscopes because they believe that major parts of life are controlled by outside forces beyond their control. They look to the horoscopes for guidance.

Believers should not look to horoscopes for guidance. Only God controls what happens, and only God knows the future. If we need advice, we should do three things: (1) read the Bible; (2) talk to wise people (Proverbs 13:20); and (3) ask God for wisdom (James 1:5). If you are worried about the future, the best thing to do is to pray and tell God about your worries, ask him to take care of you, and trust him to do it (Philippians 4:6).

KEY VERSES: *Do not let your people practice fortune-telling or sorcery, or allow them to interpret omens, or engage in witchcraft, or cast spells, or function as mediums or psychics, or call forth the spirits of the dead. (Deuteronomy 18:10-11)*

NOTE TO PARENTS: Horoscopes are closely related to occult practices. We must turn to God for guidance, wisdom, and assurance for the future.

Q 724:

Why are there spooky things like skeletons and monsters?

A: Some people like to be frightened by funny skeletons and make-believe monsters. And they like scaring others, especially at Halloween. But you don't have to be afraid of ghosts and goblins because they aren't real. Besides, God is with you and will take care of you. Keep trusting in him to protect you.

KEY VERSE: *[Moses said,] "Be strong and courageous! Do not be afraid of them! The LORD your God will go ahead of you. He will neither fail you nor forsake you." (Deuteronomy 31:6)*

Q 725:

Why do some people believe that trees, plants, and animals have spirits?

A: Some people believe that trees, plants, and animals have spirits because they are confused. Plants and animals don't have spirits, but many false religions teach that they do. Only *people* have eternal souls.

At the same time, God does want us to respect the world he created. God created all living things, including plants and animals. The Bible says that all of nature groans under the weight of our sin. And some of the psalms in the Bible say, as a figure of speech, that the trees of the fields will clap their hands in praise of God. But plants and animals don't have spirits. And even more important to remember is that we are to worship only God, not anyone or anything else.

KEY VERSES: *Let the fields and their crops burst forth with joy! Let the trees of the forest rustle with praise before the Lord! (Psalm 96:12-13)*

Q 726:

Why does the world have different religions?

A: Various religions exist for many different reasons. Most cultures know about God, but many that don't know him have tried to explain him in their own ways; they have formed their own religions.

Many people do not want to believe that there is only one way to God, so they start their own way and try to get others to join them. All of those people need to hear about God's love for them and about Jesus' dying for them.

Christianity also has many different *denominations*. A denomination is a group of churches. Some of these groups formed because the people were all from a certain country and culture or spoke a certain language (for example, German Baptist or Swedish Covenant). Other denominations exist because they hold their church services differently from others or believe in expressing their faith in a specific way.

The Bible tells us, however, that Jesus Christ is the *only* way to God. Christians may go to many different churches that speak different languages or have certain types of services as long as their beliefs and worship center on Christ and God's Word. All Christians should love and appreciate each other and work together despite their differences.

KEY VERSE: *[God said,] "Do not worship any other gods besides me." (Exodus 20:3)*

NOTE TO PARENTS: When children focus on what is "wrong" with how other Christians believe or worship, redirect their attention to their own lives. Their energy should be spent on becoming like Christ, not on correcting others.

Q 727:

What kind of holy books do people of other religions have?

A: Many religions have books of instructions or books that help people understand their own religion. Most of these religions have many, many books, not just one. These books explain the beliefs and practices of these religions.

In some ways, this is similar to how Christians use the Bible, but the Bible is also unique. The Bible has many prophecies, or predictions of the future, that have come true exactly as predicted. It also tells of many, many places and events that archaeologists have discovered to be true and accurate. Other "holy books" don't survive all these kinds of tests. The more we learn about the past, the more we learn that we can trust what the Bible says.

KEY VERSE: *Philip went off to look for Nathanael and told him, "We have found the very person Moses and the prophets wrote about! His name is Jesus, the son of Joseph from Nazareth." (John 1:45)*

Q 728:

Does God love people who don't pray?

A: God loves all people, even those who do not love him. The Bible tells of some unbelieving kings who prayed and to whom God listened. God is delighted whenever someone honors him, calls out to him, or expresses a need for him. And he invites people to come to him because he loves them; his love does not depend on whether or not a person prays.

But that does not mean that God loves everything that people do. Just because God loves people does not make all people right or good in his sight. Having a relationship with Jesus gives a person a relationship with God that not just anyone can have.

That is why God wants us to pray. It allows us to enjoy our relationship with God, to benefit from his friendship, and to see him work in our life.

KEY VERSE: *Then they cried out to the LORD, Jonah's God. "O LORD," they pleaded, "don't make us die for this man's sin. And don't hold us responsible for his death, because it isn't our fault. O LORD, you have sent this storm upon him for your own good reasons." (Jonah 1:14)*

Q 729:

Why do people worship idols instead of God?

A: Idols are simply pictures or statues of imaginary gods. Actually, most people who have idols don't worship the idols but the gods they represent. Some people, however, think that an idol itself can help them.

People want to believe in things that they can see and touch, so they make things they can see. But we cannot see God because God is spirit. As Christians, we do not make or worship idols because idols take our attention away from worshiping the one true God.

KEY VERSE: *No one has ever seen God. But his only Son, who is himself God, is near to the Father's heart; he has told us about him. (John 1:18)*

Q 730:

Why is being good not enough to get someone into heaven?

A: It is impossible to be good enough to get into heaven. Every person sins, and even one sin is too many for heaven. Heaven is perfect because God is perfect—there is no sin at all in God's presence. A person would have to be perfect to get into heaven.

That is why we need Jesus. Only Jesus can accept us into God's presence by forgiving our sin.

We are each like a pane of glass in a window. If even one tiny corner of it is broken, it is broken. We need a miracle to make us whole again. We need to believe in Jesus and invite him to save us. Then we can have our sins forgiven and be ready for heaven.

KEY VERSE: *As the Scriptures say, "No one is good—not even one." (Romans 3:10)*

Wars and Rumors of Wars

Q 731:
Why do countries fight wars with each other?

A: A war is fought when countries disagree and can't work out their problems by talking together. Sometimes a war will begin when both countries want the same thing, like a certain piece of land. Instead of talking it out, they fight. Other times, a war will begin when one country wants to take over another country.

God wants us to love others and try to get along with others. Many wars could be avoided if everyone followed God's instructions for loving others. And if each of us chooses to love God and others, we can prevent fights and make the world a little more peaceful.

KEY VERSES: *What is causing the quarrels and fights among you? Isn't it the whole army of evil desires at war within you? You want what you don't have, so you scheme and kill to get it. You are jealous for what others have, and you can't possess it, so you fight and quarrel to take it away from them. And yet the reason you don't have what you want is that you don't ask God for it. (James 4:1-2)*

Q 732:
Why do dictators push people around so much?

A: Dictators push people around because they like to have power and control over others. One of the most common sins that people commit is to use power to force people to do things their way. Because dictators are in control of everything in the country, they have a lot of power. Pushing people around is their way of abusing that power. Dictators who abuse their power are evil, and God will punish them in the end.

The Bible teaches us that the proper way to lead others is to serve them and put their interests ahead of your own. Whenever you get a chance to be in charge, even of younger brothers or sisters, think of what is best for them and do the fun things they want to do.

KEY VERSE: *When the wicked are in authority, sin increases. But the godly will live to see the tyrant's downfall. (Proverbs 29:16)*

NOTE TO PARENTS: Parental authority is the first leadership example that children have. Teach them to lead others by demonstrating service-motivated leadership.

Q 733:

Why do countries have armies, navies, and air forces?

A: It is true that some countries have armies, navies, and air forces mainly so they can attack others. But most countries have armed forces only as a defense against invasion. Their forces protect the country from other countries that might want to go to war against them.

In some countries armed forces can also help in peacetime. The soldiers are used to keep order inside the country during protests and riots and to rescue and help people during natural disasters like floods and hurricanes.

It is important to honor those who risk their lives to protect us. Most countries do this by setting aside a Memorial Day, Remembrance Day, or another holiday for people to remember the people in their armed forces. Remember to show your appreciation the next time this holiday comes around. They are "authorities sent by God to help you."

KEY VERSE: *The authorities are sent by God to help you. But if you are doing something wrong, of course you should be afraid, for you will be punished. The authorities are established by God for that very purpose, to punish those who do wrong. (Romans 13:4)*

Q 734:

Why are nuclear weapons even around?

A: Nuclear weapons were invented during World War II to gain an advantage over the Axis powers (Germany, Japan, and Italy). The government of the United States hired scientists to build a bomb that would be so powerful that the Japanese would have to surrender.

Because these weapons can kill hundreds of thousands of people at once, people all over the world have been working to get rid of them. They feel that we will only destroy ourselves if we use them.

Others know that these weapons make them powerful, so they work to keep the ones they have, or they make new ones. They feel that they would be defenseless without nuclear weapons.

This is just one reason God commands us to be kind, to forgive, and to return cruelty with kindness. Whenever we allow conflicts to escalate, or get worse, we build bigger weapons and do even more terrible things. God's way is better.

KEY VERSES: *When they refused to acknowledge God, he abandoned them to their evil minds and let them do things that should never be done. Their lives became full of every kind of wickedness, sin, greed, hate, envy, murder, fighting, deception, malicious behavior, and gossip. (Romans 1:28-29)*

NOTE TO PARENTS: The basic principles that help avoid war are the same ones that help brothers and sisters get along. Peace starts at home.

Q 735:

Why do some countries split apart?

A: Usually countries split apart when a group of people within the country wants to rule itself. It does not want to be part of the larger country anymore. Why would a group want to break away like that? Because different groups of people have different ways of life. People want to govern themselves, and certain groups don't want to be governed by other groups that have different ways of life. Sometimes groups get forced together under the same government against their will, such as in the former Soviet Union. Eventually the people's desire to govern themselves can cause the country to split.

KEY VERSES: *I have provided a permanent homeland for my people Israel, a secure place where they will never be disturbed. It will be their own land where wicked nations won't oppress them as they did in the past, from the time I appointed judges to rule my people. And I will keep you safe from all your enemies. (2 Samuel 7:10-11)*

NOTE TO PARENTS: It is important to teach our children to respect the will and desires of others, and a brother-and-sister relationship is a good place for them to start. If a brother or sister says, "Stop teasing me," or "Please stop tickling me," or "Stop crowding me," then the other should know that he or she must stop. Make respect for others a basic rule in your house.

Q 736:

Is God happy for one country and sad for the other at the end of a war?

A: God is saddened by all sin and death. In most wars, nobody wins. People from both sides are hurt and killed. Property is destroyed. Countries, cities, neighborhoods, and families are torn apart. God is not happy with any of it. He is sad about all the destruction caused by sin, including war.

But sometimes God does send war as a punishment for evil. In the Old Testament we read that some nations suffered in wars as a punishment for their sins against others. And sometimes war seems to be the only way to stop an evil dictator or an evil government. But that doesn't mean that God is happy to see nations go to war. He much prefers that people obey him, get along with each other, and avoid war altogether.

KEY VERSE: *The LORD will settle international disputes. All the nations will beat their swords into plowshares and their spears into pruning hooks. All wars will stop, and military training will come to an end. (Micah 4:3)*

Leaders and Politics

Q 737:

What are politics?

A: *Politics* is the word we use to describe governing or ruling. Politics is when people deal with one another in government. It includes trying to persuade someone else to vote your way. One part of politics involves electing government leaders. The political activities leading up to an election are called a "campaign." In a political campaign, the people who are trying to get elected try to persuade voters to vote for them through speeches, advertisements, debates, and so forth.

Governments are an important part of God's design for the world. God wants all rulers to obey him and for citizens to obey the government's laws. That is why voters should think carefully and pray often about whom to vote for. We want to pick the best rulers—the ones who will do the best job.

KEY VERSE: *Now look around among yourselves, brothers, and select seven men who are well respected and are full of the Holy Spirit and wisdom. We will put them in charge of this business. (Acts 6:3)*

Q 738:

Why can't children vote?

A: Young children are not allowed to vote because they have not had enough experience and education to have earned the right to vote. Also, they are not involved enough in society. In other words, they don't pay taxes, own land, drive a car, or run a business. In a sense, a person earns the right to vote by growing up.

The best way to become a good voter is to love and obey God with all your heart. If you know what God wants for your country, you will make better voting decisions than if you didn't know what God wants. Until then, you can pray for your leaders and voters, asking God to give them wisdom.

KEY VERSE: *Don't let anyone think less of you because you are young. Be an example to all believers in what you teach, in the way you live, in your love, your faith, and your purity. (1 Timothy 4:12)*

Q 739:

What is democracy?

A: Democracy is a type of government in which the citizens of a country elect the men and women who will lead them. These elected leaders are called representatives because they represent the people of that country—they speak for the citizens. In the election for each office (such as governor, mayor, senator, or council person), the person who gets the most votes wins the election and holds that office until the next election. In every election, the citizens can elect new leaders if they want to. Wise citizens choose their leaders very carefully because a leader's character will determine whether he or she is a just ruler.

Be sure to pray for your country's leaders. They need God's wisdom all the time.

KEY VERSES: *[Moses said,] "Be sure that you select as king the man the LORD your God chooses. . . . When he sits on the throne as king, he must copy these laws on a scroll for himself in the presence of the Levitical priests. He must always keep this copy of the law with him and read it daily as long as he lives. That way he will learn to fear the LORD his God by obeying all the terms of this law. This regular reading will prevent him from becoming proud and acting as if he is above his fellow citizens. It will also prevent him from turning away from these commands in the smallest way. This will ensure that he and his descendants will reign for many generations in Israel. (Deuteronomy 17:15, 18-20)*

NOTE TO PARENTS: In our society, most heroes are musicians, actors, and sports figures. It is good to help our children expand their list of heroes to include leaders with exceptional character. Thinking about leaders this way helps prepare children for voting and being leaders.

Q 740:

What is Communism?

A: Communism is a system in which people own property together. No one has his or her own land, business, or house; everyone owns everything together.

In governments that have been built on this idea, the state, or government, is said to own everything. The people have very little power or freedom because everything belongs to the state. The national leaders run everything and control the elections (if elections are held).

Communism is supposed to be a big group of people who govern themselves, but communist countries usually become dictatorships of the state. National leaders do whatever they want. The people themselves become servants of the leaders and have few rights or freedoms.

KEY VERSE: *When you want a certain piece of land, you find a way to seize it. When you want someone's house, you take it by fraud and violence. No one's family or inheritance is safe with you around! (Micah 2:2)*

NOTE TO PARENTS: Although some government systems are better than others, all have flaws. Only God's kingdom is perfect. Only God can rule perfectly because only God is completely unselfish, loves everyone, and always knows what is best.

Q 741:

Why do governments do things wrong?

A: Governments don't always do things wrong, even though people sometimes like to complain about the government. Government forms and programs can often be very complicated, and that's frustrating for a lot of people who have to deal with them. Of course, government leaders and officials will sometimes make mistakes and blunders. We all make mistakes. No government is perfect because no human being is perfect.

Although no government is perfect, people need government. If we didn't have leaders, laws, police officers, firefighters, tax collectors, and other government workers, every person would do whatever he or she wanted, and the country would be in a mess.

KEY VERSE: *Remind your people to submit to the government and its officers. They should be obedient, always ready to do what is good. (Titus 3:1)*

Environmental Concerns

Q 742:

How much does recycling help?

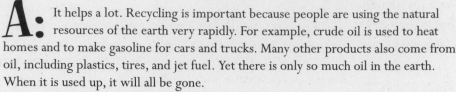

A: It helps a lot. Recycling is important because people are using the natural resources of the earth very rapidly. For example, crude oil is used to heat homes and to make gasoline for cars and trucks. Many other products also come from oil, including plastics, tires, and jet fuel. Yet there is only so much oil in the earth. When it is used up, it will all be gone.

Recycling used oil, plastic, and rubber makes these resources stretch. We don't use up things so fast. And we are able to reuse the materials to make other things. God does not want us to be wasteful.

At the same time, we don't need to fear running out of the things we need. God created us. He created this earth. He put us on this earth to live and enjoy it. He provides the things we need. If we run out of oil, it will be OK, because God will still be in charge, and he will always provide the things we need.

So recycle and don't be wasteful, but don't be afraid of running out of things either. Just be a responsible user of the good things God lets you have and use.

KEY VERSE: *"Now gather the leftovers," Jesus told his disciples, "so that nothing is wasted."* *(John 6:12)*

NOTE TO PARENTS: You may want to mention that garbage goes to landfills. Pretty soon all the landfills will be filled up with trash and garbage. Often the garbage pollutes our soil and water. We've used more nonrenewable resources since World War II than we used in all of history before. Recycling is simply a responsible way to live.

Q 743:

How can they recycle milk jugs after people step on them?

A: When items such as plastic milk jugs are recycled, they are combined with other plastic items, melted, and used to make other products. For example, recycled plastic bottles are often used to make playground equipment. Other kinds of bottles and containers are reused this way too. The bottles are *never* just washed out and refilled with milk. The government does not permit that because it would spread germs and disease. So stepping on empty milk jugs doesn't hurt recycling.

KEY VERSES: *People know how to mine silver and refine gold. They know how to dig iron from the earth and smelt copper from stone. (Job 28:1-2)*

Q 744:

Why do people litter so much when they can just throw their trash in the garbage can?

A: Some people litter by accident. They are careless or do not pay attention to what happens to their food wrappers and other trash. People who litter on purpose, however, do so because they are not showing respect for other people or the earth.

We should pick up trash instead of littering or ignoring the litter on the ground. Just because we didn't drop it doesn't mean we should say, "It's not my mess." We are all keepers of God's earth. If everyone pitched in and picked up a little, the world would be a nicer, tidier place.

KEY VERSE: *Then God said, "Let us make people in our image, to be like ourselves. They will be masters over all life—the fish in the sea, the birds in the sky, and all the livestock, wild animals, and small animals." (Genesis 1:26)*

NOTE TO PARENTS: Kids often object by saying, "But I didn't make the mess!" without realizing that their objection is irrelevant. We all live in a community, and we all share in the care of the environment. God's way is for us to look out for each other. Take your kids out with bags and gloves and clean up the litter at the school or the park and use the opportunity to teach these principles.

Q 745:

Why do people want to wreck the earth with pollution?

A: Most people don't want to wreck the earth. Instead, people pollute because they don't think about the consequences of polluting or because they don't care about the damage it might do. Some may actually believe that littering and dumping waste really don't matter, that they don't hurt anything, or that it's someone else's job to clean it up.

Some people pollute because they are just too lazy to walk to a trash can. They are more concerned with doing things the easy way than with doing what is right.

KEY VERSE: *We know that all creation has been groaning as in the pains of childbirth right up to the present time. (Romans 8:22)*

NOTE TO PARENTS: Whenever you answer a child's question about what others do wrong, be careful to guard against judging others. Help your child to focus on his or her own behavior and not judge others. God loves everyone, and we don't know why people do what they do. Pray together for the people you see doing wrong, that God will bless them with wisdom and truth.

Q 746:

Why is there so much pollution in the cities?

A: The main reason there is so much pollution in the cities is that there are so many people. Lots of people means lots of cars, buses, trucks, restaurants, stores, industry, and garbage. In most cities with all the buildings and traffic, it can be difficult to clean up right away. Sometimes events in cities (such as parades, games, concerts, and rallies) attract lots of people who litter. If one person in a field throws a wrapper on the ground, it may not seem like a big deal. But if 100,000 people in the city each throw a wrapper on the ground, that's 100,000 wrappers!

All the traffic and factories add to air pollution and noise pollution, too. In smaller towns and out in the country, there aren't as many cars, trucks, buses, and people to contribute to the pollution problems.

KEY VERSE: *Upright citizens bless a city and make it prosper, but the talk of the wicked tears it apart. (Proverbs 11:11)*

Q 747:

Why do some companies throw dangerous chemicals into rivers and oceans?

A: It used to be that companies dumped a lot of chemicals into rivers and oceans because they didn't know that the chemicals were hurting anything. But when it was discovered how harmful some chemicals can be, the government made laws against dumping them. Now if companies pollute, they are disobeying the law. Sadly, some companies continue to dump dangerous chemicals into our waterways, even though they know they should dispose of them in safer ways. They do this because it's expensive to be careful and clean, and they don't want to spend the money.

KEY VERSE: *Those who love money will never have enough. How absurd to think that wealth brings true happiness! (Ecclesiastes 5:10)*

NOTE TO PARENTS: It is easy to pollute by disposing of chemicals improperly because disposing of them properly can be time consuming and expensive. This is why many consumers routinely throw away oil, paint, and other chemicals in unsafe ways. Do your best to set a good example and dispose of these things as safely as possible, even if it is difficult or costs you money.

Q 748:

Why do people live all their lives in a city and only go out into the countryside for picnics?

A: Most people live in cities because that's where their jobs are. People need jobs to make money so they can buy food, clothes, and everything else they need. And they know it's very convenient to live close to their job. So they live near their place of work. Many people also like the busyness and the many activities to choose from in the city.

The countryside is a nice change of pace. It is a lot calmer and more peaceful than the city, and there is much less pollution there. So people like to go there occasionally for vacations and picnics. It's a nice relaxing break from their normal routine.

KEY VERSE: *That night some shepherds were in the fields outside the village, guarding their flocks of sheep. (Luke 2:8)*

Q 749:

Why do people want to cut down the trees?

A: People cut down trees

1. to make paper
2. to get wood for building houses, furniture, and other things
3. to clear land for new houses and buildings
4. to clear land for farms

It is all right to cut down trees because new trees can be planted in their place. We need paper for newspapers, magazines, and books, and paper is recyclable. We need wood for building. We need houses to live in. We need farmland to grow food.

This doesn't mean that people should cut down trees anywhere and anytime they feel like it. And they certainly shouldn't cut down trees just to be destructive. Trees provide beauty, shade, and places for birds to nest. Some trees provide flowers and fruit. And some trees help stop the wind; others help prevent soil erosion. We should take care of the trees we have.

KEY VERSE: *Joshua replied, "If the hill country of Ephraim is not large enough for you, clear out land for yourselves in the forest where the Perizzites and Rephaites live." (Joshua 17:15)*

Q 750:

If we are running out of trees, why doesn't God just make more?

A: God *is* making more trees, but it is up to us not to use them faster than he replaces them. Some trees are cut down and used for wood, paper, and other products. Other trees are cut down to make room for houses, shopping centers, roads, and other construction projects. Some people say that we are running out of trees. When God created trees and other plants, he made them with the ability to make new ones. They do this by producing seeds that fall to the ground or are planted and then grow. But it takes many years for a tree to grow to be big and tall. So people should be careful not to cut down more trees than can be replaced by the seeds. God has given human beings the job of taking care of the earth. This includes using the trees wisely and planting new ones.

KEY VERSE: *The LORD God placed the man in the Garden of Eden to tend and care for it. (Genesis 2:15)*

NOTE TO PARENTS: Faithful stewards of the earth are sensitive to the environment. This kind of question is an opportunity for you to teach your children to take good care of God's earth and its resources.

Q 751:

What can children do to help take better care of the world?

A: Sometimes it seems as though children can't do very much to make a difference in the world. After all, adults own the factories, stores, and restaurants and drive the trucks, buses, and cars. But children can help a lot. Here are a few ideas to get you started:

1. Do not litter; throw your trash away instead of throwing it on the ground.
2. Recycle paper, plastic, glass, oil, and anything else that can be recycled.
3. Take good care of your pets; they are part of God's world too.
4. Don't waste food; take only as much as you can eat.
5. Don't waste water; turn off the faucet when you're done using it.
6. Don't waste electricity; turn off the lights when you don't need them.
7. Live simply; be content with things that are a little less expensive or fancy instead of insisting on new toys or clothes.

KEY VERSE: *You put us in charge of everything you made, giving us authority over all things. (Psalm 8:6)*

Animals

Q 752:

Why are animals becoming extinct all over the world?

A: The biggest reason some animals are becoming extinct is disruption of habitat. People move in and take away the land used by the animals. Some people don't seem to care what happens to the plants and animals of the earth. They just do whatever they want, regardless of the consequences to nature. But God has given human beings the job of taking care of the world. That means taking good care of *all* of it, animals included.

Remember that this all starts with you. Take good care of your pets, don't litter so they have a clean place to live, and take good care of God's earth. After all, it all belongs to God, and we are his stewards.

KEY VERSE: *All the animals of the forest are mine, and I own the cattle on a thousand hills. (Psalm 50:10)*

Q 753:

Why does God let animals suffer from dangers in nature?

A: When sin entered the world, all of creation was damaged. Ever since that time, pain and suffering have been a part of life. People and animals suffer—no one escapes.

Probably the greatest danger to animals is other animals that attack and kill them for food. Animals eat each other because they are part of the food chain. They need the food to survive. Some animals eat only plants, but many eat other animals. For example, dragonflies eat mosquitoes, birds eat worms and other insects, cats eat mice and birds, and some big fish eat baby ducks. Some animals, called scavengers, eat dead animals that they find in the woods or along the highway. God created animals that way. If all the animals continued to live, soon the world would be filled with them.

KEY VERSES: *You send the darkness, and it becomes night, when all the forest animals prowl about. Then the young lions roar for their food, but they are dependent on God. (Psalm 104:20-21)*

Q 754:

Why do people kill animals to eat when they could just buy food at the store?

A: Many years ago, everyone had to hunt for food. They would gather plants and kill animals. Then some people began to raise fruits and vegetables and sell them. Others raised animals and sold them. Eventually, there were grocery stores where people could buy the fruit, vegetables, milk, and meat they needed to eat. But for meat to be available at a store, someone has to kill the animals.

It certainly is more convenient to buy meat at a store than to raise chickens or hunt wild pigs. But some people enjoy hunting, so they hunt deer, moose, pheasant, or some other animal instead of buying all their meat at the store.

No matter where we get our food, we should always thank God for it. The food we have is part of what God provides for us so we can live.

KEY VERSES: *God blessed Noah and his sons and told them, "Multiply and fill the earth. All the wild animals, large and small, and all the birds and fish will be afraid of you. I have placed them in your power. I have given them to you for food, just as I have given you grain and vegetables." (Genesis 9:1-3)*

Q 755:

Why are some people mean to animals?

A: Some people who don't care about animals are mean to them for fun. Other people hurt animals without meaning to when they are angry or frustrated. For example, someone might be having a very bad day. Then, when this person comes home and the pet has done something annoying, the person takes out his or her anger on the pet. We don't always know why other people are mean, but we can ask God to help us be kind and not mean. He can help us take good care of his creation.

KEY VERSE: *The godly are concerned for the welfare of their animals, but even the kindness of the wicked is cruel. (Proverbs 12:10)*

Q 756:

Do animals have feelings just like people do?

A: Animals have feelings, but they are not exactly like people. Think about your body. Animals have bodies just as we have bodies, but they're not the same kind of bodies. Humans have a unique brain structure. They can think about the future. A dog will bury a bone, but she won't sit on the porch and wonder if she has buried enough bones for retirement. It is a lot like that with feelings. A dog can feel lonely, sad, afraid, and hungry. But the dog cannot think about the reasons for those feelings. The dog only responds to certain conditions (for example, he feels alone and sad in a kennel or afraid when the thunder roars and the lightning cracks). God has given us more complex emotions that we can experience, enjoy, use, and direct.

KEY VERSE: *Do you think we are cattle? Do you think we have no intelligence? (Job 18:3)*

Q 757:

Why do people cry when their pets die?

A: Every good thing that we enjoy is a gift from God. Many people often enjoy their pets and like having them around. They grow very attached to a favorite pet. Animals are loyal, they appreciate their masters, and after they are trained, they don't give their masters much grief. Many people come to like their pets very much. Some people treat their pets as though they are members of the family. So when a pet gets lost or dies, the master feels very sad and may even cry. It is OK to cry when you lose a pet that you loved.

KEY VERSES: *[Jesus said,] "If you had one hundred sheep, and one of them strayed away and was lost in the wilderness, wouldn't you leave the ninety-nine others to go and search for the lost one until you found it? And then you would joyfully carry it home on your shoulders. When you arrived, you would call together your friends and neighbors to rejoice with you because your lost sheep was found." (Luke 15:4-6)*

Q 758:

Why do some animals look funny?

A: God is very creative. He made a huge variety of plants and animals—hundreds of thousands of kinds. And remember that *every person* is special and different. This variety is part of God's creative genius. It is part of the beauty he built into the world.

Some animals look funny because they are built a certain way to help them live in their environment and to get food. An armadillo, for example, has a hard shell that protects it from other animals. A lizard has a long, sticky tongue to help it catch flies to eat. An anteater has a long nose to help it eat ants. The giraffe's long neck helps it eat leaves from tall trees. God made all animals with amazing mechanisms for survival, and that's just one of the wonders of God himself.

KEY VERSES: *Take a look at the mighty hippopotamus. I made it, just as I made you. It eats grass like an ox. See its powerful loins and the muscles of its belly. Its tail is as straight as a cedar. The sinews of its thighs are tightly knit together. Its bones are tubes of bronze. Its limbs are bars of iron. It is a prime example of God's amazing handiwork. Only its Creator can threaten it. (Job 40:15-19)*

NOTE TO PARENTS: Encourage your children with the fact that God created them to be wonderfully unique.

Q 759:

Why do cats and dogs fight?

A: Usually cats and dogs fight because they are trying to protect their territory. It is natural for animals to compete for dominance (to see who is the strongest). Dogs and cats that are raised with each other usually don't fight. They are used to each other and get along pretty well.

KEY VERSES: *In that day the wolf and the lamb will live together; the leopard and the goat will be at peace. Calves and yearlings will be safe among lions, and a little child will lead them all. The cattle will graze among bears. Cubs and calves will lie down together. And lions will eat grass as the livestock do. (Isaiah 11:6-7)*

The Entertainment Industry

Q 760:

Why do movies have weirdos for stars?

A: Not all movie stars are weirdos. Many are normal people who live pretty normal lives. The news media don't report these normal lives. They report the abnormal ones—the weird cases. So we hear a lot about the weirdos and nothing about the rest of the normal stars. That makes it seem as though all of the movie and television actors are weird, but they're not.

Some stars act weird on purpose in order to get attention. In other words, they put on an act so newspaper and magazine stories will be written about them. They think this will help their career.

Others act weird because they have an exaggerated idea of their own importance. Because so many people tell them how great they are and because they get a lot of attention and money for doing their job, they sometimes think they can do anything they want. So they take drugs, trash hotel rooms, marry and divorce several times, and do other shocking things. The sin of pride can make people do strange things.

KEY VERSES: *[Jesus said,] "Everything [the Pharisees] do is for show. . . . They enjoy the attention they get on the streets."(Matthew 23:5, 7)*

NOTE TO PARENTS: Children often idolize movie stars and athletes for the wrong reasons. Help your children understand the difference between liking a person's skills and wanting to be like that person. We should strive to be like people who are wise and good, not like those who are popular.

Q 761:

Why do people put garbage in their heads by watching bad movies?

A: Junk entertainment is like junk food—it tastes good even though it's bad for us. Many people watch garbage on TV and in the movies because they like it, even though it is bad for them.

God wants us to be *discerning*. He wants us to recognize junk entertainment for what it is and avoid it, even if it seems fun or harmless. Ratings help many people decide whether or not to see certain movies or TV shows. A movie rated G is said to be all right for "General Audiences." In other words, people of all ages will probably not be offended or hurt by anything in the movie.

The ratings are not always right, however. That's why it is helpful to read reviews or talk with others about a movie or TV show. Some movies can have a mild rating (for example, G or PG) and yet teach some pretty bad stuff about God and life.

Be careful about what you watch because once you've watched something, you can't unwatch it.

KEY VERSE: *Fix your thoughts on what is true and honorable and right. Think about things that are pure and lovely and admirable. Think about things that are excellent and worthy of praise. (Philippians 4:8)*

NOTE TO PARENTS: What you model is what your children will become. Choose entertainment wisely; think critically about the shows and movies you consider watching.

Q 762:

Why is there so much fighting on TV?

A: One reason is that there is so much fighting in real life. Some people have not learned to control their temper, so there is a lot of fighting. God wants us to overlook insults and stay calm when people try to make us mad. Too many people think they have no choice but to blow their top.

Another reason TV has a lot of fighting is that many people like to see other people fight. A lot of people watch shows with fighting in them, so the studios produce them and the networks show them. The TV and studio bosses often say they show fighting because it is an important part of the story and they have to be realistic. That may be true, but the real reason is money.

KEY VERSE: *Good people enjoy the positive results of their words, but those who are treacherous crave violence. (Proverbs 13:2)*

Q 763:

How come people put bad movies on TV?

A: Because lots of people watch them. The moviemakers and the network bosses try to make as much money as possible. If a lot of people watch a certain movie, the television network can make a lot of money through advertising. The networks know that lots of people watch bad shows. Instead of watching bad movies, we should ignore them by changing channels or turning off the TV set. If a lot of people wrote the TV stations and complained about the bad movies, maybe the networks wouldn't show them anymore.

Remember that bad is bad no matter how many people do it. You don't have to watch bad movies just because they're popular.

KEY VERSES: *Stop loving this evil world and all that it offers you, for when you love the world, you show that you do not have the love of the Father in you. For the world offers only the lust for physical pleasure, the lust for everything we see, and pride in our possessions. These are not from the Father. They are from this evil world. (1 John 2:15-16)*

NOTE TO PARENTS: Telling children they can't watch something "because it's bad" will arouse their curiosity and often backfire. Instead, tell your children what's in the show and why it's bad, or how it will adversely affect them. This will allow them to share in the decision, or at least to see that you have good reasons for it.

Q 764:

Why do movie companies make scary movies if they know people will have nightmares?

A: Many people want to see scary movies and will pay money to see them. The companies that make these movies don't care about whether or not they are scary or bad. They just want to make money.

God doesn't want us to be afraid of monsters, demons, ghosts, and prowlers. He wants us to think good thoughts and be confident in his care for us because he loves us and created us to enjoy life. So if something you're watching scares you, stop watching it. And if you see something that bothers you, talk to your parents about it and pray together that God will protect you and give you good dreams. God does not want you to have nightmares.

KEY VERSE: *I will lie down in peace and sleep, for you alone, O LORD, will keep me safe. (Psalm 4:8)*

Q 765:

Why are some things on videos funny for adults but not for kids?

A: Some jokes are funny for adults but not for children because kids and adults have different kinds of humor. Each group finds different things funny. Also, adults have experiences that kids haven't had. They laugh at things that they know about. For example, a joke about working on the job, paying income tax, or raising children wouldn't be very funny to children. Only people who know about those situations would get the joke.

A good family movie will often include humor for the kids and for the adults so the whole family can enjoy it together.

KEY VERSE: *It's like this: When I was a child, I spoke and thought and reasoned as a child does. But when I grew up, I put away childish things. (1 Corinthians 13:11)*

NOTE TO PARENTS: Humor and laughter are gifts from God. If your children have a great sense of humor and can readily make others laugh, encourage them to use the gift wisely and not to abuse it with cruelty or offensive language.

Q 766:

Why won't parents let kids watch certain shows the kids want to watch?

A: Because God gives parents the responsibility to guide their children, and sometimes parents know something about a show that the kids don't know. Parents know that the show will have violence or swearing or will make bad things look good. They may not let their children watch those kinds of shows. Most parents also know that too much TV is not good. Good parents put limits on how much television and what shows their family can watch.

KEY VERSE: *Children, obey your parents because you belong to the Lord, for this is the right thing to do. (Ephesians 6:1)*

Q 767:

Why do people like different kinds of music?

A: People like various kinds of music because people have different tastes. Each person is unique and special—a part of the variety in God's creation. It's the same with people's tastes in food. Everyone has favorite foods. We wouldn't expect everyone to eat and like all the same foods.

Certain groups of people like certain kinds of music. People of one nationality may like one kind, and people from one area of the country may have their own musical likes and dislikes. Some people just listen to whatever is popular.

We should choose music (and other forms of entertainment) wisely, because it's something we put into our mind. God wants us to think about good things.

KEY VERSE: *Just as the mouth tastes good food, the ear tests the words it hears. (Job 34:3)*

Q 768:

Why are musicians treated like idols?

A: Everybody looks up to somebody. God made us this way so we could learn and grow into people who love and obey him. He gives us parents to start the process, and as we get older we choose others from whom to learn.

Many people choose to idolize musicians because they appear in the spotlight a lot. They are featured in newspapers and magazines and on TV and are held up as heroes. Many people look up to them simply because of all the attention they get.

Others "worship" musicians because their music makes them feel something very deeply. That is the way art works—it touches people's emotions.

And others idolize musicians because they assume that being rich and famous is important. Not all musicians are rich and famous, but those who are may appear to be especially successful or great.

KEY VERSE: *[Barnabas and Paul shouted,] "Friends, why are you doing this? We are merely human beings like yourselves! We have come to bring you the Good News that you should turn from these worthless things to the living God, who made heaven and earth, the sea, and everything in them." (Acts 14:15)*

NOTE TO PARENTS: We should choose our heroes carefully, and we should be careful not to idolize them. Encourage your children to look up to those who love God and try to do what is right. Help them to realize that no one is perfect, not even great heroes.

Q 769:

Why are there commercials all the time when good shows are on TV?

A: The commercials pay for the shows. That is, the companies that show the programs get paid by the companies that make the commercials. If the networks did not show the commercials, they would have no money to pay for the programs. A lot of people watch the very popular shows, so that is why you see so many commercials. The companies advertising want to show their commercials when a lot of people are watching.

KEY VERSE: *Do not cheat or rob anyone. Always pay your hired workers promptly. (Leviticus 19:13)*

Q 770:

When you want to have something you see on a TV commercial, why doesn't your mom let you have it?

A: Many times the products advertised on television look much better than they really are, and your parents know it. Your parents have the responsibility to guide and protect you. Their job is to teach you God's ways and God's wisdom. They may not let you have something that looks exciting on TV because they know that it isn't going to be as great as the commercial shows. Or they may know that you do not need it or that it costs too much money. Or they know that it would actually be bad for you, even if you can't imagine how.

KEY VERSE: *Then [Jesus] said, "Beware! Don't be greedy for what you don't have. Real life is not measured by how much we own." (Luke 12:15)*

Family Matters

Q 771:

Why do we have marriage?

A: God invented marriage because everyone needs someone to be close to and to love and be loved by. He also created marriage as the place for bringing children into the world. Marriage is good. In fact, God brought the first man and woman together in the Garden of Eden before any sin came into the world. God knows what is best for us. He knows that babies and children need a mother and a father to protect them and to care for them. Husbands and wives should stay together, work out their problems, and be good parents. That's God's plan.

KEY VERSE: *[Jesus] said, "This explains why a man leaves his father and mother and is joined to his wife, and the two are united into one." (Matthew 19:5)*

NOTE TO PARENTS: Emphasize God's role in making families work. God doesn't abandon families that have suffered divorce or other breakdowns. He provided us with marriage; God's plan for a husband and wife is that they will be married for life. In this sinful world, however, divorces do happen. Through his grace, God can make any family the place of protection and provision that kids need. Keep trusting God and depending on him to help you make the most of your situation.

Q 772:

Why do some moms and dads divorce?

A: God's plan is for a husband and wife to stay together and not get divorced. But all people have weaknesses. No one is perfect. That is why troubles arise in all relationships, even between two people who love each other very much.

When a man and a woman get married, they promise to stay with each other for life. They know it won't always be easy, but they want to work out their problems and stay together. When the arguments and other conflicts and pressures come, some people don't know how to handle them, and their problems get worse. Usually the problems start small and then grow. Eventually, these problems can become so big that the husband or the wife or both just give up and decide to end their marriage. Some don't try that hard; they divorce because they choose not to work out their problems.

But God wants Christians to stay married and work things out. He knows that when they do, their lives will be better for it.

KEY VERSES: *Jesus replied, "Moses permitted divorce as a concession to your hard-hearted wickedness, but it was not what God had originally intended. And I tell you this, a man who divorces his wife and marries another commits adultery—unless his wife has been unfaithful." (Matthew 19:8-9)*

Q 773:

Why do brothers and sisters fight?

A: Part of what it means to be a human being is to be sinful. In other words, no one in this world is perfect. We all do wrong things—we act in ways that displease God and get us into trouble. Sinfulness causes us to get on each other's nerves and to get angry with one another. We even argue and fight with people we love, like our parents or our brothers and sisters. God has given us rules for living. If we follow his rules, we will get along with each other.

KEY VERSES: *At harvesttime Cain brought to the LORD a gift of his farm produce, while Abel brought several choice lambs from the best of his flock. The LORD accepted Abel and his offering, but he did not accept Cain and his offering. This made Cain very angry and dejected. "Why are you so angry?" the LORD asked him. "Why do you look so dejected? You will be accepted if you respond in the right way. But if you refuse to respond correctly, then watch out! Sin is waiting to attack and destroy you, and you must subdue it." (Genesis 4:3-7)*

Q 774:

Why do some kids have stepmothers or stepfathers?

A: Stepmothers and stepfathers come into the picture whenever a parent remarries. That is, one of the parents dies or divorces the other. If the other parent gets married again, the children get a new mother or father. This person is called a *stepmother* or *stepfather*.

For example, suppose a boy's mother and father get divorced and the boy lives with his mother. If the mother remarries, her new husband becomes the boy's stepfather. Or suppose a girl's mother dies. If the girl's father remarries, his new wife becomes the girl's stepmother. If the stepfather or stepmother brings children into the family, the children of the two families become stepbrothers and stepsisters. And if the newly married parents have more children after they get married, those children become half brothers and half sisters of the children that came before them.

Divorce and remarriage can be confusing. But remember that no matter what label we give to the parents and kids in a family, they are still all part of one family. It doesn't matter how they came together.

KEY VERSE: *A wife is married to her husband as long as he lives. If her husband dies, she is free to marry whomever she wishes, but this must be a marriage acceptable to the Lord.* (1 Corinthians 7:39)

Q 775:

Why did people used to have so many kids?

A: One reason parents used to have more kids is that before modern medicine, more children died young, from disease and other problems, than die today. Parents could not be sure that their children would live. Another reason families of the past had a lot of children is that they needed many family members to help with the family work—around the house or on the farm. Modern medicine has also made it easier than ever to prevent pregnancy.

God loves families of all shapes and sizes. Today, some families do have a lot of children. But it is not as common as it used to be.

KEY VERSE: *God blessed them and told them, "Multiply and fill the earth and subdue it. Be masters over the fish and birds and all the animals." (Genesis 1:28)*

Q 776:

How are families different now from the way they used to be?

A: In some ways families are very different. Before cars and planes were invented, families were very close and lots of relatives lived together. Most families were also larger, with more children. New inventions have caused many families to spread far apart. Now people can travel long distances very quickly by car, airplane, bus, boat, or train to visit family, and they can communicate with each other on the phone and through electronic mail.

But in many ways families are still the same. Families start with a mom and a dad. The parents have parents. Kids have grandparents. And sometimes the grandparents or other relatives live with the family.

KEY VERSES: *The church should care for any widow who has no one else to care for her. But if she has children or grandchildren, their first responsibility is to show godliness at home and repay their parents by taking care of them. This is something that pleases God very much. (1 Timothy 5:3-4)*

Changing Technology

Q 777:

How fast is technology changing?

"NEW COMPUTERS" & DAY-OLD COMPUTERS SOLD HERE

A: Technology is changing very fast. Just think of some of the things that people use every day:

- Television was invented in 1926.
- Penicillin was first used to cure disease in 1929.
- The microwave oven was invented in 1947.
- The VCR was invented in 1965.
- The personal computer was invented in 1972.
- Cellular phones were first used by the public in 1979.
- The World Wide Web was created in 1990.

These recent inventions have become very important to us. And right now, as you are reading this, people are inventing new machines, medicines, appliances, computers, and other technologies that can help us even more. This all comes from the creativity God gave us.

KEY VERSE: *People should eat and drink and enjoy the fruits of their labor, for these are gifts from God. (Ecclesiastes 3:13)*

Q 778:

How did computers get so smart?

A: Computers do not think, so they aren't smart in the way that human beings are smart. Computers simply process information very, very fast. They receive and send electrical signals according to a set of rules, called instructions, built into the main chip. The computers of today seem "smarter" than older ones because they run much faster and because they have more instructions built into them. But they still just process information according to a set of rules.

Some people think that human beings are very special computers, with the "main chip" in their head. But this is not true. A person is much more than just a brain, and a brain is much more than a big computer chip. A person is a combination of body, soul, and spirit. A person is created in the image of God. Computers are just machines. They aren't anything like "smart."

KEY VERSE: *The LORD grants wisdom! From his mouth come knowledge and understanding. (Proverbs 2:6)*

Q 779:

How do computers get viruses?

A: A computer virus is a program that copies itself to another computer by attaching itself to programs or data. Computers get viruses when people load or run infected files on their computers. They are called viruses because they work like living viruses—by making copies of themselves and attaching themselves to, or "infecting," another machine. Most do this when someone opens or runs an infected file on their own computer.

Viruses don't just arise out of nowhere. People write them. Some of those who write viruses claim that it's not their fault if users get infected files. But that is just an example of how sin and selfishness can blind us to the truth. God says we should look out for each other, respect each other, and love each other because everything we do affects someone else. It is true that most viruses do not cause any damage or harm. But some are written to cause mischief or damage to data. And even the harmless ones take time and energy to get rid of. Damaging someone else's property is wrong.

KEY VERSES: *Just as damaging as a mad man shooting a lethal weapon is someone who lies to a friend and then says, "I was only joking." (Proverbs 26:18-19)*

Q 780:

How come the keys on the keyboard are not in alphabetical order?

A: Computer keyboards made today have the same layout as the very first typewriter ever made. The typewriter was invented by Christopher Sholes of Milwaukee, Wisconsin, in 1867. The layout for the keys he came up with is called a QWERTY layout because those letters are the first six letters on the top row. Sholes chose this layout because he believed it would be easy to use—the placement of the letters would make it easy to type English words quickly without jamming the parts of the typewriter. Typewriters and computer keyboards of today don't have any parts that can jam, but everyone is so used to using the QWERTY layout that we keep using it.

KEY VERSE: *Any story sounds true until someone sets the record straight. (Proverbs 18:17)*

Q 781:

Why do people surf on the Internet?

A: People "surf" the Internet for many reasons:

- Curiosity—it can be interesting; they want to see what's there.
- Education—it can be informative; they want to answer questions or learn something.
- Information—it can tell them something they need to know, such as a weather forecast, a sports schedule, or the route to a place.
- Entertainment—it can be fun; they want to listen to music, meet people, read interesting stories, or see video clips.
- Problem solving—it can help them find answers to a problem they have.
- Communication—it can be a way to send and receive messages.

KEY VERSE: *Wise people treasure knowledge, but the babbling of a fool invites trouble.* *(Proverbs 10:14)*

Q 782:

Is the Internet bad?

A: The Internet itself is not bad. It is just like any other tool, such as a hammer, a book, or a phone—it can be used for both good and bad. Almost anything can be used this way, even things that are usually used for good. A hammer can be used to build a house or hurt someone. So the Internet can be misused and used for bad purposes, just as it can be used for good purposes. Sadly, some people do use it the bad way.

By itself, the Internet is just a very big network of networks. Whether it is used for good or for bad is up to us. It has great potential for good. We each need to do our part and use it right—to the glory of God.

KEY VERSE: *Whatever you eat or drink or whatever you do, you must do all for the glory of God. (1 Corinthians 10:31)*

Q 783:

How come the olden days and these days are different?

A: First, people change the way they dress, the style of their homes, and the kinds of foods they eat. Second, and more importantly, technology keeps changing. Every year, engineers and inventors create new products and new ways of doing things. Some of these things can improve our lives, and others make things a little harder, but all of them bring change.

After the automobile was invented and became common, people didn't have to ride horses or horse-drawn buggies to travel from town to town. That was a huge change. And just think of the changes that came from airplanes, telephones, microwave ovens, antibiotics, vaccines, and computers. Then microphones, televisions, tape players, CD players, VCRs, and CD-ROM drives sure changed entertainment. Not that long ago, people didn't have any of these inventions.

But even with all the changes, many things stay the same. Human nature is the same—people still struggle and search for God. People still laugh and cry, and they are born young and grow old. A year is still 365 days, people still have to work, and each person still needs God's love and lordship. And everyone still dies.

KEY VERSE: *Don't long for "the good old days," for you don't know whether they were any better than today. (Ecclesiastes 7:10)*

Medicine

Q 784:

Why do people get sick when God is watching over them?

A: Sickness was not part of God's original plan for us. We have sickness in the world because sin brought it in. As long as we live in this world, we will have sickness. God does not promise that he will keep all pain and sickness away from us, although he does promise to always be with us.

We need to take care of ourselves and guard against sickness by eating the right foods, getting enough sleep, and exercising. When we do get sick, we should take our medicine exactly as the doctor says and pray and ask God to help us recover.

Ecclesiastes 7:14 says, "Enjoy prosperity while you can. But when hard times strike, realize that both come from God."

In heaven God will end all sickness. This life is not all there is. Don't forget about heaven.

KEY VERSE: *Our bodies now disappoint us, but when they are raised, they will be full of glory. They are weak now, but when they are raised, they will be full of power.* (1 Corinthians 15:43)

Q 785:

Why does your body feel sick?

A: When a person feels sick, that person's body is telling him or her that something is wrong. Pain and sick feelings can be a friend, an alarm system that alerts us to problems. Without these feelings, we would not know that something is wrong and that we need to do something about it (for example, eat certain foods, take medicine, or have an operation). People who don't have those bad feelings can hurt themselves more by not taking care of the problem.

KEY VERSES: *You guided my conception and formed me in the womb. You clothed me with skin and flesh, and you knit my bones and sinews together. (Job 10:10-11)*

Q 786:

What are bacteria and viruses?

A: Bacteria are one-celled living things; viruses are parasites that attack living things. Both are so small that you need a microscope to see them. Harmful bacteria and viruses are often called germs. Germs make you sick by reproducing inside your body.

Bacteria are not always harmful. *E. coli* bacteria live in your intestines and help your body break down food. Several kinds of bacteria live in the ground and break up dead leaves, sticks, grass, and other organic matter to make compost. These bacteria could make you sick if they got on your food, but they serve a good purpose in nature.

Other bacteria are very harmful; streptococcus bacteria, for example, cause strep throat, a sickness that children and adults sometimes get. Doctors treat it with antibiotics, medicines that kill bacteria.

Bacteria and viruses are everywhere, but God made our bodies to fight them off. He gave us white blood cells and antibodies. These are your body's way of staying well and of curing itself of sickness.

KEY VERSE: *Thank you for making me so wonderfully complex! Your workmanship is marvelous—and how well I know it. (Psalm 139:14)*

Q 787:

Why are doctors so smart?

A: God makes every person with talents and abilities. He makes each person unique—one person has this skill, and another person has that skill. People who become doctors have the talents and abilities to do what doctors do.

But people aren't born being doctors. They have to get a lot of training. They have to go to school for a long time and study hard. They have to learn from other doctors who have a lot of experience. Only after they have done all that are they "so smart." They know a lot because they've learned a lot.

KEY VERSE: *[Moses said,] "Bezalel, Oholiab, and the other craftsmen whom the LORD has gifted with wisdom, skill, and intelligence will construct and furnish the Tabernacle, just as the LORD has commanded." (Exodus 36:1)*

Q 788:

How does medicine make someone better?

A: Medicine helps your body heal itself. Some medicines do this by killing germs; antibiotics work that way. Some medicines help the body do what it does even better. Some medicines stop the body from doing what it should not do; some asthma medicines work that way. Doctors often know what medicines to give for each sickness. The purpose of medicine is to help your body do the healing work.

The one thing medicine cannot do is heal your attitude. You can be cured of an illness but remain angry, selfish, and bitter. Or you may not be cured physically but still be thankful, peaceful, and trusting of God. It is important to place your hope and trust in God, no matter how sick you may be. That is what Job did.

In the end, it is God who heals people. God gives us our bodies and gives us the substances that make medicines work.

KEY VERSE: *Then Isaiah said to Hezekiah's servants, "Make an ointment from figs and spread it over the boil." They did this, and Hezekiah recovered! (2 Kings 20:7)*

Q 789:

Who invented vegetables?

A: God created vegetables—they were his idea. Our bodies need certain kinds of food, just as a car needs a certain kind of fuel. You wouldn't put hamburgers into a gas tank, would you? God gave us vegetables as good food for us because that's one kind of fuel our bodies need.

In fact, vegetables have several very important jobs. First, they provide vitamins and minerals that help us grow and become strong and healthy. Without these vitamins and minerals, our body would not work right. Vegetables also give us fiber, which is the part of plant cells that your body cannot digest. Fiber carries all the other foods through your digestive system. That may sound unimportant, but without fiber, all the other food you eat would get stuck in your digestive tract.

God gave us fruits and vegetables to eat so that our bodies would work properly.

KEY VERSE: *"Test us for ten days on a diet of vegetables and water," Daniel said. (Daniel 1:12)*

Q 790:

Why is it good to exercise?

A: Your body needs exercise, just as it needs food, air, and water. Muscles need to be stretched and strengthened. The lungs need to breathe fresh, clean air. Joints need to be moved around. Blood needs to get moving. Exercise is a way of taking care of your body. Exercise also helps people lose weight by using the food, building muscle, and burning fat.

Some people today don't get enough exercise—they sit around watching TV, playing video games, or surfing the Internet for a long time. Sitting around all the time is not good for a person's health. You need to get out and use your body. Good exercise comes from working around the house, working in the yard, riding bikes, running, walking, and playing sports.

God gave us wonderful bodies, and he wants us to take care of them. And we all need exercise to do that properly.

KEY VERSE: *Physical exercise has some value, but spiritual exercise is much more important, for it promises a reward in both this life and the next. (1 Timothy 4:8)*

Q 791:

Why do people smoke?

A: People smoke because they are addicted to the nicotine in the cigarettes. Nicotine is a chemical in tobacco. Once you start putting nicotine into your body, your body starts to crave it. You start to feel like you *need* it. Smoking gives your body the nicotine it craves, and this makes it hard to stop.

People also get addicted to the experience. That is, they get used to having a cigarette at certain times of the day. It becomes a habit.

Most people who smoke started when they were very young. They may have started because they thought that smoking would make them look cool or tough or because they liked the taste. Maybe someone they knew talked them into it. After a while, however, they got tired of smoking—it's not cool anymore. But they have become addicted to the nicotine and find it almost impossible to stop.

It is important for us to take good care of our body. Smoking damages many parts of our body. God didn't make our lungs to breathe in smoke.

Try not to be too hard on people who smoke. Quitting is very difficult.

KEY VERSES: *I don't understand myself at all, for I really want to do what is right, but I don't do it. Instead, I do the very thing I hate. I know perfectly well that what I am doing is wrong, and my bad conscience shows that I agree that the law is good. But I can't help myself, because it is sin inside me that makes me do these evil things. (Romans 7:15-17)*

Q 792:

What does cloning mean?

A: Cloning means making an exact copy of a living thing's DNA, or genetic code. It involves taking the genetic code of a plant or animal and making another plant or animal from that code. Cloning bypasses the usual means of reproduction from a male and female. It's like making a photocopy of a living plant or animal, or building two houses with the same measurements.

Cloning does *not* mean making an exact copy of a person. Cloning copies only the *body,* not the soul, the spirit, or the experiences that also make a person who he or she is. Even if someone could make an exact physical copy of your eyes, knees, and brain, the clone would still be different from you. Your personality, experiences, desires, dreams, choices, and relationship with God would all be different from the clone's. It is all of these things together that make you one of a kind.

No one could ever be exactly like you. Isn't that great?

KEY VERSE: *You made all the delicate, inner parts of my body and knit me together in my mother's womb.(Psalm 139:13)*

Q 793:

Why does God let people die?

A: People die because sin came into the world when Adam and Eve sinned. In fact, everyone dies eventually. Some people die when they're young, some die when they're old, and some die when they're in the prime of life. But no matter how long a person lives, his or her life sooner or later comes to an end.

God can heal people and stop them from dying, and sometimes he does. But even a person who has been healed through a miracle from God will die someday.

But God's people know that death is not the end of the story. This life is *not* all there is. People who know God will go to live with him in heaven after they die. So it is very important for us to be ready to meet him when we die.

KEY VERSE: *We know that when this earthly tent we live in is taken down—when we die and leave these bodies— we will have a home in heaven, an eternal body made for us by God himself and not by human hands. (2 Corinthians 5:1)*

Outer Space

Q 794:

Why is there a universe?

A: *Universe* is another word for the creation— everything that God created. God created it all. He created every star, every galaxy, every black hole, every atom. And God created everything very good. We don't know why God created everything in the universe, but we do know that he had a good reason.

We also know that God designed the universe for us to live in. The Bible says that God placed the stars and the moon in the night sky to give us light during the night, and he made the sun to give us light during the day. God had us in mind when he created these things; he gave them their design so that we could live on this earth. They are a sign of God's care and love for us.

The Bible also says that the creation is evidence of God's existence (see Romans 1:20). When people look around and see the earth and all the stars, they know that these things came from God.

KEY VERSE: *By faith we understand that the entire universe was formed at God's command, that what we now see did not come from anything that can be seen. (Hebrews 11:3)*

NOTE TO PARENTS: Creation tells us something about God's power and nature. You can look out at the night sky with your children and talk about what the stars tell us about God.

Q 795:

Is outer space hot or cold?

A: Most of outer space is very cold; only the stars and the space right around them are hot. God created the universe with over a trillion stars. The stars put out a lot of heat, but there is a lot more space than stars. So anything not close to a star has almost no heat at all. The heat produced by the Sun, the star that's closest to Earth, produces just the right amount of light and heat for us to live on our planet. The air on Earth keeps the heat in. God created the earth with just the right climate so that human beings, his special creations, could live here. Earth is our home.

KEY VERSES: *When I consider your heavens, the work of your fingers, the moon and the stars, which you have set in place, what is man that you are mindful of him, the son of man that you care for him? (Psalm 8:3-4)*

Q 796:

Why do people want to fly to other planets?

A: Some people want to travel to other planets because they want to know how the universe began. Even those who believe that God created everything are curious about how he did it. The stars, the planets, and all the universe are marvelous displays of God's handiwork.

Other people are simply curious. They want to travel to other planets to see them up close, to see what it would be like to go there, and to learn all they can. It would certainly be an adventure!

KEY VERSE: *It is God's privilege to conceal things and the king's privilege to discover them. (Proverbs 25:2)*

Q 797:

If there's intelligent life on other planets, do they have teachers?

A: The universe is so big that we can't even imagine how big it is. The nearest star outside of our galaxy, Alpha Centauri, is 25 *trillion* miles from our sun, and Alpha Centauri has no planets. It is possible that God created life on other planets, far, far away. But we don't know anything about that because we have no evidence for other living beings on other planets. And even if we could travel at the speed of light, which is over 600 million miles per hour, it would take us over four years just to go to Alpha Centauri. Unless we invent some form of space travel that takes us across the galaxy faster than light, we will probably never know whether God created life on other planets. Only God knows exactly what he created far out in space.

KEY VERSE: *The LORD merely spoke, and the heavens were created. He breathed the word, and all the stars were born. (Psalm 33:6)*

Q 798:

Why do people think that beings from other planets have visited earth?

A: Some people believe that beings from other planets have visited earth. Here are some of the reasons they think so:

1. It would be exciting if it were true (wishful thinking).
2. It is one way people explain certain things that used to be hard to explain, such as how the pyramids in Egypt were built.
3. They know there is more to our existence than just ourselves, but they refuse to believe in God, so they look in outer space instead.
4. They want to connect to something that is beyond what they know or experience on earth.

Some people even think that human beings were put on earth by beings from outer space. They do not believe in God or that God created us, and this is the way they explain where we came from.

KEY VERSE: *All the Athenians as well as the foreigners in Athens seemed to spend all their time discussing the latest ideas. (Acts 17:21)*

Q 799:

Why do people want to live on the moon if they wouldn't be able to breathe there?

A: The main reason for living on the moon would be for learning—studying astronomy and trying to understand the universe better. Some people want to go to the moon to mine it. Some just want to travel and explore.

Few people really want to live on the moon, however, even if the trip were completely safe. It would cost an enormous amount of money to get there. There would be no trees, fresh air, streams, or other things to enjoy. It would also be very difficult to live and to get around. Again, the main reason for going would be to study and do research.

KEY VERSE: *Intelligent people are always open to new ideas. In fact, they look for them. (Proverbs 18:15)*

Q 800:

How do people think of things like the Hubble telescope?

A: People who invent marvelous instruments like the Hubble telescope are very talented and intelligent people. God gave them the brains and ability to think of such things. God let them learn and develop the skills to make their inventions. They read, investigated, learned, and studied hard for a long time. The skills and knowledge that people like that use to create such amazing tools come from God, and those people have used them well.

It is a beautiful part of human nature to be able to create and invent things that are useful to us. It is a part of God's image in us. It is a part of God's image in you.

KEY VERSE: *You made [man] a little lower than the heavenly beings and crowned him with glory and honor. (Psalm 8:5)*

Q 801:

Can kids be astronauts if they get trained?

A: Kids can't be astronauts because it takes so long to train for it. It takes many years of training and conditioning to withstand the rigors of space flight. Your body has to be in top shape and strong. Even if a young person were chosen to be an astronaut, he or she would be quite a bit older at the end of the training. So you might say that a kid can't be an astronaut, but a kid can train to become an astronaut when he or she is older.

Very few people actually become astronauts, although thousands try. Only the very best get chosen.

KEY VERSES: *Remember that in a race everyone runs, but only one person gets the prize. You also must run in such a way that you will win. All athletes practice strict self-control. They do it to win a prize that will fade away, but we do it for an eternal prize. (1 Corinthians 9:24-25)*

NOTE TO PARENTS: Whenever your children are interested in doing something difficult with their life, try not to discourage them from trying just because it takes a lot of effort. Instead, encourage their vision, pray with them about it, and let them know what they have to do to get there.

INDEX OF QUESTIONS

42. How did Jesus do miracles?

43. If Jesus doesn't want us to get hurt, why did he tell us to chop our hands off and poke our eyes out?

44. How did Jesus walk on water?

45. Why did the disciples tell the people Jesus was too busy to see the kids?

46. Why did Judas betray Jesus?

47. Why were the Roman soldiers so mean?

48. Why did the people say, "Come down off the cross if you are the Son of God"?

49. Why did God let them hurt Jesus?

50. Why do they call it "Good Friday" if that's the day Jesus died?

51. If Jesus died on the cross, how can he be alive today?

52. Did Jesus know that he would come to life again?

53. Why can't I see Jesus now?

54. Why did Jesus go up to heaven instead of staying here on earth?

55. Why hasn't God told us when Jesus is coming back?

SALVATION

56. Why do God and Jesus love people?

57. How can Jesus fit in my heart?

58. How do you get Jesus in your heart?

59. Why doesn't God take us to heaven as soon as we get saved?

60. Would God send nice people to hell if they are not Christians?

61. What is hell like?

62. Why is hell dark if they have fires?

63. Who ends up in hell?

64. If I swear, will I go to hell when I die?

65. Will all of my friends go to heaven?

66. Why isn't everyone a Christian?

67. Why didn't God just forgive everybody?

68. Why doesn't God just zap the bad people?

69. How long is eternity?

70. What does God want us to do?

SUFFERING

71. Why do I feel afraid if Jesus is with me?

72. Why do some people die before they are old?

73. Why are some people different from others?

74. Why does God let wars happen?

75. Why does God let us get sick?

76. Does God know about people who are hungry?

77. Who feeds people who don't have enough to eat?

78. Why do you get mad at me if you have Jesus in your heart?

79. Why does God kill nature with forest fires?

80. Why do floods and hurricanes kill innocent people?

81. Why does God send earthquakes?

82. Why do people die in hot weather?

83. Why do people commit crimes?

84. Why is the world so violent and evil?

85. Why are there so many accidents and people getting killed?

THE CHURCH

86. Why do we go to church if God is everywhere?

87. Why do we worship God?

131. Did God know Adam and Eve were going to sin?

132. If Adam and Eve hadn't sinned, would people sin today?

133. Why did Cain kill his brother?

134. How did Noah build a boat that was so big?

135. Why did God flood the whole earth?

136. Why did God put a rainbow in the sky?

137. Why did God choose Abraham to go to the Promised Land instead of someone else?

138. Why was Abraham willing to kill his own son?

139. Why did Jacob trick his dad?

140. Why did Joseph's brothers sell him?

141. Why didn't Joseph go back home?

142. Why didn't the bush burn up?

143. Why wasn't Moses afraid to go to Pharaoh?

144. Why wouldn't Pharaoh let the people go?

145. Why did God send plagues on Egypt?

146. Why did the Israelites smear blood on their doors?

147. How did Moses part the Red Sea?

148. Why did God give Moses so many laws for the Israelites to obey?

149. Why did the Israelites who left Egypt have to wander in the wilderness until they died?

THE NATION OF ISRAEL

150. Did the Israelites have lawyers and courts for their judges?

151. Was Samson a good guy or a bad guy?

152. Why did Samson tell Delilah his secret?

153. Why did Hannah leave her son at the church?

154. Why did the people want to have a king?

155. What did Goliath eat that made him so big?

156. How did David fight Goliath if he was so small?

157. Why was Saul jealous of David?

158. Why did Saul go to a fortune-teller?

159. Why did Solomon want to cut the baby in half?

160. Were prophets the people in Bible days who made lots of money?

161. Why did Elijah go up to heaven so early?

162. Why did God send the Jews to Babylon?

163. Whose hand made the writing on the wall?

164. How did Daniel sleep with the lions without being afraid?

165. Why didn't the Jews ever change their clothes while they were rebuilding the walls?

166. What's a Maccabee?

NEW TESTAMENT EVENTS AND PEOPLE

167. Did people in the Bible have Christmas?

168. How come Zacharias couldn't talk until his son was born?

169. Why did John the Baptist live in the desert?

170. Are "Beatitudes" short for bad attitudes?

171. What's a parable?

172. What does *Passover* mean?

173. Didn't the tongues of fire on the apostles' heads burn them?

174. How could the angel unlock Peter out of jail without keys?

175. How big were the worms that ate King Herod?

176. How could Peter kill and eat animals that were in a vision?

177. Why was it against the law to make friends with a Gentile?

178. Why was Saul blinded by a bright light?

223. Does God listen to any prayer, big or small?

224. Why do people say "thee" and "thou" when they pray?

225. Why do we say "amen" when we're done praying?

WHEN TO PRAY

226. Why do we call it "saying grace"?

227. What is the difference between food that we pray for and food that we have not prayed for?

228. Why do we have to thank God at every meal when he already knows we're thankful?

229. Do we still have to thank God if we don't like the food?

230. Why do we pray before we go to bed?

231. Why do we have to pray when we don't want to?

232. Why do we have to give thanks for things we don't like?

233. Why should we go to God for help?

234. Why do people wait until the last minute to pray?

235. What happens if we don't pray at all?

236. What happens if we're interrupted when we're praying?

237. What does "praying continually" mean?

238. Does praying a lot make a person better?

239. Can we pray anytime we want?

WHAT TO PRAY FOR

240. What do we need to pray for?

241. Are there some things that we shouldn't pray about?

242. Can we tell God everything we want to?

243. How come some people are asking for sunshine while other people are asking for rain?

244. Can we pray for snow so we can't go to school?

245. Can we pray for animals?

246. Can we ask God to give us things like toys?

247. Is it OK to pray to get something that our friends have?

248. Is it bad to ask God for something we don't really need?

249. If we prayed to find something we lost, would we really find it?

250. Can we ask God to help us pass a test?

251. Is it OK to complain to God?

252. When we're sad, can we pray that someone will come play with us?

253. Why do we pray to God to help us not be bad?

254. Why do we ask Jesus into our heart?

255. Do we have to pray to be forgiven?

ANSWERS TO PRAYERS

256. How can God hear our prayers from heaven?

257. If we talk to God, does he always hear us?

258. How can God hear everyone's prayers at once?

259. Does God usually give us what we pray for?

260. Does God only give us things that we need?

261. Why doesn't God give us some things we pray for?

262. How do we know God is answering our prayer?

263. Why doesn't God answer prayers right away?

264. If we're discouraged and it seems like God doesn't answer our prayers, what should we do?

265. When we pray for someone not to die and then they die, does that mean that God didn't love them?

266. If God has it all planned, can we really change it by praying for things?

267. Why does God not answer our prayers the way we want?

268. If we pray for something one night, do we have to pray for it the next night?

269. How come God answers some people's prayers and not others'?
270. Why do some people write down when God answers their prayer?
271. How does God answer our prayers?
272. When God says we can pray about anything, does he really mean *anything*?
273. Does it matter how much faith we have?
274. Doesn't God ever get tired of answering prayers?

PRAYING FOR OTHERS

275. How do we know who to pray for?
276. Does God want us to pray for our friends?
277. Do we have to pray for people we haven't met before?
278. What if kids are mean to us and it's hard for us to pray for them?
279. Why do we pray for our enemies?
280. How does praying help sick people feel better?
281. How come missionaries need so much prayer?
282. What do prayer warriors do?

PRAYING TOGETHER

283. What should a person do who feels embarrassed to pray in public?
284. If we don't like what someone prayed for, what should we do?
285. Why does God want us to pray together?
286. Do children have to pray with an adult?
287. Is group prayer more powerful?
288. Why do some people hold hands while they're praying?

BEDTIME PRAYERS

289. Do we have to pray every night?
290. What if God has already answered all of our prayers?
291. If we've prayed all through the day, do we still need to pray at night?
292. Are your daytime prayers as effective as your night ones?
293. After our parents pray with us, do we still need to pray on our own later?
294. Why did I have a bad dream when I prayed before I went to sleep?
295. Why are we sometimes forced to pray? Shouldn't we pray when we want to?
296. How can we think of something good to pray about if we've had a bad day?
297. Do we have to pray even if we're tired?
298. Is it bad to fall asleep when we are praying to God?

4 HEAVEN AND ANGELS

ANGELS

299. Where did angels come from?
300. Do angels have names?
301. What do angels really look like?
302. Do angels have hearts?
303. Do angels grow up?
304. Are angels boys or girls?
305. Do angels get tired?
306. Do angels have halos?
307. Why can't I see angels?
308. Are there people inside of angels?
309. How many angels are in heaven?
310. How did angels get their wings?
311. Can angels die?
312. Are angels our imaginary friends?

WHAT ANGELS DO

313. Do angels go to work?
314. Do angels watch television?
315. Does each angel belong to a person?
316. Are there angels in this room with us?
317. Do angels stay in the car or fly beside?
318. Do angels sin?
319. Can an angel be your friend and tell you that he is your angel?
320. Do angels just appear for an instant one minute and then disappear?
321. Can an angel be a person to us like a real person?

BAD ANGELS

322. What is evil?
323. Who is the devil?
324. Why is the devil after us?
325. Does the devil have claws?
326. What are demons?
327. Are demons red with horns and long tails?
328. Will I ever get a demon?
329. Why did God make Satan if God knew Satan would make sin?
330. Does the devil have power like God does?
331. What mean things does Satan do to people?
332. How come the devil wants us to be bad?
333. Are Satan and Jesus still at war?
334. Will God forgive Satan?
335. Can an evil spirit stop you from going to heaven?

ANGELS IN THE BIBLE

336. Why was there an angel and a fiery sword guarding the entrance to the Garden of Eden?
337. Why do some angels look like real people?
338. Who was the angel of the Lord?
339. Why are some people scared of angels?
340. Why do some angels have four faces?
341. Why did an angel come to Mary?
342. Why do angels light up and get bright?
343. Why didn't an angel take Jesus off the cross?

HEAVEN

344. What is heaven like?
345. If we went high enough in the sky, would we find heaven?
346. Why did God make heaven?
347. Is Jesus the only way to heaven?
348. Are all people nice in heaven?
349. Can you fall out of heaven?
350. Is heaven all made up of clouds?
351. Why is heaven so shiny?
352. Are the streets in heaven real gold or just painted with gold?
353. Does God have angels watching over heaven so demons can't get in?
354. Where did God live before heaven was made?
355. Does Jesus live with God in heaven, or does he live by himself?
356. Why can't we go to heaven and just see it and then come back?
357. How long does it take to get to heaven from here?

5 RIGHT AND WRONG

RIGHT AND WRONG, RIGHT?

402. Why do people do wrong when they know that it's wrong?

403. Why is it wrong to be bad?

404. How did God decide what was wrong and what was right?

405. Are things always either right or wrong?

406. It's a free country—why do we have to pay tolls?

407. Why shouldn't we take drugs?

408. If the law says something is right but God says it's wrong, who's right?

409. What are morals?

410. How can I tell right from wrong?

411. What are God's rules for right and wrong?

412. When I ask a question, why do you always tell me what the Bible says?

413. Why do some white and black people hate each other?

414. If I see someone who is poor, do I have to give that person money?

415. Is it wrong to spread rumors?

416. Is it a sin if you're not sure if something is wrong but you still go along with it?

417. What is a conscience?

418. Is it all right to laugh at dirty jokes?

419. Do I have to let little kids in my room to play when I have special stuff?

420. Is it OK to tell people to shut up if they are being jerks?

421. Is it OK to slam the door when you're mad?

422. If you say *Jesus* when you're mad, isn't that like praying?

423. Is it all right to throw rocks at someone who threw rocks at you?

424. Is it all right to say bad things if there is no one there to hear you?

425. Is thinking something bad the same as doing it or saying it?

426. Why do people litter?

TRUTH OR CONSEQUENCES

427. Why does God have rules?

428. Why doesn't God want us to have fun?

429. Is God sad when I do something wrong?

430. How do you get permission to go to heaven?

431. If you swear and you're a Christian, do you still go to heaven?

432. Why do I feel bad when I do something wrong?

433. What does God want me to do when I do something wrong?

TELLING THE TRUTH

434. Is it all right to tell a lie once in a while?

435. Is it all right to lie if you are embarrassed or scared?

436. What if I told a lie and didn't know it was a lie—is it still a lie?

437. Is it OK for Mom and Dad to lie to you about your Christmas presents?

438. If I break something that belongs to someone else but fix it, do I have to tell what I did?

439. Do all people lie?

440. Is it wrong to tell someone your parents are home when they're not?

441. Is it OK to lie, knowing you will tell the truth later?

442. Is it OK to lie to keep a friend from getting hurt?

443. What should you do if someone lies to you?

444. Is it OK to keep secrets from your friends?

445. Should I tell the truth to someone even if they won't like it?

446. If you don't like something a person wears and they ask you if you like it, are you supposed to tell them the truth?

447. If lying is a sin, why did some people in the Bible tell lies?

SCHOOL DAYS AND TV DAZE

448. Why is it wrong to do something if all the other kids do it?
449. Should I tell on other kids?
450. Is it wrong to watch music videos?
451. Why do some people make music with bad words?
452. Is it OK to listen to bad music groups if you don't listen to the words?
453. Why don't you let us watch certain TV shows?
454. On TV, why do people who aren't married live together?
455. What if one parent says you can watch a certain movie, and then the other one says you can't?
456. Is it wrong to leave your homework till the last minute so that you can watch TV?
457. Why do people say things that aren't true about the stuff they sell on commercials?

GETTING ALONG WITH YOUR FAMILY

458. Why do I have to obey my parents?
459. Is it wrong to put my fingers in my ears so I can't hear my parents?
460. Is it OK to beg for things from your parents?
461. Why is it wrong to complain when my mom asks me to do something?
462. If my parents are arguing, is it OK to tell them to stop?
463. Is it OK to tell secrets to parents?
464. Is it OK to hit my brother back if he hit me first?
465. Is it OK to bug my sister?
466. Is kissing wrong?
467. Is it OK to drive my dad's car for four seconds?
468. Do I really have to eat my vegetables, or are my parents just making sure I clean my plate?
469. Why do I have to do chores?
470. Why do I have to brush my teeth?
471. Why is it not good to talk to strangers?
472. Can I do whatever I want when I'm older?

FAIR AND SQUARE

473. Is it OK to say you tagged someone in tag when you really didn't?
474. Is it OK to cheat at a game when the game is called "Cheat" and that's what you're supposed to do?
475. Why is it wrong to look at someone's spelling test and write the words down?
476. What's so bad about cheating in sports?
477. Is it cheating when you let the other team win when their team wasn't playing that well?
478. If I cheated and I won, do I have to tell?
479. When you're playing a game, is it OK to fool the other players?
480. Why do people cheat just to win a stupid game?
481. What should I do if someone cheats me?

WHAT'S YOURS ISN'T MINE

482. Why is it wrong to steal things?
483. Is it OK to steal something back from someone who stole it from you?
484. Is it OK to keep a toy that belongs to someone else if they don't ask for it back?
485. Would it be wrong if your friends told you something was for free, so you took it, and then you found out later it wasn't really free?
486. If it's wrong to steal, why do they call it "stealing bases" in baseball?
487. Is it wrong to copy computer games?
488. Is it wrong to keep money that you find on the street?
489. Is it stealing if a poor person takes food?
490. Is it stealing to borrow someone else's stuff without asking?
491. What if someone is shoplifting and it is your friend—what do you do?
492. What if you find something that doesn't belong to you and you can't find who it belongs to—is that stealing?

6 MONEY MATTERS

MONEY DOESN'T GROW ON TREES

493. Where does money come from, God or people?

494. Why is there such a thing as money?

495. Why don't people just trade for what they need?

496. When was money invented?

497. Why are those little pieces of paper worth so much?

498. Why are there all different kinds of money?

499. Where does the money go when you buy what you want?

500. Why isn't a dollar worth a dollar anymore?

YOU CAN BANK ON IT

501. Why do we put our money in the bank when we have to keep going back there to get it?

502. How much money are we supposed to put in the bank?

503. Why do we have to put money in the bank when we have our own piggy banks?

504. What does the bank do with everyone's money?

505. What happens to my money if the bank gets robbed?

506. Why do banks give interest?

507. What are accounts?

508. How can we buy things with a check instead of money?

509. How does a check bounce?

510. Where does all the money in the bank machines come from?

IN GOD WE TRUST

511. Is it all right to pray to God for money?

512. How do I trust God for money?

513. Why doesn't God just give us money when we need it?

514. Why are some people rich?

515. Do billionaires still need to trust God for money they need?

516. Why doesn't God take rich people's money and give it to the poor people?

517. How do poor people get poor?

518. Why doesn't the government just print more money in factories and give it to the poor?

519. Why didn't God give us money right away when my dad lost his job?

520. Why does God sometimes wait until the last minute to supply our needs?

521. If God owns everything, why doesn't he keep it all in heaven?

522. If God owns everything, why do people sell stuff like it is their own and charge however much they want for it?

523. Why did Jesus talk about money when he didn't have very much?

524. Did Jesus ever have problems with money?

525. Is money one of the most important things in life?

526. If salvation is free, why do we have to buy a Bible?

LIVING AND GIVING

527. What is tithing?

528. Why do I have to give money to church?

529. How much should a person give to the church?

530. Why do some people keep all their money to themselves instead of giving some to God?

531. Where does the money I give to church go?

532. How does God get the money that I give to him?

533. Do we have to give money to poor people?

534. Is it wrong to see poor people on the street and not give them any money?

535. Where does all the money from fountains and wishing wells go?

A PENNY SAVED

536. What is the reason for learning to save money?
537. What should we know about saving money?
538. What is the quickest way to save money?
539. If I put money in a savings account, can I get it back?
540. Is it selfish to save money?
541. Why do some people hide their money?
542. Is the stock market a place where you buy animals?
543. How can retired people go on trips if they don't have a job?
544. How much do investments cost?

GOTTA HAVE IT

545. Why do parents sometimes not let kids buy what we want, even when we have enough money for it?
546. Why can't I have all the things I want?
547. Why do people fight over money?
548. Why do people want more money if they already have lots of it?
549. Is buying a lottery ticket the same as gambling?
550. Why do people play the lottery if they probably won't win?
551. Does money make people bad?
552. Why can't my parents just get a loan instead of waiting for payday?
553. If people keep buying lots of things, won't they run out of money?
554. Why do people spend money they don't have?
555. What are taxes?
556. What does the government do with all the taxes we pay?
557. Why is there so much tax on prices?
558. Why should you pay property taxes if you already own your house?
559. Why do people get bored with something they just bought?
560. Why do people waste their money on dumb things?

GIVE ME SOME CREDIT

561. Are credit cards good or bad?
562. How do credit cards work?
563. Why can't I have my own credit card?
564. What happens if a person doesn't pay a credit card bill?
565. Is it wrong to borrow money?
566. Why do people have to pay interest on money they borrow?
567. What is a mortgage?
568. Why are there bills to pay?
569. What if I don't have enough money to pay my bills?
570. Should I borrow money from the bank or from my friends?

FROM ALLOWANCE TO PAYCHECK

571. Why do some kids get their allowance free and others have to earn it?
572. Why do some kids get huge allowances and others don't get any?
573. How come I don't get enough allowance to buy anything?
574. Why do kids get less money than adults?
575. How are kids supposed to earn money?
576. Where does the money that bosses pay come from?
577. What does minimum wage mean?
578. Should people stay at a good-paying job that they don't like?
579. What should people do if they do not get paid enough at their job?
580. Why do athletes get paid so much money to do something that's fun?
581. How will I know what I want to do when I grow up?

WHEN THE BUDGET WON'T BUDGE

582. What is budgeting?

583. Why do people have to budget their money?

584. Why can't parents afford a lot of things?

585. Why do some people spend every cent they get right away?

586. Why do people spend their money on little things and not on the important things?

587. Why is it that when I want to buy something I am always short of cash?

588. Does God get angry when I spend my money foolishly?

589. How do I know what is wise to spend my money on?

HONESTY IS THE BEST POLICY

590. Would it be right to keep the money if someone paid too much?

591. What should a person do if the bank machine doesn't give the right amount of money?

592. What if the waiter gives me a kid's meal free because he thinks I'm younger than I really am?

593. Is it really finders keepers?

594. If I try to pay my friend back and he forgot I borrowed some money, is it wrong to keep it?

595. Why do some people trust me and lend me money?

596. Why do some salesclerks steal money from the cash register?

597. Is it OK to use Canadian coins in American vending machines?

7 FRIENDS AND SCHOOL

MAKING FRIENDS

598. How do I make friends?

599. When you're making friends, how do you know what to say?

600. I want to have nice friends, but how do I know if kids are nice?

601. Where can I find some friends?

602. What should I do if I'm scared to go up to someone and say, "Hi, do you want to be my friend?"

603. Why can't I have everyone as a friend?

604. Why do some kids not want to have friends?

605. How should I treat kids who are different?

606. Why do parents not like your friends just because they have green hair or something?

607. Why don't parents just let you pick your own friends?

608. If I'm supposed to love everybody, why am I supposed to stay away from certain kids?

609. Sometimes when I hang around with my friends, they do something bad. What should I do?

610. What should I do when my old friends don't like my new friends?

BEING A GOOD FRIEND

611. What's the difference between being best friends and just being friends?

612. Can you have more than one best friend?

613. My friend's parents are getting a divorce. What can I do?

614. Why do friends get mad at you when you tell the truth?

615. Is it wrong to stop telling my friends about Jesus even when they won't listen?

616. When you are talking with people, how do you know that they are actually listening to you?

617. Why do friends talk behind your back?

618. Why won't my friend let me play with his stuff?

619. Why can't I go over to my best friend's house very often?

620. Why don't my parents let me go to special places with my friends?

621. Why should we always have to rescue our friends when they get in trouble?

622. What should I do if my friend turns on a show that I'm not allowed to watch?

623. If some of my friends are doing something that I think is bad, should I tell my parents?

HANDLING FRIENDSHIP DIFFICULTIES

624. Why do friends let each other down?

625. If a friend asks me to keep a promise and it's something wrong, should I do it?

626. Why can't my best friend stay here with me and not move away?

627. Why would your friends expect you to lie for them?

628. Why don't your friends like you just for who you are?

629. Why do you have to do whatever your friends want, or they get mad?

630. Why can't friends just get along instead of fighting and arguing with each other?

631. Why do my friends break their promises to me?

632. When one of my friends is picking on someone, what should I do?

633. If my friends ignore me, should I ignore them?

634. Why do some people want to be friends one day and not the next?

635. What can I do when one of my best friends used to like me but now hates me?

GETTING ALONG WITH OTHERS

636. Is it OK to think that you are better than somebody else if you really are better?

637. Why are some kids so messy?

638. Why do some kids get their own way when they cry and get angry?

639. Why do some kids always try to be first?

640. Should I stand up for myself around pushy kids?

641. Why do some kids just have to talk in class? Why can't they wait until recess?

642. Why do kids wreck my things for no reason?

643. Why do some kids act tough?

644. Why do some kids say bad things about others?

645. Why are some kids bullies?

646. Should I stick up for someone who's being bullied?

647. If you know a friend is going to do something wrong, should you try to stop the person?

648. What should I do when kids are mean to me?

649. Why is it so hard to love your enemies?

650. How can I love my enemies?

651. Is it wrong to hate people if they're nerds?

652. When kids tease me, is it OK to tease them back?

653. Why don't other kids ever do what I say?

FITTING IN AT SCHOOL

654. Why do some kids dress so weird?

655. Sometimes I'm afraid to go to school. What should I do?

656. Why do kids always want to dress according to different fads?

657. What's so bad about wanting to wear clothes that are in style?

658. Why does everybody want to do things that other people do?

659. What should I do if other kids laugh at me for going to church?

660. Why do you have to be good and obey in school?

661. Why are some kids so big and other kids so small?

662. What if I don't like the music that everyone else listens to?

663. I feel so stupid in some subjects. What can I do?

664. Why do some kids swear?

665. What should I say if someone makes fun of the Bible?

DEALING WITH THE DESIRE TO BE POPULAR

666. How does someone become popular?

667. Is it OK to be popular?

668. Do you have to wear makeup or dress cool to make people like you?

669. How do you get someone to like you if you aren't as popular as everyone else?

670. Why do kids think something is cool one day and stupid the next?

671. Why do some kids all dress, talk, and act the same?

672. Should I get a cool nickname?

673. Do you have to be good at a sport to be popular?

674. If someone isn't popular, how come others think less of him or her as a person?

675. Why does my friend always want me to ask people what they think about her?

676. Should I hang out with popular people to become popular?

RELATING TO TEACHERS

677. Why is it that some teachers are nice to other kids but mean to me?

678. Why do some teachers let you get away with stuff while others give you trouble when you drop a pencil?

679. Why do teachers make it easy for some kids to get good grades and hard for others?

680. Why do teachers give so much homework?

681. Why won't the teacher let me sit next to my friend?

682. Why do we have to respect teachers?

683. Why are some children suspended from school?

684. Why do kids often take advantage of a substitute teacher?

685. Why don't teachers just get to the point instead of blabbing on and on about the subject?

686. Why do my friends get fun teachers and I get mean ones?

687. Why doesn't the teacher ever choose my papers or pictures to put on the wall?

688. Why do some teachers have rules that don't even make sense?

SUCCEEDING IN CLASS

689. Why do we have to study subjects that we might not need to know when we grow up?

690. If you have already studied something, such as addition, why do you have to keep studying it?

691. Why do some people find a subject hard, and others find it easy?

692. Is it OK to stay up late on school nights if your friends do?

693. How can I stop daydreaming and pay better attention in class?

694. Do you need to learn math only if you want to be a pilot or a construction worker?

695. Why do we have to learn geography and history?

696. Why are grades so important?

697. Why do people cheat?

698. How can I do better in spelling?

699. The kids around me keep getting me into trouble. What can I do?

700. I want to get A's, but my friends say getting good grades is dumb. What should I do?

701. When kids miss a lot of school, how do they pass?

702. Why do we have to study computers?

CHOOSING ACTIVITIES

703. Why don't I have enough time to play?

704. Why don't we have gym class every day?

705. When you are home during the summer and nobody is around, what can you do to have some fun?

706. My parents want me to play soccer, but I hate it. What should I do?

707. I like playing the piano, but I hate practicing. Should I quit?

708. Why do my parents want me to be involved in so many things?

709. Why does my coach care so much about winning? It's not fun anymore.

710. How can I get better at art?

711. I want to be with my friends. Why do we have to go to church so much?

8 OUR WORLD

ANIMALS
752. Why are animals becoming extinct all over the world?

753. Why does God let animals suffer from dangers in nature?

754. Why do people kill animals to eat when they could just buy food at the store?

755. Why are some people mean to animals?

756. Do animals have feelings just like people do?

757. Why do people cry when their pets die?

758. Why do some animals look funny?

759. Why do cats and dogs fight?

THE ENTERTAINMENT INDUSTRY
760. Why do movies have weirdos for stars?

761. Why do people put garbage in their heads by watching bad movies?

762. Why is there so much fighting on TV?

763. How come people put bad movies on TV?

764. Why do movie companies make scary movies if they know people will have nightmares?

765. Why are some things on videos funny for adults but not for kids?

766. Why won't parents let kids watch certain shows the kids want to watch?

767. Why do people like different kinds of music?

768. Why are musicians treated like idols?

769. Why are there commercials all the time when good shows are on TV?

770. When you want to have something you see on a TV commercial, why doesn't your mom let you have it?

FAMILY MATTERS
771. Why do we have marriage?

772. Why do some moms and dads divorce?

773. Why do brothers and sisters fight?

774. Why do some kids have stepmothers or stepfathers?

775. Why did people used to have so many kids?

776. How are families different now from the way they used to be?

CHANGING TECHNOLOGY
777. How fast is technology changing?

778. How did computers get so smart?

779. How do computers get viruses?

780. How come the keys on the keyboard are not in alphabetical order?

781. Why do people surf on the Internet?

782. Is the Internet bad?

783. How come the olden days and these days are different?

MEDICINE
784. Why do people get sick when God is watching over them?

785. Why does your body feel sick?

786. What are bacteria and viruses?

787. Why are doctors so smart?

788. How does medicine make someone better?

789. Who invented vegetables?

790. Why is it good to exercise?

791. Why do people smoke?

792. What does cloning mean?

793. Why does God let people die?

OUTER SPACE

794. Why is there a universe?
795. Is outer space hot or cold?
796. Why do people want to fly to other planets?
797. If there's intelligent life on other planets, do they have teachers?
798. Why do people think that beings from other planets have visited earth?
799. Why do people want to live on the moon if they wouldn't be able to breathe there?
800. How do people think of things like the Hubble telescope?
801. Can kids be astronauts if they get trained?

FOCUS ON THE FAMILY®

Welcome to the Family ——————

Whether you purchased this book, borrowed it, or received it as a gift, thanks for reading it! This is just one of many insightful, biblically based resources that Focus on the Family produces for people in all stages of life.

Focus is a global Christian ministry dedicated to helping families thrive as they celebrate and cultivate God's design for marriage and experience the adventure of parenthood. Our outreach exists to support individuals and families in the joys and challenges they face, and to equip and empower them to be the best they can be.

Through our many media outlets, we offer help and hope, promote moral values and share the life-changing message of Jesus Christ with people around the world.

Focus on the Family MAGAZINES

These faith-building, character-developing publications address the interests, issues, concerns, and challenges faced by every member of your family from preschool through the senior years.

For More INFORMATION

 ONLINE:
Log on to
FocusOnTheFamily.com
In Canada, log on to
FocusOnTheFamily.ca

 PHONE:
Call toll-free:
800-A-FAMILY
(232-6459)
In Canada, call toll-free:
800-661-9800

THRIVING FAMILY®	**FOCUS ON THE FAMILY CLUBHOUSE JR.®**	**FOCUS ON THE FAMILY CLUBHOUSE®**	**FOCUS ON THE FAMILY CITIZEN®**
Marriage & Parenting	Ages 4 to 8	Ages 8 to 12	U.S. news issues

Rev. 3/11

More Great Resources
from Focus on the Family®

Raising a Modern-Day Princess
Inspiring purpose, value, and strength in your daughter
by Pam Farrel and Doreen Hanna
Help your daughter journey into womanhood with a healthy self-image and knowledge of who she is in Christ! Coauthors Farrel and Hanna stress the importance of creating a rite-of-passage ceremony for your young woman; provide helpful tips, and offer an entire chapter for father figures.

The 21-Day Dad's Challenge
Three weeks to a better relationship with your kids
Edited by Carey Casey
Take the 21-Day Dad's Challenge, and in just three weeks, learn habits that will have an eternal impact on your kids, your family, and your community. You'll be challenged by the best: like Tony Dungy, Josh McDowell, Randy Alcorn, and more. Let's get started!

Voyage with the Vikings
The Imagination Station® book series #1
by Marianne Hering and Paul McCusker
Journey with cousins Patrick and Beth as they travel to Greenland in 1000 AD through Mr. Whittaker's popular invention, the Imagination Station. You'll meet with Leif Eriksson, his father Erik, polar bears, and lots of adventure.

FOR MORE INFORMATION

 Online:
Log on to FocusOnTheFamily.com
In Canada, log on to FocusOnTheFamily.ca

 Phone:
Call toll-free: 800-A-FAMILY
In Canada, call toll-free: 800-661-9800

BPZZXP1